ed Road:
ge Music Trail

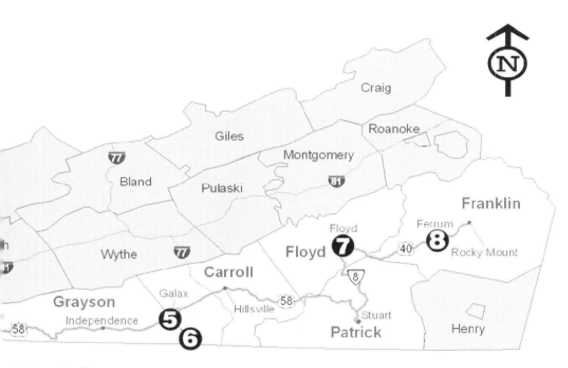

KED ROAD

5 REX THEATER & OLD FIDDLER'S CONVENTION, GALAX

6 BLUE RIDGE MUSIC CENTER, CARROLL/GRAYSON COUNTIES

7 THE FLOYD COUNTRY STORE & COUNTY SALES, FLOYD

8 BLUE RIDGE INSTITUTE AND MUSEUM, FERRUM

Grazing Along the Crooked Road

Recipes and Stories - Past and Present

Betty Skeens and Libby Bondurant
www.crookedroadcookbook.com

Read, cook, and enjoy the journey along the Crooked Road!

Blessings,
Libby Bondurant
&
In Loving Memory of Betty Skeens

ISBN: 978-1-891029-56-1
Copyright 2008 by Betty Skeens and Libby Bondurant
The contents of this publication may not be reproduced without the written consent of the authors.

First Edition October 2008
Second Edition April 2009

Cover art courtesy of artist Patricia Robin Woodruff
www.InnerArtSpirit.com

Giclee' reproductions of original artwork may be obtained at:
Art Under the Sun Gallery
302 S. Locust Street (under the Winter Sun)
Floyd, VA 24091
540-745-PENS
www.ArtUnderTheSun.org

HENDERSON PUBLISHING
811 Eva's Walk, Pounding Mill, VA 24637

Mountains of Virginia

…And on the eighth day, after His day of rest, God began scattering talents about to different parts of the world He had made. Some would be known for their beautiful beadwork, some for painting pictures that touched the heart. Many would have a great gift for wood, others for fabric and lovely woven articles. And on and on, over the entire world, with music a part of them all. In a place where the mountains sometimes rise sharply, though not the tallest in the world, but are noted for their blueness or their beauty, He added extra music. The winters would be long and hard, the summers would require much work, and the people's souls would depend on it for survival. Across these mountains a love of stringed instruments was liberally sprinkled. In one area, an extra measure fell from his hand. "Shouldn't you take that back and spread it out more?" asked the angel who assisted Him. "I suppose I could," He replied. "But much has been given and much will be shared in these mountains. I will leave it as it is. They will know what to do with it." And they did.

Dedication

To our husbands, Dickey Bondurant and Robert Skeens, who have been patient beyond their natures during the writing of this book. Often they ate fast food or whipped up a sandwich as we collected excellent recipes that we didn't have time to cook.

To the folks who have followed a long tradition of connecting to others through the sharing of recipes and stories – we won't forget you. You have made this work a joy.

In Memory of Betty Skeens
12/4/46 – 2/27/09

Her children arise and call her blessed;
Her husband also, and he praises her;
"Many women do noble things,
But you surpass them all."
Charm is deceptive, and beauty is fleeting;
But a woman who fears the LORD is to be praised.
Give her the reward she has earned,
And let her works bring her praise at the city gate.
-*Proverbs 31:28-31*

Strong, creative, loyal, funny, sometimes stubborn, often corny but never boring. You taught us to follow our dreams and to never take no for an answer. By watching you we learned to value those around us and the importance of lending a helping hand to a friend in need. You never stopped learning, growing, and loving. The time we spent and the memories we made will be forever cherished in our hearts and minds. This is your legacy.

Your loving family.

The Authors

Betty and Libby met through church and the friendship of their daughters. Working together in church activities such as with the youth group, Christmas plays, and in a United Methodist Women's Circle helped develop a common ground. In addition, there was an antique and collectibles stage when much scouring of flea markets and yard sales took place and the pair maintained a booth at a local antique mall. Overlapping this was a crafts making period when many "found" objects took on a new life, especially old rusted anything and everything, which was nailed to barn board birdhouses. This was the most fun of any of the joint projects the two had undertaken until the cookbook / storybook, which has been an adventure they'll never forget! In fact, they plan to be the most entertaining two old people in the nursing home with anecdotes and tales of mishaps on the road.

Thank You...

We extend appreciation to our families and friends who have encouraged us during the creation of this book. To Linda Martin, Iris McGrady, Carolyn Haynes, Virginia Young, and Pat Jones - the ladies who have spent time reading and editing this manuscript – your help has meant more than we can possibly express. A special thanks goes to our church family at Pleasant Grove United Methodist for testing recipes, thereby providing a fantastic covered dish meal and wonderful fellowship. The last chapter of the book is due to Jane Poore, who had the idea of incorporating "Friends," allowing extra contributions.

The cover painting by Patricia Robin Woodruff was done with this book in mind, though unbeknownst to us. We thank you for adding your special touch. Finally, our regards go to Ken Henderson who completed this book under difficult circumstances, remaining ever amiable and gentlemanly to the end. You're a trouper!

Table of Contents

Dickenson County 1
Wise County..41
Lee County 81
Scott County 109
Washington County...141
Grayson County 175
Carroll County...217
Patrick County 257
Floyd County 301
Franklin County 341
Friends 391

Disclaimer

Every attempt has been made to secure permissions. If there were inadvertent omissions, please accept our apologies.

This book is not a scholarly work. It is a book of recipes, recollections, and stories told to us by people who were there, or heard it from others. We regret inaccuracies in dates or other details if they are found.

Dickenson County

Dr. Ralph Stanley Museum - Clintwood, Virginia

Table of Contents

Angel Cake..5
Applesauce Cake, Princess Stanley's..............................5
Baked Apple Dumplings...6
Baked Country Ham..6
Best Carrot Cake...8
Betty's Chicken Soup..9
Blueberry Cream Pie...9
Bread & Butter Pickles for Microwave........................10
Chocolate Éclair...12
Coconut Caramel Sundae Pie......................................12
Cracklin Bread...13
Creamy Chocolate Pie...15
Creamy Snicker Salad...15
Crème Puff Cake...16
Crock Pot Apple Butter...16
Curried Cider-Pork Stew...17
Dandelion Salad..19
Doke..21
Easy Cereal Bars...21
Fried Green Tomatoes...21
Grandmother Large's Jam Cake..................................22
Gritted Corn Bread..22
Ham Delights..23
Ham Hocks and Collard Greens with Cornmeal Dumplings.........24
Homemade Soap...24
Meatloaf (Sunday)...25
Molasses Cake...25
Molasses Stack Cake...26
Moonshine Fruitcake...27
Peach Cobbler...29
Peanut Butter Cookies...30
Pepsi Roast..30
Pickled Corn..30
Pickled Vegetables..31
Pork Chops with Barbecue Sauce...............................31
Quick and Zesty Vegetable Soup................................35
Shrimp Butter..36
Squirrel and Dumplings in a Dutch Oven...................36
Sugar Cured Ham..37
Vinegar Butter...37
Yeast Cornbread..38
Zesty Meatballs...38

Visiting Dickenson County

Rarely have two young men had so much fun from rocking chairs.

We arrived in Dickenson County late in the afternoon of July 3, 2007. Two days of our first *recipe gathering* road trip were completed and a bed and a shower sounded good. By the time the motel was reached, Clintwood had made an impression. People were strolling and stopping to chat on the streets, chairs on porches contained what appeared to be families and neighbors visiting. Amazing! A movie set of small town America. Libby and I fell more in love with Southwest Virginia.

Too rejuvenated to stay in our room, we toured the town. At the Children's Park, we met Mr. A.C. Steffey and his young grandson, struck up a conversation and found common ground right away because my brother-in-law is a Steffey. We traced family trees long enough for his wife to wave and drive away *("It's not too far for me to walk home,")* and continued until his daughter-in-law came back to pick up son and father-in-law. During the conversation, we learned about a re-enactment by the local Sons of the Confederacy at the cemetery that night.

An after dark stroll through old gravestones sounded too good to miss so we ventured up the steep hillside where the cemetery is located. There, costumed guides and re-enactors told the stories of people long buried. A most moving and lovely portrayal was of a wife and mother left behind during the Civil War to cope as best she could.

Next morning we overslept and awoke to more bustle and noise than expected. Independence Day and almost time for the parade! Just up the hill from our room, in a small square of shade provided by a large sign, sat two wooden rocking chairs. Fascinated, we watched, expecting to see an elderly couple enjoy the parade from the excellent viewing seats. Not so… it was two young teenage boys. Rarely have two young men had so much fun from rocking chairs. They waved and shouted at passers-by, who yelled back and sometimes stopped for a few words. Girls were whistled at, guys walked by and talked a spell, and a good time was being had by all. The air around them fairly bristled with energy. We were pressed, getting ready for the day and spending so much time checking out the action beyond our door.

Photo courtesy of Jonnie B. Deel Library
Left to right: Willie Fleming, Retha Grizzle, and Susie Counts

The Appalachian Quilt of Our Lives

Each piece of fabric in this quilt comes with a story about why it was chosen. All were contributed by local people and illustrate the pride and culture of the Appalachian community. It is a project of the Learning Co-op, a program of the Fourth World Movement in Appalachia. *(www.4thworldmovement.org)*

The quilt is now on exhibit at various locations in the United States and in other countries, carrying with it stories of the lives of people in Appalachia.

Angel Cake
Shirley Hawkins – Haysi, VA

1 box Duncan Hines Angel Food cake mix
1 (20 oz.) can crushed pineapple

Mix together with mixer. Must use one-step angel food cake mix. Bake at 350° for 35-40 minutes or until dry – do not over bake. This recipe seems just too simple, but it is simply delicious. Diabetics dream also.

Topping: Combine together and spread on cake.

1 small Cool Whip
1 can crushed pineapple, drained
1 small sugar free instant vanilla pudding

"Grandma Princess and husband, Del Stanley had a nice apple orchard in their back yard. She was a wonderful cook and used apples liberally in her recipes. My husband fondly recalls the taste of her fresh apple butter on hot biscuits. But his favorite treat at her house was this Applesauce Cake."

Applesauce Cake, Princess Stanley's
Gayle Stanley – Clintwood, VA

2 cups self-rising flour	1 cup brown sugar
¼ tsp. cloves	2 eggs
½ tsp. nutmeg	1 cup raisins
1 tsp. cinnamon	1 cup chopped nuts
2/3 cup butter	1 cup applesauce

Sift flour and spices 3 times, set aside. Cream butter until soft. Add sugar to butter and mix until light and fluffy. Mix in eggs. Add nuts and raisins, mixing well. Add flour mixture and applesauce alternately. Mix until smooth. Pour into pans and bake at 350° until done (about 30 minutes for two 9-inch round pans, a little longer for an oblong pan.).

O, weary Moms,
mixing dough,
Don't you wish
that food would
grow?
A smile would
come, I know,
to see.
A bread bush or
a casserole tree!

Baked Apple Dumplings

Mozelle Steffey – Clintwood, VA

6   cooking apples – chopped
1   stick margarine
1 ½ tsps. cinnamon
1   cup sugar
1   (12 oz) 7 Up
1   can of 10 biscuits

Roll biscuits thinly and fill with chopped apples. Seal edges and place in a 9 x 13 inch pan. Combine 7 Up, sugar, margarine and cinnamon. Boil for 2 minutes. Pour over dumplings and bake at 325° for about 30 minutes.

> Early settlers found wildlife plentiful amongst the steep hills, valleys, and streams of the area. Growing crops was sometimes hard but these were hardy people, who passed endurance to the next generation.

Baked Country Ham

Charlie Fleming

Cut hock off ham. Use about the top 6 inches of ham. Soak this overnight in cold water, changing if needed.

1 can Pepsi cola
1 small can (individual size) pineapple juice

Place ham in cooking bag. Pour mixture over and bake at 350 degrees about 4 hours or until ham begins to pull back from bone. Delicious! Your guests won't leave nothin' but the bone!

The 100th county formed in Virginia, Dickenson is known as "Virginia's Baby." It was carved from Russell, Wise, and Buchanan counties in March 1880. (Virginia now consists of 95 counties.)

Around In The Mountain

According to Charles Fleming, he was raised in one of the least known communities of Dickenson County. Located off Camp Creek, on what is now called Ventura Road, his family lived in the last house before going into Wise County, or the first upon entering Dickenson, according to which way you were traveling. "Each little section of the county is named for its location, a family, or some landmark like a rock or creek," he says. "But places like Fox Town, Caney Ridge, Frying Pan, and Smith Ridge are generally known, while for some reason, we weren't."

The two-room Swindall School he attended was a three-mile walk until the fourth grade when a bus route began. After that, through graduation from high school, it was only a mile each way to catch the bus. Of course the bus came by at 7:00 AM and delivered them back at 5:00 PM on the last run of the day.

Fleming left his mountain home but, like many others, has come back – and begun the process of telling his own and the community's stories in a book to be titled, *Around in the Mountain,* where we can learn about two rather rough characters, Heinen and Kal Fleming, who were ancestors and early settlers. They fought the law at a place near Pound Gap called the Battlegrounds. The law won and Heinen was killed. The irony is that Kal later wound up in law enforcement and was a police officer for many years.

Grandfather Fleming, called Ticky George, earned his nickname during a foxhunt. After listening to the dogs run and drinking enough anti-freeze from a jar to get sleepy, he lay down near the fire and dosed off. His dogs came back and lay down beside him. Whether he actually got up with ticks or not isn't known but the name stuck. It was said that Ticky knew more than most veterinarians about healing livestock and was often called upon by farmers, though his methods were sometimes unorthodox.

A rooster-fighting pit was located at the Battlegrounds during much of Fleming's growing up years. "Back then, there were people who made their living from cock fighting. We didn't think too much about the bad aspects of it as kids, just something we took for granted, but now I wouldn't want any part of it."

"Us youngsters used to sneak over there to watch. You walked up a path that looked like a hunting trail, but it opened up into cleared land with several buildings. They sold hot dogs and hamburgers and drinks. Many prominent people came there to bet and fight their roosters. I've seen liquor and money passing hands – roosters fighting, blood flying, roosters dying. We once brought some dead roosters home and cooked them, thinking they shouldn't be wasted. We found out how tough they really are."

Best Carrot Cake
Sue Mullins – Clintwood, VA

Numerous communities evolved within the county. They usually centered around a small one or two-room school, a church, a store, and perhaps a post office. Often the church served as a school, also. Many of the early schools only operated two or three months, due to weather and the students being needed at home.

2   cups sugar
¾   cup buttermilk
¾   cup vegetable oil
3   eggs, beaten
2   tsps. vanilla extract
2   cups all-purpose flour
2   tsps. baking soda
½   tsp. salt
2   tsps. ground cinnamon
2   cups grated carrots
1   cup chopped walnuts
1   (8 oz.) can crushed pineapple, drained
1   (3 ½ oz.) can flaked coconut

Combine first 5 ingredients; beat well. Combine flour, soda, salt and cinnamon; add to sugar mixture, stirring well. Add carrots, walnuts, pineapple and coconut; stir well. Pour batter into 3 greased and floured 9-inch round cake pans. Bake at 350° for 35-45 minutes or until a wooden pick inserted in center comes out clean. Pour Buttermilk Glaze over warm cake layers. Let cool in pans 15 minutes; remove from pans and let cool completely on wire racks. Spread Cream Cheese Frosting between layers and on top and sides of cake.

Buttermilk Glaze:
1   cup sugar
½   cup buttermilk
½   cup butter
1   Tbsp. light corn syrup
½   tsp. baking soda
1   tsp. vanilla extract

Combine first 5 ingredients in a large saucepan. Bring to a boil over medium heat; stir in vanilla.

Cream Cheese Frosting:
1   (8 oz.) pkg. cream cheese, softened
½   cup butter or margarine, softened
1   (16 oz.) pkg. powdered sugar, sifted
1   tsp. vanilla extract

Combine cream cheese and butter; beat at medium speed with an electric mixer until smooth. Gradually add sugar, beating until light and fluffy. Stir in vanilla.

Betty's Chicken Soup
Original Recipe from Betty Stanley - Clintwood, VA

- 4 chicken breasts, split in half, cooked and cut into pieces
- 6 potatoes cooked & drained
- 2 cans kidney beans – drained
- 1 can green beans – drained
- 1 can peas – drained
- 1 can corn – drained
- 1 large can tomatoes
- 1 can cream of chicken soup
- 1 tsp. onion powder
- 1 tsp. dried basil
- Salt & pepper to taste

Add all ingredients together. Simmer for 1 hour. Serve with crackers or bread.

"I received this recipe from my mother-in-law, Marjorie Jarstfer. It is her son, Daniel's, favorite dessert. Once after Daniel had left home for college, his parents came to visit. Marjorie told Daniel to get some whipped topping and he knew what that meant. She was bringing Blueberry Cream Pie with her. I make this delicious pie every year for Daniel's birthday. It is now my oldest daughter, Danelle's, birthday favorite as well."

Cheerfulness and contentment are great beautifiers and are famous preservers of good looks.
-Charles Dickens

Blueberry Cream Pie
Donna Jarstfer –Haysi, VA

Pick and wash 1 quart of blueberries (frozen can be used but it is better with fresh berries). Make a smooth paste of the following ingredients:

- ½ cup cold water
- 5 Tbsp. flour
- ½ cup sugar
- Pinch of salt

Bring to a boil:
- 1 cup blueberries
- ½ cup sugar
- ¼ cup water

When boiling, add the flour paste and stir until it thickens. Remove from stove and cool. When cool, add the remaining 3 cups of raw blueberries and put into a 10-inch baked pie shell. Refrigerate. When cool, garnish with sweetened whipped cream or whipped topping.

It's All Good Café

After several years of living away, Beverly Creger has found that you can come home again. "I found I could come home and like it, too," she says. Her husband, Jerry, who originally hails from Bristol, seems to have found a niche in Clintwood at their progressive restaurant, *It's All Good Café*, as well.

"School friends, family, and so many people we know live here," says Beverly.

Customers are discovering that the meals really are all good. (The authors of this book can vouch for several items.) A full size dessert or a mini-size one - often all you'll have space for – can make the visit complete.

Some early games were "base" games like: Stink Base, Round Town, and Straight Town. Marbles were played, but rarely could they "keep" the ones they won – that would have been gambling.

Bread & Butter Pickles For Microwave
Kathy Harrison, Haysi, VA

4	cups sliced cucumbers (¼")
1 ½	cups sliced onions (¼")
1	cup sugar
½	cup white vinegar
1	tsp. salt
½	tsp. mustard seeds
¼	tsp. turmeric

Mix last 5 ingredients & pour over cucumbers & onions in large microwave bowl. Do not cover. Microwave on high for 10-12 minutes, stirring after 5 minutes. Cook till cucumbers are tender and onions are transparent. May take longer than 10-12 minutes. Ladle into hot pint jar and hot lids, then let cool. Can double this recipe (more than 8 cups of cucumbers are fine and maybe 2 cups onions.) Takes about 20 minutes in microwave. Make sure liquid is boiling. This will make 4 pints of pickles.

Always do right.
This will gratify some people and astonish the rest.
  -*Mark Twain*

Ken Childress and Jimmy Mullins

They've picked and sung and been friends for forty-five years. Friends, not companions, as Jim stressed to an audience. "Me and Ken ain't companions. We don't even like each other, but for economic reasons we get up on stage to play and sing together occasionally."

Only in the past five years have they performed together publicly. "If we were going to do this," says Ken to Jim one fine day, "why in the world didn't we start a little sooner?"

Why indeed? Both are talented – Jim is a great old time guitar picker and singer and Ken possesses an unusual voice. Numerous songs by Ken have accompanied couples tying the knot and even more folks have been sung or spoken over as they slipped into eternity.

At the moment, negotiations are ongoing as to whether Ken will speak at his best friend's funeral. At one service where Ken presided, Jim is sure he saw him reading. "The Primitive Baptist believe that words are given to you and that's what I believe," he says.

'Well," replies Ken, "I'm not sure I can think of anything good to say on the spur of the moment. How about you give me ten days notice so I'll have time to think up something worthwhile about you?" It's still under discussion.

Great lengths have been gone to over the years in the effort of getting each others goat, which must have consumed a good deal of time since neither stays the winner for long.

One day they planned to meet for lunch about 1:00. Jim arrived first and was asked by several people where's Ken and how's Ken, etc. Due to diabetes, part of Ken's leg had to be removed and a prosthesis used. "His wife's got his leg," Jim explained. "He went to spreeing and staying out til all hours and she took his leg away from him. I think maybe she's giving it back today."

When Ken came through the door, he was greeted with "Hey, Ken! Glad your wife gave your leg back!"

An announcer at WMMT radio station found the story worth telling on the air. "For months," laughs Ken, " I couldn't go anywhere without somebody saying, 'Good to see you – glad Caroline let you have your leg today."

There's closeness among the people of Dickenson County. It was commented on by a number of people we spoke to but can be felt in the interaction as well. Perhaps it's a shared history, or left over from the isolation of years ago. The connection extends to the mountains, creeks, and valleys, as well as to each other. It is a lovely thing.

Chocolate Éclair
In memory of Caroline – Ken Childress, Clintwood, VA

1 box graham crackers
1 large Cool Whip
2 (3 oz.) boxes French vanilla instant pudding
3 cups milk

Line a 9 x 13 inch pan with crackers. Mix 3 cups milk with 2 boxes of pudding. Blend or fold in Cool Whip. Do layers of crackers and pudding, end with crackers. Top with chocolate sauce.

Chocolate Sauce:
½ cup cocoa
½ stick margarine
¼ cup milk
1 cup sugar or Splenda
1 tsp. vanilla

Mix cocoa, sugar, and milk. Cook to slow boil, approx. 1 minute. Remove from heat; add margarine and vanilla. Whisk well. Let cool before adding to the top of pudding. You may use sugar-free ingredients except for cocoa.

Coconut Caramel Sundae Pie
Sheila B. Phipps – Clintwood, VA

¼ cup margarine
1 (7 oz.) pkg. coconut
½ cup chopped pecans
1 (8 oz.) pkg. cream cheese
1 (16 oz.) Cool Whip
1 can Eagle Brand condensed milk
2 graham cracker crusts
1 jar caramel ice cream topping

Melt margarine in large skillet. Add coconut and chopped pecans; cook until golden brown,stirring frequently. Combine softened cream cheese and condensed milk; beat until smooth. Fold in whipped topping. Layer ¼ of the mixture in each pie shell. Drizzle ¼ of the caramel over the whipped topping mixture and sprinkle with ¼ of the coconut mixture. Repeat layers. Cover and freeze until firm. Let pies stand at room temperature 5 minutes before serving. Can also use chocolate ice cream topping instead of caramel.

Sheila Phipps says she has had the same address for forty-two years. " In addition," she adds with a grin, " I've also had the same husband and the same job for all those years!"

Breaks Interstate Park

The Breaks Interstate Park is the end of the Crooked Road Heritage Music Trail – or the beginning of the Crooked Road, depending on whom you're speaking to. Either way it is a wondrous place to visit. You can come for the day or stay a week. Fishing, swimming, horseback riding, hiking, and various other outdoor activities will keep the whole family busy. The glass walled Rhododendron Restaurant is open from April to December and offers a fantastic view as you enjoy great food. Gospel singings take place Memorial Day weekend, Fathers Day, and Labor Day Weekend. Music is usually scheduled each Saturday night during the summer.

www.breakspark.com   *800-982-5122*

"When you render lard from a hog (render is cooking fat down to a liquid), the solids that are left are placed in a cheese cloth. The cheese cloth is squeezed until most liquid is removed. This is called Cracklins."

Cracklin' Bread
Izetta Fleming - Clintwood, VA

1 cup cracklins
2 cups cornmeal
½ cup flour
buttermilk
water

Mix ingredients with enough buttermilk and water to make batter thin enough to pour. Pour into well greased pan. Bake at 400° until golden brown.

As we ate lunch at the Rhododendron Restaurant, our waitress, Brittany, regaled us with stories of living in the area. She was from the Kentucky side and asked if we came across Rt. 80 where the road is a higher altitude, narrow, and can get dangerous during winter storms or summer fog. To help us get our accent right, she explained that the risky section of road is called "high narrows" but should be pronounced *high narrs*.

Roy and Plinia Deel

Haysi (Hay-Sigh) was named for Charles Hayter and J.C. Sifers, who had established a trading post in the vicinity early on. The two names were later combined for the post office located inside their general store.

However, a great tidbit of folklore exists about a ferryboat operator named Silas who shuttled people across the water in pioneer days. It seems that if someone arrived and found him on the opposite shore, they'd yell, "Hey, Si!" to get his attention, allegedly giving the town it's name.

Before cars were everyday, going to church served several purposes. Spiritual, of course, but spirits in need of fellowship and social interaction was reason enough to walk long distances in one's best clothes. This went double for young, unmarried girls and boys who could flirt and strike up friendships and escape from daily work. One such young couple met just after WWII.

"My Mother, Plinia (pronounced Pliny) and her brother, Lawrence, walked several miles, maybe ten, to the Russell Prater Church over in Buchanan County where she was to meet up with an aunt that happened to be about the same age. Since there was little in the way of entertainment in the country, the two girls competed for and often stole boyfriends from each other.

A fine looking fellow in a sailor's uniform showed up, causing hearts to flutter. 'That sailor boy is going to walk me home when I leave here,' said the aunt, who dropped her handkerchief, bobby pins and various things that the quarry ignored as he walked right by.

When church was over, the sailor approached Plinia and asked the all important question, 'May I walk you home?' The answer was yes since her brother was along, making it suitable.

After the second time of being walked home by the sailor, her mother questioned her closely. 'Who is that boy?' On being told that she didn't know, the mother replied, 'Well, you better find out if you want him to keep walking you home!'

Took three walks, but finally the sailor's watch got turned over (with a bit of finagling by Pliny) and she saw a name, Roy, which was reported to her Mother. Pretty quickly her last name became Deel - the same as his - and more than fifty years later they're still together and have a gleam in their eyes when they tell this story."

Roy Deel came from a family of teachers (his father and three brothers) and taught 30+ years in Haysi. His daughter, Cathy Harrison is very proud of both her parents and told us this story at the Library in Haysi where she works. Across the street, Roy and Pliny are immortalized as part of the Haysi town mural that faces a small park.

Creamy Chocolate Pie

Rita Surratt-Clintwood, VA

1 cup sugar	2 egg yolks
1/3 cup cocoa	2 Tbsps. butter
1/3 cup flour	1 tsp. vanilla flavoring
2 cups milk	dash of salt

Beat egg yolks and cook with other ingredients until smooth. Pour into baked pie crust. Add meringue if desired.

Mountain Art Works

www.mountainartworks.net

Mountain Art Works in Haysi provides good food, music, and locally crafted items in a homey atmosphere. Every Thursday night any and all musicians are invited to come in and jam, while diners enjoy listening or do a little dancing. Families are welcome. Entertainment is usually provided on Friday and Saturday nights, as well.

Creamy Snickers Salad

Jane Moore – Mountain Art Works, Haysi, VA

1 (8 oz.) cream cheese
1 jar (7 oz.) marshmallow crème
1 (8 oz.) Cool Whip
  diced apples (any amount)
  diced Snickers candy bars (any amount)

Blend cream cheese and marshmallow crème; fold in Cool Whip. Add diced apples and candy bars. It takes about 5 minutes and is delicious. (Mildred Deel of our Lions Club shared this recipe with me.)

The Lord is my rock, and my fortress, and my deliverer; my God, my strength, in whom I will trust; my buckler, and the horn of my salvation, and my high tower.
Psalm 18: 2

Crème Puff Cake

Kathy Harrison – Haysi, VA

1   cup water
1   stick margarine
1   cup self rising flour
4   eggs
2 ½ cups milk
1   large box vanilla instant pudding
1   (8 oz.) cream cheese (softened at room temp.)
1   (8 oz.) Cool Whip

Add margarine to water and bring to a boil. Boil until margarine melts. Remove from heat and stir in flour. Add one egg and stir until mixture begins to become dry. Add second egg and repeat until 4 eggs are thoroughly mixed. Spread in a 9 ½ x 13 inch pan. Bake at 400° for 30 minutes. Remove from oven and press down crust with hands. Let cool.

Mix pudding and milk. Before it gets thick add cream cheese and beat well. Pour over cooled crust and spread Cool Whip over pudding mixture. Serves 12.

The heavens declare the glory of God: and the firmament sheweth his handiwork.
Psalm 19:1

Crock Pot Apple Butter

*Chris Deel, Flat Top Guitar for **Basic Grass** – Haysi, VA*

8   cups of thick apples (cooked with no lumps)
4   cups sugar
1/8 cup vinegar
2-3 drops cinnamon oil
3   cinnamon sticks

Cook on high 5 hours, then cook on low 5 hours.

Curried Cider-Pork Stew

Carol Sadler, submitted by: Mavis Sowards, Clintwood, VA

- 2 lbs. boneless pork shoulder
- 3 medium red and/or green crisp-tart cooking apples
- 1 Tbsp. cooking oil
- 1 large onion cut in thin wedges
- 2 tsps. curry powder
- 1 can chicken broth (14 oz.)
- 2/3 cup apple cider or apple juice
- ¼ tsp. salt
- ¼ tsp. ground black pepper
- 12 ozs. baby carrots with tops, trimmed or packaged peeled baby carrots
- 2 stalks celery, sliced
- 1½ lbs. butternut squash, peeled and cubed (2 cups)
- Sour cream, shredded orange peel, snipped fresh oregano and/or freshly ground pepper (optional)

Trim fat from pork; cut pork in 1 inch cubes, peel, core and chop 2 apples; set aside. In a 4-qt. Dutch oven, brown pork half at a time in hot oil; return all pork to pan. Add chopped apples, onion, and curry powder. Cook and stir 2 minutes, add broth, cider, salt, and pepper. Bring to boiling, reduce heat, and simmer covered for 30 minutes, stirring occasionally.

Add carrots and celery to pork mixture; return to boiling. Reduce heat; simmer covered 20 minutes, stirring occasionally. Cut remaining apples in ¼-inch thick wedges. Add apples and squash to pan and cover; cook 10 to 12 minutes or until pork and vegetables are tender. Serve with sour cream, orange peel, oregano, and pepper. Makes 6 servings. Cook 1 hour.

Carol didn't use the sour cream, orange peel, oregano, or pepper and it was delicious!!!

Railroads came to the mountains in the late 1800's. This provided construction jobs, first of all, and then a means to ship out coal and lumber, forever changing the area. The people of the region have paid a heavy price for the coal industry.

Falling in the Well
Mavis Sowards

"Daddy and Mommy were going over to a neighbor's farm to work in tobacco. I wanted to go but they didn't let me. Now, I didn't want to work; I just wanted to ride the old mare. So I was mad about being left behind and looking to cause trouble.

There were fifteen in our family and I was number twelve. Mama said that out of the whole lot, I was the worst. But we all pulled pranks and tried to scare each other, even our parents. Hard work was just a way of life; singing and playing made us basically a happy family.

So, looking to do something mean that morning, I saw my brother Jim going into the outhouse. I waited til he had time to get sorta comfortable, then I started throwing rocks. That'll give you a jolt, taking care of business and a big rock going *kur-thump* right by your head. He came flying out, fastening up his overalls, and grabbin' rocks to throw back. He was burning me up so I took off for the cornfield and hid in a corner of the rail fence.

There, I hatched a plan. It involved the hand-dug well that us smaller children were not allowed to go near alone. The well was 80 ft. deep. Our father had walled it all the way down with fieldstone. The zinc bucket was let down by a rope handle and was supposed to be used cautiously.

Our older sisters had to look out for us younger ones and practically raised us because Mommy worked right alongside Dad all the time. They took over the work around the house, too, when needed.

I walked past my sister, Faye, who was sweeping the yard. (Yes, the yard had to be swept. Grass couldn't grow with 15 kids and chickens and other animals roaming around!) Went on in the kitchen and told another sister, Lee, who was cooking, that I wanted some water. "Go ahead and get some and go on out," she said.

"This ain't fresh. I want some fresh water."

"You can't get it and I don't have time. Just drink that," Lee answers.

"Can I take the bucket out to Faye?" I counter. Lee decided I could.

I walked right past Faye with the bucket, toward the well. "You can't draw water," she tells me. "Lee said I could," I replied.

She washes her hands of the situation and goes on sweeping. I wind the bucket carefully down about halfway. Then I position myself on the side away from Faye, so that my head is downhill and my feet are sticking up over the top of the rock wall around the well. I reach up and let that bucket go and it clangs and makes a terrible racket as it beats from side to side. As the noise attracts Faye's attention, I start screaming and jerk my feet down. From her side, it looks like I have fallen into the well.

"Mavis fell in the well!" Faye yells to the others, her voice full of fright. She comes flying around the well as white as a sheet. Upon spying me lying on the ground, the white quickly began to be replaced by red that started at her neck and crept into her face as realization made fear turn to anger.

A broom can be a terrible weapon, I found out. I mean to tell you she was swiping me and stayed right behind me as I circled the house screaming at the top of my lungs. Jim came up from the barn and propped on the gate, enjoying the show. 'Help me, Jim!' I hollered on one round and 'do something, Jim!' on another.

"What can I do?" he replied, happy that I was getting what he figured was coming to me.

Out of breath, I shouted, 'You could (pant) open the gate (pant, pant) the next time I come around!'

He didn't, but I spied a little hole under the fence and dived for it. I got hung and Faye was just wearing me out while I was stuck. I shucked out of my overalls that were about two sizes too big anyway and took off in my feed sack underwear. (We called them droopy-drawers because they had drawstrings to keep them tight and that often loosened.)

Smack dab in front of me came the preacher with a saw on his shoulders that he was bringing for Daddy to sharpen. "How're you doing, little girl?" he asked kindly.

"Fi..fi..fine," I whimpered, and took off for the barn. Boy, was I in for it now. Greeting the preacher in my droopy drawers on top of my other sins. Crying myself to sleep was my only consolation.

Hours later, wrapped in dread, I started toward the house. Somebody had felt sorry for me and hung my overalls on the gatepost. Supper found a subdued Mavis at the table, waiting for the ax to fall.

"How did things go around here today?" asked Mama. I was scared to death. Nobody said anything and the meal went on.

Jim looked at Faye and whispered, "Open the gate!" They snickered. Boy, did I eat crow that day, even though they didn't tell on me. They saved it to hold over my head. That caused me to have to be good for a right long time. But… not *too* long…

Dandelion Salad
Viva Lea Stanley

Clean and wash enough dandelion greens for a large bowl	2 Tbsps. flour	½ cup water
4 slices bacon	3 Tbsps. vinegar	1 large beaten egg
	1 Tbsp. sugar	Salt & pepper to taste

Cut bacon into small pieces and fry until crisp. Add water; mix the beaten egg with salt & pepper, flour, vinegar, and sugar. Add to the bacon and cook over low heat until dressing is thick. Just before serving, add the hot dressing to the greens and toss. Serve with fried trout and hot cornbread or hot rolls. Makes 4 – 6 servings.

Ralph Stanley Museum and Traditional Mountain Music Center

We learned a lesson in relativity (the distance of a quarter mile ain't the same to out-of-towners as to natives) while exploring winding roads looking for the site of Ralph Stanley's Festival and the home of Willie and Cathy Neece, whom we'd met at the Museum. At one stop for directions, an amused fellow stated as I waved my arms and babbled while explaining where we'd been (lost!) "You ain't from around here, are you?"

Though Clintwood, VA, has traditionally been better known as a town one stumbles across than a destination, the state of the art Ralph Stanley Museum has changed that concept somewhat. Opened on October 16, 2004, the museum features headphones for visitors that allow them to plug into music selections and Dr. Ralph Stanley's narration of his childhood, early career, and some milestones in bluegrass music history.

Stanley, who received an honorary Ph.D. from Lincoln Memorial University in Harrogate, Tennessee, grew up singing spirituals in the McClure Primitive Baptist Church. That haunting and timeless sound from childhood has traveled the world through the music that he and his band have performed for over fifty years.

A soundtrack album for the movie, "O Brother, Where Art Thou," in 2000 won five Grammys, two Country Music Associations Awards and sold millions of CD's. It brought attention to bluegrass and traditional singers and their music, including Dr. Stanley who was 77 at the time. That publicity was perhaps an impetus in getting the world-class museum that now serves as a resource for preserving traditional mountain music and cultural programs of the area.

The museum is located in the historical Chase House, built by attorney Roland E. Chase in 1904, the first brick house in the county. The house later became a boarding house and cafeteria and after that, a funeral parlor. The town of Clintwood bought the house as part of its revitalization project. Many organizations and grants have been instrumental in accomplishing the feat of transformation from rundown to redesigned and rejuvenated.

Knowledgeable and agreeable, Director Aaron Davis and Assistant Director Pam Morris provide top-notch guidance for the Museum. Their assistance adds the sparkle to your visit. Though located several steps up from street level, the building is handicapped accessible from a parking lot in back of the Museum. *www.ralphstanleymuseum.com*

Jettie Baker Center

Mullins Theater thrived in the late 1940's when it was new, but was vacant and rundown by the 1990's when the town decided to revitalize. With federal, state, and local funding the 350-seat (none of them bad!) building became a showplace that can host musical and community events, plays, and conferences. Well-equipped with top of the line lighting and sound, a great stage, and backstage rooms that make some in bigger venues look shabby, the center is an asset to the community and a great place to take in a show.

Easy Cereal Bars
Shirley Hawkins –Haysi, VA

- 4 cups Grape Nuts cereal
- 1 cup oatmeal
- 1 cup almonds or pecans
- 1 cup dried cranberries, dried Cherries, or raisins
- ½ cup chocolate chips (optional)
- ½ cup sugar or Splenda
- 1 cup Karo syrup
- 1 ½ cups peanut butter

Combine and stir the first 5 ingredients together and set aside. Combine the remaining 3 ingredients together in a saucepan and bring to a boil. Boil for 1 minute. Add this to the dry ingredients and stir well. Line a 9 x 13-inch pan with aluminum foil and spray it with vegetable oil spray. Spread the mixture in this pan. Cool, cut into squares, and remove from the pan. Makes 24 squares.

Fried Green Tomatoes
Barbara Vanover, Clintwood, VA

Tomatoes
Flour
Shortening
Salt & pepper
Sugar

Slice tomatoes about ¼ inch thick. Coat each piece with flour. Put in a skillet of hot melted shortening. Salt and pepper to taste. Sprinkle a generous amount of sugar on each piece of tomato. When brown, turn over and sprinkle on more sugar. Fry until tender.

Doke
Jessie Mullins

- 1 cup hot coffee
- sugar & cream to taste
- 1 Tbsp. butter
- 1 baked home-made biscuit

Put biscuit and butter in hot creamed and sugared coffee. Eat while hot. Father always ate this.

"This is a recipe from my great-grandmother Lydia Large. I remember my Grandmother Bessie Large making this cake, as my great-grandmother Large had already passed before I was born. Anytime I hear or see the words "Jam Cake" I remember my late grandmother who always had leftover food in her oven and refrigerator whenever anyone dropped by her house."

Grandmother Large's Jam Cake
Cathy Stanley

2 cups sugar	1 cup buttermilk
3 cups plain flour	4 cups jam
1½ cups butter	1 box raisins
6 eggs	1 can nuts
2 tsps. nutmeg	2 tsps. baking soda
2 tsps. cinnamon	2 tsps. baking powder

Melt butter; add eggs and sugar, and mix well. Add dry ingredients, then milk and jam. Flour raisins and nuts and mix well. Bake 2 hours in greased and floured tube pan at 300°. Put pan of water under cake pan in oven for moisture.

"Mountain people made their own gritters. They took tin, usually a coffee can, and flattened it out. Then they drove nail holes all over it and fastened it to a smooth board with the sharp side out. It worked."

Gritted Corn Bread
Helen Mullins Fields

2 cups gritted corn	salt to taste (2-3 pinches)
2 pinches soda	buttermilk (enough to make a batter)

Mix and bake in 8 or 9-inch iron skillet in 400° oven. The bread will be somewhat sticky or "doughy," more like spoon bread than regular corn bread. Delicious!

Note: Corn should be past the tender, milky stage – firm but not hard.

A Sunbeam
to warm you,
A Moonbeam
to charm you,
Laughter
to cheer you.
Faithful friends
near you.
A sheltering
Angel so
Nothing can
harm you.
And whenever
you pray,
Heaven to
hear you.

-An Irish Blessing

Helen Mullins Fields

Helen Mullins Fields, who has seen her ninetieth birthday come and go, was second from the baby in a family of thirteen children and the only one still surviving. She vividly recalls details of everyday life on the farm where her Mother, Father, and the three youngest children lived. It was located on a strip of bottomland near the entrance to Garden Hole, on the road that leads to Breaks Interstate Park. Constant work was required to keep food on the table and to feed the animals, but she remembers it as being a special time. The older children had married and started their own families, but what a good time was had when they all came to visit!

"I can still see my Mother working in the fields until time to go in and cook dinner. Then she would pull ears of corn to take to the house to shuck and grit into meal for our bread. It was wonderful - I can taste it right now!"

> "Something was there, a special spirit, during my early years that I wish we had today. Maybe we looked more to the Lord back then."
> - *Helen Mullins Fields*

Ham Delights

Sheila B. Phipps – Clintwood, VA

3   cans Hormel chunk ham, chopped
1   sm. onion, sauté in ham juice
1   tsp. Worcestershire sauce
3   Tbsp. poppy seeds
1 ¾   sticks butter, melted
1   pkg. shredded Swiss cheese
24   party rolls

Mix together and spread on party rolls. Wrap in aluminum foil and heat in 300° oven until hot, about 25-30 minutes. Great appetizer for family get togethers. Left over ham works well, also.

Good corn meal is required for good corn bread. Because we were lucky enough to meet Carl and Alice Counts, we brought home some that was a hit. The corn seed has been kept from year to year in her family for generations and is almost a burgundy color when ground by Carl. Different and absolutely delicious!

Ham Hocks & Collard Greens with Cornmeal Dumplings

Ethel Silcox, submitted by: Rita Surratt, Clintwood, VA

1½	lbs. ham hocks	1½ cups water
2	lbs. collard greens	salt to taste
2	cups cornmeal	

Cook ham hocks in 1 ½ cups water until tender. Add salt to taste. Wash and drain 2 lbs. fresh collard greens and put into pot with ham hocks and cook 15 minutes.

Make cornmeal dumplings by adding enough water to meal to make dumplings, pat out like a small pancake, stiff enough so they won't fall apart. Drop into boiling ham and collards. Don't stir dumplings. Cook 5 minutes.

"It's recognized that women of the mountains were artisans, often from necessity, with their crocheting, quiltmaking, sewing, spinning, and rugmaking. But the men were artistic with rail fences, rock walls, the way they laid out the fields, and built cabins and furniture. What they often created was harmony."
-Anita Belcher

Homemade Soap
Retha Grizzle, Haysi, VA

1   can lye
2½ pints cold rainwater
6   lbs. clean fat (lard, tallow, or shortening)

Slowly add lye to cold water, stirring to dissolve. Melt fat and let cool (Lard - 85°, Tallow - 110°). Pour lye solution into melted fat in a thin steady stream, with slow even stirring. Continue stirring until a thick wooden spoon can stand on its own. Pour into cardboard or wooden box lined with plastic wrap. Let stand for 24 hours. Remove and cut into bars. Keep in dry room for 2 weeks to cure.

Sunday Meatloaf

Gayle Stanley – Clintwood, VA

- 3 lbs. ground beef
- 1 large onion (thinly diced)
- 6 slices white bread (crumbled into small pieces)
- 2 small sweet peppers (chopped)
- 3 eggs
- ¼ cup milk
- 1 bottle chili sauce
- 1 small can tomato sauce
- Salt and pepper to taste

Mix all ingredients and put into greased pan.

Topper Sauce:

- 1 large can tomato sauce
- 3 Tbsps. yellow mustard
- 5 Tbsps. red vinegar
- ½ cup water
- ½ cup brown sugar

Mix and pour over meatloaf. (This will be thin). Bake for 1 hour at 400^0.

Molasses Cake

Tina & Savannah Church - Clinchco, VA

- ½ cup of molasses
- ½ cup buttermilk
- ½ cup sugar
- ½ cup oil
- 2 eggs
- 1¾ cup of self rising flour
- 10 tsps. ginger

Put all ingredients in bowl and stir until smooth. Put in two 8 inch pans. Bake at 350° for 35 minutes. Split layers and spread cooked apples or applesauce in between layers (I use applesauce). If using applesauce, add sugar and nutmeg to taste before putting between the layers. Eat, it is yummy!

May the road rise to meet you.
May the wind be always at your back.
May the sun shine warm upon your face;
The rains fall soft upon your fields.
And, until we meet again,
May God hold you in the palm of his hand.
 -Irish Blessing

Molasses Stack Cake

Janie Bise – Clintwood, VA

> "On a trip to the Breaks Park, Charlie and I stood with his Mother and Father, looking at the mountains and the river flowing on each side. His Dad commented that they always liked to come here this time of year because it was about now that the water pressure collected and built up enough under the mountain that it lifted slightly to let the water run out. 'If you watch close, you might just see it today,' he said. Before we left, I could have sworn I saw them rise a bit!"
> *-Izetta Fleming*

1 cup molasses
¾ cup sugar
2 sticks margarine, softened
½ cup boiling water
1 Tbsp. baking soda
1 Tbsp. ginger
1 egg, beaten
6 cups plain flour
   pinch of salt (1/4 tsp.)
   applesauce
   apple pie spice

Mix molasses, sugar, and butter. Add egg, beating all thoroughly. Add the boiling water, then add the soda, ginger, and salt which has been sifted with 4 cups flour. Mix well; add the other 2 cups of flour. Cover with paper towel and let set 30-45 minutes. Work like biscuit dough on a pastry cloth. Keep putting flour around the dough and working it in being careful not to add too much. Roll dough into a long roll and pinch off small amount. Press into a 9-inch cake pan which has been sprayed with Pam. Bake 10 minutes at 350°. Makes 10 layers. Put layers together while warm with warm spiced applesauce between layers of cake.
Use one teaspoon apple pie spice per quart of applesauce.

Old-fashioned Molasses Stack Cake

"When Mountain couples got married everyone in the community baked a layer of cake and covered the top with applesauce. Then they would bring the layer of cake to the wedding. The layers would go into a stack of cake hence the layered wedding cake became known as a stack cake. The couple's popularity was measured by how high their wedding cake was." *-Gayle Stanley*

"This is the recipe my Great Aunt Martha used. She used to make her cakes during Thanksgiving and hide them until Christmas. We would usually find her stash before Christmas and steal one out. The last time we found them hidden in her old wringer-type washing machine. I remember the sweet taste of that cake!"

Moonshine Fruitcake
Gayle Stanley – Clintwood, VA

2 ½   cups chopped nuts (pecans or walnuts or a mixture of both, also mixed between whole and chopped)
1   pkg. (8 oz.) whole pitted dates, chop into two or three slices each. The chopped dates are not as good as the big chunks are in this recipe.)
1   cup dark raisins
1   container (8 oz.) red candied cherries
1   container (4 oz.) candied pineapple
1 ½   cups candied mixed fruits and peels
1 ¼   cups unbleached plain all-purpose flour
1 ¼   cups white sugar
1   tsp. baking powder
½   tsp. salt
6   eggs
2   Tbsps. brandy or a good drinking rum
    moonshine or other whiskey (for pouring on the cakes)

Preheat oven to 300°. Put a pan of hot water in the oven on the lower shelf below the cakes to keep them moist while baking and to

A kitchen is a friendly place, Full of livings daily grace. And rich in dignity is she Who shares its hospitality.

keep the fruit in the cakes from sticking to the pans. To prepare pans, cut brown paper or parchment liners for sides and bottoms of two bread loaf pans. Grease the pans with solid Crisco shortening or spray with Pam. Then arrange the paper liners inside the pans and grease the paper liners or spray with Pam. This step is very important to keep the fruit in the cake from sticking to the inside of the pan.

Combine all nuts and fruits in a very large bowl. Beat eggs with brandy until light, pour over fruit mixture, and then blend in thoroughly. Let the fruit soak in the rum mixture while you mix the dry ingredients and prepare the pans.

Mix together flour, sugar, baking powder, and salt. Set aside.

When you are ready to mix the cake batter, sprinkle the dry ingredients over the fruit mixture; mix well with heavy spoon to a doughy consistency. Spoon mixture into pans, press down firmly until nuts and fruits are almost covered with batter. Bake at 300° for 1 hr. and 45 min.

Remove the cakes from the pans when you get them out of the oven. (Do not wait 10 minutes as you would for other types of cakes.) Invert the pan with a thump onto the counter top on a plate to release the cake. Peel away the paper liners from the cake immediately while it is hot. If you wait too long the cake will cool, and the fruit will stick to the liners and pull chunks out of your cakes.

When cakes are thoroughly cool, dribble a little moonshine or any other whiskey, over the cakes, then soak clean cheesecloths in some moonshine or whiskey and wrap each cake in the cheesecloth. (You may use men's undershirts for wrapping cloths if cheesecloth is not available.) Place the cakes in containers with tight-fitting lids, or wrap in heavy aluminum foil. Store in a cool, dark place for four weeks. But, you may eat the cakes right away, or at any stage along the process. However, the longer the cakes sit, the softer and more flavorful they will become.

I like God's mathematics – He can take one-tenth and do more with it than I can with ten-tenths. Tithing takes the worry out of living.

> Old Saying: You can't keep trouble from coming but you don't have to pull it up a chair to sit on.

Mamaw's Peach Cobbler

Sunday dinners at Mamaw's will never be forgotten. Food, fun, and fellowship were always in abundance.

My grandmother gave birth to twelve children. Those children all had many children as well. On any one Sunday, as many as fifty people were in and out of her house to share in food and conversation. Aunts, uncles, sons, daughters, cousins, nieces, nephews, grandchildren, great-grandchildren, and great-great grandchildren all gathered around the table.

Among the delectable foods that were served, peach cobbler was my favorite. I was the grandchild that my grandmother made peach cobbler for. I liked it fresh out of the oven, two hours old, or two days old. (Although it rarely ever lasted that long) Mamaw would always remember me and tell the others, "Save some of that cobbler for Rita Jean!"

My family is from the southeastern corner of Kentucky. I am a coalminer's granddaughter. My ancestry goes back to Scotland and Ireland. Hard work, commitment to God and family, and a sense of community was bred into us. Food and the sharing of it was at the top of the list. Almost everything was shared over food.

As my grandmother began to age and arthritis crippled her hands, cataracts dimmed her eyesight, and cancer weakened her body, I began to wonder how much of her life we all really knew. I spent a lot of time the last seven years of her life asking her questions about her life as a child, about raising children, and about the recipes of some of my favorite foods she prepared.

"How about giving me the recipe for your peach cobbler?" I asked.

"Recipe? I don't have a recipe for it, I just make it, child," she replied.

"Well, can you let me watch you the next time you make it?"

"Why, sure."

She didn't use measuring spoons or cups. As she added each ingredient I would have her pour her handful, pinch, or shake of ingredient into a measuring cup or spoon. It took a little time but was well worth it. Every time I make peach cobbler, I think back to those days of having my dear Mamaw, Louellen Lafferty Porter, with me and once again, I share in her life. - *Rita Jean Belcher*

Peach Cobbler

Louellen Lafferty (Mamaw) Porter's recipe

1 cup flour (self-rising)
1 cup sugar
1 cup milk
1 stick butter
2 cups fresh or frozen peaches

Heat oven to 350°. In a bowl, mix flour, sugar and milk. Melt butter in an 8x8 pan in the oven. Pour flour mixture into hot buttered pan. Pour peaches on top of flour mixture. Bake for 30 minutes or until top is brown and peaches are bubbly.

"I share these cookies with people who come by. Everyone thinks they are great but kids love when you add 2 cups of chocolate chips to this recipe."

Peanut Butter Cookies

Edna Gulley, Appalachian Women's Alliance Center, Clinchco, VA

2 ½ cups plain flour	½ tsp. salt
2 sticks butter	1 ½ tsps. vanilla
1 cup brown sugar (packed)	1 cup peanut butter
1 cup white sugar	3 large eggs
1 tsp. baking soda	

Preheat oven at 375°. Combine butter, sugars, eggs, and vanilla and beat well. Add flour, salt, and soda, mix all ingredients together. Roll into balls and place on cookie sheet. Bake for 10 minutes. They are good!

A sad fact of life; too many square meals often make round people.

Pepsi Roast

Myrtle Mullins - Clintwood, VA

1 3 or 4 lb. beef chuck roast	1 pkg. onion soup mix
1 pkg. brown gravy mix	1 can golden mushroom soup
1 can Pepsi	

Coat slow cooker with nonstick spray and place roast in cooker. Mix together brown gravy mix, onion soup, mushroom soup, and Pepsi. Pour over roast and cook until tender.

Pickled Corn

Izetta Fleming

Start with 2 gallons of water or enough water to cover corn. Put coarse salt in water. Stir until dissolved. Place egg on top of water. If egg floats, you have enough salt. (Be careful, do not break egg.)

Cook corn on cob until barely tender and cool quickly. Place in crock. Put a plate on top of corn and a rock on top of plate to weigh it down. Cover crock with cloth. Tie down with a string. Can be kept all winter in a cool place.

"You can use any kind of vegetables you like to make this recipe. Put the veggies in raw and you decide the amount you use of each vegetable. I use a gallon jar and put in refrigerator until all are eaten. This is good to snack on."

Pickled Vegetables
Kathy Harrison, Haysi, VA

1 quart white vinegar
1 cup canning salt
1 ½ cups Mazola oil
 cauliflower
 carrots
celery
onions
banana peppers
(hot if you like)
cabbage

Heat the vinegar, salt, and Mazola oil until it boils. Simmer for 10 minutes and pour over raw vegetables.

Pork Chops with Barbecue Sauce
Jimmy Mullins - Kenneth Childress - Clintwood, VA

2 Tbsps. sugar
2 Tbsps. Worcestershire sauce
½ cup white vinegar
½ cup catsup
¼ cup butter
1 tsp. salt
¼ tsp. pepper
1 tsp. paprika
1 Tbsp. prepared mustard
6-7 pork chops

Place chops in baking dish. Combine all ingredients and bring to a boil. Pour over chops. Cover and bake at 350° for approximately 1 hour.

To believe only in possibilities is not Faith, but mere philosophy.
If anything can be done, experience and skill can do it.
If a thing cannot be done, only Faith can do it.
Faith is Fear that has said its prayers.
Faith is not contrary to reason, but rather, reason grown courageous.

Ol' Barney

by Mavis Soward
(as told to Betty Skeens)

"Daddy had a team of mules he had raised from colts that he just thought the world of. Ol' Barney and Ol' Noah is what we called them and we accused Daddy of thinking more of them than us children. "You'd sell one of us before you'd sell one of them ol' mules," we told him.

"I reckon it'd be easier to replace a kid than to find a good mule," he would reply.

One Saturday evening Dad was feeling really bad and was lying down. He was getting older and I was the only one left at home. (Even my younger siblings had married, causing me to dance in the hog trough three times.) "Mavis," he told me, "you're going to have to feed and take care of the mules this evening, because I'm not able to."

I was going to milk anyway, so I said okay. I sorta dreaded it because Ol' Barney was frisky, even though he was getting older, too. He would kick your head off or bite cha' if he got half a chance.

When I got out there, Ol' Barney was standing there with his head drooped almost between his front legs, moaning. I could tell something bad was wrong with him.

Running back into the house, I told Dad, "Something's wrong with Barney! He looks like he's about to fall over."

"Call Elmer Smith, I'm not able to go out and check him," he said. Elmer was the County Extension Agent and had often come out to the farm when we needed help with the livestock.

When I got Elmer on the phone, he said, "Mavis, I can't come tonight. I'm just leaving to take some boys to Blacksburg for a poultry-judging contest. Tell me how he's acting and maybe I can tell you what to do for him."

After my description, Elmer told me he thought Barney had colic and I could take care of him. "What am I to do?" I ask.

"Give him a dose of mineral oil," he instructed me.

"And how am I supposed to do that?" I reply.

"Get a long-necked bottle and pour it down him."

"Oh, no, I'll not try that! That ornery ol' mule will bite my arm off!" I answer.

"Well, you'll have to go the other route, then," Elmer says. "You'll have to put it in his back-end."

"What?! How in the world am I supposed to manage that?"

"You've got that old log barn over there, with some big chunks out of the wall," he tells me. "Back his rear up to one of those holes and tie him in place. Get you a funnel and insert it from outside the barn. Pour the mineral oil in and it will help break up the gas bubbles and relieve the colic."

I pass the information along to Dad. "Mavis, I can't help you, I'm too sick. You'll have to manage by yourself."

Things went a little better than I anticipated. Barney was fairly docile and backed up pretty easily. I stationed a rail in front of him to keep him in the corner. A search of the outbuildings yielded nothing in the way of a funnel, however. It was getting dark by now and I was getting more flustered. I spied an old fox horn of my brother's and noticed it was open at both ends. It even had the right general shape, being smaller on one end, somewhat like a cow's horn. "Maybe this'll do," I think.

Neither could I spot anything in the tool shed that was clearly labeled *mineral oil*. Mostly, they were faded and it was hard to see by now, anyway. Finally, I spotted a bottle that looked right and headed back to the barn and Barney's rear end, knowing that if he wasn't so sick, I wouldn't even attempt what I was about to do. After a little work, I got that horn in place and remembered that Elmer hadn't said how much mineral oil to use. Since I only intended to do this one time, I turned it up and used the whole thing.

In a split second, Ol' Barney's moan turned to a scream. I stood in shock as he broke the rail in front of him and burst out the door like a bullet. Out into the barnyard he went, where he began jumping up and down like he had springs on the bottom of his feet. Up and down, up and down, and every time he hit the ground, that fox horn would blow. Then he took off down the holler as hard as he could go with me trying to catch him.

Our neighbors down the road had a bunch of foxhounds that thought someone was calling to the hunt, so they managed to get out and came after him, barking as hard as they could. They passed me right off. There we went, Barney in front jumping and tootin', the dogs barking close behind, and me bringing up the rear.

My uncle came along in a car and slowed beside me. "What is going on?" he yelled. "I'm after ol' Barney," I yell back.

"Get in the car," he said.

We take off and hit the hard top headed into Clintwood. That mule and them dogs go right on through town toward Pound. Cars lined up behind us while Barney was still up ahead tootin' and the dogs still barking. Everybody was yelling and cheering, adding to the commotion.

My uncle said we might as well turn around 'cause nobody was going to catch that mule with dogs after him. I was crying and going on, dreading to go tell poor Dad what had happened to his favorite mule. It was especially hard after smelling of the bottle left lying on the ground. It reeked of turpentine…

Anyway, two days later we heard about Ol' Barney. Seems he'd made it through Kentucky clear to the Ohio River, still tootin' and with the foxhounds still behind. The drawbridge operator heard the tooting and thought it was a tugboat; he began

> "Seems he'd made it through Kentucky clear to the Ohio River."

raising the bridge just as Barney and the dogs got about mid way. It threw the lot of them right into the water below. Mule and dogs went under, never to surface alive. Some fishermen nearby swore that when Barney went under, he was playing taps.

It was later told that the bridge operator lost his job. They said if he couldn't tell the difference between a tugboat and a mule with a horn up his behind, he sure didn't need to be in charge of raising and lowering a bridge.

Basic Grass

Dale Boyd, bass; Chris Deel, Guitar; Harmon Roy Johnson, banjo; Gary Edwards, mandolin and fiddle.

"My husband, Gary Edwards, has a bluegrass band, *Basic Grass*. It is made up of Gary Edwards, who plays the mandolin and the fiddle, Chris Deel, who plays the guitar, Harmon Roy Johnson, who plays the banjo, and Dale Boyd, who plays bass.

The band was named *Basic Grass* on the spur of the moment. This group was getting ready to go on stage and realized they didn't have a name. So my husband said, "They want to know the name of the band, what are we going to call it?" I thought for a moment, and then said "*Basic Grass*." All the members agreed and so it stuck and we love it. Some of the members have changed since then but my husband's band has remained *Basic Grass*.

They have played at several of the places that are noted along the Crooked Road. They play also a lot of benefit shows for free to aid a good cause. Sometimes they are requested to sing at funerals which they do willingly. They also play for the senior citizens and at nursing homes. My husband plays music for the fun of it. He enjoys it and wants to pass this joy on to others. I am so proud of this band, *Basic Grass*."

Quick and Zesty Vegetable Soup
Ruth R. Edwards, Birchleaf, VA

1 (1 lb., 13 oz.) can Veg-All mixed vegetables
1 (10 oz.) can cream of celery soup
1 (15 oz.) can turkey chili/beans
1 (8.5 oz.) can peas & carrots
1 (10.5 oz.) can chicken with rice soup
1 (10 oz.) can diced tomatoes and green chilies
1 (14.5 oz.) can whole tomatoes (chopped)
1 soup can of water

Mix all ingredients together. Bring to a boil. Cook 10 minutes. This soup makes a quick and easy warm up for a cold winter evening. It's a tasty treat anytime.

The Hog Toother

"I was eighteen when Charlie and I got married and we were making our first visit to his parent's house. Lying on the porch was a strange looking tool. "What's this for?" I naively asked my new father-in-law.

"Well, honey, that's a hog toother," he replied. "Sometimes you have a sow that's getting a little old, a good ol' breeder, and her tooth will fall out. You take that tool and pick up the tooth and put it back in. Her gums will latch back around that tooth, and she'll breed another few years."

Pity for the poor old sow filled me. I felt so sorry for that poor hog having to make babies till she fell over 'cause they kept putting her teeth back in.

It was a while before I found out it was a hog ringer- to put a ring in the nose of a hog to keep them from rooting under the fence.

-Izetta Fleming

> Whenever you see food beautifully arranged on a plate, you know someone's fingers have been all over it
> *-Julia Child*

Shrimp Butter
Betty Stanley – Clintwood, VA

1	(8 oz.) cream cheese
1½	sticks of butter
3	Tbsps. mayonnaise
1	Tbsp. onion, chopped finely
1	Tbsp. lemon juice
2	small cans shrimp-drained

Mix cream cheese & butter together until smooth. Then add rest of the ingredients. Chill for about 1 or 2 hours. Serve with crackers of your choice.

Salt your food with humor, Pepper it with wit, And Sprinkle over it the charm of fellowship. (But don't poison it with the cares of life!)

"This is nothing fancy but it's truly a soldier's feast. This is one of my favorite recipes that we fix when re-enacting or doing living histories at school. The kids get a kick out of the squirrel because it's something that they have never had before."

Squirrel and Dumplings in a Dutch oven
Creg Barton, 1st Sgt. Cumberland Mtn. Rangers - Clintwood, VA

2	squirrels cut into serving size pieces
1	onion chopped
1	bay leaf
1	large can of biscuits
	salt & pepper to taste

Place squirrels, onions, bay leaf, salt, and pepper into Dutch oven. Cover with water and cook until squirrel is done. Then roll out the biscuit dough very thin, cut into 1 x 4 inch pieces, add these to Dutch oven, cover, and cook until dumplings are firm.

Refresh stale potato chips, crackers, cereal, or other snacks by putting in microwave for 30-45 seconds. Let stand for 1 minute to crisp.

Sugar Cured Ham
Clay Trent, submitted by: Izetta Fleming - Clintwood, VA

2 cups coarse salt
2 Tbsps. black pepper
1 Tbsp. red pepper
2-2 ½ lbs. brown sugar
1 ham from 200 lb. hog
meat should feel warm

Mix together the first 4 ingredients. Lay warm ham on brown paper large enough to wrap ham. Rub in mixture until it starts to melt. Wrap the ham up in paper. Then wrap in cheese cloth. Let lay for 48 hours at room temperature. Drop ham in cloth bag. Hang with knee down.

Vinegar Butter
Viva Lea Stanley

1 cup sugar
2 Tbsps. cornstarch
¼ cup vinegar
¾ cup water
2 Tbsps. butter
1 tsp. vanilla
pinch of salt

Combine cornstarch, sugar, and salt. Mix the vinegar and water in a sauce pan. Slowly add cornstarch mixture. Bring to a boil. Add butter and vanilla. Cook until thick. Serve over hot biscuits or toast.

Advice to a wife about her husband: You have to lean on him on one side…. And prop him up on the other.

Dickenson County mural for 4-H. There are many beautiful murals in Dickenson County.

Yeast Cornbread
Gayle Stanley – Clintwood, VA

"I found this recipe many years ago. It's really different. Bake it in loaf pans and then it can be sliced just like "white" bread."

1	cup milk
6	Tbsps. sugar
2	eggs, beaten
3 ½	cups unbleached plain all-purpose flour
1 ¾	cups yellow cornmeal
2	pkgs active dry yeast
2	tsps. salt
1	stick butter
½	cup warm water

Scald milk; stir in salt and butter. Cool to lukewarm. Pour warm water into large bowl; sprinkle in the yeast and stir until dissolved. Stir in milk mixture, eggs, flour, and cornmeal. Beat about 2 minutes until well mixed. Batter will be very stiff. Pour or spoon into two 9 x 5 x 3-inch well greased loaf pans. Cover and let rise in warm place until double in size. Bake at 375° for 30-35 minutes.

Zesty Meatballs
Sheila Phipps – Clintwood, VA

"I make these for my family at Christmas. They are wonderful to have for a family gathering."

3	lbs. ground chuck	¾	cup Worcestershire sauce
3	med. onions, finely chopped	¾	cup sugar
1 ½	cups soft breadcrumbs	¼	cup plus 2 Tbsps. vinegar
1 ½	tsps. salt	3	(8 oz.) cans tomato sauce
¾	tsp. pepper		fresh chopped parsley
1 ½	tsps. chili powder		vegetable oil
¼	cup plus 2 Tbsps. milk		

Combine first 7 ingredients. Mix well, shape into 1 inch balls. Cook meatballs in hot oil until lightly browned; drain. Place meatball in a 9 x 13 x 2-inch baking dish. Combine remaining ingredients in a medium saucepan; bring to a boil. Cook over low heat for 1 minute, stirring constantly. Pour sauce over meatballs. Bake at 325° for 30 minutes. Garnish with parsley, if desired. Yields about 6 dozen.

Jim Scott Mullins

Mullins family members are born singing. The babies don't just blow spit bubbles - they blow shape note spit bubbles. Then they gurgle the appropriate sound of that note, the way Dock Mullins taught all his kids, church members, and whoever happened by to sing.

Well… that may be stretching truth a bit, but not too much. Music and singing is as much a part of their lives as breathing. Dickenson County hills and hollers have echoed Mullins voices for over a century and the community gatherings, churches, and funerals graced by their singing would be impossible to count. The music is real, it's heartfelt, and it's sound reflects the heart of the mountains.

Formally, the music began in the 1930's with Dock Mullins. His son, Hie and wife, Frances, reached a greater audience through radio station WNVA in Norton, VA. Several states and the Lincoln Center in New York got acquainted with the Mullins Family through a play, "New Ground Revival," written by Ron Short for Appalshop's Roadside Theater. Billy Gene, who sang with his parents, Hie and Frances from an early age, took his family to perform during the play.

"There's a connection you make with people through music," states Scott Mullins, youngest son of Billy Gene and Myrtle Ann Rose Mullins and current leader of the Mullins Family Singers. Though not serious about singing until his late teens, he gradually realized the importance of the music that had been a part of everyday life. The leadership role fell to Scott upon the death of his father and grandfather within a year of each other. Now his life's work is to promote and protect mountain music, that of his family as well as the work of other artists of the region. In that spirit he formed Mountain Tone Music Workshop and has worked with local 4-H youngsters to complete a CD titled, *"Mountain Tyme."* He produced *"Laboring Soldier"* a tribute to his father, Billy Gene, who was a preacher, coalminer, and singer/songwriter.

Scott's maternal and paternal grandfathers were ministers, often working for the Lord in the same area. "My Aunt Annabelle used to call them Paul and Silas," he laughs.

The family music is sometimes sung a cappella but often accompanied with acoustic instruments. He says, "I love it more than anything. I guess I couldn't have avoided it anyway because singing was just part of our household. There was always records playing or the family rehearsing."

> "I feel it's up to someone to preserve and pass on the musical legacy of our forefathers. For me, it clearly defines who I am in a world where there's so many uncertainties - hard times, struggles, and tragedies."
> -*Jim Scott Mullins*

Scott Mullins (center) performing at the 4th of July Celebration in 2007 at Clintwood, VA.

Jim and Jesse McReynolds playing for fans at the Carter Stanley Memorial during the early days of their career.

Take Time For 10 Things

1. Take time to work...It is the price of success.
2. Take time to think...It is the source of power.
3. Take time to play...It is the secret of youth.
4. Take time to read...It is the foundation of knowledge.
5. Take time to worship...It is the highway of reverence and washes the dust of earth from our eyes.
6. Take time to help and enjoy friends...It is the source of happiness.
7. Take time to love...It is the one sacrament of life.
8. Take time to dream...It hitches the soul to the stars.
9. Take time to laugh...It is the singing that helps with life's loads.
10. Take time to plan...it is the secret of being able to have time to take time for the first nine things.

Wise County

Contents

Baked Butternut Squash..........44	Hawaiian Pineapple Cake..........57
Baked Spaghetti..........44	Jack's Bread Recipe..........59
Biscuits..........44	Microwave Peanut Butter Roll..........60
Bologna Sandwich Filling..........44	Million Dollar Pie..........60
Breakfast Casserole..........45	North Carolina Squash..........61
Brine Mixture for Pickled Corn, Beans, Mixed Pickles or Kraut..........45	Oatmeal Pie..........61
	Old Fashioned Stack Cake..........61
	Peanut Butter Pie..........64
Broccoli Macaroni..........46	Pineapple Bread..........64
Cherry Winks..........47	Pineapple Rice..........64
Chicken and Dumplings..........48	Pizza Casserole..........66
Chicken and Rice..........49	Potato Cakes..........66
Chocolate Marshmallow Candy..........49	Potato Doughnuts..........66
Corn Flakes Chicken..........51	Red Velvet Cake..........67
Cornmeal Bread..........52	Rump Roast..........68
Cornmeal Gravy..........53	Salisbury Steak with Onion Gravy..........68
Country Ham Bone Soup..........55	Shoo Fly Pie..........68
Creamy Dutch Apple Dessert..........55	Squash and Apple Bake..........70
Diet Coke Cake..........55	Squash Relish..........71
Donna's Baked Ziti..........56	Strawberry Shortcakes..........71
Easy Fudge..........56	Taco Soup..........72
Easy Southern Chicken Casserole..........56	Tomato Pie..........73
Fried Apples..........56	Truffles..........73
Fried Corn..........57	Zucchini "Crab" Cakes..........73
Ham and Pork Loaf..........57	

By the third weekend in October, the trees covering the hillsides of Wise County are putting on a spectacular show. What better time for Home Craft Days, a folk life festival that celebrates Appalachian culture? Begun in 1972 by folklorist Roddy Moore and George Reynolds on the Campus of Mountain Empire Community College, it continues to bring together the finest traditional craftsman, musicians, storytellers, and food vendors. www.homecraftdays.org

The Wise County Historical Society

In 1990, Dorothy Witt heard that a group of Lee County Citizens was having meetings to write a history. Since Dorothy had lived in Lee County and had relatives still living there, she started attending the meetings. During these meetings, she decided it would be good if Wise County could have a book also. From this decision, The Wise County Historical Society came into being. Everyone in Wise County owes Dorothy a big "thank you."

On November 7, 1991, fourteen interested people from different areas of the county met in the conference room of the Wise Appalachian Regional Hospital to discuss the writing of a book. We discovered that this was not an easy thing to do, but we were a determined group. We traveled all over the county gathering histories, spreading the word, and learning a great deal.

Our committee of fourteen grew to sixty-one and, with the help of Ron Montgomery of Lee County, the Society became a corporation. We now have over nine hundred members scattered all over the United States, Puerto Rico, Australia, Spain, and England.

The Heritage of Wise County and City of Norton Volume 1 was our first book though it is no longer in print. We began collecting information about the six thousand men from Wise County who served during World War II. Their histories and over three thousand pictures were part of the book, *Veterans of WWII*.

Orchards used to grow in much of the county. Apple production was the biggest industry in Wise and we honored that with a book titled, *Apple Blossoms of Yesterday*.

In 1996, we began publishing *The Appalachian Quarterly*, a 112-page magazine with lots of history, folklore, feuds, funny sayings, and human-interest stories.

A great deal of information was added when the 1100 page *Heritage II* was completed in 2001. *Between Brothers* tells the story of the men who fought in the Civil War. It was hard to imagine that Rhonda Robertson and Lillian Gobble, who did the research, were able to collect so much information after all these years.

Our office is open five days a week in the courthouse, with volunteers willing to help you with research. The only charge is for copies that are made. Feel free to visit us or join our group in preserving the history of our county.

May God send you good fortune, contentment and peace. And may all of your blessings Forever increase.
-*Irish Blessing*

Baked Butternut Squash
Lois Adkins - Appalachia, VA

1 butternut squash
½ stick melted margarine
½ cup brown sugar
walnuts

Wash and split butternut squash in half, clean out all the seeds. Place in pan. Bake 1 hour in 350° oven. Mix ½ stick melted margarine and ½ cup of brown sugar. Pour over squash, sprinkle with walnuts. Heat another 15 minutes and serve.

Biscuits
Mary Bryan -St. Paul, VA

2 cups self-rising flour
2/3 cup shortening
buttermilk

Preheat oven to 450°. Cut shortening into flour with hand or fork. Add enough buttermilk to make a stiff dough. Roll out and cut and place on baking sheet. Bake until golden brown.

"This is very good with a bowl of lima beans."

Baked Spaghetti
Wanda Manicure –The Wise County Historical Society - Wise, VA

1 cup chopped onion
1 cup green pepper
1 (4 oz.) can mushrooms
1 (28 oz.) can tomatoes with liquid
1 lb. ground beef cooked and drained
12 ozs. spaghetti cooked and drained
2 cups shredded cheese
1 can cream of mushroom soup (undiluted)

Sauté onions and green peppers in butter; add tomatoes and mushrooms. Add ground beef and simmer uncovered for 10 minutes. In greased 13 x 9-inch dish, put ½ of the spaghetti and ½ of the tomato mixture and sprinkle with 1 cup shredded cheese. Repeat this layer again. Pour soup on top and sprinkle with remaining 1 cup shredded cheese. Bake at 350° for 30-45 minutes.

Bologna Sandwich Filling
Wanda Rose – The Wise County Historical Society -Wise, VA

1 ½ to 2 lbs. fat free bologna
4 hard-boiled eggs
½ cup chopped onion
½ cup (more if you like) pickle relish
2 Tbsps. mustard
¼ to ½ cup salad dressing or mayonnaise

Grind or use food processor to chop bologna. Chop eggs fine. Mix all the above with mustard and salad dressing. Refrigerate to let flavors mix. Spread on bread or bun and enjoy.

Breakfast Casserole

Glenda Collins - Lonesome Pine Office on Youth - Coeburn, VA

1	lb. lean sausage	1½	cups grated cheese
12	eggs	½	cup milk
6	slices white bread		

Crumble and brown sausage. Rinse and drain, then place in 9x13 inch casserole dish. Put eggs, ½ of the cheese, milk and the bread in a blender. Blend until thoroughly mixed. Add salt and pepper to taste. Pour this mixture slowly over the sausage. Sprinkle with the remaining cheese. Bake at 350° for about 30 minutes until light brown and knife inserted in center comes out clean. This serves about 15. Have on hand, chopped tomatoes, green onions, extra cheese, salsa and sour cream when serving. Note: use mild or hot sausage to your taste.

Brine Mixture to Pickle Corn, Beans, Cukes or Kraut

Freddy W. Elkins - Wise, VA

1	gallon cold water	1	cup vinegar
1	cup iodine-free salt	½	cup sugar

Mix all the ingredients well and pour over the corn, beans, cucumbers, or cabbage after they have been prepared and put into canning jars. Put lids on loosely but do not seal. Set in a cool place for 7 days or until it reaches desired sourness. Screw the tops down tightly and process for 10 minutes in a kettle of boiling water. In the making of mixed pickles, the cucumbers should be cooked until the green color is gone. The same for pickled beans.

In honor of Wise County's 150th birthday, Paul Kuczko, director of the Lonesome Pine Office On Youth, conceived the idea of a book and CD project called *Music of Coal*. After two years of collaborative effort, it was released in 2007. Historical pictures, liner notes, and forty-eight songs combine to tell a haunting story of bituminous coalmining in the southern Appalachians. www.lpoy.org

Broccoli Macaroni

Betty Belcher - Pound, VA

1   box macaroni and cheese dinner
1   (8 oz. to 10 oz.) package of frozen chopped broccoli (cooked and drained)
1   can mushroom soup
1   can mushrooms (optional)
    cheese

Prepare macaroni & cheese dinner as directed on box. Mix the cooked and drained broccoli with macaroni. Add mushroom soup and mushrooms (if desired). Put in a baking dish and cover with cheese. Bake at 350° until cheese melts. This is good!

Freddy Elkins

The Curator at the Harry W. Meador Coal Museum is imminently qualified to identify and explain the uses of items on display. Freddy Elkins worked in the coalmines for thirty-one years. He is the son of a miner. He was raised in Bold Camp, near Pound, VA. One of his earliest memories is of his father's dinner bucket, which always held a treat for Elkins and his siblings. "My Dad worked in the evenings and got home after we were asleep. Whoever got up first in the mornings (and I tried to be first) ran to Dad's dinner bucket. He would have maybe Beechnut chewing gum, hard candy or peppermints – sometimes something left over from his dinner. But always a little treat for us, even if it was a pork chop biscuit. My mother, Ruble Elkins, saw to it that he had extra in his dinner bucket because he had to work so hard. Even if we ate beans for dinner, she would cook meat to pack his dinner bucket."

Miner's hat and dinner buckets on display at the Harry W. Meador Coal Museum

If righteousness is in the heart, there will be beauty in the character,
If beauty is in the character, there will be harmony in the home.
If harmony is in the home, there will be order in the nation.
If order is in the nation, there will be PEACE IN THE WORLD.

Cherry Winks

Dorothy (Dot) Hale - St. Paul

2¼ cups all-purpose (plain) flour
2 tsps. baking powder
½ tsp. salt
¾ cup butter or margarine, softened
1 cup sugar
2 eggs
2 Tbsps. milk
1 tsp. vanilla flavoring
1 cup chopped nuts
1 cup finely cut, pitted dates
½ cup finely chopped maraschino cherries
2½ cups corn flakes – crushed to 1 ½ cups
15 maraschino cherries cut into quarters

Stir together flour, baking powder and salt. In a large mixing bowl, beat butter and sugar until light and fluffy. Add eggs. Beat well. Stir in milk and vanilla. Add flour mixture and mix until combined. Stir in nuts, dates, and cherries. Portion dough by using a level measuring tablespoon. Shape into balls. Roll in corn flake crumbs and place about two inches apart on greased baking sheet. Press down slightly and put maraschino cherry quarter on each. Bake 8 – 10 minutes at 375°.

   "I was about thirteen when my father died. He moved a rock in the mines where he worked and something poisonous came up in his face, I think he called it "black damp." It took the hide right off his face and hands. He went to Dante to see the doctor early the next morning and stopped at some kinfolks' house to wait until time for the doctor to come in. He just slumped over in a chair and fell dead right there. He was 56 years old.
   At that time, nothing could be proven about what killed him. My mother was left with five girls to raise and no income. (Our three brothers were already grown.) We could eat if we worked, because we had chickens, hogs, cows, and raised a garden. There was no electricity so Mommy didn't have many bills. For heat we had a fireplace and a cook stove that had to have fuel. Three of us slept in a bed and I always tried to get in the middle because it was the warmest place to be.

Twentieth Century Southwest Virginia was defined by the coal industry and continues to be affected greatly today. The Harry W. Meador Coal Museum serves to educate visitors and offer a glimpse into the heritage of coal mining in the area. The renovated building was once the library and study of John Fox, Jr.

We lived at Moorefield and the coal trains used to stop a little ways down the track to change lines or wait for another train or something. I would climb up on the train car and throw coal off until the train started to move. I remember being afraid it would bump me off. Then we'd get a bucket and fill it up with the coal and carry it up to the house. I was a tomboy and the only one with the nerve to climb the cars so I did it often. We probably would have been colder than we already were, otherwise. We were poor as could be but it was during the depression and everybody was. Nobody knew any better; it was just a way of life.

When I was older, but still a teenager, Mommy bought each of us a dress from Dean's, down on the western front. The store had pants for women that had just come in style. I wanted a pair so bad. I sold my sister my new dress and bought the pants. Mommy almost didn't let me wear them, but finally with some begging, she did. I loved those pants way more than a dress!" ...Dot Hale

Happiness depends,
As Nature shows,
Less on exterior things
Than most suppose.
-*William Cowper*

Chicken and Dumplings
Fannie Steele – The Wise County Historical Society -Wise, VA

1   cooking hen (a cooking/stewing hen is best, you can use large fryer breast)
1½ tsps. salt
1   tsp. baking powder
2   cups milk (either buttermilk or sweet)
1   Tbsp. butter
2   lbs. plain flour
     water
¼   tsp. black pepper

Cook chicken until tender in enough salted water to cover chicken. Take chicken out of pot and set aside. Place about 2 pounds of flour in a large mixing bowl. Make an indenture in middle of flour with hands, leaving some flour on the bottom of bowl. Add a little butter (about 1 Tbsp.), baking powder, salt, milk, and mix with hands to the consistency of biscuit dough, and then mix some more according to whether you want light and fluffy dumplings or chewy and firm dumplings. The more you mix and pat, the stiffer the dough becomes.

Roll out on a board and cut with biscuit cutter or cut into strips, or pinch off about a Tbsp. at a time and drop into the boiling chicken gruel. If gruel has cooked down, add a little more water to the pot. Let cook until done.

While the dumplings are cooking, take chicken off bone. Place chicken back in pot with finished dumplings and add black pepper and mix all together and let simmer a few minutes to heat the chicken back up. Enjoy!

Chicken and Rice
Bobbie Jean Elkins

2	cups raw rice	1	pkg. onion soup mix
1	can cream of celery soup	1	can cream of mushroom soup
1	tsp. dry parsley flakes		
8-10	chicken breast cooked and cut up	1½	to 2 cups water
		1	tsp. curry powder

Mix together rice, soups, water, parsley and curry powder and place in a 13 x 9 x 2-inch baking dish. Place cut up chicken on top.
Sprinkle with onion soup mix. Cover with heavy-duty aluminum foil and bake for 2 hours at 350°. Ummm good!

Chocolate Marshmallow Candy
Helen E. Hobbs

1½	cups sugar	1	(12 oz.) bag milk chocolate chips
1	stick oleo	1	jar marshmallow cream
1	small can cream	1	cup black walnuts

Combine sugar, oleo, cream and marshmallow cream in pan and cook over medium heat. Stir until it comes to a boil. Boil 5 minutes, stirring constantly. Remove from heat and add chocolate chips. Beat and add nuts, if desired.

> *"Judge not another from our high and lofty seat. Step down into the arena where he and his problems meet."*

Life is what we make it. Always has been. Always will be.
- *Grandma Moses*

The Santa Train
Photo by Gary Hale

You will find as you look back upon your life that the moments you have really lived are the moments when you have done things in the spirit of love.

-Henry Drummond

Excitement is in the air along a 110-mile section of railroad track from Shelby, Kentucky to Kingsport, TN on the Saturday before Thanksgiving. For sixty-five years the young and the young at heart have waited in anticipation. The Santa Train is coming! And yes, Santa himself is standing on the back platform, waving and throwing goodies to the crowd.

What began as an act of generosity to the people of Southwest Virginia and eastern Kentucky as thanks for shopping in Kingsport, Tennessee has become a longstanding tradition. The first Santa Train ran in 1943 when the Merchant's Bureau of Kingsport (now Kingsport Chamber of Commerce) and the Clinchfield Railroad put the idea together.

In the early years, Santa threw goodies from the back of the moving train. Greta Sue Skeens Tongue remembers going with her brothers to wait for the train at Hamlin, midway between Dante and St. Paul, VA. "That was one of the highlights of the Christmas season. We didn't have a lot going on then, so the Santa Train was something exciting to look forward to. I don't think it was so much the candy, just seeing Santa Claus on the red caboose and the spirit of the holidays. You had to scramble for the goodies!"

CSX Transportation now owns the railroad, which has become more safety conscious. Toys and other items are thrown at designated stops along the route, though the train has been known to make an unscheduled stop for a large crowd. Fifteen tons of gifts are distributed each year through the cooperative effort of CSXT, Food City and the Kingsport Chamber of Commerce.

Celebrities such as Allison Krouse, Travis Tritt, Naomi Judd, along with various state, local, and federal government officials of all levels have ridden the Santa Special. Patty Loveless, who remembers the train from her childhood in Pikeville, KY has been the celebrity guest three times and chronicled her memories in a song she wrote titled, (what else?) "Santa Train."

The train pulls out of the station at 7:30 in the morning in order to be in Kingsport by 3:00 p.m. for Mr. Claus to continue his journey on a float in the Christmas parade. After all, it's the beginning of the busiest time of year and Santa has to be about his work.

> We should practice patience with the faults of others, They have to try to be patient with ours.

Corn Flakes Chicken
Lora Beth Belcher

peanut or vegetable oil	½ cup all purpose flour
4 boneless skinless chicken breast	¼ tsp. red pepper
2 cups cornflakes, crushed	salt and pepper to
1 egg, well beaten	taste

Season crushed corn flakes with red pepper. Mix salt and pepper with flour. Dust chicken in flour and dip in beaten egg, then roll in corn flakes. Fry in oil at 350° until golden brown.

The six most important words in the English language:
   I admit I made a mistake
The five most important words: You did a good job.
The four most important words: What is your opinion?
The three most important words: If you please.
The two most important words: Thank you.
The one most important word: We
The one least important word: I

Cornmeal Bread
Ron Short - Big Stone Gap, VA

"You cannot get any more basic than this recipe and you cannot get any more country! And, even though the recipe seems simple it takes practice and skill to create both dishes. If you can bake cornbread, then go ahead and do it to suit yourself. If you cannot, here is the basic recipe."

2 cups of your favorite cornmeal mix. *(Yes, I said cornmeal mix; White Lily, Martha White, whatever. You can grind your own cornmeal and mix the baking powder and soda if you want, but I'd advise the cornmeal mix.)*

1¼ - 1½ cups of buttermilk or sweet milk *(Some cornmeal mixes are labeled buttermilk mixes, so don't add buttermilk to them.)*

1 egg well beaten or about 1/8 cup of fake eggs *(Now, the egg is optional, and you can use it or leave it out.)* **But, the sugar is not optional!** *(Mountain people do not put sugar in cornbread. If we could afford cake, we'd be eating cake.)*

¼ cup of oil or bacon grease *(Some folks like to heat the grease and then pour the hot grease into the mixture to start the rising process. And, then they set the skillet —oh yeah, I forgot to mention you can't really bake cornbread without a seasoned and well greased iron skillet, about 10-12-in. diameter—set it on the hot eye for a while to fry the bottom of the cornbread and start it to turn brown.)*

Bake in a 400° oven or cook stove for approx. 30-35 min. *(After about 25 min. check the cornbread to see if the top is turning golden brown. When it gets a few shades darker take it out of the oven and turn the skillet upside down. The cornbread should drop easily onto a dinner plate—if not, you need to work on your skillet seasoning. If all went well, the bottom is one shade of dark golden brown; about the color of good ale.)*

No soil upon earth is so dear to our eyes,
As the soil we first stirred with sticks, making mud pies.
-Author unknown

Cornmeal Gravy
Ron Short - Big Stone Gap, VA

Ron Short

In a separate iron skillet, **fry up some bacon or side meat**. When the meat is crispy done, set it aside to eat with the gravy and cornbread. (*O.K., you don't have to eat the meat. You can go straight to about ¼ cup of oil*).

Heat grease or oil until it sizzles when you **sprinkle cornmeal into it.** Turn stove to medium heat. Stir in about **½ to ¾ cup of cornmeal mix and fry it**, stirring all the while, until it turns brown. You should have a loose, bubbly browned cornmeal paste mixture.

The four basic food groups for mountain folks are: grease, greens, grits, and gravy.
 -Ron Short
(Beans gotta come in somewhere!)

Pour in about **4-5 cups of milk.** (*You can use whole or skim milk, whichever you prefer but poor folks used to mix a half can of evaporated milk with about 3 cups of water*). Pour milk in slowly, stirring actively all the while. Bring to a boil and keep stirring. When the gravy begins to thicken, keep stirring until the mixture is thoroughly cooked. (*Cornmeal gravy does not thicken like flour gravy but it will attain gravy status. When and how long you cook it depends on your own eye and some experience. Don't overcook it, as the gravy tends to break down if it is cooked too long*).

Now fry yourself up a couple of good old brown hen eggs and get your bacon or side meat. (*O.K. you don't have to eat the meat but once in your life you ought to try this meal to see how wonderfully tasteful this combination of very basic ingredients can be*).

Crumble up a chunk of cornbread onto a plate and add gravy to taste. Pile the fried eggs on top of this and see how good poor folks used to eat and still do as often as we can.

Down on the Farm
Ron Short - Big Stone Gap, VA

Cornmeal bread and cornmeal gravy,
They'll make you fat but won't make you lazy,
Talkin' 'bout the good ole things down on the farm.
Rabbit stew and squirrel maybe,
They'll drive you wild but won't drive you crazy.
Talkin' 'bout the good ole things down on the farm.

London, England, Paris, France,
Ain't none of them places stand a chance.
Talkin' 'bout the good ole things down on the farm.
I don't care' 'bout Betty Crocker's Gold Medal,
Ain't nothin' no better than my Mama's iron kettle.
Talkin' 'bout the good ole things down on the farm.

"Cat head" biscuits and fried chicken,
Make ya' give your whole arm a lickin'.
Talkin' 'bout the good ole things down on the farm.
Fried squash, fried 'maters,
Fried corn and fried taters.
Talkin' 'bout the good ole things down on the farm.

Apple pie and blackberry jam,
Made me sweet as I am.
Talkin' 'bout the good ole things down on the farm.
Wild turkey and Wild "corn",
They'll make you glad that you was born.
Talkin' 'bout the good ole things down on the farm.

How did I git to be a hundred years old?
Well, when I moves, I moves slow.
When I sets, I sets loose.
And when I worries, I goes to sleep.
  -*Attributed to an Appalachian mountain woman*

When Daddy cooks, he doesn't read
The cookbooks Mother seems to need.
He doesn't fuss with pies or cakes,
He never roasts or boils or bakes,
He doesn't use a rolling pin,
Or measure level spoonfuls in,
He doesn't watch the oven clock.
He doesn't fill the cookie crock.
But we watch him with admiring eyes
While Daddy fries and fries and fries!
-*Author unknown*

Country Ham Bone Soup
Nina Mullins - The Wise County Historical Society - Wise, VA

1 ham bone cooked in 3 quarts water for 30 minutes
When cool enough to handle remove meat from bone and cut in small pieces. Return to kettle and add the following ingredients:

1	cup sliced carrots	1	(10 oz.) pkg. frozen lima beans
1	cup diced celery	1	(16 oz.) can peas
½	cup chopped onion	1	(16 oz.) can tomatoes
1	(10 oz.) pkg. whole kernel corn		

Simmer for 30 minutes and add:

2   cups elbow macaroni

Cook an additional 10 to 15 minutes and salt and pepper to taste. Yields about 15 servings. May be frozen for use another day.

Creamy Dutch Apple Dessert
Mona Elkins

- ¼ cup butter or margarine
- 1 ½ cups graham cracker crumbs
- 1 (14 oz.) can Eagle Brand milk
- ¼ cup Realemon reconstituted lemon juice
- 1 can Comstock or Thank You brand apple pie filling
- 1 (8 oz.) cup sour cream
- ¼ cup chopped walnuts or pecans
- ½ tsp. ground cinnamon

Preheat oven to 350°. In a 10 x 6-inch shallow baking dish melt butter in oven. Sprinkle in crumbs; stir well. Press on bottom of dish. In medium bowl, mix together sweetened condensed milk, sour cream and lemon juice. Spread evenly over crumbs. Spoon pie filling evenly over creamy layer. Bake 25 to 30 minutes or until set. Cool slightly. In small dish, mix together nuts and cinnamon. Sprinkle over pie filling. May be served warm or cold. Refrigerate leftovers. Variations: Omit cinnamon. Substitute blueberry, cherry or peach pie filling.

Diet Coke Cake
Ms. Sherry - Big Stone Gap, VA

- 1 chocolate cake mix
- 1 can diet Coke or diet Dr. Pepper

Mix cake and coke together. Bake in oil sprayed pan at 350° for about 35 – 45 minutes. Cool & serve. (If you want to use white cake, just use diet Sprite).

Donna's Baked Ziti
Donna E. Coxe

- 1 (1 lb.) box ziti noodles
- 1 (16 oz.) container ricotta cheese
- 4 cups mozzarella cheese
-   parmesan cheese
- 2 lbs hamburger
- 1 medium jar Ragu of choice

Preheat oven to 350°. Brown hamburger in skillet and add Ragu; let simmer while preparing noodles for 15 to 20 minutes. Cook noodles in medium sauce pan until slightly tender; drain. Mix in ricotta cheese and 2 ½ cups of mozzarella cheese. Place in sprayed baking dish. Cover with hamburger mixture, sprinkle remaining mozzarella cheese on top. Place in preheated oven and bake until brown on top.

Easy Southern Chicken Casserole
Clara Elkins

- 2 cups cooked chicken, deboned and skinned
- 1 can cream of mushroom soup
- 1 can cream of chicken soup
- 1 can cream of celery soup
- ½ cup margarine, melted
- 1 cup sour cream
- 1 roll Ritz crackers, crushed

Place cooked chicken in a 13 x 9 x 2-inch baking dish. Mix sour cream and soups. Pour over chicken. Mix cracker crumbs with melted margarine. Sprinkle on top of casserole. Bake at 350° for 25 minutes or until lightly browned.

Fried Apples
Nancy Steffey - St. Paul, VA

- 5 to 6 apples, Granny Smith preferred
- 1 cup sugar
- 3 Tbsps. butter

Slice apples, leaving on peel if preferred. Melt butter in skillet and add apples and sugar. Stir occasionally, about ten minutes.

Easy Fudge
Janice E. Collins

- 1 (16 oz.) jar creamy peanut butter
- 1 (16 oz.) can vanilla cake icing

Put peanut butter in a Pyrex bowl. Microwave for 2 minutes. Stir cake icing slightly while peanut butter heats. After 2 minutes pour icing into peanut butter. It will begin to set up. Dump into an 8 x 11 inch Pyrex baking dish. Cool and cut into squares.

Ham and Pork Loaf

Phyllis Williams – The Wise Gallery Quilters - Wise, VA

1 lb. ham, ground	2 eggs
1 ½ lbs. lean pork, ground	½ to 1 cup milk
1 cup bread crumbs	
black pepper (doesn't need salt)	

Heat oven to 325° and use a 13 x 9 inch baking dish.
Mix the above ingredients together, make into two loaves and place in 13 x 9-inch baking dish.

1/3 cup vinegar	¾ Tbsp. dry mustard
1 cup brown sugar	½ cup water

Boil these ingredients together for 5 minutes to make syrup. Place baking dish on large cookie sheet. Keep bottom of cookie sheet covered with water. Baste every 15 to 20 minutes with syrup. Bake for 1 ½ to 2 hours.

Hawaiian Pineapple Cake

Renda Salyers - Norton, VA

- 2   cups all purpose flour
- 2   eggs
- 2   cups sugar
- ¾   cup chopped pecans
- 1   (20 oz.) can crushed pineapple
- 2   Tbsps. baking soda

Put pineapple in separate bowl with baking soda and let foam. Mix flour, sugar, eggs and nuts together. Stir pineapple into flour mixture (do not use mixer). Bake at 350° for 30-40 minutes.

Icing

1 stick butter	1 box confectioners sugar
1 (8 oz.) cream cheese	1 tsp. vanilla flavoring

Mix with mixer and pour over cake while warm.

Fried Corn

Faye Deaner - St. Paul, VA

Corn from 5 ears
Drippings from 3 slices of bacon, fried crisp
½ cup evaporated milk

Cook corn in 1 cup water until water evaporates. Pour bacon drippings over corn. Add milk and cook until corn is almost dry.

William M. (Uncle Billy) Robinette II
Submitted by: Renda Salyers – granddaughter

High up on Stone Mountain above Benge's Gap at a place called Robinette Field; a boy child was born on March 25, 1856, the same year that Wise became a county. He lived with his parents in a typical pioneer log cabin. During farming season everyone labored in the fields.

"Uncle Billy," as he came to be called, met and married Malissa Holbrook from Bull Run, located between Coeburn and St. Paul. They established a farm near what is now Lonesome Pine Country Club, and reared a large family of fourteen – seven boys and seven girls. Upon his death at seventy-eight, each of his children received forty acres of land.

At age 26, Uncle Billy preached his first sermon at Little Stone Gap. For the next fifty-two years he preached for the love of God, never accepting money, and supported his family by farming. He held the pastorate of four different Primitive Baptist Churches for forty-five years: Little Stone Gap, Laurel Grove, Grab Orchard, and Blue Springs. He was one of the staunchest pillars and a founder of the Three Fork's of Powell's River Baptist Association. His was the old time preaching of the hills, his voice floating out over congregations or funeral crowds with such hypnotic power that even the forests seemed to listen.

Whenever a call came to serve, the task at hand was dropped, whether it was plowing, hoeing, or whatever. Whether it was to go pray by a sick bed or perform a marriage ceremony, he went unhesitatingly. Malissa, a devoted wife and mother and surely a true companion, cared for the family and their homestead while Uncle Billy was absent for his church duties.

In the days before automobiles, it was not unusual for him to walk twenty miles to a church and then deliver his sermon. Sometimes the hills and mountains were traveled by horseback. His reputation as a preacher was not confined to Wise County or the state of Virginia. He traveled and held protracted meetings in Kentucky, West Virginia, Tennessee, and North Carolina, as well as other parts of Virginia.

His last sermon was preached at Blue Springs shortly before his death in 1934 at age seventy-eight. About fifteen hundred people came from all directions and different states to assemble in the front yard (and adjoining fields) of Uncle Billy and Malissa's home for the funeral ceremony. Reverend John Smith held the memorial service, assisted by the Reverends Wolfenbarger of Tennessee, Evans of Russell County, and Mullins of Buchanan County. Internment was in the family cemetery in beautiful Powell's Valley; Malissa was laid to rest there with him in 1946 at age eighty-eight.

-Originally written by: Willie Frances Miner

Jack's Bread Recipe

Jack Turner – The Wise County Historical Society -Wise, VA

Introduction: If you require exact measurements, you might as well skip to another recipe!

Get a pretty good-sized bowl and put in a little molasses or brown sugar. Add a quart or two of warm water (if your elbow likes the temperature of the water, the yeast will also). Add some yeast. I use bottled yeast that I keep in the fridge and dip out a spoonful or so, or you can use 1 package of yeast. Cover (but not with a tight fitting lid).

Hug a kid or call a friend.

Stir in whole-wheat flour and maybe some rye flour (if you like rye) or maybe some buckwheat flour (if you like the darker color) a cup at a time until you get a slurry (consistency of mud or wet cement – I like for it to splash around a bit if I use a mixer to smooth it up). Cover.

Note: if your slurry is half way to the top of the bowl, put a pan under it to catch spillage in case it rises that much. If your slurry fills more than half the bowl, you might want to consider swapping to a bigger bowl.

Leave it alone for a day or two; three or four if you and the house enjoys the aroma.

Stir in some salt (say ½ Tbsp. to 1 Tbsp.) and some oil (say ½ cup to 1 cup).

Stir in bread flour (whole wheat if you insist, but expect long rising time) one cup at a time until you get dough that doesn't stick to the bowl.

Turn it out on a floured surface and knead it – and keep kneading it (sprinkle more flour as necessary) until you like the way it feels. Some people get fancy with their kneading techniques, but the main idea is to keep folding the dough back into itself.

Cover it with a cloth and go finish the book you were reading.

Fill greased baking pans about half full of the dough and let it rise again.

Run a knifepoint about half an inch deep lengthwise along the top of the loaf (or score any way you think it'll look good).

Bake in the middle of a 350° oven for about 1 hour (less time if you have small loaves; more time if you have big loaves).

Microwave Peanut Butter Roll
Crystal E. Kirby

2 ½ cups white sugar	2 egg whites
½ cup light corn syrup	1 tsp. vanilla
½ cup water	1/8 tsp. salt

Combine sugar, syrup, water, and salt in large microwave bowl. Microwave on high for 5 minutes. Stir well. Microwave 9 to 9 ½ minutes more. <u>*Do not stir.*</u> Beat egg whites while candy is cooking. Slowly pour hot mixture over egg whites and beat until mix holds shape and loses gloss. Roll out on pastry sheet. Sprinkle with powdered sugar. Spread with peanut butter softened in microwave. Roll up and slice. Store in airtight container.

Million Dollar Pie
Mary Holyfield (AKA: Aunt Doll)

2 graham cracker pie crusts
1 (8 oz.) Cool whip
1 can Eagle brand milk
¼ cup lemon juice
1 (15 oz.) can crushed pineapple, drained
1 cup chopped pecans

Mix together and pour into graham cracker pie crusts. Chill and serve.

The official Virginia State Outdoor drama, "The Trail of the Lonesome Pine" is also the longest running outdoor drama in Virginia. Begun in 1964, it is presented Thursday – Saturday evenings from late June to August. The wooden benches that have served for forty years are currently being replaced. www.trailofthelonesomepine.org

---

If at first you don't succeed, You're running about average.

Chief Benge, a Chickamauga warrior, was the last leader of the Cherokee resistance to the onslaught of the white man into their territory. Though the methods were sometimes cruel, he and his band were fighting to preserve the heritage of their people.

North Carolina Squash

Kathy Osborne – Wise, VA

4-5 med. Squash
1 small onion, diced or ½ tsp. onion flakes.
1 cup sour cream
1 can chicken soup, undiluted
½ pkg. Pepperidge Farm herb stuffing
½ stick oleo, melted

Cook the squash with onion in small amount of salted water; drain and place in baking dish. Combine sour cream and soup and pour over squash. Mix oleo with stuffing and sprinkle on top. Bake at 350^0 for 30 minutes.

Oatmeal Pie

Karen Elkins

3 eggs
2/3 cup sugar
1 cup brown sugar
2/3 cup oatmeal
2/3 cup coconut
2/3 cup milk
1 tsp. vanilla
2 tsps. margarine

Blend ingredients: pour into unbaked pie shell. Bake at 350° for 35-40 minutes until knife comes out clean. Makes 2 pies.

Old Fashioned Stack Cake

Ann Hughes – The Wise Gallery Quilters - Wise, VA

2 eggs
½ cup shortening
1 cup molasses
1 cup sugar
½ cup buttermilk
3 cups plain flour
2 tsps. ginger
1 tsp. cinnamon
½ tsp. all spice
1 tsp. baking soda
1 tsp. salt

Mix first five ingredients and beat well. Combine dry ingredients and add to first mixture to make soft dough. Pat out small amount into an iron skillet to make thin layers. Bake 10 minutes at 350°. Do not over bake. Stack layers with apple butter or dried fruit cooked with sugar and spices and allowed to cool. Leave top layer plain.

Shelled or unshelled nuts and seeds keep better and longer stored in the freezer. The unshelled nuts crack more easily when frozen.

That's Just Roscoe

Sue L. Vaughn – Big Stone Gap, VA

In the fall of 1966, I began teaching in Wise County, Virginia, as a part of President Lyndon B. Johnson's Aid to Appalachia program. Along with a reading teacher and the bus driver, I traveled in a school bus that had been converted into a classroom on wheels. We served seven little schools surrounding Coeburn, Virginia, bringing music and reading once a week to the lives of the "educationally deprived" youngsters of the poverty-stricken southwest Virginia mountains. I was young, incredibly naïve, and full of the vigor that only those born to teach possess.

Our first stop was at Tom's Creek School, which sat on the top of a hill, directly across from the coal mine of the same name. I went into the building to teach music to the first- and second-graders, while the reading teacher brought her charges out to the bus for instruction.

My first lesson was rhythms, using all sorts of rhythm instruments, recorded music, songs such as *The March of the Toy Soldiers* and several of Sousa's marches. The children responded as only six- and seven-year-olds can – with unbridled enthusiasm. I was euphoric! My first day was going to be a success!

However, I noticed a little boy sitting in the back of the room, isolated from the rest of the children. He didn't touch the musical instrument I had given him. But his blue eyes sparkled and his grubby little fingers moved with the beat of the music. He was without doubt the dirtiest little child I had ever seen. His hair was matted and greasy; his clothes had never seen soap and water; his shoes, barely covering his feet, were ragged, too large and tied with rough twine. His neck was so caked with grime that I wondered if anyone had ever held him down and scrubbed it like my grandmother did mine. All in all, he was a sad sight, a filthy little urchin in a classroom full of clean and shining faces.

After class, I questioned the teacher about him. Her reply startled and troubled me. "Oh, that's just Roscoe. He doesn't know anything. His whole family is retarded. He just comes to school so he can have a hot meal every day. He doesn't even talk. Don't mind him, Honey."

I left Tom's Creek but couldn't get Roscoe off my mind. How did the teachers at the school know he was retarded? Had he ever been tested? Had he just been shoved into the corner because of his family? What could I do to help him? I was sure I had seen him respond to the music. Had anyone even tried to help him?

When we arrived back in Coeburn, I made some inquiries. The principal at the high school told me that the family was an infamous one in the area. There was incest, alcoholism, mental illness and various other problems in the clan. Most of the agencies that tried to help had long since given up, because the grandfather, the patriarch of the group, was one to shoot first and ask questions later when "strangers" came too close to the home place.

The following week, as the bus pulled into Tom's Creek, the teacher I had talked to during the last visit was waiting eagerly on the front steps, smiling broadly.

As I approached her, she said, "I couldn't wait to tell you. This morning when Roscoe got here, he grabbed my dress, gave it a tug and said, 'Today's the day the music teacher comes.' I didn't even know he could talk, much less tell one day from another. It seems you and your musical instruments turned on a switch or something."

With tears of joy in my eyes, and prayer of thanksgiving in my heart, I walked into the classroom for only the second time. Roscoe was sitting in the front row, still filthy, still different from the other children, but with blue eyes sparkling as he waited for the *music teacher*.

As the year progressed, I took clothes to Roscoe, convinced the teacher to help me clean him up (in a washtub in the cafeteria, but that's another story), and watched as he began to blossom. His hair was a silky, platinum blond that women around the world would envy; his skin was peaches and cream. When the clothes began to look ratty, I brought more. The teacher made him change before he went home, because she said the other kids at home would take them or they would "just disappear" if he didn't.

Roscoe learned to read, learned his alphabet and his numbers, and showed an artistic nature that was superior to most of the other children in the class. He became a part of their games at recess and was no longer looked upon as "different."

I taught in the program for two years and was proud to see Roscoe progress.

When I left to return to school in Tennessee, I lost track of him. I have no idea what happened to him, but I believe music – and soap and water – changed a life and maybe even a clan.

To soften rock-hard ice cream, microwave at medium-low (30% power) for about 30 seconds. Test with a paring knife before adding any additional time.

Peanut Butter Pie

Elsie Green – The Wise Gallery Quilters - Wise, VA

3 Tbsps. peanut butter
½ cup confectioners sugar
1 (8 oz.) cream cheese
1 (8 oz.) Cool Whip
1 Tbsp. vanilla

Mix all ingredients together and place in graham cracker crust. Refrigerate for at least 2 hours.

Pineapple Bread

Joyce Powers

3 eggs
1 cup cooking oil
2 cups white sugar
1 (16 oz.) can crushed pineapple
1 tsp. vanilla
3 cups self-rising flour
1 tsp. cinnamon
   walnuts or pecans, chopped

Beat eggs and add oil, sugar, pineapple, and vanilla. Mix well and add flour, cinnamon, and nuts. Mix well. Pour into 2 greased loaf pans and bake at 350° for 1 hour. Enjoy!

Pineapple Rice

Wanda Rose – The Wise Gallery Quilters - Wise, VA

1 cup rice
2 cups water

Use a 2 quart kettle with tight fitting lid. Place rice in cold water and let come to boil. Put lid on kettle, cut heat to simmer, and cook for 15 minutes. Remove from heat and add the following ingredients.

2 Tbsps. butter
½ cup sugar
1 (15 oz.) can of crushed pineapple with juice
   pinch of salt

Pour into 2 quart casserole, cover generously with marshmallows and bake at 350° until marshmallows brown.

The Wise Gallery Quilters

(Left to right) Joyce Shepherd, Ann Hughes, Phyllis Williams, Elsie Green, Wanda Rose, Mary Bingman and Ruth Bond

The Wise Gallery Quilters came about as a direct result of Hurricane Hugo. Pat Gates, a friend of Nancy Baugh, lived in Sumter, SC, a town that was hit hard by Hugo. Gates got in touch with Baugh and said, "The people of Southwest Virginia have been so good to help us down here, I want to come up and do a workshop on making 'Quilts in a Day.'

Helen Hamm, director of The Charlie Harris Library Gallery gave permission to hold the workshop there. When the big day came, the gallery was full of potential quilters.

Pat Gates brought all materials for the quilt, along with snap together quilt frames, a type no one had seen before. With help from the audience, the quilt was indeed finished at the end of the day and presented to the library gallery for a fundraiser.

From that presentation sprang the Gallery Quilters, who began with fifteen members. Besides teaching people to construct quilt tops and quilt them, members have made lap robes for nursing homes as well as designing and creating a quilt for the town hall. Their efforts have bought lights for the gallery and a wireless sound system for the library, and helped purchase a microfilm reader.

Quilts have been made and given to the Friends of the Library, The Library Gallery, and the Wise County Historical Society as fundraisers. They also sponsor children for the Dolly Parton reading program.

Though several members have died or are in poor health, two original quilters still attend. One devoted 87-year-old lady broke her hip in 2007 and was back attending meetings in three months. (Note: Just goes to prove quilting is good for your health!)

Each Monday at 1:00, the Gallery Quilters meet to keep the craft alive while having a good time. Anyone who is interested is welcome! *-Wanda Rose*

Experience is a wonderful thing. It enables you to recognize a mistake when you make it again.

For hiking enthusiast, the fifteen-mile Chief Benge Scout Trail follows Mountain Fork and Little Stony Creek through parts of Wise and Scott Counties. There are a wide variety of plants to see along the dirt footpaths, old railroad grades, and a few steep climbs that pass High Knob and Bark Camp Lakes, three tall waterfalls, and pools along Little Stony.

Pizza Casserole
Amanda E. Jackson

1 lb. ground beef	2 cups rotini macaroni
1 small chopped onion	1 (15 oz.) jar spaghetti sauce
mozzarella cheese	pepperonis

Brown ground beef and chopped onion. Cook macaroni until tender. Layer hamburger and macaroni in baking dish. Pour spaghetti sauce over it. Top with cheese and pepperonis. Bake at 350° for 30 minutes.

Potato Cakes
Neva Bryan - St. Paul, VA

2 cups cold mashed potatoes	1 tsp. sage
1 egg	1 tsp. black pepper
2 heaping Tbss. of flour	¼ cup cream
	hot water

Mix all ingredients together with enough of the hot water to make mixture consistency of hot mashed potatoes. Fry in hot oil or lard on medium heat until brown.. Use a large spoonful for each cake.

Potato Doughnuts
Jill Elkins

3 cups flour	1 cup hot mashed potatoes
1 egg	1 cup sugar
½ cup milk	¼ tsp. nutmeg
2 ½ tsps. baking powder	1 tsp. vanilla
1 Tbsp. butter	

Measure sugar and butter and add to hot mashed potatoes and egg. Mix well. Add rest of ingredients. If dough is too soft or sticky; add more flour. Roll and cut with doughnut cutter and fry in hot oil, 325° to 350°, until light brown on both sides, about 3 minutes. Shake in powdered sugar or glaze with frosting. Can also use cinnamon and sugar.

Red Velvet Cake

Josh Belcher

2	cups sugar	2 ½	cups cake flour
2	sticks butter, at room temperature	1	tsp. salt
		1	cup buttermilk
2	eggs	1	tsp. vanilla flavoring
2	Tbsps. cocoa powder	½	tsp. baking soda
2	oz. red food coloring	1	Tbsp. vinegar

Preheat oven to 350°. In a mixing bowl, cream the sugar and butter. Beat until light and fluffy. Add the eggs one at a time and mix well after each addition. Mix the cocoa and food coloring together and then add to sugar mixture; mix well. Sift together flour and salt. Add flour mixture to the creamed mixture alternately with buttermilk. Blend in vanilla. In a small bowl, combine baking soda and vinegar and add to mixture. Pour batter into three 8 inch round greased and floured cake pans. Bake for 20 to 25 minutes or until a toothpick inserted into the center comes out clean. Remove from oven and cool completely before frosting.

Icing for Red Velvet Cake

1	(8 oz.) pkg. cream cheese	1	(1 lb.) box confectioners sugar
1	stick butter, softened		
1	cup melted marshmallows	1	cup marshmallow cream

Blend cream cheese and butter together in a mixing bowl. Add marshmallows and sugar and blend well. Fold in marshmallow cream. Spread between layers and on top and sides of cooled cakes.

The Southwest Virginia Museum Historical State Park

The Southwest Virginia Museum Historical State Park depicts the "boom and bust" era of the late 1800's and early 1900's when railroads came to the area. It was hoped that with the rich coal and iron ore deposits of the area, Big Stone Gap would become the "Pittsburgh of the South." The builder of the house that now serves as the museum, Rufus Ayers, served as Virginia's Attorney General in 1885. Craftsmen who built the locally quarried, hand chiseled, limestone and sandstone exterior walls were paid seventeen and a half cents an hour.

An empty plastic thread spool is a good gadget for imprinting a flower design into sugar cookies. Simply press the spool into the cut-out cookie before baking.

Rump Roast
Joyce E. Powers

1	large rump roast	2	Tbsps. flour
12	green olives		salt
1	onion		black pepper
1	can tomato soup and	½	can water

Poke several holes in roast. Stuff olives in holes. Roll roast in flour. Brown in skillet on stovetop. Salt and pepper to taste. Put in crock pot. Add 1 can tomato soup and ½ can water. Add onion. Cook overnight on low.

Salisbury Steak with Onion Gravy
Jill Elkins

1½	lbs. ground chuck	¼	cup catsup
	salt and pepper to taste	½	tsp. mustard
1	egg, beaten	1	tsp. Worcestershire
1	can condensed onion soup		sauce
½	cup bread crumbs	½	cup water

Mix together ground chuck, salt, pepper, egg, ½ can onion soup, and bread crumbs. Form into patties and fry in skillet over medium heat until done. Transfer patties to saucepan. Mix together remaining ½ can onion soup, catsup, mustard, Worcestershire sauce, and water. Pour over patties and simmer 20 minutes. Gently stir occasionally.

Shoo Fly Pie
Mary Bingman – The Wise Gallery Quilters – Wise, VA

Mix for crumbs and topping:
1 cup flour
½ cup sugar
1 Tbsps shortening

1 cup molasses
1 egg beaten
¾ cup cold water
1 tsp. soda in ¼ cup hot water

Combine remaining ingredients with ½ cup of the crumb mixture and pour in prepared pie crust. Top with remaining crumbs. Bake 35 minutes at 375°.

Sidebar:

When milk begins to resemble yogurt, it's spoiled. When yogurt starts to look like cottage cheese, it's spoiled. Cottage cheese is spoiled when it starts to look like regular cheese. Regular cheese is nothing but spoiled milk anyway, and can't get any more spoiled than it already is. Just cut the mold off and eat the rest!

Cheeses should be served at room temperature – about 70 degrees.

Ron Short

Ron Short was raised by the waters of Big Branch in Dickenson County and saw his first brick house on a trip to Big Stone Gap as a youngster. His dad threw him in the river as a method of teaching him to swim. Later in life, he questioned his father, "Dad, why did you throw me in, you knew I couldn't swim?"

"Well," replied his dad, "it was the quickest way to find out how much you did know so I wouldn't have to teach you everything!"

Short is a talented communicator: musician, storyteller, playwright, actor, director, and on and on, - who sticks to his roots. He works with Roadside Theater, a touring theater group that affirms the stories of Appalachia, links those stories to the histories of other cultures in America, and helps other communities across the U.S. to discover their own cultural resources. The plays are presented internationally, as well as nationally.

On a day in August 2007 when the heat shimmered between two mountains and nary a breeze drifted by, the Carter Family Memorial Festival took place in Poor Valley. No one perspired that day, everyone sweated. Buckets. But musicians played, people danced and ate and froliced. We spotted Ron Short under a tent with his string band class from Mountain Empire Community College, picking and singing. We approached him and though he was busy and didn't know us from, well…say, um… Martha Stewart, he was gracious and agreed to send a recipe. We got somewhat hysterical when Short told the story of Long Noah (Noey) because we found it hilarious. This is pretty much how it was told to us. If you feel the need, put the saltshaker on stand-by.

The more you count the blessings you have,
The less you crave the luxuries you haven't.

Long Noah (Pronounced Noey)

When I was a young boy, maybe 8 or 10, there was a preacher in the county who held services at different churches. He was tall and lanky and everybody called him Long Noey. Now they didn't call him that because he was long and thin, but because of the amount of time he preached. He expounded way beyond anybody's capacity for paying attention and on into the time when stomachs began to growl.

One Sunday, Long Noey was at our house and heard me say that I would *never* eat a particular food. He must have heard me say it before because he took me to task. "Boy, don't never say never. You don't know what you might do under different circumstances."

Then he continued with a story to confirm his point. "When I was growing up people still believed in making a medicinal tea from sheep dung. It was used for a croup, to help measles break out, maybe pneumonia, and various things. I told Mommy not to ever, under any circumstances, try to make me drink that stuff. 'I'll *never* take that sheep dung tea,' I repeated time and time again. That was that, until I got sick and thought I was going to die.

Several of us got sick at the same time. Mommy doctored us as best she could but I kept getting worse. Finally, it got so bad, I said weakly, 'I might could drink some of that sheep dung tea.'

But she didn't hear me, or was too busy. Much later, when I was sure I was going to die, I repeated it, with the same results. Finally, with my last ounce of strength, I sat up in bed. 'Mommy, I think I could drink some of that sheep dung tea, if you'll fix me some,' I whimpered and fell back on the bed exhausted. I drifted off.

A little later I came back around to see Dad come in from outside with a small bucket of sheep droppings. Mommy was putting water on the stove to boil. "Mommy," I called out weakly, "if you'll bring it to me, I might could chew on one of them there pills while you get the water boiling for the tea!"

So, son, take it from me. Don't *never* say *never*!

Squash and Apple Bake

Ruth Bond – The Wise Gallery Quilters –Wise, VA

- 1 lbs. Butternut squash
- ½ cup brown sugar (packed)
- ¼ cup butter melted
- 1 Tbsp. flour
- 1 tsp. salt
- ½ tsp. cinnamon or mace
- 1 sliced apple

Cut each squash in half. Remove seeds and fibers, peel squash, and slice into ½ inch pieces. Arrange squash in the ungreased 12" x 8" baking dish and top with apple slices. Stir together the dry ingredients and sprinkle over top. Pour melted butter on top and cover with foil. Bake for 50 to 60 minutes in a 350° oven.

"This is very good with fresh vegetable dinner and home-made cornbread."

Squash Relish

Freddy W. Elkins -Wise, VA

1 cups diced yellow or zucchini squash
1 cups diced onions
1 Tbsp. salt

Mix together and let set for one hour. Drain.

Vinegar Solution
½ cup of chopped green pepper
1 ¾ cups sugar
1 cup of vinegar
½ tsp. of mustard seed
½ tsp. of celery seed
½ tsp. of turmeric

Mix and bring to a boil. Drop squash and onions into boiling vinegar solution. Immediately put into canning jars, place lids on them and set aside to seal.

Strawberry Shortcakes

Sue E. Cantrell

1   quart strawberries, sliced
1   cup sugar
1/3 cup shortening
2   cups self-rising flour
1   Tbsp. sugar
¾   cup milk
1   (12 oz.) Cool whip

Mix strawberries with cup of sugar and let set for an hour. Preheat oven to 450°. Cut shortening into flour and 2 Tbsp. sugar until it looks like fine crumbs. Stir in milk until blended. Smooth dough into a ball on lightly floured surface. Knead 20 to 25 times. Roll out ½-inch thick. Cut with 3-inch cookie cutter. Put 1 inch apart on ungreased cookie sheet. Bake 10 to 12 minutes or until golden. Cut in half across. Spread with margarine. Fill and top with Cool whip and strawberries.

The more I study nature, the more I stand amazed at the work of the creator. -Louis Pasteur

Long strings of beans hanging to dry were a familiar sight in pioneer homes. White varieties (White Hasting, Cornfield, White Half-Runners, etc.) are best for drying because they stay light after cooking, while the darker beans look really dark. Either variety can be used, though. To cook, I wash them well and soak them in water overnight. (Note: beans double in volume when soaked.) Pour off that water, add fresh and parboil for 15 minutes. Pour off water again and continue cooking with fresh water and seasoning. This is powerful good eating.
-Bobbie Jean Elkins

"I have only been clogging for a little over two years now. I started because my granddaughter, Grace, had seen some of her friends clogging and thought it would be fun. All of her friends' mothers clogged with them so she wanted me to clog with her. I thought it would be good exercise, boy was I right!!!! It is also lots of fun. Our teacher, Velisa Stallard, has been doing this since she was in school; she loves it and makes it fun for us. We have performed for numerous occasions, Christmas parades, Home Craft Days, Trail of the Lonesome Pine, and at the Carter Fold. We also performed for a group from Ireland, England, and others that were touring the Crooked Road. There are around 30 of us in class and we have a blast! -Tammy Puckett

Taco Soup

Tammy Puckett – Coeburn, VA

1 lb. ground beef
1 large onion, chopped
1 (15 ½ oz.) cans Mexican-style chili beans, undrained
1 (15 ½ oz.) can whole kernel corn, undrained
1 (15 oz.) can tomato sauce
1 ½ cup water

1 (14 ½ oz.) diced tomatoes, undrained
1 (4.5 oz.) chopped green chilies
1 (1¼ oz.) taco seasoning mix
1 (1 oz.) ranch style dressing mix

Toppings:
Fritos
Shredded cheese
Shredded lettuce
Chopped tomato
Sour cream

Cook beef and onions in a Dutch oven over medium high heat until meat is browned and onions are tender, stirring until meat crumbles; drain. Stir beans and next 7 ingredients into beef mixture; bring to a boil. Reduce heat and simmer, uncovered, 15 minutes, stirring occasionally. Spoon soup into bowls and top with desired toppings.

The Lord is good, a strong hold in the day of trouble; and he knoweth them that trust in him…Nahum 1:7

Tomato Pie
Renda Salyers – Norton, VA

- 1 can Grand biscuits or crescent rolls
- 1 or more tomatoes
- 1 green pepper
- 1 onion
- 1 stick of butter
- mayonnaise
- mozzarella cheese

Line the bottom of a 13 x 9-inch baking dish with biscuits (separate and press edges together to form crust). Slice tomatoes thin and place on top of biscuit dough. Sauté onions and pepper in butter and place over tomatoes. Spread enough mayonnaise to cover the onions, peppers and tomatoes. Top with shredded mozzarella cheese. Bake at 350° until biscuits are done approximately 15 to 20 minutes.

Truffles
Joyce Shepherd – The Wise Gallery Quilters –Wise, VA

- ½ cup whipping cream
- 1 (8 oz.) dark chocolate or chocolate chips
- ¼ cup butter
- 2 tsps. vanilla
- cocoa
- nuts
- white chocolate, melted

Combine whipping cream and chocolate or chocolate chips and stir over low heat until melted, cook for 2 to 4 minutes. Stir in butter, cool, and add vanilla. Refrigerate until firm. Form into 1 inch balls, roll in cocoa or nuts, or dip in melted white chocolate. Place on wax paper and let harden.

Zucchini "Crab" Cakes
Kathy Obsorne – Wise, VA

- 1½ cups grated, raw, unpeeled zucchini
- 1 cup Pepperidge Farm herb stuffing
- 1 egg, beaten
- 1 Tbsp. Old Bay seafood seasoning
- 1 Tbsp. melted oleo

Mix well and form into patties. Fry in oil on both sides. Drain on paper towels. May be frozen.

In 1937, under President Roosevelt's WPA program, a community recreational facility called Country Cabin was built in Norton, VA. It served to carry on the music and traditions of the Appalachian Mountains. The building is now a National and State Historical Landmark.

Across the street is Country Cabin II, where the traditions of music and dance continue each Saturday night and Mountain Clogging is taught. A non-profit corporation whose name states their mission manages it: Appalachian Traditions, Inc.
www.appalachiantraditions.net

Life in Duncan Gap

Fannie Steele - Wise, VA

We lived in the Duncan Gap area of Wise County, Virginia, about seven miles from the town of Wise. I still live on the same farm but in a different house. I was born in 1934 just after the depression days and we didn't have all the things that are now thought of as necessities; however, we didn't miss them because we never had them. We lived in a big white house with a big porch, about as far back in Wise County in the mountains as you can go without being in Dickenson County.

We didn't have a road all the way to our house, except for a path my Father, Mother, and older siblings had dug. It was big enough to get a sled over that was pulled by a horse. If we had to have furniture or anything big, such as sacks of feed for the cows, chickens, horse, or pigs, my Dad and Mom would go buy it and they would set it out at the top of the hill where we parked our pickup truck. Poppie then would go gear up the horse and sled and back up the hill he would go, load up the sled and haul the merchandise to the house or barn.

I remember so well, and still can smell the fresh aroma of clean *underskirts* and gowns draped over chairs in front of the fireplace, "seasoning out" from the cold, frosty clothesline. Mommie was never one to let us put on clothes that weren't "seasoned out" in winter because of catching colds or pneumonia. The "underskirts" were made from feed-sacks, which sometimes had in large black print, the head of a pig or cow on them. This usually washed out after a few washings. We began to get "flowered" feed sacks, which had pretty floral print on them that Mommie made some of our dresses from, as well as her aprons and bonnets. They were very pretty. Flour sacks came on the scene sometime during my growing up. They were also a floral print and if you could get enough alike, dresses, curtains, and bonnets would be made. They were of a finer, more closely threaded material. I really liked my "feed-sack" dresses until one or two of the children in school made fun of them. After that, I was just a little self-conscious about wearing them, even though they were pretty. Many children wore them. Mommie kept them washed and ironed so neat. We also had "store bought" dresses, or dresses made from material purchased from the store. But the feed-sack dresses are the ones that have stuck in my mind.

We had a big, long kitchen with a wood cook stove, where Mommie cooked the most delicious meals, especially on Sundays when we would have company from Church. We would have chicken and dumplings, homemade biscuits, beans–either green beans or dried, depending on the season, and always some kind of potatoes, either mashed or fried and we always had apple butter or cooked apples, jelly, and a wonderful homemade yellow cake with egg-white frosting.

The stove had a "warming closet," where we kept food for latecomers, and Mommie dried apples in it. A water tank in the stove kept warm water for hand washing before meals, washing dishes, and for baths. We also kept a teakettle of hot water on the stove. Our table was a long one with a homemade wood bench in back where the children sat. Homemade wooden chairs were kept around the other sides.

In the springtime, Mom would take a water bucket and a kitchen knife and walk alongside our road and up or down into the fields, to pick greens. She would pick just about everything–young, tender plantain, dandelion, violets, old field lettuce and creecy, mouses ear, lamb's quarter, and other varieties of greens. She would have brown soup beans boiling with fatback in them on the cook stove and would cook the greens and then fry them in meat grease. She would fry potatoes and make corn bread and we would eat like kings…probably better.

Poppie had built a dairy into the hillside of our kitchen yard. We kept our milk and butter in a corner of the dairy in a box that Poppie had made with rock. This building served a two-fold purpose: it kept our dairy products and Mommie's "can-stuff" nice and cool and was a haven from bad storms. My Mother was afraid of storms, and when it looked like a bad one was coming, she threw coats or quilts over our heads and headed for that dairy. Poppie, on the other hand wasn't afraid of anything and would hardly ever go with us. On occasion, he would go to please Mommie. I was always afraid to look out from the dairy, thinking the house would be flattened to the ground and Poppie gone.

From time to time, Mommie would send me with a pan to the dairy to get "pickle-stuff" from the jars. We usually got them out with our hands which Mommie made sure was clean. Sometimes I would have to plunge my hands almost up to my elbows into that cold brine. Then they would start itching and burning. I couldn't wait 'til I washed that brine off my hands and arms. Mommie liked her dairy and took pride in her canned food lined up on the shelves. She scrubbed the cement and sand floor until it was clean enough to eat from.

We carried water from a spring that Poppie had dug out of the ground in sandrock. It was under the hill in a hollow, so it was quite a chore to carry all that water up the hill to the house, although it wasn't very far. This chore fell to me after the other children were gone, due to me being the youngest. Mom was very thrifty and caught rainwater in tubs and barrels that she had sitting "under the leak" to wash clothes and bathe in. We always had a cow or two and plenty of milk and butter. We also had chickens and eggs. We raised pigs to butcher for winter. Poppie kept a good horse. He raised

Mommie coming from the dairy

(grew) corn and hay for the animals. We had a big garden and Mom canned plenty of food, such as beans, apples, cucumbers, tomatoes, and big jars of mixed pickles, sour kraut, pickled corn, and pickle beans. Sometimes she would make soap from meat scraps. It was "strong," that is, it smelled bad, but it sure got the clothes clean. There was never a need for much to be purchased from the store. We bought flour, meal, beans, sugar and salt, and little more.

Another chore that fell to me often was to pick up chips from where the wood was cut. I would take a box or an old dishpan to put the chips in. This made wonderful kindling wood to start fires. On the edge of the chip yard grew "hardychokes" (Jerusalem Artichokes). They grew high and had a bright yellow bloom on them. When I got hungry between meals, I would run to the chip yard and dig up a bunch of "hardychokes." They looked like roots. We would wash them and eat them raw. They tasted somewhat like a raw potato, but better. I also was sent frequently to the plum trees to pick up luscious red plums that had fallen from the trees. They were bright red with golden flecks in them, and the ground would be covered with them. I have never tasted plums so delicious since those trees died out.

We could hardly wait until berry picking time. We put on bibbed overalls, long sleeve shirts and hats, grabbed a bucket and off we went into the berry fields. My older married sisters, Blanche, Hattie, and my sisters, Letha and Jean, my brother Cowan, and nephews and nieces and Mamma all picked. The best and sweetest berries were near the woods in the shade. We called them "shade berries."

Mamma would can the berries for blackberry dumplings or cobblers for winter. Raspberries ripened a little earlier and were not as plentiful as blackberries. We also went "strawberry picking." Wild strawberries are absolutely the sweetest and best!

My sister Jean, and I built "playhouses" until she outgrew them. I had to either build them alone or play with my nieces and nephews, who were close to my age.

We built some of them on a big rock down near

Left: My cousin, Carrol Lane, Baby Dimples, and me

Jerusalem Artichoke

the spring. We used small rocks for our stove, chair and beds. We hunted moss for our carpets and used can lids for our plates and kettles and sticks for spoons.

My sister, Letha, who lived and worked in the Washington, DC area, brought home to me a beautiful doll with dimples, a pink coat and hat and white shoes. Letha called it "Baby Dimples," so that is what I called it. I loved that doll! I thought it was the prettiest doll I had ever seen and kept it until I was grown, then passed it on to one of my nieces.

"Poppie" worked in the mines at different times. Sometimes I wouldn't see him for quite awhile. He worked over in Jenkins, Kentucky, and I don't know how he got there and back. We didn't have an automobile at the time. He also worked on the "WPA" when Roosevelt got things going after the depression. He helped build roads in the area. The people who worked for WPA were automatically tagged as "working on the road." Finally he went to Fairfax to work in defense work, and I didn't like it a bit! I thought "Mr. Fairfax" was a man that was taking my Poppie away to work for him. He worked in the Washington, D.C. area for some time. He and Mom always managed to raise a garden, and corn, oats, and hay to feed the animals.

My father was a good blacksmith and worked for the State Highway Department as their blacksmith for several years. We had a blacksmith shop near our back porch in the yard where Poppie made our hoes, hammers, chisels and other tools so he could shape the iron and other metals. I helped him by pumping the bellows, to blow air on the fire to make it red and glowing hot, so he could shape the iron and other metals. He later used another type blower that connected to the forge as I turned the handle. While the iron was red hot, he would then hammer it and shape it to his liking, then dunk it into a bucket of water, tempering the iron.

My Mother kept things going on the home front while Poppie was away at work. She raised a garden and carried on with everyday chores. I remember that she and my sisters and brother would go to the barn and gear up "Old Nell" and hitch her to the sled to go to the woods and get wood for our stove and fireplaces.

I used to get my homework by the light of oil lamps at the kitchen table. Of course, we had no refrigerator, so our leftovers went into the bottom of our kitchen cabinet. It was a large wood structure that sat at one end of the kitchen near a small bedroom. It held dishes, silverware,

Poppie and Old Frank

and had a flour bin with a sifter in the bottom of it. When my Mom needed flour, I would turn the sifter handle and flour would come out of the bottom, sifted nice and smooth.

When WWII was going on certain foods were rationed. I remember having "ration stamps." Families were allowed a certain amount of a specific food, such as sugar. I don't remember the other rationed food, but I do remember we couldn't buy butter, only margarine, and it was white. Little yellow pills came with the margarine and I can still see my Mother dropping the pills into the white margarine and mixing it to turn it to a nice golden color. We never had to buy much margarine though because we always kept a cow, however sometimes when they were expecting a calf, the cow would be "dry" for a while until after the calf was born, and she would "come fresh."

During this time, there were pictures of "Uncle Sam" everywhere, and people were very patriotic. In the pictures, "Uncle Sam" would point his finger and say, "Uncle Sam wants you!" Another saying was, "Buy War Bonds and Stamps and help win the War!" There was a lot of talk about a "Victory Garden," wanting everyone to raise a garden to help with food supplies. I think shoes were also rationed, and people would swap their food ration stamps for shoe ration stamps.

Uncle Sam Wants You!

Both my brothers were in WWII and that took a toll on my Mother. She worried and prayed, and prayed and worried. We had to walk quite a way to our mailbox, but she would go nearly every day, wanting to hear from her sons. When she wouldn't hear for some time, she would ask the mailman, "are you sure there is no letter for me today?" Both sons came home from the War.

In one of our bedrooms there was a Victrola "Talking Machine," which stood near a window. It was a tall thing, and had a large head that was placed on the record, which played Bluebird, RCA, and Columbia records. On one side was a crank that we had to wind up. When it began to run down it made a funny, whining sound and we would have to wind it again.

Before we got a radio, I would go with my sisters and brother to our married sister, Blanche's, home to listen to the *Grand Ole' Opry* on Saturday nights. She would make chocolate fudge or popcorn and we would sit around and talk and listen to Minnie Pearl saying, "How-dy, I'm just so proud to be here!" Then Roy Acuff sang "The Great Speckled Bird," and Ernest Tubb "I'm Walking the Floor Over You." Sometimes Mommie would go with us. We finally got a radio and played it sparingly because when the battery went down, it was a while before we got another one. The battery was almost as big as a car battery and sat in back of the radio. When it became weak we would warm it up in front of the fireplace and encourage it to last a little while longer.

We received catalogs from Aldens, Sears and Roebuck, Spiegel, and Montgomery Ward. Once in a great while, Mom would order from one of the catalogs. It seems that Aldens was less expensive and Spiegel was the most expensive. Pretty dresses and hats were ordered from these catalogs, especially around "August Meeting" time when the ladies wanted to look their best. The catalogs sure came in handy for multi-purposes—they kept us entertained for hours. The pretty ladies and children in the catalogs made wonderful paper dolls and last but not least, they were a necessary item in the outhouse.

I went to school at Duncan Gap from "primer" through sixth grade, primer being before first grade. My nephew, Billy, and I passed the primer and first grade both the first year. I remember walking to school which was about a mile, and on hot days, after they paved the road, It would almost burn our feet. We had to do a lot of feet scrubbing before we went to bed those nights.

Sometimes, we took half gallon lard buckets of milk and bread crumbed in. We sat them under the schoolhouse floor to keep cool. Homemade biscuits with fried ham or shoulder meat stuffed in the middle and an apple butter biscuit made a good lunch. The school gave out apples and nuts in the wintertime, a one-time distribution until they ran out. The aroma of the apples filled the room and made me hungry. We could hardly wait until evening when we would get one each.

The school was located in the Gap and sat just across the road from the church. There were two rooms called the "Big Room" and the "Little Room." It had a front porch and was heated with a pot-bellied stove. A well house covered the well where we drew water for the school. It usually took two children to pull up the water from the deep well.

About once a year, some men would come to the school and put oil on the floors. We children would pull off our shoes and slide all over the floor in our bare feet. We would laugh and slide and have the best time! Needless to say, our feet would be an oily, greasy mess, but some of it would wear off as we played in the dirt schoolyard and walked home barefoot.

"All day meeting and dinner on the ground" was a community affair in the summertime. These memorial meetings, held each summer, lasted most all day on Sunday. They were held near - or at- family cemeteries in memory of the loved ones that had passed on. Several preachers would speak and then the food would be spread on sheets and tablecloths on the ground. Everyone would eat and after that there would be more preaching. This practice still is going on at the Gap, but I believe the food is eaten at homes or the church now instead of the cemetery.

Diet rules for cheating:

If you eat something and no one sees you eat it, the calories don't count.

Cookie pieces contain no fat – breaking causes a process called *fat leakage*.

When you eat a candy bar and drink a diet soda, the calories in the candy bar are canceled out by the diet soda.

Calories don't count when you eat with a friend, as long as they eat more than you do.

Stuff licked off a utensil while preparing something else (ex. Peanut butter, ice cream, cookie dough) don't count because you're in the process of preparation.

Movie related foods are part of the entertainment package deal, therefore don't count.

If you're on a color diet - green, yellow, etc. – remember, chocolate is a universal color and may be substituted for any other food color.

Calories are units of heat; therefore frozen foods can't have calories.

Lee County

Contents

Apple Crisp...................................83
Applesauce Cake.......................83
Black Walnut Cake....................85
Coal Miner's Garden.................85
Cherry Dessert..........................85
Chili Con-queso Dip..................86
Corn Pudding............................88
Cranberry Crème Salad..............88
Daddy's Breakfast Crumbles......89
Farmer's Fruit Cake (1922)........89
Fresh Peach Pie........................90
Fried Molasses..........................90
Grandma's Slaw Dressing..........90
Hot Apple Cider........................91
Ice Box Rolls............................91

Lemon Walnut Drizzle.....................92
Old Fashioned Corn Light Bread......92
One Bowl Chocolate Cake..............93
Orange Cake...................................93
Ozark Apple Pudding......................95
Peanut Streusel Pie.........................95
Perfect Boiled Eggs........................95
Popcorn Balls.................................96
Red Eye Gravy...............................96
Road Side Lemonade......................96
Snow Ice Cream...........................102
Strawberry Cake...........................103
Swedish Apple Pie........................103
Sweet Potato Casserole.................106
Texas Sheet Cake..........................107

Schoolhouse Window at Hensley Settlement
- Used by permission of Harold Jerrell

Harold Jerrell has been the Agricultural Extension Agent for Lee County since 1984. Before that he worked as a seasonal park ranger for the Cumberland Gap National Historical Park and taught school. His long-time interest in photography has escalated in the past few years and he has won a number of awards, one that landed his photo on the cover of the March 2006 Virginia Wildlife Magazine. He enjoys photographing cultural and historical scenes, especially in the Southern Appalachian Mountains.

Apple Crisp

Pat Houck – In memory of Aunt Ethel – Rose Hill, VA

4	cups pared, sliced apples	1	tsp. cinnamon
¼	cup water	1/8	tsp. salt
¾	cup all-purpose flour	1/2	cup butter
1	cup sugar		ice cream for topping

Place apples in lightly greased 10 x 10 x 2-inch baking dish and add water. In bowl, sift flour, sugar, cinnamon, and salt, using a pastry blender; cut in butter until mixture resembles coarse crumbs. Sprinkle over apples and bake at 350° for about 45 minutes. Serve hot with ice cream.

"This was a family tradition at our house. We always had this cake at Christmas time when I was growing up in Calvin, VA. This was my mother, Pearl Wade's recipe."

Applesauce Cake

Wilma Wade Parsons - Jonesville, VA

2½	cups hot applesauce	1	tsp. cloves
2	cups white sugar	1	tsp. allspice
2	cups chopped nuts	4	tsp. soda
2	eggs, beaten	1	lb. raisins
1	cup butter or shortening	4	cups flour
1	tsp. cinnamon		

Cream sugar and butter. Add soda to hot applesauce. Mix dry ingredients together and add to first mixture. Bake in a tube pan about 1 hour at 350°. Let cake cool completely. Wrap cake with wax paper and Reynolds wrap. Make the cake about two weeks before you plan on serving it. This will make the cake very moist.

Were there no God, we would be in this glorious world with grateful hearts and no one to thank.
-Christina Rossetti

Hensley Settlement, established in 1904, where about one hundred people lived in isolation until the mid - 1900's, is located on a remote plateau nearly 1,000 ft. higher than the Pinnacle Overlook in Cumberland Gap National Park, which is 2,440 ft.

I Called Her Aunt Ethel

Pat Houck - Founding Member, Wilderness Road Dulcimer Club - Rose Hill, VA

"As far as I know she never performed for anyone but Uncle Mel."

"She wasn't my Aunt, but I called her that. I called her husband Uncle Mel. They were my neighbors when I was growing up in the 1940's and 50's in Ewing, VA, in Lee County. Their house sat just across Indian Creek from where our house sat and I saw them almost every day of my life. They didn't have children and I often wondered why because they would have made great parents. I know, because they were good to me.

Aunt Ethel was a musician. She played the piano. As far as I know she never performed for anyone but Uncle Mel. In the evenings, after the day's work was done, she played for him. I think she never knew, but she played for me as well.

Like most kids my age, I had a bicycle and I had a mother who watched over me carefully. I was allowed to ride my bicycle along a route my mother specified. The route she chose for me was the country road, which ran in front of our house, across Indian Creek, and around a curve where Uncle Mel and Aunt Ethel's house sat.

On those summer evenings long ago I was treated to the sound of melodies that the evening breeze carried to me through open windows as I rode my bicycle past Aunt Ethel and Uncle Mel Thompson's house. As I passed by I could see her at the piano and I could see Uncle Mel sitting in his favorite chair. During those times, I believe Aunt Ethel wouldn't have felt more satisfaction had she been playing the piano in a packed concert hall. After all, she was playing for the love of her life and who could be more important than that?

Long after Aunt Ethel and Uncle Mel died and long after I was no longer a young girl riding my bicycle on a route designated by my mother, I learned to play the Appalachian Mountain Lap Dulcimer. When my husband gave it to me for my 60th birthday I learned to play simple melodies. As I played the dulcimer for him in the privacy of our home, my thoughts carried me back to the white frame house where Aunt Ethel played the piano for Uncle Mel.

In 2005, I, along with Joan Porter of Rose Hill and Pam and Terry Lewis of the Wheeler Community, founded the Wilderness Road Dulcimer Club in Rose Hill, VA, Lee County, in an effort to preserve that part of our musical heritage.

Black Walnut Cake

Betty Falin – Ben Hur, VA

1	can crushed pineapple (don't drain)		
2	cups self-rising flour	2	cups sugar
2	eggs	1	tsp vanilla
2	tsps. soda	½	cup walnuts

Grease and flour long pan, mix ingredients and pour in pan. Bake 30 to 35 minutes in 350° oven.

Frosting
1   (8 oz.) cream cheese (softened)
1   stick margarine
1 ¾ cups powdered sugar or more
1   tsp. vanilla
½   cup walnuts (I use <u>our</u> fresh cracked walnuts)

Mix well and put on cake while it is hot. I let my cake cool about 10 to 15 minutes before I put icing on.

Cherry Dessert

Lula Belle Reasor – Pennington Gap, VA

2	cans sour cherries and the juice	slivered almonds
1	white or yellow cake mix	(enough to cover top)
1	stick melted margarine	Dream Whip

Pour the cans of sour cherries and the juice into a large flat pan. Pour the contents of a cake mix over this but don't stir. Drizzle the melted margarine on top of cake mix. Top with slivered almonds. Bake at 350° for 35 to 40 minutes. Cut in squares and top with Dream Whip. Best if served a little warm.

Coal Miner's Garden

Submitted by Sharon Sarver

Place several pieces of coal in an old dish. Sprinkle 4 Tbsps. of salt over the lumps. Then spread 4 Tbsps. of water over the coal and salt. Next pour 2 Tbsps. of bluing and 1 Tbsp. of ammonia over the mixture.
Sprinkle a few drops of Mercurochrome or food coloring in various spots. To keep growing, add 2 Tbsps. of ammonia every 2 days.

This is a fun recipe for children.

Dr. Daniel Sheffey Reasor

My great-grandfather, Dr. Daniel Sheffey Reasor, who was born in the Turkey Cove community of Lee County, entered the Confederate army at the age of twenty-three. He was part of the 64th Mounted Infantry of the Virginia State Militia and attained the rank of 2nd Lieutenant before being captured during a skirmish at Cumberland Gap.

For two years Dr. Reasor (known as D.S. to friends and family) was held at Johnson's Island, a Northern prison camp at Sandusky, Ohio. As a prisoner of war, he acquired medical training. It is not known how or why this happened to a POW except that possibly there was a severe shortage of medical personnel and he was required to serve as an apprentice at the camp.

At the end of the war, great-grandfather swore allegiance to the United States government and was allowed to return to Turkey Cove where he farmed progressively, served as a dentist and medical doctor, and was a leader at the Deep Springs Baptist Church. D.S. married Elizabeth Pennington Skaggs and together they raised seven children. Today their descendants are scattered about the country. Many well-respected men such as he helped develop Lee County by their commitment to family and community.

In 2001, the Lee County Board of Supervisors passed a resolution to name the U.S. 58A bridge over the Powell River east of Dryden, VA in honor of Daniel Reasor. The dedication took place in 2004 and my family was very excited about the event. We had over one hundred relatives there for the event. *-Lula Belle Reasor*

The Cumberland Gap changed hands four times during the Civil War. Though no major battles were fought there, several skirmishes took place.

Chili Con-queso Dip
Elaine Davis, Ben Hur, VA

1 lb. ground chuck	¼ cup chopped green onion
1 (8 oz.) can tomato sauce	1 tsp. Worcestershire sauce
1 (4 oz.) jar green chili peppers, drained and chopped	1 lb. Velveeta cheese, cut up

In a large skillet, brown meat. Add green onion. Cook over low heat until tender but do not brown. Add tomato sauce, chili peppers, Worcestershire sauce, and cheese. Cook, stirring occasionally until all cheese is melted. Serve in a chafing dish over low heat. Serve with corn chips. Makes 1 quart. "This is simple and very good!"

Bluegrass Memories
As told by: Frances Robertson Inwood

"I sort of fell into bluegrass and traditional music," states Frances Inwood, laughingly. "A friend in college during the early 70's asked if I'd like to spend the weekend with his parents and go hear him play at a festival with the Dixie Travelers. After that I went to Myrtle Beach where another friend played bass for James Monroe, Bill Monroe's son, who had started his own band, *The Midnight Ramblers.*

James was called to the stage and needed someone to watch the record table while they were on and he appointed me just because I was standing there. After doing that, I began to think, hummm… maybe I can work my way to these festivals. Often there was a need for someone to work the gate. Otherwise, I'd be at James Monroe's table selling records, guitar picks, and photographs suitable for framing.

The festivals were sort of like a circuit, each weekend you saw many of the same people. It was loads of fun, meeting all the musicians. Bluegrass people are mostly genial and accessible, willing to shake hands and pose for pictures."

Many of the singers and musicians touring then have names that are well known or remembered today - Mac Wiseman, Curley Ray Cline, Ralph Stanley, Keith Whitley, Ricky Scaggs, Jimmy Martin, Charlie Waller, and scores more. Bill Monroe traveled in a bus with steer longhorns adorning the hood, which was forever breaking down. "I believe James Monroe was in a Winnebago." Many honest-to-goodness hippies attended the festivals along with older folks. Inwood fondly remembers the Ralph Stanley Festival near McClure before it was improved as being in a place as "steep as a cow's face," but with great music and crowds of fans. That was also the festival where Little Roy Lewis of the Lewis Family Singers told the crowd that he had 'run the bus's battery out blowing his horn at his own tail lights.'

"Paul Davis told me this story. Who knows if it was true? A lot of kidding went on. It seems that during a raid on a still somewhere in the mountains of Virginia, Mac Wiseman was spotted running away. Being pretty distinctive looking, he'd be hard to mistake. May possibly have been getting medicine for his voice."

Working the gate paid enough to attend the next show, but sometimes it was located as much as a mile from the stage area where food

Because of working for James, my first trip to the Grand Ol' Opry was as the guest of Bill Monroe, thank you very much! Going in through the back door of the Ryman was sooo neat and impressed me greatly at the time. I've asked my son whether he would state this fact in my obituary, but so far he declines with, "That might be a little tacky, Mom."
-*Frances Robertson Inwood*

and drinks were available. "Consistently, the nicest, most thoughtful group that came through was Jim and Jesse McReynolds. They never failed to stop and ask if we could use some coffee or a coke, or if we needed change. They would hand something right out the window. Other groups were willing to do something if I flagged them down and asked, but Jim and Jesse always offered first. That meant so much when you were stuck a mile away from everything."

Great stories and great memories and pictures to share from a happy and carefree time of life, along with one regret: "I never had my picture made with Kenny Baker."

The 20,000-acre Cumberland Gap National Historical Park, located on the borders of Tennessee, Virginia, and Kentucky contains the natural break in the Appalachian Mountains that was the easiest route for Indians and migratory animals. Between the late 1700's to early 1800's, it is thought that as many as 300,000 settlers traveled through the Gap on the way west.

Corn Pudding

Recipe of Evelyn Robertson-Frances Inwood-Ewing, VA

2	eggs, separated	½	tsp. salt
2	Tbsp. sugar	4	ears corn
2	Tbsp. flour	¾	cup sweet milk
4	Tbsp. butter		

Beat egg yolks, beat in sugar, flour, butter, and salt. Add milk. Thinly cut corn from cob and scrape the cob. Add corn to mixture. Fold in stiffly beaten egg whites. Pour into greased baking dish. Bake at 350° for 35-45 minutes or until congealed. Serve immediately. Note: 1 can drained whole kernel corn may be used instead of fresh corn.
Yields: 4-6 servings

"This recipe is from an aunt of mine. I got it about 43 years ago."

Cranberry Crème Salad

Lula Belle Reasor – Pennington Gap, VA

1	(3 oz.) pkg. cherry gelatin	1/3	cup chopped celery
3	Tbsps. sugar	1/3	cup chopped walnuts
1	cup boiling water	1	cup sour cream
1	can whole cranberry sauce		

Dissolve gelatin and sugar in boiling water and add cranberry sauce. Chill until thick, but not firm. Add other ingredients and mix well. Use 8-inch pan.

"This recipe was brought over to Virginia from Kentucky. I still fix this occasionally. Delicious and filling with a good cup of coffee".

Daddy's Breakfast Crumbles

Sharon Sarver in memory of Henrietta Lewis Logan

bacon
cornbread
2-3 eggs
salt and pepper

Fry bacon in pan. Remove bacon. Crumble last night's cornbread into bacon grease. Break 2 or 3 eggs over bread; scramble or fry. Salt and pepper to taste. Sprinkle water over mixture until moist. Stir. (Do not let this get dry.)

Farmer's Fruit Cake (1922)

Elaine Davis, Ben Hur, VA

3 cups dried apples	1 ½ cup milk
2 cups molasses	2 eggs
1 cup butter	4 cups flour
1 cup sugar	4 tsp. baking powder
1 cup seedless raisins	nuts
3 tsp. mixed spices	1 tsp. vanilla

Soak the apples overnight, chop and cook slowly until tender. Cream the butter and sugar, add the eggs one at a time, then the apples and molasses, raisins and milk. Sift flour, baking powder, and spices; add to apple mixture. Beat well and add vanilla. Pour into a well-greased pan. Bake in slow oven 350° on center rack for about one hour. Note: English walnuts or black walnuts may be added.

Sprinkled with love,
Garnished with care,
Prepared with my heart,
For generations to share.

About Closed Hands

A closed hand can't receive.
Even God himself cannot give you or I any more than we are mentally, emotionally, and spiritually conditioned to receive. If our hands are already full of ourselves then God can't fill them.

Grandma's Slaw Dressing

Sharon Sarver

Cook until thick.
½ cup vinegar
½ cup sugar
butter, size of walnut
2 eggs, well beaten

Add when cool:
1 cup whipped cream

A little more laughter
A little less worry.
A little more kindness
A little less hurry.

Fresh Peach Pie
Mary Lou Carter – Pennington Gap, VA

2½	lbs. fresh ripe peaches, peeled and sliced thin		
4	oz. white sugar	2	oz. lemon juice
3	Tbsps. corn starch	1	pie shell
¼	tsp. salt	1	oz. unsalted butter
		8	oz. streusel topping (below)

Combine peaches, sugar, cornstarch, salt, and lemon juice in a large bowl. Let set 15 minutes. Spoon into pie shell. Cut butter into small pieces and dot on top of peaches. Cover with topping. Bake at 400° until bubbly hot and topping is brown, approximately 45 minutes.

Streusel Topping

2	lbs. all purpose flour	11	oz. brown sugar
2	tsps. cinnamon	8	oz. white sugar
2	tsps. salt	1 ½	lb. cold butter

Combine all dry ingredients. Cut in butter. Use for muffins, fruit pies, or quick breads. Makes a lot. Freeze to use later. No need to thaw or make a fraction of the recipe.

Fried Molasses
Ginger Sullivan - Pennington Gap

1	cup molasses	butter
	baking soda	iron skillet

Pour abut one cup molasses into iron skillet. Turn stove eye to medium high heat. When molasses begin to boil, sprinkle a pinch or two of baking soda over the top. Stir. They will turn a golden color. Pour quickly into bowls or plate. Mix a pat or two of butter into the molasses and eat with homemade biscuits. Umm....good!

Hot Apple Cider
Elaine Davis, Ben Hur, VA

2 quarts apple cider	1 small orange, studded with cloves
1 pint cranberry juice	
¾ cup sugar (some like less)	2 cinnamon sticks
1 tsp. whole allspice	

Combine all ingredients and boil on high heat for 1 hour, then turn to low and simmer for 4 to 8 hours.

"The Peters Brothers, Arthur and J. C., were born and raised in a small town in Southwest VA, and their music is influenced by their rural background and by the uncles in their family who played "back porch style" mountain music when they were growing up. They began to play and sing Bluegrass when they were in their teens, and have continued to play and sing for 55 years or so, playing the old Bluegrass tunes. They know just about all the old songs, and they love to jam with other musicians. This recipe was J. C. and Arthur's mother's recipe."

Dr. Thomas Walker first recorded an expedition to Cumberland Gap in 1750, though his name is not generally known. Daniel Boone is the name most often associated with discovering the Gateway to the West.

Ice Box Rolls
Pat Peters – wife of Arthur Peters

Scald together and cool:
1 quart sweet milk   1 cup lard (1 stick Crisco shortening)
1 cup sugar

Add to lukewarm mixture:
1 cup mashed potatoes   1 pkg. yeast

Sift together:
1 tsp. soda
1 tsp. salt   1 tsp. baking powder
**   Enough flour to make stiff dough**

Let mixture sit overnight in refrigerator. Next day roll out, brush with melted butter, and let stand at room temperature for at least 3 hours. Bake at 375° for about 12 minutes. Makes 4 – 5 dozen rolls.

Need a warm place for bread dough to rise? A slow cooker can do the trick!

Mary Lou Carter plays the banjo and drives from Lee County to Mt. Rogers school in Grayson County, about two hours, to take lessons from Emily Spencer and play at the jam session with other talented musicians.

Lemon Walnut Drizzles
Mary Lou Carter – Pennington Gap, VA

1   bag of Betty Crocker Sugar Cookie Mix
    (may substitute 1 yellow cake mix)
1   egg   1   stick melted butter

Combine these 3 ingredients, and then add:
1   (3oz.) box of instant lemon pudding
1   cup chopped nuts (optional)
½   bag of white chocolate chips
2   Tbsps. lemon juice

Drop by tablespoon (or roll into balls) onto lightly sprayed cookie sheet. Bake 375° for 10 minutes on top rack. Let cool. Mix 1 ½ cups powdered sugar with enough lemon juice to make drizzle glaze.

Old Fashioned Corn Light Bread
Elaine Davis – Ben Hur, VA

2 cups water   1 tsp. salt
Bring this water and salt to a boil in a 4-quart saucepan.

"This recipe is over 100 years old and is very, very good."

2 cups cornmeal   2 cups cold water
Moisten cornmeal with cold water and stir into the boiling water. Cook for 2 to 3 minutes until thick mush is formed. Take from stove and add the following:

3 cups cold water   1   cup sifted flour
2 cups cornmeal   1 ½ cups cornmeal

Mix well and sprinkle 1 ½ cups cornmeal over mixture but do not stir. Tie a cloth over the saucepan and put in a warm place for 24 hours or until sour enough to bubble. Then add:

2 cups sugar   ½ cup melted shortening
Preheat oven to 300°. Mix well. Pour into a greased stem cake pan and cook for 1 ½ hours. Leave bread in the pan until it is cold. It will slice nicely.

One Bowl Chocolate Cake
Mary Lou Carter – Pennington Gap, VA

2 cups plain flour	1 tsp. baking powder
2 cups sugar	1 tsp. salt
2 tsps. soda	½ cup Hershey's cocoa

Stir all of this together. Now add:

2 eggs beaten	1 cup oil
1 cup buttermilk	1 cup hot water

Stir well: then add 1 cup hot water as the last thing and stir well. Spray pan with non-stick cooking spray. Pour into bundt pan, 13 x 9 x 2 inch, or tube pan. Bake 350° for 35 minutes.

> Jesus Christ the same yesterday, and today and forever.
> *-Hebrews 13:8*

Orange Cake
Recipe of Dorothy Griffith, submitted by Elaine Davis

6-8 orange peels dried and beaten into a powder (reserve some for frosting)	3 cups sugar
	3 eggs
	1 stick real butter melted and cooled
4 cups self-rising flour	
3 cups sweet milk	1 tsp. vanilla

Preheat oven to 350°. In a mixing bowl add milk, sugar, eggs, and butter. Mix well. Add flour and orange peel powder a little at a time until the consistency of cake batter, and add vanilla. Pour into 8 or 10-inch cake pans. Mom would use a 10-inch cast iron skillet. This makes 2 round cakes (cool to touch).

Frosting

4 cups whipping cream	1 tsp. vanilla
½ tsp. lemon juice	orange peel powder
sugar to taste	

Whip the cream until it starts to get thick. Add sugar to taste, vanilla, and some of the orange peel powder. Frost the cakes.

> *"Mom always had a cow, so she always had the cream that came off the milk. Now you can buy whipping cream from the store.*

In Honor of My Mother, Dorothy Griffith

> Who can find a virtuous woman? For her price is far above rubies.
> *-Proverbs 31:10*

I find it hard to put Mom's recipes on paper. You see, my Mom is 80 years old now, and did not learn to read and write because she had to work in the cornfields back when she was a girl. She said they went into the fields at dawn and came out at dusk.

She married at fourteen. My Dad was in his twenties. She thought she would get married and would not have to work as hard as she did at home, but got into worse than ever. They had sixteen children – ten boys and six girls. Twelve of us are left. Times were so hard on large families during the 50's, 60's, and 70's. I was born in 1960.

We all worked hard. We had to, to survive. Some of the things I cherish the most in my life are the days helping to cook the meals at our house. Some of the favorite things I learned were making biscuits, apple butter, and churning butter and the process of getting it into butter molds. Harder things were cooking fresh chicken, (from the pen to the table on Sundays!) rendering lard, and all the canning. We ate what was raised in the many large gardens we had and canning food was a way for us to survive the winter months.

Mom sold eggs, butter, anything she could do to get enough money to buy flour, coffee, pinto beans, sugar, and salt. By the time I was ten, my parents had ten of us in school at one time.

Flour sacks were what many of my dresses were made of. Oh, they would itch me to death at church on Sundays!

Our playground was the mountains, grapevines our swings, and the creek near our house was our swimming pool. We had nothing but each other and the love of our parents. But if I could put into words the things my mother has taught me over the years, it would be a Bible in itself. I know of no stronger woman that the Lord has placed in my life.

At Christmas, we never got gifts but our mother would go to the local country store and bring back a box filled with apples, oranges, and one large peppermint candy stick. Each of us got an apple and an orange and she would break up that big red and white peppermint candy stick and give each of us a piece. Someone would read the story of Christ. I would call him baby Jesus.

We always kept the orange peels for Mom to lay on the shelf of that old cook stove to dry out. Around the first of the year, she would take the orange peels that were good and dry and beat them until they were like a powder and use it to bake a cake. Oh, that smell of orange cake baking, I can never forget! - *Elaine Davis – Ben Hur*

Ozark Apple Pudding

Mary Lou Carter – Pennington Gap, VA

- 2 eggs
- 1½ cups sugar (makes a bit too sweet for me, I use 1 cup only)
- 4 Tbsps. flour
- 2½ tsps. baking powder
- 1½ cup (finely) chopped apples (may increase to 2 cups)
- ¼ tsp. salt
- 1 cup broken nuts – your choice
- 1½ tsps. vanilla

Beat eggs and sugar until smooth and add vanilla. Mix dry ingredients together and add to egg mixture. Stir in apples and nuts. Pour into a greased sheet cake pan. Bake 350° for 35 minutes. The "cake" will rise and then fall to create a crunchy top. Serve with ice cream!

Peanut Streusel Pie

Wilma Wade Parsons – Jonesville, VA

- 1/3 cup peanut butter
- ¾ cup confectioners sugar
- 1 baked pie shell
- 1/3 cup all-purpose flour
- ½ cup sugar
- ½ tsp. salt
- 2 cups scalded milk
- 3 egg yolks slightly beaten
- 2 Tbsps. margarine
- ½ tsp. vanilla

Blend peanut butter with confectioners sugar until mealy. Sprinkle two-thirds of mixture over baked pie shell. Combine flour, ½ cup sugar, and ½ tsp. salt. Stir in scalded milk-stirring constantly until thickened. Stir small amount of cooked filling into the egg yolks. Combine with remaining hot mixture and cook several minutes longer. Add margarine and vanilla. Pour into pie shell. Top with meringue. Sprinkle remaining peanut butter and confectioner sugar on meringue. Brown meringue in 350° oven.

Perfect Boiled Eggs

Virginia Sullivan's method - submitted by: daughter, Ginger Sullivan

Number of eggs desired

Place any number of eggs into saucepan. Cover with cold water and bring them to boil on medium heat. When water comes to a boil, turn off heat and let them remain in water for 20 minutes. Pour off water, crack each egg and add cold water. Let the cracked eggs remain in cold water for a few minutes; peel each one. With this method there will be no green yolks and the whites will be tender and good.

Popcorn Balls

Submitted by Sharon Sarver in memory of her mother, Henrietta Lewis Logan

Pop enough corn to make 5 quarts. Keep popped corn hot and crisp in slow oven (300° to 325°)

2	cups sugar	½	tsp. salt
½	cup light corn syrup	1	tsp. vinegar
1 ½	cups water	1	tsp. vanilla

Combine sugar, corn syrup, water, salt, and vinegar together. Cook to hardball stage. Add vanilla. Pour syrup slowly over popped corn. Mix well to coat every kernel. Press into balls or leave as is. Use fat on hands if necessary. Makes 15 to 20 balls.

Red Eye Gravy

Louise Holman – Pennington Gap, VA

grease from ham
2 Tbsps. brown sugar   **¾ cup coffee**

Fry ham and remove it from skillet. In the skillet add 2 Tbsps. brown sugar, stir in ¾ cup coffee and bring to a boil. Boil gently uncovered 2 – 3 minutes or until slightly thickened and a reddish brown color. Scrape the skillet to loosen any crusty bits.

Road Side Lemonade

Louise Holman – Pennington Gap, VA

6	cups water	8-9	large lemons
1 ½	cups sugar		ice cubes

In a 3 qt. saucepan, combine 2 cups water and the sugar. Bring to a boil. Reduce heat to low, stirring occasionally, and cook until sugar dissolves, 1 – 2 more minutes. Remove sugar syrup from heat and let cool 5 minutes. Cut lemons in half and squeeze out juice. Strain and remove seeds and pulp. Stir lemon juice into sugar syrup in a 2 ½ qt. container. Combine 4 cups water and the lemon syrup and cover. Put in refrigerator and chill. Serve over ice cubes in glasses. Makes about 2 quarts.

The only known "temple mound" in Virginia is in Lee County. Early Indians built the well-preserved site sometime during the period 1200 – 1600 AD. It can be seen from old Rt. 58 near Roseville.

Growing up in a Mining Camp

As I get older, I often think back to my childhood and the wonderful memories of growing up in a coal camp. It was like a small town or village where we knew everybody and had freedom to roam. In a big ball field, we played ball with children that we saw at school and went to church with. The grown-ups knew and tolerated all us children and we felt safe and secure in our little world.

I grew up in Calvin, a coal camp near Keokee, VA. When I was born in 1935, we had electricity and plumbing in our house. Calvin had its own water system so I never lived in a house without modern conveniences, including a bathroom. There was a commissary, a post office, a theater, and a boarding house. Our little town contained everything a child needed, even a neighbor who would take me with her to milk the cow.

Stoneface Rock, said to mark the entrance to a Cherokee Indian holy ground, is located just minutes from Pennington Gap, VA.

When someone got sick, neighbors pitched in to care for them and their families. I remember a lady who died with a baby and my mother kept it a while until the father got things straightened out. Nobody had ever heard of welfare.

Sundays were for going to Grandma's house. My three brothers and my sister and I looked forward to that and didn't expect anything different.

My Daddy was head of the carpenter shop for the mines. He had to go inside to repair anything that needed it, along with work in the shop. Mama raised a big garden that we helped her can, and we killed a hog to have meat in the winter.

Us kids attended elementary school in the camp, and went to high school in Keokee. The old commissary there was turned into a school gymnasium.

I knew my husband from the time I was about thirteen years old, but we never dated until we were in college. I dropped out after one year and went to Ohio to work because Daddy was on short time and couldn't afford to keep me in school. I found a job on Monday and had to go to work on Wednesday, but didn't know how to ride the trolley. My cousin took me to work until I figured it out.

Now, my husband has died and I am living back home in Lee County. I like being here and sometimes I go look at the place where Calvin used to be. It was shut down in 1954 and houses were sold for $50 each, providing the person would move them off the company land. When I go back to where that world existed, I try to picture our house and the ball field and all the places that were so familiar to a young child, but they can't be found anywhere except in my memories. - *Wilma Wade Parsons*

Happy Hollow
Originally written by Henrietta Lewis Logan – Submitted by daughter, Sharon Sarver

Being the fifth child in a family of seven sort of puts you in the middle where you can learn from the older ones and boss the younger ones. That kinda' evens things out. This was my situation.

The four of us who were the youngest were born in the little cabin home that was snuggled between two small hills outside of Pennington Gap, VA. Dr. Pearce delivered us and I think his fee was twenty-five dollars. My father called this place Happy Hollow.

Until I was about fourteen years old, we had no electricity or a telephone. We used the outdoor john and took our baths in a big zinc tub on Saturday night. The furniture was mostly handmade. We had a dining room table with chairs and stools. In the living room, we had a big table that we sat around at night and got our lessons for school. We played games and worked on projects, etc. by the light of a kerosene lamp.

We did not have fine furniture, but our home contained good books. The Holy Bible headed the list and was read to us regularly. We were often required to memorize large portions of it. In the living room was a long bookcase that held a set of Compton's Encyclopedias, a set of O. Henry's writings, another set of literature books and a dictionary. We had an Ellington piano and most of us took piano lessons. Some of us took these lessons more seriously than others… (My sister, Cora, did well. She taught piano and played the pipe organ in the Methodist Church for 25 years.) We younger children enjoyed the *Child Life* magazine and the older ones got the *American Magazine*.

Early in my life, children in our family took lessons in elocution. Bertie Fletcher was our teacher and she was a good one. Each spring she entered all of her pupils in a speaking contest. Medals were awarded to the ones best in their category. We worked hard on these contests because competition ran high. The recitations had to be done by memory; using the right expression was emphasized.

When I was in the Primer class, I won my first medal for a recitation called "An Accident." As a senior in high school, my recitation of "The Happy Prince" by Oscar Wilde, won a countywide speaking contest. It took fifteen minutes to recite. I owed this success to my sister, June, who trained me.

My older brothers and sisters spoke in contests, too, and brought home their share of the prizes. One night in particular, both my brother, Marsh, and sister, June, brought home the countywide speaking medals. When my Uncle Henry brought them home that night, he blew the car horn all the way up the hollow. Everybody was so happy and proud!

I don't know exactly how my family managed financially to give us the advantages they did, such as speech and music lessons, but I know it must have been a sacrifice. How my mother accomplished all she did as scarce as money was, I'll never know. She could do the most with the least of anyone I ever knew. Mama was a great lady in many ways.

The years we children grew up were mostly the years of the Great Depression. During these lean years, we were more fortunate than some because my parents owned our home and raised most of our food. We had cows, chickens, and hogs. We grew apples, peaches, and grapes, and always had a big garden. My father dug holes in the back yard and lined them with straw to store potatoes and apples. They were covered with lots of dirt. On a cold winter's night, Daddy would get apples out of the hole and we would eat them around the fireplace with some popcorn. We had a wire popcorn popper and if you weren't careful, you would get it too close to the fire and burn the popcorn. We ate it anyway. By the way, those apples that were dug from the hole were always cold and had an earthy taste. Good, Good, Good!

When the weather became cold enough, it was time for the hogs to be slaughtered. I always hated to hear the shots go off that killed the hogs, so I would cover my ears until it was over. When this was done, the men would dip the hogs in scalding water and scrape the hair off. Then they would string them up, split them open, and cut them up. The hams and shoulders were seasoned and hung from the ceiling in the smokehouse. The bacon was cut in big slabs ready to be fried or used to season a pot of brown pinto beans. It also went into the smoke house.

Inside the kitchen, the women folk were busy. The fat had to be cut up, placed in big kettles, and rendered into lard. This lard was stored in big cans. Sausage had to be ground and made ready for canning. There was no refrigeration down on the farm!

All this was greasy, hard work but to smell the sausage frying in the pan, the cracklin' cornbread baking in the oven, and the anticipation of tasting the fruit of your labors was compensation of a sort.

After all the meat was done up, it was time for our annual indoor rib roast – one of the most important events of the year. My father would place two stools on either side of the big fireplace. On a long metal pole, he would hang the whole sides of ribs. These would be slowly turned by hand in front of the fire until they had finished cooking. Big bread pans were placed underneath the ribs to catch the drippings. The ribs were seasoned with salt, pepper, and sage.

The aroma would begin to fill the house where all our kinfolk would be joking, laughing, and singing around the piano. The preacher and his family would be invited, too.

Mama would spread the big long table with a cloth and bring in other delicious foods from the kitchen. I remember cracklin' cornbread, potato salad, her good mustard pickles, baked beans, dried fruit stack cake, and lots of good hot coffee for the adults and milk for the kids. The preacher would say the blessing and everyone would dive in.

Most illnesses and minor ailments were taken care of with home remedies. It had to be a new baby or something very serious to send for a doctor. One time I stepped on a rake that put three holes in the bottom of my foot, but didn't need to go to the doctor for a little thing like that. Mama just poured on the turpentine. "Oow!" I screamed - and yelled and danced around for a while - then limped for a few days with a rag tied about my foot. Before long, I was well again.

If needed, we sent for Grandma Gish, who would stay overnight or longer if the situation was serious enough. When Grandma arrived, the first thing she did was administer a dose of castor oil so your "innards" were cleaned out good. That was a *must* in Granny's book. If you had pneumonia or a bad chest cold, Grandma would make a mustard plaster and apply it to your chest. This application would loosen up most people's lungs to release the phlegm. I wouldn't be surprised if it took the hair off a man's chest; it sure made your skin red as fire. Another remedy Grandma relied on heavily was Black Draught to keep you "regular." It was a dark, dry powder. She would put some in the palm of her hand, lick it, and take a sip of water

My father had his own remedies. In the springtime, he would take a round of Calomel to "purge" his insides. If he had a cold, he rubbed lard and kerosene on his chest. Another cold remedy was Dr. Pepsin's Cough Syrup. I sort of liked a dose of that, maybe because it was sweet. Oh, yes, there was Ungentine for burns, Iodine for cuts and a flaxseed poultice for drawing out splinters. Mama had a little remedy that worked every time – when one of us fell or got hurt, she kissed the hurt, a soothing ointment.

Her other remedy was a little tougher. Whenever we needed a good "lickin" for some wrongdoing, my mother would take us around back to the currant bush. She would break off a keen little switch from this bush and administer it to our back and legs. We had red stripes for a day or two but one thing was certain, whatever we did to deserve our "lickin," we thought twice before we did it again. That Currant bush was all the psychology that my parents knew to use but it worked. My Mother and Daddy didn't turn out perfect children but we grew up to be seven God-fearing, law abiding citizens. All of us had utmost respect for our parents and I don't think we ever got many licks that weren't deserved. Some were overdue.

The very mention of the word Christmas brought hope, joy, expectation, and activities of different kinds to the Lewis household. It wasn't gifts so much as all the other things like numerous relatives whose lives intertwined with ours at festive holiday occasions. We took part in plays presented by our church. Our family would gather around the piano and sing the beautiful carols of Christmas. Scriptures pertaining to Jesus' birth were memorized and we shared food from our "security closet."

My brothers usually went to find a live cedar tree. Sometimes it wasn't too straight or we had to turn the bad side to the wall. It was put into a bucket with rocks around the base to help it stand up straight. We decorated it with strings of popcorn, colored rope, and icicles. To us, it was beautiful to behold.

Mama's kitchen began to take on sweet delicious odors. A big fruitcake was made early, though there was no wine added to give it flavor. That was a no-no at our house. Another favorite cake was a Lady Baltimore, with white icing filled with candied fruits, raisins, and nuts. It was often served with Mama's boiled custard at one of our big family dinners. To please us children, Mama taught us how to make candied popcorn balls. They were so pretty and *so* good.

When Christmas morning finally came, we were up bright and early to check our long cotton brown stockings that had been hung on the mantel. The house would be cold because the fires had not yet been built. We didn't care. We just shivered in our shirttails and enjoyed the moment. The presents were under the tree unwrapped with our names on them. Our stockings were filled and running over with oranges, apples, candy, and nuts. To this day, when I smell oranges, I am reminded of Christmas because that was the only time we had them. The wonderful morning was topped off with a delicious breakfast of boiled fresh ham and gravy, biscuits, and homemade preserves. None of us received a lot of gifts, but what wonderful times these were!

Appalachian African-American Culture Center

Ron Carson and Jill Carson

Ron's great, great, great grandmother, Rachel Scott, donated the land where the building sits. His grandfather used to walk up the hill every morning to stoke the fires and made the same walk each evening to bank them. His mother was in the first class to attend the little brick school, the first and only primary school for blacks in 1940 in Lee County. Ron Carson was part of the last class of students to leave the school on a September morning in 1967 when Eddie B. Beatty arrived and said, "You guys are going out to the white schools today. It's just not right; all the other schools are integrating. So this year, you will begin school at Pennington Elementary and High School." They went, to become history as the first integration of schools in Lee County.

Carson and his wife, Jill, bought the brick building in 1988, the same year they moved into their new home across the road on land once owned by Rachel Scott and still in his family. The next question after acquiring the building was, "What will we do with it?" Jill, who was raised in Boston, Massachusetts, experienced a bit of culture shock upon moving to Appalachia. She has developed great respect for the people, especially through the oral history project, and finds the plight of older miners "heart-wrenching." She is forward looking and strives to broaden the scope of the culture center, tackling such issues as racism through story swaps and workshops.

The building was renovated with a grant from the Appalachian Community Fund. Jill and Ron began taking oral histories from older black people and held a very successful memorabilia night, when numerous items from the school were brought and donated back to the center. Black history programs were organized and presented at local schools and a Race Unity Day, which drew a large participation, was begun at a park in Jonesville and continues each year.

A suspicious and devastating fire in 1994 destroyed almost all the oral histories and artifacts that the Carson's had so diligently collected. Starting over was extremely hard and they are still struggling to regain what was lost. Both Jill and Ron have jobs and lead busy lives, but the center has become a symbol: of the past that should be remembered and learned from, and of a future that can be shaped by a vision shared by enough people.

Appalachian African-American Culture Center

"I love being back in Pennington Gap. It is quiet and peaceful and lots of good people here. You couldn't drag me out of here!"

Snow Ice Cream
Louise Holman – Pennington Gap, VA

½   cup sugar
¼   cup cream, milk or evaporated milk
1   tsp. vanilla
1   Tbsp. cocoa (optional)

Mix all together. Then add snow until it's the consistency of ice cream. Eat and enjoy!

Strawberry Cake

Jill Carson – Pennington Gap, VA

1	box white cake mix (Duncan Hines)
1	big box strawberry Jell-O
4	tsps. flour
½	cup cold water
1	cup Wesson oil or Crisco oil
4	eggs
1	cup frozen strawberries (thawed)

Mix dry ingredients with water and oil; add eggs one at a time beating after each. Add strawberries. Bake 10 minutes longer than directions on box.

Topping
- ¾ stick of butter
- ¾ cup of confectioners sugar
- 1 cup strawberries

Let come to a boil, cool slightly then pour over the cake.

Swedish Apple Pie

Louise Holman – Pennington Gap, VA

½	cup flour	1½	cups diced apples
¾	cup sugar	½	cup chopped walnuts
	Dash of salt	1	egg beaten
2	tsps. baking soda	1	tsp. vanilla

Mix together flour, sugar, salt, and baking powder. Then add apples and walnuts. Beat egg with vanilla, add to mixture and stir. Spread in a well-oiled 9-inch pie plate. Bake 25 minutes at 350°. Serve warm with vanilla ice cream or whipped cream. Serves 6 – 8.

Settlers moved into the mountainous area and created a little village called Crab Orchard in the late 1700's. Timber and farming were a way of life until the Keokee Coal and Coke Company was organized in the early 1900's. Industrialization brought a modern town and a better life to local farmers and immigrants and became known as Keokee.

On Black Lung

Mary "Mother" Jones, an activist during the late 1800's until her death in the 1930's was known as *the Miner's Angel*. Her war cry became famous, " Pray for the dead and fight like hell for the living."

Ron Carson's stepfather, grandfather, and great-grandfather all worked in the mines. At the height of the coal boom, there was a fairly large population of African-Americans who came to get work. Now there are less than one hundred in the whole county. "We are a minority within a minority," he says.

But Ron's concern is for black lung victims and he functions as an advocate for them regardless of race. "Almost every miner who has spent ten years working in a mine will suffer from Black Lung, a disease caused by inhaling coal dust," says Carson. "There are two types of Coal Worker's Pneumoconiosis (CWP). The most common is Simple black lung, which causes blisters, lesions, and/or nodules about the size of a dime. With Complicated black lung the lesions will be the size of a half-dollar and contract the sufferer's lungs. Air gets in but the lungs cannot push it back out. Oxygen is often required."

The National Institute for Occupational Safety and Health (NIOSH) did a study across the nation and found that Lee and Buchanan counties are hot spots for Complicated CWP, with more cases than any other coal producing state. Still, it is extremely hard to win a black lung case. Medical care is very necessary for anyone with the disease because it can affect other organs such as the heart and kidneys; however, decent care is often hard to come by without insurance. Therefore, proving CWP and receiving a medical card that guarantees treatment is a more important benefit than receiving the monetary compensation each month.

In 1990, Carson was one of three people who began a Federal Black Lung Program at Stone Mountain Health Services in Jonesville with a $68,000 grant. Today there are fifteen employees at three sites and the grant has risen to $780,000. They work alongside physicians to get the best medical treatment possible, a pulmonary rehab program, and prevention of infection, as well as helping establish a black lung claim.

"We are the only source in the tri-state area of Kentucky, Tennessee, and Virginia to process claims fulltime – and free of charge. And when we win, we take no fee. Our purpose is to give the miners or widows of miners a voice that they don't have otherwise."

The Department of Labor identifies the responsible operator – the last coal company the miner worked for at least a year. That operator carried insurance with an insurance carrier who employs high caliber lawyers to contest any claims. These lawyers are paid $100,00 up front to defend the case. It's hard to get local lawyers to take cases because they tend to drag on and on and there's little money to be made.

Three key elements have to be taken into consideration and proven to win a case:
1. Prove the presumption that the former miner actually has black lung. Insurance company doctors and lawyers attribute the problem to cigarettes, asbestos, raising chickens, or in some cases – being Melungeon and having sarcoidosis.
2. Evidence of nodules through x-ray and test read by B-Readers who are trained to verify the evidence.
3. That the miner is totally disabled by the CWP – the hardest to prove. Because of legislation approved in January 2001, there is now a limitation of two pieces of evidence from each side. This is helpful to the miner because each reading of evidence costs $60.00 apiece, a hardship for them, whereas the responsible operator could produce any number.

"We have led the nation the past five years in securing black lung benefits," states Carson. "Since 2000, some 480 awards have been secured over the whole coalmining region. That is the most rewarding thing we can see – helping someone who needs it so badly." *-Ron Carson*

Martin's Station, a living history museum with costumed interpreters, is part of the Wilderness Road State Park. Connecting Martin's Station with Cumberland Gap, there is a 10-mile hiking, biking, and equestrian trail that roughly follows Daniel Boone's Wilderness Road.

Wilderness Road State Park, one of the newest in Virginia, is farther west than Wheeling, WVA, Pittsburgh, PA, or Canton, Ohio. Used by permission of the Park and Marty McConnell.

Sweet Potato Casserole

Joy Fleenor's Recipe -Laura Lawson – Pennington Gap, VA

A good low sodium spice blend for your saltshaker:

**1 Tbsp. dry mustard
1 tsp. garlic powder
1 1/2 Tbsps. onion powder
1/2 Tbsp. ground pepper
1/2 Tbsp. thyme, crushed
1 tsp. sage
1/2 tsp. marjoram, crushed
1 Tbsp. paprika
1/2 tsp. basil, crushed
1/2 tsp. ground oregano**

3 cups mashed sweet potatoes
1 cup sugar
2 eggs
½ cup milk
1/3 tsp. salt
1/3 cup butter
1 tsp. vanilla

Mix and pour into a buttered baking dish.

Topping
1/3 cup butter
½ cup flour
1 cup brown sugar
1 cup chopped nuts

Mix ingredients and spread over sweet potato mixture. Bake at 350° for about 25 to 30 minutes.

"I grew up thinking I was Scots-Irish. With red hair and green eyes, there was no reason to think otherwise. But while doing genealogical research, my uncle and I found that there were three Kennedy brothers who split their loyalties during the Civil War. Two fought for the North and one for the South. One northern brother was killed and the other two never reconciled. Brent Kennedy, who has done extensive research on the Melungeon people, is a descendant of the brother who fought for the Union and I am a descendant of the Confederate Kennedy. At a reunion in the 1990's, we Kennedy's officially ended the rift after 130 years. Because of Brent Kennedy's research, and because he has a disease called sarcoidosis, doctors were able to diagnose my health problem, which is the same disease.

These days, it has become fashionable and popular to come from a Melungeon bloodline and many set out to prove their heritage. That was not the case in years gone by when they were often shunned and ridiculed because of their dark skin and hair. But America is the great melting pot and the Melungeon people are the original melting pot. They were here when the English came. It's a wonderful thing that there is now pride in our heritage, though we don't know the whole story of our ancestry yet." **-Laura Lawson**

Texas Sheet Cake

Laura Lawson – Pennington Gap, VA

2	sticks of butter	4	tsps. cocoa
1	cup water		

Preheat oven to 375°. Heat until boiling. Remove from heat and add the following ingredients. (Mix well each ingredient one at a time).

2	cups flour	2	eggs
2	cups sugar	1	tsp. baking soda
½	tsp. salt	1	cup sour cream

Bake for 30 minutes in a 13 x 9-inch pan.

Frosting
1	stick of butter	6	Tbsps. milk
4	Tbsps. cocoa		

Heat until butter melts. Remove from heat and add:

1	box confectioners sugar	1	tsp. vanilla

Beat until smooth. Pour on cake while hot.

This organization is dear to my heart because of my grandson, Tony Biggs, Jr. who has Down Syndrome. It is an advocacy group formed by parents of children with special needs, working for a brighter tomorrow.
.... *Laura Lawson*

G.I.R.A.F.F.E
Giving
Individuals
Resources and
Advocacy
For a
Fulfilling
Education

Deb's Fruit Market

"One morning I decided to do something different, so I bought a fruit market," laughs Debbie Jones. And what a great place to trade! There's a deli, meat is ground daily, and chili is homemade for the 80-cent hot dogs. Lunch can be bought or a deli tray ordered for a gathering and, oh, yeah….you can buy fresh fruits and vegetables or shuck beans by the pound. Definitely a fun stop while visiting Pennington Gap!

The Good Shepherd Quartet

For twenty-three years, David Fannon, Jim Clark, Mike Mooney, and James Hartsock traveled and sang close four-part harmony as the Good Shepherd Quartet. Their 'a Capella and impeccable timing made them well known over much of the east coast. Twice they were invited to sing at the Grand Ol' Opry. The quartet retired in 2006, but has revamped and will be doing limited engagements again. They are recreating their old-time sound, which makes their fans quite happy.

Dr. AnneMarie Mackway-Girardi

Courtesy: Powell Valley News

Dr. AnneMarie Mackway-Girardi has long been interested in healing with the use of plants and holds a PhD in Pharmacology and a DO in Osteopathic Medicine.

" I feel that my basic science training enabled me to be a better physician, and continues to help me in understanding how plants help us. Many of our "fancy" modern medicines are derived from plants, either entirely, as is Lanoxin for heart failure, or originally as with penicillins and cephalosporins. We have so much still to learn."

Since moving to Lee County from Pennsylvania, she has learned more from studying the medicines used by the Cherokee Indian tribes. According to Dr. Mackway-Girardi, the Cherokee were very sharing of their knowledge with the white settlers who first came among them. Many of their remedies saved lives in the mountains where there were no doctors. Some continue to be used today. She feels very grounded in the area and is known as the "Medicine Woman" at festivals held at Wilderness Road State Park.

Scott County

Contents

Apple Butter Bars.................................112	Hominy with Soda..........................126
Aunt Cleo's Hoecakes.........................112	Jewish Coffee Cake.........................127
Baw Baw Vermillion's Tomato Gravy..114	Never Fail Dumplins.......................127
Broccoli Dish......................................114	Oatmeal Cake..................................128
Butta Beans..115	Old Fashioned Banana Pudding.......128
Cabbage Au Gratin.............................120	Opossum and Sweet Potatoes.........130
Corn Casserole...................................120	Peanut Butter Fudge........................131
Cream Crunch....................................121	Pecan Pie Bars.................................132
Crunchy Tossed Salad........................122	Pickled Beets...................................132
Dandelion Wine..................................121	Pickled Eggs....................................132
Florence's Fruit Salad........................122	Pineapple Pie...................................134
Fresh Apple Cake...............................123	Pumpkin Butter................................134
Fried Green Tomatoes........................124	Sweet Potato Pudding......................134
Gages Chicken or Shrimp Curry.........125	Taco Soup..135
Ginger Bread......................................126	Wheat Loaf......................................135
Home Made Yeast..............................126	

"A Window Into the Past"

A window of the cabin birthplace of A. P. Carter and his seven siblings. His brother, Ermine's three children were also born there and in recent years, donated the cabin to be relocated to the grounds of the Carter Fold. Originally located in Little Valley, it was moved and restored by a painstaking and costly process, involving numerous professionals. It is open to the public when the Fold is operating.

The Carter Family Fold
www.carterfamilyfold.com

In 1974, Janette Carter began hosting weekly music shows in the general store her father, A.P. Carter, had built in the1940's. She was carrying on the traditional music of the Carter Family while fulfilling a promise made to him before his death in 1960. Within two years the small store building was burstin' at the seams and would no longer hold the number of listeners who came each week.

A decision was made to build a larger venue and with help from her sister Gladys, brother Joe, and other members of the extended Carter family, a center was begun near the store. Joe Carter designed the rustic building and contributed a name, the Carter Family Fold. Neighbors, friends, and family pitched in to help construct the 880-seat amphitheater, built with the lay of the land. Acoustic music and lots of dancing by all ages take place each Saturday night in a family oriented atmosphere. A number of improvements have been made in the past few years but the general atmosphere is homey and relaxed.

The non-profit Carter Family Memorial Music Center, Inc. – the official name for the Fold – was formally established in 1979. Building what can be considered an arts center twenty miles from the nearest town was a pretty innovative idea. The fact that it repeatedly draws crowds from all over the U.S. and abroad is remarkable and a tribute to the importance of the Carter's influence on traditional and bluegrass music. It is also a tribute to Janette Carter, who directed the business affairs, performed each week, and kept the show running smoothly.

Many prestigious awards have been bestowed on Janette Carter because of her devotion to preserving Appalachian music. She and her brother, Joe Carter, were dedicated keepers of the flame; close-knit family members have always supported their work and continue on in their absence.

Folks enjoying good times at the Carter Fold.

Both Joe and Janette Carter lived to see the restoration of the cabin where their father and his seven brothers and sisters were born. It was designated a National and State Historical landmark in it's original secluded location and carried both designations to it's new location. Although the process involved in moving the cabin to the grounds of the Fold near the general store was complicated, it was accomplished in 2004. Visitors may now go

Opening soon ~ Estillville Bed and Breakfast ~ named to honor the original name of Gate City.
Call 276-386-7447 for information

inside the cabin as well as the museum located in the general store.

This question was asked of Rita Forrester, Janette Carter's daughter who carries on her Mother's work: When your Mother started the music at the general store, do you think she ever imagined its far-reaching influence?

"I don't believe Mom did fully realize the far-reaching influence of what she started. Her main objective in doing what she did was fulfilling a promise she made to her dying father. It surprised all of us when shows quickly outgrew the one-room store and the Fold building had to be built. I remember her saying we would probably never fill it! Of course, we did fill it and it has now been enlarged beyond its original size."

Apple Butter Bars
Jan Jenkins – Gate City, VA

1 ½	cups plain flour	2 ½	cups quick cooking oats
1	tsp. soda	1 ½	cups sugar
1	tsp. salt	1	cup melted butter or margarine
1	pint apple butter		

Sift flour, soda, and salt together. Add other ingredients and spread ½ the mixture in bottom of a 9x12-inch baking dish. Press into pan. Spread 1 pint apple butter over top. Sprinkle remaining mixture on top and press down lightly. Bake 45 minutes at 350°. Can be refrigerated overnight and baked the next morning. Enjoy!

"Cleo McNutt, my aunt, was the oldest daughter of Myrtle Vermillion. She was also a musician and played old time music. She made a recording with The Log Cabin Entertainers.*"*

Aunt Cleo's Hoecakes
Marianna Roberts – Hiltons, VA

1	cup self-rising cornmeal	2	eggs
1	cup self-rising flour	1	Tbsp. sugar
¾	cup buttermilk	¼	cup vegetable oil or bacon grease
1/3	cup, plus 1 Tbsp. water		

Mix all ingredients except oil. Heat oil and or bacon grease in iron skillet over medium heat. Drop mixture by large Tbsp. into hot skillet. Brown until crisp; turn and brown on other side. Drain on cloth. Left over batter will keep in refrigerator for up to 2 days.

Myrtle Vermillion

My grandmother, Myrtle Porter Vermillion, was the first female to ever make a record playing the Autoharp. She played and sang with the Magic City Trio at dances and events in Southwest Virginia. The trio she recorded with also included John R. Dykes, who played the fiddle and G.H. "Hub" Mahaffey, who played the guitar. Their group made several recordings at the Brunswick Studios in New York from March 8 – 10, 1927, beating the famous Bristol recordings by a few months. Also present on the trip to New York that March in 1927, was the famous banjo player and singer, Doc Boggs, and a preacher by the name of Johnson.

Out of some 800 contestants heard in February 1927 at the big 100-room Hotel Norton in Norton, VA, they were chosen to record and represent this Appalachian area. Many other now-famous musicians and singers performed at that same audition in Norton including A.P. Carter and the Carter Family, the McReynolds Family from Coeburn (grandparents of Bluegrass stars Jim and Jesse), the Shepherd Brothers, who later recorded for Champion, and Byrd Moore, one of the most recorded guitarists of his time.

Nancy Addington Porter, Myrtle's mother, was a close relative of Maybelle Addington Carter. She was also kin to Sara Carter on the Dougherty side. As cousins growing up together near the Addington Frame Church in the Midway Community outside of Nickelsville, VA, they often played and sang together. My mother, Verna "Queenie" Vermillion, the youngest living child of Myrtle and Schuyler Vermillion, remembers when Sara Carter would come over to their farm by the Holston River and stay a few days. She recalls listening to her mother and Sara Carter singing and playing music together.

I once found a small photograph-poster inside a book at my grandmother's home in the late 1970's of Dykes Magic City Trio. My mother, who was five or six at the time, was pictured with them. The poster read, The Magic City Trio and the Little Dancing Queen." That was how my mother acquired the nickname Queenie that everyone knows her by today. (My grandfather, Schuyler, was noted for his dancing as well.)

The Magic City Trio, by the way, was named for the city of Kingsport, TN, which was a model, or planned city. I don't know why the trio didn't record at Bristol later that same year. I know that they were invited back to New York to record again but Mr. Dykes declined to go, perhaps remembering that he had been robbed at Grand Central Station on their first trip. They didn't make much money from their recordings because they were paid a flat fee (neither Dykes nor any of them knew about royalties). However, their trip to New York by train was probably one of the greatest adventures of any of their lives. As the winning contestants of the auditions, their trip was paid by Brunswick.

I am proud of Grandmother Vermillion and her brave endeavors in early old-time music. All who knew her loved her. This was especially true of her husband, Schuyler, who encouraged her trip to New York while he stayed home to keep up the farm and take care of three children. None of the band members could drive, so Schuyler Vermillion was the chauffeur for the band when they traveled. Dances were often held at their farm on the Holston River. A room would be cleaned out and people often danced till milking time next morning.

I continue the tradition and hope to do my part to keep my rich musical heritage alive. I love playing and singing the old time tunes that were performed by my grandmother and her friends with my group, the Appalachian Dream Spinners. It reveals something of the soul of the mountains we are part of. -*Marianna Roberts, Granddaughter*

"My grandmother, Myrtle Vermillion, made this for me when I would go for a visit. The smell would wake me up early in the morning."

Baw Baw Vermillion's Tomato Gravy
Marianna Roberts – Hiltons, VA

- 2 **ripe red tomatoes, diced**
- ½ **stick real butter**
- 1 **tsp. salt**
- ½ **tsp. black pepper**
- 2 **Tbsps. self-rising flour**
- 2 **cups milk (fresh from the cow back then)**

Sauté tomatoes and butter in an iron skillet. Add flour and cook until mixture thickens. Remove from heat for 5 minutes. Add milk slowly to thickened mixture. Add black pepper and salt. Cook over medium heat until gravy starts to boil. Let boil for 1 minute. Serve with pone bread or biscuits. Umm! Good!

Broccoli Dish
Helen Smith – Gate City, VA

4 **cups of chopped broccoli**	**Dressing:**
2 **cups raisins**	1 **cup mayonnaise**
1 **cup cashews**	2 **tsp. vinegar**
¼ **cup chopped onion**	1/3 **cup sugar**
Mix all the above well.	Mix all and pour over broccoli just before serving.

The Ivy Cottage

The Ivy Cottage is an Antique Store located on the main street of Gate City in a building that once housed the Taylor Theater. It was built in the early 1900's and eventually bought by the Taylor brothers - Ralph, Malcolm, and Bascom. They sold it to S. C. Dougherty in 1959. He used it for a Western Auto Store and later it became a craft and antique store known as Southern Treasures. After Southern Treasures it was called Country Charm. The Ivy Cottage took over in June 2005, with twenty vendors offering an excellent selection of items. A walk down memory lane can be taken by stopping by 143 West Jackson Street any day except Sunday. As you take your walk, you will notice that the floor slants downhill slightly, as befits the old theater.

While gathering information about the old theater, Mr. Ron Blackburn, now living in Michigan, stopped by The Ivy Cottage. Imagine our surprise when he told us he had run the projector for the Taylor Brothers in the early 1940's. It was great to talk to someone that had actually worked here. We hear lots of stories from people who remember coming on Saturday and watching movies all day for a dime. Times sure have changed! *-Helen Smith*

Rosie Calhoun displays her crocheted pieces in the Ivy Cottage in Gate City, VA

"Though I was born and raised in New Jersey, my grandfather's roots in Virginia brought me back. Turns out most of my ancestors are from the Old Dominion. Scott County was named for my great-grandmother's uncle, General Winfield Scott. I've been a Magistrate in Scott County for twenty years and love my job." -Pattie Hensley

"Butta Beans"
Pattie & Jerry Hensley – Hiltons, VA

2	cans baked beans	1	onion chopped
1	can dark kidney beans	12	slices of bacon
1	can lima beans	½	cup vinegar
1	can butter beans	1	cup dark brown sugar

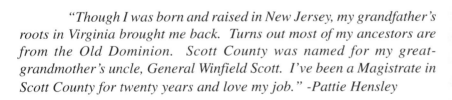

Cook bacon; sauté onion in small amount of bacon grease; combine vinegar and brown sugar; put all beans in baking dish; add vinegar and sugar mixture and onions; crumble bacon over top. Bake at 350° for 1 hour.

Jerry Hensley

Jerry Hensley discovered his life's work and calling when he was about three or four years old. His mom, Lois, took him from Cleveland, where they lived, to Akron, Ohio to see her cousin in concert. The cousin's name happened to be June Carter. She performed with Carl Smith, her husband at that time, and young Jerry was hit right between the eyes with a desire to be a performer. Immediately, he begged for a guitar and finally got a cheap one but no lessons. At about twelve years old, he began taking lessons and continued for nine months until he broke his wrist. That was the end of his formal music training.

Jerry Hensley relaxing on screen porch at home

Moving back to Poor Valley where their Carter kin lived provided an education in the form of Joe Carter that would have been unlikely from any music teacher. Though Hensley was practicing Beatles and Bob Dylan songs, Joe often visited and began picking with the young teenager. Before long Joe Carter introduced him to fiddle tunes and the Carter style of picking – called the Carter Scratch – that was made famous by Maybelle Carter. "I fell in love with that," says Hensley, who continued to play electric guitar as he picked up acoustic.

"Poor Valley was different in those days. We knew everybody up and down the road and were kin to most of them. People came by and stayed for hours. Watching television wasn't done much as you only got two channels at best. Joe Carter was a real visitor. He'd play Parcheesi, or Yahtzee, or Rook or just pick and sing, and stay for supper. There were some cutthroat Rook games throughout the whole neighborhood, especially during the winter. You wouldn't believe how those wonderful good-hearted, honest people would cheat and fuss during some of those Rook games."

November 1968 stands out in Hensley's mind because he and Joe Carter went to the Kingsport Civic Auditorium to see Johnny Cash. Also on the show were Carl Perkins, the Carter Family, and the Statler Brothers. "I was impressed by all the acts," states Hensley, "but when John walked out, I was dumbstruck. He had a stage presence that could only be equaled in my mind by Elvis, who I saw perform in his prime. I'll never forget either of those experiences. And all I could think was Good Lord - this is what I gotta do!"

"Joe had written a couple of songs for John so I got to meet him and help demo the songs for him that night. When he liked my playing and said, 'You should consider moving down to Nashville to get into the music business,' boy, that was all this kid needed to hear."

It was 1970 when Jerry Hensley actually moved to Nashville to work for Cash who was doing a weekly television show at the time. Since there was no opening for a musician, Jerry picked up the guest for the show each week and took that celebrity out to John and June's lake house for lunch. He did odd jobs and yard work, etc. until being hired on as a musician by Tommy Cash. At that time, Tommy Cash had the #1 song on the charts, *Six White Horses*, but didn't have a band. "Tommy was a riot, and the three years I played for him were the most fun I ever had on the road. We were a bit irresponsible but I was young and unmarried and most of the other band members were single."

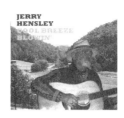

A great traveling CD. It has been on a number of road trips with us and has become one of the favorites while winding along crooked roads or even cruising on interstates. www.jerryhensley.com

After that Hensley put together a band called "Poor Valley" and struck out on his own. One day a call came that he couldn't pass up. Carl Perkins, who opened the show, and then played backup for Johnny Cash, needed to take time off to be with his dad who was sick. Could Jerry come and finish the dates for that tour?

"The first date with John was the Ohio State Fair and we played to 35,000 people. I hadn't even had a rehearsal."

This short-term arrangement lasted eight years, during which time Jerry opened the show in beautiful and exciting venues and met interesting people. "I've been in the room with some pretty important people, but when John came in, every head would turn to him. This happened even if the President of the United States was in the room. John had a charisma that can't be explained and I don't think it can be acquired. You have it or you don't, and he did."

"John began going through a difficult period and fired his long-time bass player, Marshall Grant. Two years later, he fired me and two other guys.

Grant had moved on and was managing the Statler Brothers. After about a year, he asked me to try out for their band and I was hired to open for them and play guitar. I stayed with them for nineteen years until they retired in October 2002. That was a great run.

Earlier, I began an acoustic album just for fun and because my mother had always wanted me to do one. Anita Carter, my cousin and good friend, sang on two of the tracks. She had the most beautiful voice I ever heard in my life. Jimmy Fortune, one of the best voices around, sings on a couple. I decided to put one of John's songs on the CD and he sang *Flesh and Blood* with me. By the way, he was never one to say, 'I'm sorry.' The way he apologized years after firing me was by calling up and asking if I'd play on an album for him."

Though Hensley says he has "gotten happy with retirement," he stays busy. There's family, always music, fishing, the lovely mountain where he and Pattie live, and dressing up in leather as a cowboy to enter six-gun and lever action rifle shooting contests. How much fun can that be for a fan of old westerns??

Flo Wolfe

There might be a more pleasant way to spend a hot afternoon but it would take some thinking to come up with an equal idea. Sitting in Flo Wolfe's yard in one of her porch swings, talking about this and that, is about as good as it gets. Yes, I said yard because her porch won't hold all her swings. As grandchildren have come along and the family has grown, her husband became quite ingenious about providing more comfortable seating underneath the big shade trees.

Flo lives in the shadow of the Carter Family Fold in more ways than one. It's nearby and she works there on Saturday nights, but the history is part of her life. "We come from the non-singing side," she laughs. "My mother, Gladys, was the oldest child and told us about entertaining Joe by playing in the creek while her parents, A.P. and Sara, made a recording in Bristol, VA in 1927." *(Which became legendary, by the way.)*

Though he was Wolfe's uncle, Joe lived with them often during her growing up years and was more like a sibling. He was full of mischief and the two farm kids got into trouble for things like punching holes in the hog guts during hog killing time. She recalls that he caught a wharf rat and tied it on to her cat's tail and had the poor cat running around like a crazed varmint. He could make animal sounds so well he could call a cow right up to the porch or start a catfight just for sport.

"Farming was our way of life," says Wolfe. "Daddy would go help the neighbors kill hogs and they'd come help us. We had to work, too, but there were two things I didn't like to do. The main thing I hated was suckering tobacco and the other was plucking chickens. I always tried to get my mother to just skin them."

She may not sing or be famous, but sitting in a porch swing talking to Flo Wolfe gives you hope. She embodies what is good about America – love of family, loyalty, being a good neighbor, following the principals of the Bible as the natural order of things, and having fun along the way. When she grins a certain way, you're almost sure Joe Carter didn't think up all that childhood mischief by himself!

"Blessings are not to hoard, but to share. As Christians we are blessed to share our blessings with others."

Preserved Children

Take 1 large field, half a dozen children, 2 or 3 small dogs, a pinch of brook and some pebbles. Mix the children and dogs well together; put them on the field, stirring constantly. Pour the brook over the pebbles; sprinkle the field with flowers; spread over all a deep blue sky and bake in the sun. When brown, set away to cool in the bathtub.

Broadwater Drug Lunch Counter

"What do you want?" demands Jackie Tipton to any lunch counter customer who takes a seat at Broadwater Drug in Gate City. There's nary a notepad in sight, but she delivers the order back with "Here, eat it and be glad to get it!" No, she's not mad; it's just her way. She has an award for grouchiness on the wall and lives up to it. Many of the orders are the same from day to day, especially from the regulars. Tipton can be counted on to be consistent, too. "How're you today?" questions a gentleman as he straddles a stool. "Don't ask," she snaps back.

Jackie Tipton

"I give everybody a hard time, I don't care who they are," she states flatly. "If the president came through, which I'm not expecting him, but if he did, he'd be treated just like everybody else."

Jackie and co-worker, Kay Falin, work well together and make all the salads - potato, tuna, chicken, and macaroni. Hamburgers are pattied by hand when ordered, from ground round. Lemonade is freshly made by the tasty glassful. Broadwater Drug, along with the lunch counter, has been at the same location since 1951 and they have no desire to be a fast food joint. B.J. Broadwater, who started the business in 1948, no longer owns it but usually comes by for a midday meal. Tipton worked for him and they get along fine; he knows what to expect, as do the new owners, Tony Street and Brack Slate.

Tipton has a "blue light special" board with pictures of policeman who come in often, along with their children. "I help 'em out with candy and stuff for special events and try to be on their good side."

When a customer requested potato salad, the conversation went like this: "We're out of potato salad," replied Jackie.

"Guess I'll take something else," he says.

"Guess you will," she answered.

At the end of the day that we visited, a television crew is expected. Tipton takes it in stride. "I've been on channel 5 before and in newspapers. I'm in a cookbook."

After raising five children, being grandmother to seven, and great-grandmother to one, Tipton is proud of her age. "I'm just glad the good Lord has seen fit to let me live to be 64 years old - without a customer killing me. I plan to keep on working as long as I can put one foot in front of the other."

Jackie is amiable and shows signs of a generous spirit as she sits at the table talking to us. As we finish up and mention that we need to be going, she announces, "About time, you can't sit around here all day!"

Upon departing, I can't help but ponder what sort of sparks would fly if Flo, of *Mel's Diner* fame and Jackie, of Broadwater Drug fame somehow wound up working at the same lunch counter.

Cabbage Au Gratin
Flo Wolfe – Hiltons, VA

Plant a few sprigs of dill near your tomato plants to prevent tomato worms on your plants.

1 head cabbage, cut up, boiled and drained
1 can cream of celery soup
¼ cup milk
1 cup grated American cheese
1 cup crushed crackers or breadcrumbs
½ cup melted butter

Boil cabbage 10 minutes and drain. Place in baking dish. Mix celery soup, milk, and cheese together. Heat until cheese melts. Pour over cabbage, top with crackers or breadcrumbs. Pour melted butter over top. Bake at 350° for 30 minutes.

"There used to be a bus route between Bristol and Gate City with a stop in Bruno where we live, and one at Fido, about five miles up the road. I guess McMurray's Grocery was downtown Bruno." -Mavis Hatton

Corn Casserole
Mavis Hatton – Hiltons, VA

1 can cream style corn
1 can whole kernel corn (drained)
1 (8 oz.) sour cream
1 stick butter, melted
1 pkg. Jiffy corn muffin mix

Mix corn with sour cream, ¾ of the butter, and ¾ of the corn muffin mix. Pour into a casserole dish. Sprinkle remainder of corn muffin mix on top and drizzle remainder of butter on top of that. Bake at 350° for 30 minutes or until golden brown.

Cream Crunch
Jackie Tipton – Gate City, VA

1	cup of Splenda
1 ½	cups of honey graham crackers crushed
1	(8 oz.) cream cheese
2	large Cool Whip (12 oz.)
1	large box of sugar free instant vanilla pudding
1	large box of sugar free instant chocolate pudding
3	cups milk
2	cups pecans
1 ¼	sticks of butter, soft

Preheat oven to 350°. Mix graham cracker crumbs, butter, and pecans together, and line the bottom of 13 x 9 inch pan with mixture. Bake for 5 minutes, no longer. Take out and cool completely. Mix cream cheese, Splenda, and 6 ozs. of Cool Whip together. Spread this over graham cracker crust.

1st layer: Mix together vanilla pudding, 1 ½ cups milk, 6 ozs. of Cool Whip and spread over cream cheese mixture.

2nd layer: Mix together chocolate pudding, 1 ½ cups milk, 6 ozs. of Cool Whip and spread over 1st layer of pudding. Top with remaining cool whip. Sprinkle crushed graham cracker crumbs on top. Refrigerate for at least 12 hours.

Spray garbage bags with ammonia to prevent dogs from tearing the bags before they're picked up.

"This recipe is over 100 years old."
Dandelion Wine
Audrey Maddox – Gate City, VA

4	quarts dandelion flowers	4	lbs. sugar
1	gallon water	½	yeast cake
6	lemons		

Place the dandelion flowers in the water, bring to a boil and stir. Remove from heat. When lukewarm add six lemons and four lbs. sugar and one half yeast cake. Let stand ten days until fermenting ceases. Bottle and seal.

Crunchy Tossed Salad

Nancy Odel – Nickelsville, VA

Dressing:
- ½ cup salad oil
- ¼ cup sugar
- 2 Tbsps. vinegar
- 1 tsp. salt
- ½ tsp. pepper

Mix above ingredients together in a jar with a tight fitting lid; shake well. Chill for one hour.

Salad:
- 1 bunch Romaine Lettuce
- ½ head Iceberg Lettuce (sliced)
- 1 cup coarsely shredded cabbage
- 6 green onions (sliced)
- 3 ounces sunflower seeds
- 4 ounces sliced almonds
- 10 strips bacon cooked and crumbled

Toss above ingredients together. Just before serving, add 1 cup or more chow mein noodles. Add dressing, toss and serve. Makes a big bowl and best to use the same day.

> For the Lord is good, His mercy is everlasting.
> -Psalms 100:5

"Florence's Fruit Salad"

Pattie and Jerry Hensley – Hiltons, VA

- 2 small boxes tapioca pudding
- 1 large can pineapple chunks
- 3 small cans mandarin oranges
- 3-4 bananas
-   Maraschino cherries
-   orange juice

Drain and reserve juice from pineapple and mandarin oranges; add orange juice to make 3 cups and add to tapioca pudding; cook pudding and juice slowly to a bubbling boil; when it gets a little thick, let cool. **Layer**: Pineapple, bananas, mandarin oranges & cherries; cover sparingly with pudding; repeat twice and cover with remaining pudding. Cool in refrigerator.

> "Florence's fruit salad was passed to me via my sister, Linda. Florence was a parishioner at my sister and brother-in-law's first church in Buckingham County, VA."
> -Pattie Hensley

Steve Brooks

For ten years Steve Brooks has been director of Virginia Forest Watch (www.virginiaforestwatch.org), a grass roots coalition of individuals and environmental groups throughout the state. The organization is committed to protecting National Forests and the natural ecology and biodiversity within the boundaries of these Public Lands. VAFW holds the belief that resource extraction such as logging, mining, and grazing, etc. is harmful to, and inappropriate use of, America's National Forests.

In 2008, he is stepping down as director of VAFW to become more active in the Clinch Coalition. (www.clinchcoalition.net) Their mission statement is: *To protect and preserve the forest, wildlife, and watersheds of High Knob and surrounding areas.* The Clinch District, one of the most beautiful and diverse areas of the Jefferson National Forest, encompasses High Knob and Bark Camp Lake.

An immediate concern is the fire tower at High Knob, a landmark since 1939 that was burned down on Halloween 2007. With the support of federal and local organizations and individuals, the Coalition is working to replace the tower, build an education center, and to improve other facilities in the National Forest that will increase public awareness of the area and promote tourism.

The biodiversity of Southwest Virginia is second only to Hawaii. Brooks and numerous others would like to see it sustained for future generations, along with the natural beauty of the area. Healthy forests and unpolluted streams… isn't that a work worth doing?

> We don't inherit the land from our ancestors; we borrow it from our children.
> -Native American proverb.

Fresh Apple Cake

Rosie Calhoun – Gate City, VA

- 1 box yellow cake mix
- 2 tsp. cinnamon
- 3 cups chopped apples
- 1 cup sugar
- 2 tsps. vanilla
- 1 cup butterscotch chips
- Heath brittle for topping

Mix cake mix as directed on box, add all other ingredients except Health brittle chips. Pour in 9 x 13 inch pan. Put Heath brittle chips on top. Bake 1 hour at 350°.

Mustard Seed

Robin Norris and Kay Quellen

"I've got the best job in the world," says Robin Norris. "It's the most rewarding, satisfying job I've ever done." The job is running the unique café/coffee shop located on Jefferson Street in downtown Gate City, VA.

Through a bout with cancer five years ago, she met the former owner of the then antique shop who was looking to sell. After completing chemo, Norris decided to buy the antique business and two years ago turned it into a café that features a few antiques. "With the antique shop came debt and the necessity of constantly restocking. Only by the grace of God was I able to meet obligations each month, not to mention having $7,000 as start-up for the café."

"Kay Quellen and I developed the recipes. We began with a small amount of chicken salad and now make thirty pounds each day. People have learned to love our quiche pies, though they were doubtful at first. We call ourselves "two chicks in a kitchen." Kay always seems to be working with chicken and me with eggs."

The trials of life have made Norris stronger and given her a new spirit, she believes. Losing a husband to cancer and then facing it herself forced her to look inward and outward to God, and to now appreciate family and friends more. After all, look what life can offer when you go forward with the faith of a mustard seed

Fried Green Tomatoes

Marianna Roberts – Hiltons, VA

*"Good with homemade soup, beans, and fried potatoes. And, of course, a big pone of corn bread!" Marianna is a member of the **Appalachian Dream Spinners Band.***

3-4	medium green tomatoes		vegetable oil
	salt to taste	1	egg
1	cup flour	1	Tbsp. sugar
1	cup cornmeal		sprinkle of Cayenne
1	tsp. black pepper		pepper
	butter		sprinkle of dill (optional)

Slice tomatoes to desired thickness. Sprinkle with salt. Lay aside and allow time for salt to draw water out of tomatoes. Mix flour, cornmeal, sugar, and peppers. Dip tomatoes in egg, then coat with flour and cornmeal mixture and fry in a mixture of vegetable oil and butter until golden brown. Add more vegetable oil and butter as needed. It is optional if you want to add a dash of dill to fried tomatoes.

Gage's Towne House Restaurant

Expect the unexpected in Southwest Virginia. Does a Caribbean cuisine mixed with country ham and biscuits sound good? Drop by Gage's, located in a beautiful old home in Nickelsville for that and more than you'd expect – Alaskan whitefish, Jamaican jerk shrimp, and southern fried chicken – offered fresh from Nazim Hack and wife, Judy Gilmer. There's a Friday Seafood Feast running from 11 am – 10 pm, special events and music often, and always out-of-the-ordinary food. Call 276-479-1900 for info.

Gage's Chicken or Shrimp Curry

Judy Gilmer & Nazim Hack – Nickelsville, VA

- 2 Tbsps. Patak's Curry Paste (available at Food City or Kroger under specialty foods)
- 1 Tbsp. olive oil
- 1 lb. boneless chicken breast or 1 lb. raw peeled and deveined shrimp
- ½ cup buttermilk
- ½ cup of your favorite mixed vegetables

Sauté chicken or shrimp in pan with the olive oil over medium heat on stove. Add curry paste and stir to mix. Add buttermilk and mixed vegetables. Stir to mix and cover with lid. Let simmer for 5 minutes. Stir occasionally. Serve immediately over Basmati Rice or real mashed potatoes. Hot sauce or chutney may be served on the side if desired. Enjoy your curry in the mountains!

Wayne Culbertson

Wayne Culbertson has been painting since his mother bought a paint by number set when he was eight years old. What the original picture was has been forgotten but the paint created a cocker spaniel. A painter who works mostly in oils but uses all mediums, a sculptor, a luthier who builds violins – some of which are replicas such as a hardanger fiddle – and a history buff / reenactor who cooks bread over an open fire, Culbertson is in his own words, "a jack of all trades." Oh, and he builds primitive pieces from old wood and some reproduction pieces. And Johnny Cash bought two of his violins back in the 1980's – from Scott Jewelers, a watch repair shop that sells some musical instruments.

Home Made Yeast

Wayne Culbertson – Gate City, VA

Boil 2 ounces of hops in 4 quarts of water for 30 minutes. Strain into an earthen bowl and let cool to 90°. Add a small handful of salt (¼ cup), ½ pound of brown sugar (1 cup). Add some of the liquid to 1 pound of flour (4 cups) to make a paste, and then mix all well together. Set aside in a warm place (80°-85°) and let it stand for 2 days, stirring often. Strain well, bottle and cork. Let sit 1 to 2 days before using. The yeast will keep for several weeks in a cool place. It should be shaken before using. Use 1 cup of liquid in place of one cake of yeast or 2 packages of yeast.

Ginger Bread

Audrey Mattox – Gate City, VA

½	cup sugar	1	tsp. soda
½	cup butter	1	tsp. cinnamon
½	cup shortening	1	tsp. ginger
1	egg	½	tsp. cloves
1	cup molasses	½	tsp. salt
2	cups all-purpose flour	1	cup hot water

Cream together shortening and butter and then add sugar. Add beaten egg and molasses. Add dry ingredients. Add hot water. Beat until smooth. Bake in a greased, shallow pan for 35 minutes in a 350° oven.

Hominy With Soda

Audrey Maddox – Gate City, VA

1	gallon white or yellow shelled corn	2	gallons water
8	Tbsp. (heaping) soda		salt

Place corn in a stone jar or enamel kettle; add water and soda. Let stand for 15 hours. Bring to a boil in the soda water and cook about 3 hours or until husk loosens, adding more water if necessary during the cooking time. Drain, add clear water, and rub off excess hulls. Drain. Cover with water. Add 1 tsp. salt to each quart of hominy; cook until tender. Pack in containers and freeze.

Bush Mill

Bush Mill has stood beside Amos Branch, whose waters power the wheel, since 1896, ready to grind a turn of grain between stone burrs for local residents. For many years it just stood, unused. Due to the Bush Mill Project, the historic landmark is being restored repaired and in use again. The project is a school-based enterprise with support from the Nickelsville Ruritan Club and cooperation from several organizations. Four millers in the area are passing their skills to youth involved in the program. In addition, the youth are learning to own and operate the mill as a business.

Jewish Coffee Cake

Jean Hettman – Gate City, VA

½ lb. butter or margarine	2 tsps. baking soda
3 cups flour	2 tsps. baking powder
2 cups sugar	2 tsps. vanilla
4 eggs	1 tsp. salt
1 pint sour cream	

Topping
1 cup sugar
1 tsp. cinnamon

1 cup chopped nuts

Grease and flour a 10 x 14 inch pan. Cream together the butter, eggs, sour cream, sugar and vanilla. Mix the flour, baking soda, baking powder, and salt together. Add it to the creamed mixture and mix for about 10 minutes. Mix the topping ingredients together. Stir half of the topping in the cake batter. Sprinkle the other half on top of the cake. Bake 45 min. in a 350° oven.

"Popular Cabins" near Dungannon served beer, which probably explained their popularity. As well, they served as a small general store.

Never Fail Dumplins'

Barbara Larkey – Hiltons, VA

1 cup flour
2 tsp. baking powder
1 egg

milk
dash of salt

Mix flour, baking powder, egg, and salt together. Add enough milk to make stiff batter. Drop by spoonfuls into stew. Put top on and cook for 20 minutes without removing cover. Chopped parsley may be added to batter. This makes about 10 dumplings. You may double this.

Before you spray dandelions, remember: Young, tender dandelion leaves make an excellent addition to salads, or can be cooked like spinach. Pick the leaves before the flowers appear, otherwise they'll be bitter. Dandelion wine can be made from the flowers. The roots may be roasted and ground as a coffee substitute. Dandelions are a good source of iron and vitamin A. (Never use plants that have been sprayed with weed killing chemicals.)

Mom (Janette Carter) always loved to cook. Bill Clifton, long time performer at the Carter Fold, said the first time he ever met Mom, he went with her Dad, A.P. and sister, Gladys and husband, Milan, to Mom and Dad's house in Bristol. Mom was cooking a birthday dinner for her brother, Joe. Bill said they all gathered and patiently waited for Joe and his wife, Nancy, to arrive. When they didn't come, Mom phoned to see what was wrong. Joe had completely forgotten about the invitation and gone hunting. Bill said Mom had cooked a wonderful dinner with an elaborate birthday cake. Everyone ate and enjoyed the meal except the birthday boy, who was a no-show!
-Rita Forrester

Oatmeal Cake

Nell Kendrick – Gate City, VA

1	cup oatmeal	2	eggs	
1 1/3	cup boiling water	1 ½	cups flour	
½	cup margarine or butter	½	teaspoon salt	
1	cup white sugar	1	teaspoon soda	
1	cup brown sugar	1	teaspoon cinnamon	

Pour boiling water over oatmeal and let stand 20 minutes. Cream together margarine and sugars; beat in eggs one at a time. Add the oatmeal. Stir together flour, salt, soda, and cinnamon. Stir into creamed mixture; pour into a greased, floured 13 x 9 -inch pan. Bake at 350º for 30-35 minutes. Add the following topping to warm cake.

6	Tbsps. margarine or butter	¼	cup cream or milk
1	cup brown sugar	1	tsp. vanilla
1	cup chopped nuts (pecans)	1	cup coconut

Mix together and spread on top of cake. Broil until lightly browned. (This freezes well)

Old Fashioned Banana Pudding

Joann Vicars – Bristol, VA

¼	cup flour	3	eggs
1/8	tsp. salt	1	tsp. vanilla
¾	cup sugar	4	bananas
2	cups milk	1	box vanilla wafers

In a double boiler, mix flour, salt, sugar and milk. Cook while stirring about 15 minutes. Remove from heat and add beaten egg yolks. Return to double boiler and cook 3 minutes more. Remove from heat and add vanilla. Layer wafers and bananas. Pour pudding over wafers and bananas and repeat layers.

Meringue
3 egg whites   2 Tbsps. sugar

Beat egg whites and add sugar. Beat until forms stiff peaks and put on top of pudding. Brown in oven.

Audrey Maddox

"My parents were married in 1898. They were poor as church mice but very ambitious for us," says Audrey Mattox, who was born in 1913. "They wanted all five of us to get an education. Both were bright people although they weren't educated."

There was a local high school, Shoemaker, and Mattox only had to walk about a mile to get there. The county acquired buses in 1931 but she never rode one because you had to live farther than a mile to be allowed to ride. She attended Berea College during the depression and began teaching "whatever they needed taught" in 1937. "I mostly taught English and history in Junior High, but many times it was science and biology, or even sociolology.

"My great-grandfather ran a legal distillery in Gate City. He had an orchard and used the fruit to make the beverages. His sons all fought in the Civil War. My great uncle who had apprenticed with a doctor, told about using a cave over in Cumberland Gap as a hospital and having to take off a lot of arms and legs there. He said they were sometimes reduced to eating parched corn.

Dr. Baker was our doctor and he drove a one-horse buggy. Sometimes when he was passing by, he'd stop in and 'look us over' to make sure we were okay. He and my great-uncle would mix herbs and roots to make medicine during the summer when my uncle would come home from out west. Mother would let my uncle use the kitchen to cook everything except skunk oil. He had to go down behind the barn to render that."

Dray wagons used to meet the train to pick up and deliver items that had been ordered throughout the community. A 100-year-old Ginkgo tree in Maddox's front yard was sent from China and delivered by a dray wagon. The owner of the land at that time was said to have carried water from the creek for the tree because he thought the well water might be too cold.

All of Mattox's siblings have enjoyed long productive lives. The youngest to pass away was 89 years old. To what does she contribute their longevity? "I think it was the good food we ate growing up. Everything was grown on the farm and we had plenty of milk and butter."

> Mother's homemade vinegar: Wash sour apples and cut out all the bad spots. Crush them and place in a crock. Cover with water and leave until they ferment. Strain through a cloth and you have good vinegar with a bit of an apple taste.
>
> *-Audrey Mattox*

Opossum and Sweet Potatoes

Audrey Maddox – Gate City, VA

1	opossum (about 2½ pounds)
2 ½	tsps. salt
	black pepper to taste
	flour
½	cup water
4	medium sweet potatoes or yams
¼	tsp. salt
2	Tbsps. sugar

Trim excess fat from opossum and discard. Wipe with damp cloth, pick off any clinging hair, then wash quickly inside and out with warm water. Drain thoroughly. Rub salt mixed with pepper well into the opossum inside and out. Sprinkle inside and out with flour. Lay the opossum on its back in a roasting pan with a tight-fitting cover. Add water, cover and bake at 350° from 45 minutes to one hour, until opossum is about half done. Split peeled potatoes in half lengthwise and place in pan around opossum. Add more water if needed. Cover and cook about 20 minutes longer. Remove cover and sprinkle the potatoes with ¼ tsp. salt and the sugar. Continue cooking uncovered until both potatoes and opossum are brown and tender. Serves 3 to 4.

Dungannon Days

"I loved growing up in Dungannon. When I married, we lived in Ohio three years, but I couldn't be satisfied so we moved back home. I guess there wasn't a lot to do but we had candy makings, played cards and checkers, and it was a big deal to go to ball games at the school. Going out of town was unusual.

I had an older brother and three sisters. My brother was good for getting us into trouble. He once told me a bad word to call my father (he said Daddy would like it), who was up on a ladder at the time. My father questioned me as to what I had said and when I repeated it, he climbed down and straightened me out with a keen switch. I don't think my brother got the switch but he should have! When I was a teenager and wanting to smoke, my brother would give me two cigarettes to

"I loved growing up in Dungannon."

polish his shoes. Then he'd tell Mom I was out behind the house smoking. It seemed I never learned because I'd do it again when he asked.

My mother did beautiful needlework and quilts. When I was older, she sold pieces at the Cave House in Abingdon. I used to take her there to deliver things.

My Dad was a superintendent at a coalmine and on Christmas they'd give every employee a bag of oranges, apples, nuts, raisins, and things. We were so excited when he brought that home. That was our Christmas present. We'd trade around with each other to get what each of us liked.

I went to work in a coal mine when they first started hiring women. That's an experience I'll never forget. The area I worked in was 31 inches high and had to be crawled all day, shoveling a belt line. By the end of the week, my knees were like raw hamburger even though I was wearing kneepads. At the end of the last day I worked, I had to go around and gather up all the lunch buckets. Another girl helped me or I never would have been able to do it. One week was enough for me." -*Nancy West Osborne*

Our Creator would never have made such lovely days, and given us the deep hearts to enjoy them, above and beyond all thought, unless we were meant to be immortal.
-*Nathaniel Hawthorne*

Peanut Butter Fudge
Nancy Osborne – Gate City, VA

5	cups white sugar	1	pint marshmallow crème
1	stick margarine	1	pint peanut butter
1	can evaporated milk	2	tsp. vanilla

Combine the sugar, margarine, and evaporated milk. Cook over medium heat for 9 minutes, stirring often. Remove from heat and add the marshmallow crème, peanut butter, and vanilla. Stir and pour into buttered pan. Makes 5 lbs. of fudge.

Pecan Pie Bars

Rosie Calhoun – Gate City, VA

2 ¾ cups flour	4 Tbsps. melted margarine
4 Tbsps. brown sugar	2 tsp. vanilla
½ cup butter	1 cup pecans

Filling:
1 cup brown sugar
4 eggs
1 cup corn syrup

People are lonely because they build walls instead of bridges.

In small bowl, mix flour and brown sugar. Work in butter until dough holds together. Press into bottom of 9 x 13 inch baking dish. Bake 12 to 15 minutes at 350° or until firm.
    In bowl, beat brown sugar and eggs, add corn syrup, pecans, melted butter and vanilla. Mix well. Pour over crust. Bake at 350° for 25 minutes or until lightly browned. Cool in pan and cut into bars.

Pickled Beets

Gladys McMurray – Hiltons, VA

beets	1 qt. sugar
1 qt. vinegar	1 pint water

Wash and boil beets until tender. Drain beets and slip off skins. Combine the vinegar, sugar and water. Heat until it comes to a boil. Add beets. Let return to a boil and boil 10 minutes. Put in jars and seal.

Pickled Eggs

Helen Smith – Gate City, VA

1 dozen hard boiled eggs, peeled while hot
1 cup vinegar
¾ cup Kosher Vinegar
1 tsp. salt
   red food coloring (desired color)

Mix together the vinegars, salt, and food coloring. Add eggs and simmer until eggs are a deep pink. Place in jar and cool. Cap and refrigerate.

These are the McMurray sisters - Patsy Larkey, Mavis Hatton, Joann Vicars, and mother, Gladys McMurray & dog.

Meeting the McMurray's

Nothing about traveling and compiling this cookbook is equal to the friends we've made. Some have been met in unusual ways. While winding along route 58 between Bristol and the Carter Fold, we passed a neat white building on the side of the road with a sign that read, "McMurray's Grocery." Thinking we'd get a coke (any drink is a coke in the mountains!) and meet the owners, we turned around in a dangerous curve and drove back. Instead of a country store as expected, two sisters and a sister-in-law were setting up a yard sale for the next day. That's all it took to entertain us. But there was more. The ladies' jovial manner and interest in our project made us feel like long lost cousins who'd dropped into a family reunion. Before long, another sister showed up and made the afternoon even more entertaining by announcing that her picture couldn't be taken because she didn't have on underwear. Try keeping your eyes to yourself after an announcement like that! Everyone giggled like schoolgirls. Pictures were taken. We met the Mother and the dog. And the afternoon was one to remember with a grin. In the mountains, one can be married, have children and grandchildren, but locally you'll still be so and so's girl or sister or brother. Holding to tradition, we remember our visit as the time spent with the McMurray girls.

Gladys McMurray is 89 years old. She and her husband, Virgil, were the proprietors of McMurray Grocery on Hwy. 58 in Bruno, VA. She used to cook pickled beets outside over an open flame for at least half a day.

Pineapple Pie

Rosie Calhoun – Gate City, VA

- ½ cup lemon juice
- 1 small Cool Whip
- 1 (20 oz.) can crushed pineapple (do not drain)
- 1 can Eagle Brand milk
-   graham cracker crust

Stir milk and lemon juice until thick, and then add Cool Whip and pineapple. Pour into graham cracker crust. Refrigerate over night.

Pumpkin Butter

Audrey Maddox – Gate City, VA

- 3 cups cooked, mashed fresh pumpkin
- 1 cup sugar
- 2 Tbsps. butter
- ½ tsp. ground cinnamon
- ¼ tsp. ground ginger
- ¼ tsp. ground nutmeg
- ½ tsp. vinegar

Combine all ingredients in a heavy saucepan; mix well. Cook over low heat for 1 hour. Serve with toast or biscuits. Yields: 2½ cups.

Sweet Potato Pudding

Helen Smith – Gate City, VA

- 3 cups mashed sweet potatoes
- ½ cup white sugar
- ¼ tsp. salt
- 1 cup milk
- ½ cup margarine
- 1 tsp. vanilla
- ½ cup butter melted
- 1 cup coconut
- ¼ cup flour
- 1 cup chopped pecans

Mix the sweet potatoes, sugar, salt, milk, margarine, and vanilla. Spread into a 13 x 9 inch greased baking dish and heat until bubbly hot. Remove from oven. Mix together the melted butter, coconut, flour, and chopped pecans, then put on top of sweet potatoes. Bake for 30 minutes at 350°.

> A holy life will produce the deepest impression. Lighthouses blow no horns; they only shine.
> *-Dwight L. Moody*

Taco Soup

Renita Probst – Gate City, VA

1 lb. ground beef
1 cup chopped onion
3 cans chili beans, with juice
1 can corn
1 can diced tomatoes
1 (8 oz.) can tomato sauce
   optional – can of peppers (jalapeno or whatever kind you like)
1 package taco seasoning mix
1 package hidden valley ranch mix

Brown ground beef and onion. Drain. Add rest of ingredients. Cook in crock pot.

Wheat Loaf

Wayne Culbertson – Gate City, VA

1 cup milk
4 Tbsps. honey or maple syrup
1 cake yeast
2 cups white flour, sifted
1 Tbsp. salt
3 Tbsps. butter
1 cup warm water
4 cups whole wheat flour

Scald milk; add salt, sweetening, butter and ¾ cup warm water. Stir well. Cool to luke warm. Dissolve yeast in remaining ¼ cup of luke warm water add to rest of liquid. Mix dry ingredients, add liquid, and beat with spoon until a textured ball. Knead for 10 minutes until smooth. Set aside in bowl covered with towel in a warm place. Let rise for 1 hour or until double in size. Remove from bowl, punch down, and shape into loaf. Let rise again in well-greased pan. Bake at 350° for 50 to 60 minutes. If crust is brown before time is up, cover with foil. This recipe is good for all yeast breads. Just change flours. For German rye add fennel seed and molasses as sweetener.

Homeplace Mountain Farm and Museum depicts life on an 1840's homestead in the Southwest Virginia Mountains. They offer demonstrations and tours, as well as Highland Games Scottish Festival in mid-July.
www.virginiastar.net/ceilidh/homeplace.htm

Glimpses of Yesteryear

If I close my eyes and drift, I can still see and smell and feel life as it was growing up in Dungannon in the 1940's and 50's:

My very first memory is of lying on the painted wooden floor and looking at a linoleum rug and thinking how spotless it was. The evening sun was shining through the window making everything so bright…

I loved going to take corn to the mill with my dad in our old green '39 Chevy truck. Mr. Stallard, the miller, ground it into corn meal and kept a portion of it for his own use. That's how we paid him for grinding our corn. One of my jobs was to shell corn for the chickens and for the mill. I would place the ear of corn into the sheller and turn the handle by hand. The corn came out a spout near the bottom and into a bucket or pan.

When we went to S.I. Osborne's store, the smell of freshly oiled floors met you at the door. Of course, there was a stove and many men sitting around it and counters on both sides of the store and all the merchandise on shelves on the walls. The clerk had to get each can or item with a long-handled stick with a clasp on it… Items were charged on an account for the year and you paid when the tobacco and cattle were sold in the fall… You got a set-up when your bill was paid. I remember a pretty bowl with gold flowers on it, the only one I remember. I think it was a smaller one than usual and that is why I remember it so well.

My playmate, Johnny Ray, and I drank lots and lots of water through onion stalks – straws were still a novelty in the 1940's. Mama told us to quit and I did but he kept on till he got a little sick. We thought it great fun. I can still taste the onion water…gourmet, huh?

When I was little we had nickel cups of ice cream with a picture of a movie star on it and they looked like they had the most beautiful red lips even though it was in black and white. One day I decided to paint my lips red - with fingernail polish. I was real classy until I had to peel it off. Mother warned me, too, but what good did that do?

We got a kitchen sink and daddy made me a playhouse out of the box it came in. I can yet feel myself cutting the holes out for the windows and see the crepe paper curtains I decorated them with.

Shirley Wolf and I roasted potatoes and onions on a stick over a fire built under a tarp in the heat of summer. Yum, yum! We would walk each other home – back and forth – till one of our mothers put a stop to it.

The Blevins's lived between us. They were an older couple and they grew celery in sawdust around the cistern house. Mrs. Blevins made the best sugar cookies and wonderful yellow cake with homemade caramel icing. I stayed with them after school if my parents were late getting home.

I remember walking around out by our cistern house eating radish and butter sandwiches…man, they are good. The best, or the worst, thing I ever found in our cistern house was a quart jar full of baby mice. They were living in there.

Out below the cistern house is where I was determined and set out to prove to mama that she didn't have to wait for daddy to come home and wring a chicken's head off. I could do it! Well, I swung and swung that poor chicken until it's neck was about a foot long and it was still alive and I was screaming and Mama had to cut it's head off with a butcher knife and then she was screaming and it flopped forever and wound up way down the hill in the weeds.

Mama and I made cheese by pouring bucket after bucket of milk in with a rennet tablet purchased at the drug store. We mashed and mashed the whey (water) out of it for days and days until we had the most heavenly cottage cheese one could imagine. Then we mashed some more and wrapped it in cheesecloth and let it age and we had a tiny little round of cheese no bigger than a dinner plate and about 3 inches thick. Daddy loved it with brown sugar on it and I do too, the perfect desert to any meal.

I was watching Roy and Dale as usual at 11 A.M. on Saturday morning and my stomach was hurting. It soon became apparent my periods had started, making me mad as could be. I cried and cried because I was only eleven and now I'd have to be grown up and not watch my favorite shows like Lash LaRue and Poncho and Cisco and Roy and Dale Evans.

My cousin Joe was a boy and could farm and drive a truck and do things I wasn't supposed to since I was a girl and ladies didn't do things like that, at least not when we were starting out. I was so jealous. I was expected to be a secretary or a teacher – that was my choice. Once daddy was plowing with a big turning plow and went over to the fence to talk to somebody. I talked him into letting me plow a round. I hung the point of the plow under a rock that wasn't about to be moved and the leather strap that you wear around your waist almost pulled me in two. I'm still proud of doing it, though Mama got mad at Daddy for letting me.

Mrs. Lou Farmer always baked heavenly apple pies – stacked 5 or 6 high. They were extremely thin, with fine tart applesauce. They could be placed one on top of the other on a plate. She sliced through the stack and drizzled honey over the top – they were to die for…Her house burned and that was the only time I ever saw my Daddy run.

My grandmother was noted for her biscuits and strawberry jam. She told Mama that she did not like baking them three times a day because the boys ate too much butter when she did. She could sell the butter, you know. My Daddy used to take her over to Coeburn to sell eggs and butter. When I was in college, I had the privilege of staying with a family that bought from them.

Once I got a beautiful multicolored rubber ball. Our cow ate it. I was so mad at that cow. Later, she fell in the spring around in the holler and broke her neck. Somehow I talked Daddy into cutting her open to find the ball and it was still there. But all the glorious swirls of color were gone.

My Daddy loved tomato gravy over cold biscuits. It was slightly thickened and sweetened with brown sugar. His favorite Sunday night supper was cold corn bread crumbled in a glass of cold milk. Our big meal was dinner, of course. Mother's dad, my grandfather, loved fluffy dumplings made in spring peas. He called it *pon hoss* although I have no idea why.

It was a thrill to top the hill on my walk home from the school bus and hear the silage cutter going. It cut up corn stalks and corn and put them into the silo for the winter where it would ferment and smell really good and yeasty. Right after silage time was molasses making time. That was grand.

The cane was ground into juice by a horse walking in circles, which operated the juice mill. The cane had to be hand fed into the mill. Then the juice was boiled in a long rectangular copper pan until it foamed and foamed. We all got stalks of cane cut slanting like a spoon so we could skim off the foam and eat it. All the foam had to be skimmed off; otherwise the molasses would be dark and strong.

Hog killing was a ritual when it got cold enough. I always had to grind up sausage that first night. It was hard work, but we always had fried tenderloin and gravy and biscuits for supper that night. Later, Mama would fry up sausage cakes and can them for the coming year. Daddy salted down the shoulders and hams and middlins' and then traded the hams for spiced luncheon meat because they didn't think it was as bad for them as the salty ham.

Christmas time came and Daddy cut a cedar tree on the farm and Mama whipped Angel Flake washing powder to make snow that looked like Cool Whip. We put it on the tree and branches that decorated the mantle and maybe the windows. One Christmas Eve about dark, I heard loud stomping on the front porch just like Daddy was stomping snow off his boots, but he was in the kitchen. Mama and I were in the living room. We went to the door and all we heard were sleigh bells in the distance, going up the hill. Still gives me a chill.

Mama always baked a stack cake with dried apples between the layers, which were sorta' like sugar cookie dough sweetened with molasses. It has to set about a week to be good and then it's the cat's meow! She baked a hen for every holiday in the year, Christmas, Easter, Thanksgiving, everything. But the stack cake was just Christmas.   *- Jenette Chapman*

Picking Parlor

If you like to pick and need someone to pick along with, here's your sign! The Pickin' Parlor, or Leonard's Music Store if you want to be formal, is open every day in Weber City behind the Scott County Bank. There's a Tuesday night jam from 7 – 10 and a Saturday morning session from 10 am – 1:00 pm. However, any time you stop by, you're apt to find someone picking and grinning. Harold may even be frying up corn bread if you're lucky.

The Pickin' Parlor in Weber City

Natural Tunnel

William Jennings Bryan called the tunnel "the eighth wonder of the world." Trains daily travel through the 850 ft. Natural Tunnel, as they have for over a hundred years, while Stock Creeks flows alongside as it has for a million years. The area has been a State Park since 1971, offering camping, swimming, hiking, musical concerts, plays, and a chairlift into the Stock Creek Gorge for a view of the Tunnel. There's a visitor center offering many types of interpretive programs and Cove Ridge Center, a conference and educational center with dormitory type lodging. You can join a Wild Cave Tour led by a naturalist or canoe the Clinch with an organized canoe and kayak group. www.naturaltunnel.info

May you always have work for your hands to do.
May your pockets hold always a coin or two.
May the sun shine bright on your window pane.
May the rainbow be certain to follow each rain.
May the hand of a friend always be near you.
And may God fill your heart with gladness to cheer you.
-Irish Blessing

The Dykes Magic City Trio in 1927. (L to R) John Dykes, Myrtle Vermillion and Hub Mahaffey.

The Appalachian Dream Spinners 2005. (L to R) Anita Gibson, Dwight Bishop and Marianna Roberts (grandaughter of Myrtle Vermillion.)

About Salt...

Table salt has additives to maintain its white color and to keep it from clumping. Iodized salt provides iodine, an essential mineral.

Pickling Salt is additive free so it won't cloud pickling liquids or brines. It is a finer grind than table salt.

Sea Salt is obtained by evaporating seawater. It may contain slightly more trace minerals than table salt.

Seasoned Salts are blends of salt and other seasonings, such as celery, garlic or onion.

Kosher Salt tastes about half as salty as table salt. It is coarse ground and additive-free.

Rock Salt is often used for freezing ice cream. It's an inedible, coarse-ground salt.

One teaspoon of salt contains about 2,000 mg of sodium.

Salt is mentioned at least thirty times in the Bible.

Washington County

Contents

Apple Dumplings..............................143	Orange French Toast......................155
Buchanan Inn Crabbies.....................143	Oriental Crunch Salad....................156
Butterscotch Pie................................144	Parsnip Fritters...............................156
Canned Jalapeno Peppers..................144	Parsnips, Stewed.............................157
Caramel Icing....................................146	Peanut Butter Chocolate Dessert......157
Chicken Salad Casserole...................146	Peanut Butter Cookies....................158
Chili..148	Pig Lickin' Cake..............................158
Coconut Chews.................................148	Pinto Bean Pie.................................158
Corn Bread Pie..................................149	Plain Soft Custard...........................159
Fried Bluegill....................................150	Pretzel Salad....................................159
Fruit Cheese Ball..............................150	Pumpkin Cheesecake......................164
Hershey Bar Layer Cake...................151	Refrigerator Ginger Bread...............165
Oatmeal Cake...................................151	Sour Dough Bread..........................165
Old Fashioned Buckwheat Cakes......152	Strata Milano..................................166
One Egg Cake..................................153	Summer Salad.................................166
Onion Bread.....................................153	Swiss Chocolate Cake.....................168
Orange Croissant Soufflés.................154	Taffy..168
	White Chocolate Rice Krispie Treats..................170

White's Mill

Photo by Frank Young - Lasting Impressions
Used by permission

Frank is a 26-year veteran of the US Air Force, where he traveled extensively. Photography has been a hobby since 9th grade when he got his first $5.00 Kodak Brownie Camera. Other hobbies include hiking and traveling. He started LASTING IMPRESSIONS photography to share and sell his photos, which mostly feature historic, scenic, nature, and military subjects. Frank lives in Foscoe near Boone, NC with wife, Virginia, a retired nurse. Whenever possible, they enjoy spending time with their 3 daughters and their families including 8 grandchildren.

Apple Dumplings
Eloise Buckles – Meadowview, VA

Standard Pastry – Two Crust Pie
2 cups sifted plain flour	2/3 cup plus 2 Tbsps. Crisco
1 tsp. salt	¼ cup water

In a mixing bowl blend flour and salt. Cut in shortening until the size of large peas. Sprinkle with water a tablespoon at a time mixing lightly with a fork until all the flour is moistened. Gather dough together with fingers so it cleans the bowl. Press into a ball.

Roll out pastry a little less than 1/8 inch thick, and cut into 7-inch squares. This pastry makes 6 dumplings. Pare and core a medium tart, juicy apple for each dumpling. Then prepare syrup.

1 cup sugar	3 Tbsps. butter
2 cups water	¼ tsp. cinnamon

Boil together for 3 minutes. Fill cavities of apples with mixture:

½ cup sugar	dot with butter, 1 Tbsp.
1 ½ tsps. cinnamon	

Lift carefully the apples and place a little apart in baking dish. Pour hot syrup around dumplings. Bake at 425º for 40 to 45 minutes.

"Apple, apple dumpling my first choice," cry all the husbands with one voice. "Apple for the filling, sugar and spice, wrap it up in pastry, count me twice."
—*Eloise Buckles*

Buchanan Inn Crabbies
The Buchanan Inn - Jim & Annette Goode – Damascus, VA

- 6 English muffins, split in half
- 1 (7 oz.) can crab, drained
- 1 (5 oz.) jar Kraft Old English Cheese
- 1 stick of butter, softened
- ½ tsp. garlic powder
- 1 ½ tsps. mayonnaise

Mix all ingredients and spread on 12 English muffin halves. Place on cookie sheet and freeze. Put in zip lock bag when frozen. When ready to use, thaw desired number of halves. Cut each into fourths. Bake on cookie sheet at 350° for 8 – 10 minutes.

Butterscotch Pie
Sheila & Frank McMurray – Abingdon, VA

1 cup brown sugar
¼ cup flour
1 cup cream
2 eggs yolks
½ stick melted butter
1 tsp. vanilla
1 cup boiling water

Combine sugar, flour, and cream. Mix and add water, yolks, butter, and vanilla. Cook over medium heat until thick. Pour into 9 inch baked pie shell.

"This recipe given to me by Joe Carter, son of A. P. Carter."

Canned Jalapeño Peppers
Jerry Larkey – Bristol, VA

Jalapeno peppers
brown vinegar
chopped garlic
2 tsps. oregano
olive oil

1. Cut peppers long ways and remove seeds. Be sure to wear gloves.
2. Place in big crock or jar and cover with brown vinegar.
3. Let stand for 10 days.
4. Pour vinegar off and put in jars.

Fill jars with one layer of peppers and one layer of chopped garlic until full. Add 2 tsps. of oregano and fill remainder of jar with olive oil. Seal jar and let stand 42 days before eating.

Among the counties that were split from Washington were: Dickenson, Wise, Lee, and Scott. In 1776, Washington County would have extended to what is now Kentucky and West Virginia as well as North Carolina and Tennessee.

The Widener Sisters

After working in factories and taking care of their parents, sisters Anna (74) and Grace (79) Widener settled into their retirement to relax. But that proved difficult. Work was too much a part of their lives. "We were just plain bored," they say.

Anna and Grace Widener

"We take time about with our sisters a-cooking meals for the family," says Anna. "One day when our nephew, Darryl, was there, Grace asked him if there was anything we could do at the new motel (Hampton Inn) they were building in Abingdon. Darryl spoke to the owner about us running the breakfast bar, who said as far as he was concerned we had the job. We didn't fill out an application or anything. We've been here nine years, now."

They enjoy meeting the travelers and have made friends with many who are regulars. Initially, they were hesitant about coming up with a recipe for our book. But after thinking a bit, Grace decides to share a Carmel icing recipe given to her by "someone who's been dead for years."

"That's a good one," responds Anna.

After writing it down hurriedly, Grace begins to repeat it verbally. Just to be sure, Anna called up sister, Josie (82) who is the boss over the kitchen, but out with bursitis. Josie looks up her copy and interjects ingredients and instructions over the cell phone via Anna. Turns out Grace did forget one ingredient: evaporated milk. "We use Pet," she stresses, as Josie continues the recipe by phone. Both agree on the general directions and Grace tells us that it takes right at 20 minutes to reach a soft-ball stage. "I timed it one day just so I'd know," she says.

When the last step, beating it until thick, is explained, Josie sends word across the airwaves, "Beat the dickens out of it is what you do!" she emphasizes.

All agreed the icing was worth the effort it takes to make it, but each had their own opinion as to the best cake to serve it on. "Chocolate is best," we hear from Josie but Grace is sure that spice compliments it better. Anna likes both but thinks it is also good with a plain yellow cake. We didn't hear from Mary, (77) who works on Saturdays but has been in bad health.

Caramel Icing
Anna & Grace Widener – Abingdon, VA - Hampton Inn Breakfast Room

2	cups sugar	1	tsp. vanilla
2	sticks butter	¾	cup Pet evaporated milk

Put sugar, butter, and evaporated milk in pan big enough to boil. Get it good and hot. Set it off for 1 hour. Stir once in a while. Put back on stove, boil 20 minutes or until a soft ball forms in water. Take off stove and add vanilla. Beat until thick enough to go on cake. Beat the dickens out of it! Good on spice cake, but it is best on chocolate cake.

Chicken Salad Casserole
Tammy Martin – Emory, VA

> "Ya got time to breathe, ya got time for music."
> *-Briscoe Darling*

- 4 cooked (boiled) chicken breasts, shredded
- ½ cup to 1 cup celery, parboiled
- ½ cup mayonnaise
- 1 can cream of celery soup
- ½ can to 1 can cream of chicken soup
- 2 Tbsps. finely chopped onions, sautéed
- 1 Tbsp. lemon juice
- 2 cups grated cheddar cheese
- 1 cup slivered almonds
- 1 small can Chinese noodles (or crushed potato chips)

Mix everything lightly (save 1 cup of cheese for top). Pour into 9 x 13-inch baking dish. Top with noodles and remaining cheese. Sprinkle with paprika. Bake 25 minutes at 350°.

Tammy Martin - Hammered dulcimer, Irish Bodhran player and vocalist for *"Fire in the Kitchen"* band. **www.fire-in-the-kitchen.com**

Trying to decide between butter and marjarine? Consider which you trust, a scientist or a cow.

Damascus

Damascus, VA is the little town that *could*. A boomtown in the early twentieth century due to timber and industries such as an extract company and flooring plant that sprang from up alongside, to a depressed area in mid-century, to a trail town of renown by the twenty-first century. Surrounded by rugged, scenic mountains on all sides and inhabited by a community of people who are in tune with their lovely and diverse corner of the world, the town sits in a unique sort of crossroads.

Aptly billed as Trail Town, USA, Damascus is crossed by the 34-mile Virginia Creeper biking and hiking rail trail that runs from Abingdon to Whitetop Station. "Creeper" was the nickname given to the steam locomotive that ran from 1901-1957 when it was replaced with a diesel engine that continued until 1977, the year the rails were dismantled.

The Appalachian Trail is a continuously marked path over 2100 miles long, from Springer Mountain in Georgia to Katahdin Mountain in Maine. Main Street in Damascus is part of the trail. Early on the town embraced the often scruffy hikers who came through. The United Methodist Church has operated a hostel since 1976, offering a bath and place to sleep for a donation to help with electricity. Many times the local postmaster has opened the post office to hand a much needed package of supplies to a thru hiker who arrived after it was closed.

A 4,247-mile long road cycling trail, the TransAmerica, which reaches from Oregon to Yorktown, VA, passes through town on Rt. 58. Iron Mountain trail can be hiked into the Mount Rodgers National Recreation Area. Two driving trails bring travelers through town – The Daniel Boone Wilderness Trail and the Crooked Road Musical Heritage Trail. For birders, there is Virginia's Birding and Wildlife Trail.

In 1987, the first Trail Days took place to celebrate the fiftieth anniversary of the Appalachian Trail with about 10 vendors and hikers who returned for a reunion. By 2008, it's an official three day affair but events stretch over more than a week. It's family friendly and features such things as a hikers parade and talent show, concerts, interesting programs and speakers, as well as over 150 vendors as part of the celebration. Backpacking tents are pitched side by side, making a temporary tent city. The First Baptist Church offers free showers and free meals at different times.

New adventurers are appreciating places once roamed by Cherokee, Shawnee, and in 1759, by Daniel Boone. More modern perhaps, but still seeking wilderness in which to travel and test one's mettle. Damascus didn't grow as famous as it's namesake in Syria by becoming the steel-producing city dreamed of by General John D. Imboden when he changed its name from Mock's Mill in the 1880's. But perhaps it has fulfilled a destiny he could never have foreseen.

Chili
Lindsey Massie – Glade Spring, VA

1 pound hamburger, browned	½ tsp. black pepper
1 tsp. garlic powder	1 cup water
1 Tbsp. chili powder	1 tsp. vinegar
2 Tbsps. brown sugar	1 small onion, chopped
½ - 1 tsp. salt, adjust to taste	14 ozs. ketchup

Brown hamburger meat and onion, drain. Add rest of the ingredients and cook slowly for 20 to 25 minutes.

"I have been on the Board at White's Mill for almost 4 years. Since I live so close to the Mill, I was asked to head up the operations committee. I spent a lot of time with the miller and learned by asking questions and helping out. The miller took another position in October 2007 and my brother and I have been milling since then. We have learned by reading books, asking Old Timers what they remember of the Mill and by our own experiences. It has been great fun and we can hardly wait until White's Mill is restored and back on waterpower again! Corn flour makes a rich, smooth cornbread. We have a sheet of recipes that we hand out at White's Mill." -Jennifer Kling

Coconut Chews
Jennifer Kling – Abingdon, VA

1 (14 oz.) can sweetened condensed milk	¼ tsp. salt
2 tsps. Vanilla	3 cups shredded coconut
1 cup corn flour	½ cup chopped nuts

Preheat oven to 325°. Mix well. Drop from a teaspoon onto greased baking sheet. Bake for 12 to 15 minutes until golden brown on the edges. Allow to cool slightly before removing from baking sheet.

Daniel Boone and Nathaniel Gist camped in the area that is now Abingdon while on a hunting trip. Wolves came out of a cave and attacked their dogs leading Boone to name the place Wolf Hills. The grotto can be still seen behind the Cave House Crafts.

Corn Bread Pie
Teddy Helton – Bristol, VA

1 lb. ground chuck
1 large onion
1 (16 oz.) can chopped tomatoes
1 (6 oz.) can tomato paste
½ tsp. salt
½ tsp. black pepper
½ tsp. chili powder
1 (11 oz.) can Green Giant mexicorn
1 (16 oz.) can kidney beans

Topping
3/4 cup self-rising cornmeal
1 Tbsp. self-rising flour
½ tsp. sugar
1 egg
1 Tbsp. vegetable oil
½ cup buttermilk

Teddy Helton is bass and guitar player for *"Fire In The Kitchen"* band.
http://fire-in-the-kitchen.com/

Brown ground beef and onion in large skillet. (I use an iron skillet so I can put the skillet in oven.) Add all other ingredients, mix well. If not using iron skillet, transfer mixture to casserole dish. Mix topping and spread on meat mixture. Bake in 350° oven about 20 minutes or until cornbread on top is done.

Fishing for Bluegill

"Fishing for bluegill is fun, because the fish are scrappy. They love to put up a good fight. And they're easy to catch. Just grab some earthworms and a line with a bobber and head out to the lake.

I fish around the lakes of Washington County, where I live just off The Crooked Road: Virginia's Heritage Music Trail. My favorite place to hide away is Hidden Valley Lake on Brumley Mountain, near the site of where the Chestnut Grove Quartet played near Little Moccasin Gap. There my daughter, Abigail, caught the biggest bluegill I had ever seen – almost nine inches long – and she was only five years old at the time!

Hidden Valley Lake eventually flows down to the North Fork of the Holston River, the same watercourse that flows through the valley where The Carter Family comes from.

Remember: Bluegills are not big. So you'll need to catch quite a batch before you can go home and make a meal. I usually figure about five – fried - make up enough to satisfy, so long as you serve some French fries and some slices of fresh, homegrown tomatoes on the side. Add iced tea, and you've got the perfect meal."

-Joe Tennis

Garden Bath
Brenda Sauls – Bristol, VA

2 Tbsps. dried rose petals
1 Tbsp. dried lavender flowers
2 Tbsps. orange peel, grated
1 tsp. rosemary
2 bay leaves, crushed

Place all ingredients in bath bag, and place in bath while water is running. You will be surrounded with a sweet – scented garden.

Joe Tennis is the author of four books featuring places along The Crooked Road, including *Beach to Bluegrass,* an illustrated collection of tales, music, and legends along Highway 58; *Southwest Virginia Crossroads,* an illustrated history and guide to 17 counties and profiles of Crooked Road attractions; *Sullivan County, Tennessee,* an illustrated history featuring Bristol and the Birthplace of Country Music; and *The Marble and Other Ghost Tales of Tennessee and Virginia,* a collection of legends from Abingdon, Damascus, Bristol, and Big Stone Gap.

Fried Bluegill
Joe Tennis – Bristol, VA

10 bluegills
1 egg
4 ozs. milk
4 ozs. water

flour
cornmeal
canola oil

Clean bluegill by gutting, scaling and cutting off head. Then place cleaned fish in egg wash – a mix of one beaten egg, a little milk and a little water. Then dust egg-washed fish in a mix of flour and cornmeal. Toss in a frying pan – at medium heat – with plenty of canola oil. Fry until golden brown, drain and serve. Servings: Two (about five fish per person).

Fruit Cheese Ball
Patsy Larkey – Bristol, VA

1 (15 oz.) can fruit cocktail, drained
2 (8 oz.) cream cheese (softened)
1 (5.1 oz.) box French vanilla instant pudding

Mix all ingredients, roll into ball, and then roll in nuts or coconut. Serve with graham crackers.

Hershey Bar Layer Cake
Deane Fletcher – Glade Spring, VA

1 box devil's food cake mix	3 eggs
1 small box instant chocolate pudding	¾ cup oil
	1 ½ cups milk

Combine dry ingredients. Add eggs, oil and milk. Mix until smooth. Pour batter into 3 round cake pans. Bake for 20 minutes at 325°.

Frosting:

1 (8 oz.) pkg. cream cheese	1 (16 oz.) Cool Whip
1 cup powdered sugar	6 Hershey bars, grated
1 cup sugar	

Soften cream cheese, add sugars and mix well. Add Cool Whip and gently mix until blended. Add 5 ½ grated Hershey bars. Frost cake. Sprinkle remaining ½ grated Hershey bar on frosted cake. Keep in refrigerator.

Oatmeal Cake
Phyllis Helton – Bristol, VA

1 cup quick oats
1 1/3 cups boiling water
Mix and set aside to cool.

2 eggs	1 tsp. vanilla
1 cup white sugar	1 tsp. soda
½ cup shortening	1 1/3 cups flour

Cream sugar and shortening then add eggs. Mix in cooled oats, vanilla, soda, and flour. Bake 35 minutes at 325°.

Topping

1 cup brown sugar	2 eggs yolks
1 stick margarine or butter, melted	1 cup pecans (chopped)
	1 cup coconut

Mix brown sugar and butter. Heat until sugar is dissolved. Add the egg yolks, pecans, and coconut. Spread topping on cake and broil just long enough to brown topping.

To thine own self be true, and it must follow, as the night the day, thou canst not then be false to any man.
—William Shakespeare in Hamlet

Abingdon, VA

The cobblestone streets of Abingdon often have names that reflect businesses of yesteryear: Tanner, Brewers Alley, and Court St. for example. History abounds here; the arts and gracious living are part of the heritage. Good manners still matter, as does good food. It has been named one of the best 100 small towns in America and you'll see why once you visit.

Artist can be observed working in many mediums at the Arts Depot or at the William King Regional Arts Center, which features four museum-standard galleries. There are antique shops and other galleries to browse as well as historic buildings to enjoy. The oldest building in Abingdon is the Tavern, built in 1779, that has served as a courthouse, post office, cabinet shop, a pub, a stage office, and a hospital during the Civil War, among other uses. It is now a restaurant.

In earlier days, an area behind the Courthouse was called the Jockey Lot. On court days, it was the place for men and boys to trade horses and mules, or guns and knives if they could work out a deal. Proper ladies did not go there on court days.

A beautiful old Victorian house on Main Street, circa 1858, has been a Co-Op called Cave House Crafts since 1971. Artisans who live within a 50-mile radius sell outstanding handcrafted products here. www.cavehousecrafts.org

Sixteen-day festivals are somewhat longer than normal in the south, but the Virginia Highlands Festival has been held since 1948. The first two weeks in August see more than 200,000 tourist and locals mingling to take in events of an amazingly eclectic variety. There truly is something for everyone. www.vahighlandsfestival.org

Old Fashioned Buckwheat Cakes
Recipe from White's Mill, Abingdon, VA

1 cake yeast
1 egg
1 tsp. salt

   buckwheat flour
1 cup luke hot water
   sweet milk

Dissolve yeast in 1 cup of luke hot water, pour into mixing bowl, and add flour and water until you have the desired amount, beat well. Set where warm to rise overnight. The next morning break an egg into this and add enough salt to season, thin with sweet milk, beat real hard for several minutes, and fry on greased griddle.

"My great, great grandmother gave me this recipe."

One Egg Cake
Renee Winningham

1	cup sugar	1	cup milk
1	stick butter	1	tsp. vanilla
1	egg	2	cups flour (around)

Cream sugar and butter, beat well. Add the egg and beat well. Add flour and milk; starting with flour and ending with flour. Add flavoring and mix well. Bake at 350° until done. This is great topped with berries.

Onion Bread
Recipe from White's Mill – Abingdon, VA

1	cup of chopped raw onions	3	cups flour
1	cup water	1	tsp. salt
1	pkg. dry yeast	1	Tbsp. sugar
1	tsp. sugar	1	Tbsp. melted butter

Cook 1 cup of chopped raw onions in a cup of water until soft. Strain, keeping the liquid. In ½ cup of water dissolve 1 pkg. of dry yeast and 1 tsp. of sugar – when frothy; add 3 cups of flour and 1 tsp. of salt, 1 Tbsp. of sugar and 1 Tbsp. of melted butter. Add the onions and enough of the liquid to create stiff dough, kneading until smooth. Place the dough in a greased bowl, cover and let it rise until it doubles in bulk. Punch down, reknead and form into a large round hearth-type loaf and allow it to rise an hour. Cut several slashes in the top of the loaf with a sharp knife. Bake for 40 minutes at 375°.

Round the Mountain: Southwest Virginia's Artisan Network, a non-profit organization, is working to connect venues, artisans, and potential customers for the benefit of all.
www.roundthemountain.org

Barter Theatre

The building that houses the State Theatre of Virginia, the Barter Theatre, began life as Sinking Springs Presbyterian Church in the early 1830's. The first known minister, Charles Cummings, was called the "fighting Parson" and appears to have had a theatrical bent; carrying a rifle that he leaned against the pulpit while preaching.

During the depression, in 1933, Robert Porterfield brought 22 fellow actors to his hometown and began work on an ingenious idea. Plays would be presented to local folks for produce, chickens, or whatever would be worth the admission price. The Barter Company cleared $4.35 at the end of the first season, along with a weight gain among the actors, and two barrels of jelly.

Playwright George Bernard Shaw requested spinach as royalty for his plays since he was a vegetarian but others, such as Noel Coward, accepted Virginia hams.

Productions are presented year round. Once during each year the Barter takes donations as admission to a performance to honor their heritage.

Inn on Town Creek, located one block from the historic district, is beautifully landscaped and furnished with antiques. The Inn has two suites, each with it's own private entrance off the covered porches. There are three spacious bedrooms with private baths. Full breakfast included with room. Innkeepers are Dr. Roger and Linda Neal.
www.innontowncreek.com

Orange Croissants Soufflés
Linda Neal – Abingdon, VA

10	cocktail croissants
9	ozs. orange marmalade
1 ½	cups heavy cream (not half & half)
3	ozs. fresh squeezed orange juice
8	eggs
1	tsp. plus a splash almond extract

Cut croissants in half lengthwise and place bottom halves in a 12 x 10 inch baking dish. I use a large round stoneware baking dish. Thin marmalade with orange juice and spoon over each bottom half, saving a little to be used as glaze. Replace croissant top. Beat eggs, cream, and almond extract. Pour over top of the croissants. Spoon thinned marmalade over top. Soak overnight or freeze. Thaw before cooking. Remove from refrigerator at least 45 minutes before cooking. Bake 25 minutes at 350°. Serve hot with powder sugar sprinkled on the top to garnish. Serves 8 to 10. Serve with maple syrup to pour over it like French toast. Enjoy!

Orange French Toast

Jim & Annette Goode – Damascus, VA - The Buchannan Inn at Green Cove Station

The Toast

6 slices of French bread, 1–1½ inches thick	1 tsp. vanilla
4 eggs	1/8 tsp. nutmeg
2/3 cup orange juice	¼ tsp. cinnamon
1/3 cup milk	½ stick butter
¼ cup sugar (scant)	orange zest
	Cool Whip or whipped cream

In a large bowl with electric mixer, beat eggs, orange juice, milk, sugar, vanilla, nutmeg and cinnamon. Pour some of the liquid into a 9 x 13 inch casserole dish, lay the bread on top, and pour on remainder of the liquid. Be sure each piece is covered well with the liquid. Batter is really plenty for 8 pieces. Cover dish with plastic wrap and refrigerate overnight. Preheat oven to 350°. Place butter on a 15 x 10 x 1 inch baking sheet, place in oven until butter is melted. Place prepared bread in a single layer on the melted butter. Bake 10 minutes. Turn the slices over and bake 10-12 minutes until the underside is golden. Serve immediately with a small amount of warm orange syrup, orange zest and Cool Whip or whipped cream. Have a dish of pecans and a pitcher of extra syrup on the table.

The Syrup

1 stick of butter
½ cup sugar (scant)
1/3 cup orange juice concentrate (This is ½ of 6 oz. can)

In medium saucepan, combine butter, sugar and orange juice. Cook and stir over low heat until butter is melted and all ingredients are combined well. Do not boil. Cool for 10 minutes, and then beat until thick. Syrup can be made ahead of time and refrigerated, then warmed. Also, left over syrup can be frozen until needed.

The town of Abingdon was name for Martha Washington's ancestral home of Abingdon Parish.

Oriental Crunch Salad

Brenda Sauls – Bristol, VA

> A recipe that is not shared with others will soon be forgotten, but when it's shared, it will be enjoyed by future generations.

- 1 (16 oz.) vacuum bag shredded cabbage
- 6 chopped green onions (tops too)

Dressing:

- ½ cup sugar (I use Splenda)
- ½ cup oil
- ¼ cup tarragon vinegar
- 1 Tbsp. soy sauce

Mix dressing and refrigerate until ready to use.

- 1 stick of butter
- 5 ozs. sliced almonds
- 4 ozs. sunflower seeds
- 2 (3 oz.) Ramen instant noodles, any flavor, do not use flavor packet

Break up noodles and place in pan. Melt butter, add brown noodles, almonds, and sunflower seeds. Drain on a paper towel after browning. You can prepare the three mixtures ahead of time, even the day before. Keep cabbage and dressing refrigerated (separately) and the noodle mixture in a zip lock bag until just before serving. Fifteen minutes before serving, mix the cabbage and onions together in a bowl, place the noodle mixture on top of cabbage and onions and top with dressing. Mix thoroughly.

Parsnip Fritters

Mary Blevins – Green Cove, VA

Boil 4 or 5 parsnips; when tender, take off the skins and mash them fine. Add to them a teaspoonful of wheat flour and a beaten egg. Put a tablespoon of lard or beef drippings in a frying pan over the fire, add to it a teaspoon of salt. When boiling hot put in the parsnips made into cakes with a spoon. When one side is a delicate brown, turn to the other. When both are done, take them on a dish put a very little of the fat in which they were fried over and serve hot. These resemble very nearly the taste of salsify (oyster) roots, but will generally be preferred.

"The Parsnip recipe came from The Original White House Cook Book –Edition 1887."

Parsnips, Stewed

Mary Blevins – Green Cove, VA

After washing and scrapping parsnips, slice them about half an inch thick. Put into saucepan of boiling water containing enough to barely cook them. Add a tablespoon of butter, salt, and pepper; cover closely. Stew them until the water has cooked away, watching carefully and stirring often to prevent burning, until soft. When done they will be a creamy straw color and deliciously sweet, retaining all the vegetable goodness.

Peanut Butter Chocolate Dessert

Deane Fletcher – Glade Spring, VA

24	chocolate cream-filled chocolate sandwich cookies (Oreos or other brand)
2	Tbsps. butter or margarine, melted
1	(8 oz.) pkg. cream cheese, softened
½	cup peanut butter
1 ½	cups confectioners' sugar
1	(16 oz.) frozen whipped topping, thawed
15	miniature peanut butter cups, chopped
1	cup cold milk
1	(3.9 oz.) pkg. instant chocolate pudding mix

Crush 20 cookies, toss with butter. Press in 9 x 13-inch ungreased pan. In mixing bowl, beat the cream cheese, peanut butter and 1 cup confectioners sugar until smooth. Fold in half of the whipped topping. Spread over crust. Sprinkle with chopped peanut butter cups. In another mixing bowl, beat the milk, pudding mix and remaining confectioners sugar on low speed for 2 minutes. Fold in remaining whipped topping. Spread over peanut butter cup layer. Crush remaining cookies, sprinkle over the top. Cover and chill for at least 3 hours. Yields: 12-16 servings.

If you don't read the newspapers, you are uninformed.
If you do, you are misinformed.
-Mark Twain

Bonnie's Family Restaurant

After working as a waitress 17 years, Bonnie Jones bought a restaurant that was being sold and she became known for her home cooking and homemade pies. Many race fans visit when they come to the Bristol Motor Speedway and locals drop by often for the specialties such as Pinto Bean Pie. "I enjoy the restaurant business," states Bonnie. "But I'm not sure what is worse, being a waitress or being the owner!" 276-669-3361

Peanut Butter Cookies
Jennifer Kling – Abingdon, VA

½ cup butter
½ cup peanut butter
½ cup brown sugar
½ cup white sugar
1 egg
1 tsp. baking soda
½ tsp. salt
½ tsp. baking powder
1 ¼ cups corn flour

Preheat oven to 350°. Mix well. Drop from a teaspoon onto greased baking sheet. Press flat with a fork. Bake for 12 to 15 minutes. Allow to cool slightly before removing from baking sheet.

Pig Lickin' Cake
Madison Massie – Glade Spring, VA

1 box yellow cake mix
1 (11 oz.) mandarin oranges, not drained
4 eggs
½ cup cooking oil

Mix together and bake at 325° for 30 minutes in a 9 x 13 inch pan.
Frosting:
1 (12 oz.) Cool Whip
1 (8.5 oz.) crushed pineapple, drained
1 large box vanilla instant pudding, dry

Mix slowly and let set until cake is cool. Spread on cake. Refrigerate.

Pinto Bean Pie
Bonnie Jones - Bonnie's Family Restaurant – Bristol, VA

1 cup mashed pinto beans
1 cup chopped pecans
1 tsp. vanilla
1 stick butter or margarine, melted
1 small can coconut
2 eggs, beaten
1 ½ cups sugar

Preheat oven to 300°. Mix all ingredients together and pour into prepared pie shells. Bake for 45 minutes. Cool for 30 minutes or until set.

"It was hard for me to decide what recipes to send you. Since I am 81 years old, I thought about the ones I had enjoyed for years with my family. I am still active in FCE Club. In 2006 I received my certificate for 60 years of membership. It is 61 now and I have enjoyed every year with club work. This recipe is from "The American Woman's Cookbook" 1943 Print. I have used this recipe for Christmas Day since 1944 served with White Coconut Cake."

Plain Soft Custard
Eloise R. Buckles – Meadowview, VA

2	cups milk		
2	whole eggs or 4 egg yolks	4	Tbsps. sugar
1/8	tsp. salt	½	tsp. vanilla

Scald the milk in the top of a double boiler. Beat together slightly the eggs, sugar and salt. Add the hot milk to the egg mixture, mix thoroughly and return to the top of the double boiler. Cook over hot water stirring constantly until the egg coats the spoon. Add vanilla. Serve cold topped with whipped cream.

Pretzel Salad
Brenda Sauls – Bristol, VA

2	cups crushed pretzels	2	cups Cool Whip
1	stick margarine, melted	1	(6 oz.) pkg. strawberry Jell-O
3	Tbsps. sugar		
1	(8 oz.) pkg. cream cheese	2	cups boiling water
1	cup sugar	2	(10 oz.) frozen strawberries

Mix together crushed pretzels, margarine and 3 Tbsps. sugar. Press into a greased 9 x 13-inch pan. Bake 10 minutes in a 350° oven. Let cool.

Filling:
Mix together cream cheese and 1 cup sugar. Add Cool Whip. Spread over cooled pretzel mix. Mix together Jell-O and water. Add frozen strawberries; chill until syrupy. Pour over cheese mixture and refrigerate until ready to serve. Cut into squares and serve.

I will lift up mine eyes unto the hills, from whence cometh my help. My help cometh from the Lord, which made heaven and earth.
-Psalm 121:1-2

(L to R) Sammy Shelor, banjo; Linda Lay, bass; David Lay, Guitar; and Gale Shockley, mandolin.

Linda Lay

Is it any surprise that someone noted for clarity and richness of voice was born in Bristol, VA, where the *Big Bang of Country Music* took place? With impeccable timing on the bass as well as on her vocals, Linda Lay delivers an impressive performance wherever and whenever she takes the stage.

Lay was playing the guitar by age eight, taught by her father who played mandolin. She credits Gene Boyd, known as the fiddling barber, for teaching her to play the bass, her instrument of choice. Her family's band is where Lay cut her teeth as a performer and she later spent twenty years as lead singer for *Appalachian Trail,* while still working a regular job and raising children.

When the National Council for Traditional Arts (NCTA) created the "Masters of the Steel String Guitar" tour and needed a vocalist, they looked no further than Linda. The Virginia Foundation for Humanities and Arts also named her a Master Vocalist, though she states that she does not read music. Maybe that's what makes her singing appear so natural as to be called a "Gift." It certainly is to the listener.

Green Cove Station

After winding through scenic Grayson County, we spent the night at the cozy Buchanan Inn in Green Cove with Innkeepers Jim and Annette Goode. They made us feel so welcome that our breakfast next morning turned into a two-hour conversation after they joined us for coffee.

Stopping by Green Cove Station on the Virginia Creeper Trail. Photo by Robert Skeens

Annette Goode has vivid childhood memories of the train station that her grandfather, William (Mr. Buck) Buchanan, owned that served as a post office, general store, and Western Union office from 1914 to the 1970's. The men who came to wait for the mail swapped stories, chewed the fat (talked) and chewed tobacco. The old wood stove was rarely without tobacco juice trailing down the sides where the spitter had missed the mark (stove door) slightly, causing the spitee to sizzle - a homey sound in those days.

The men often partook of a big orange soda and a moon pie while waiting. Goode recalls a new item her grandfather got in, peach tarts. A local mountain man came in and decided to try one. He took a bite and proceeded to chew and chew. The others watched and said nothing. Another bite and extended chewing period – then another and another until the tart was gone. Finally, a comment, "That's got to be the toughest pie crust I ever et'!

"Well," replied one of the regulars dryly, "you ate the cardboard, too!"

Music was part of life in the mountains and Goode remembers her mother, also her teacher at the three-room Green Cove Elementary School, bringing in musicians for the children. *Uncle Zeke and the Tennessee Hill Toppers* is the only band's name she can still recall but there were several. Later, Goode happily attended school in Damascus, glad to have a different teacher than her mother, who always knew what the homework was.

Through the years, numerous schoolteachers boarded with the Buchanan's. Mary, Annette Goode's grandmother, daily cooked 25-50 lunches for the passengers and crew of the Virginia Creeper from the 1920's to the 1960's, keeping her four daughters and often the boarders busy. These lunches cost $.50 and might consist of fried chicken, ham biscuits, home grown vegetables, and dessert, along with coffee in a coke bottle.

When television came to the Green Cove area, an elderly lady visited Mrs. Buchanan one day and the conversation turned to patience. "The person who has the most patience of anyone in the world must be whoever teaches those little pigs to dance and sing on television!" the visitor proclaimed, referring to the Valleydale advertisement. The statement amuses Annette today as it did her grandmother years ago.

Mr. Buchanan is remembered by local children as being generous and always handing out a treat to them. "He was so good-hearted he almost gave away the store," states his granddaughter. "During hard times, he would say, 'if we can eat, our neighbors will eat, too,' and he tried to see that everyone did."

The last train ran in 1977 and Goode's mother, Eleanor Edwards, donated the station and general store to the U.S. Forest Service in 1992. It is used as a Visitor and Education Center for the Virginia Creeper National Recreation Trail.

O. Winston Link often visited Green Cove and in 1956, took one of his famous steam engine pictures there, "Maud Bowing to the train." He married Conchita Mendoza at the Station. To commemorate the fiftieth anniversary of the occasion, a celebration was held and a marker was placed in the spot where he stood to take the photo. Four of the six people in the original picture were able to attend the event.

Luckily, we thought to ask the Goodes if they'd recommend someone we should contact for recipes or stories. "Go down to the "dump" and ask Mary Katherine Blevins," they suggested. "Everybody stops by there and talks to her."

While we didn't meet *everybody* at the recycling center, we did meet Mary, Joe Blevins, and Skip Blackburn – the person credited by some for putting Green Cove on the map. He was instrumental in starting art exhibits by local artisans and high school students in the Station, which he manned five years for the Forest Service after retiring and moving home to Green Cove. Blackburn conceived the idea of a marker for the spot where O. Winston Link stood to snap the picture of Maud bowing to the Virginia Creeper and worked to see it completed.

Mary Blevins, who does beautiful stained glass, never wanted to move away from her childhood home, though seven of her ten siblings did. She graduated from the River Rock School in Damascus in the same class as Skip Blackburn.

The visit was genial and somewhat crowded with five people in the small building. (Indeed, it appeared that every body does drop by, as several of those bodies stuck heads in to say hello. There was nowhere to stand.) We

Mary Blevins at the "Dump".

discussed mountain dialects, ground cherries, growing up in the area and going away to find work, finally touching on local "haints."

Booger Rock is one place where natives never want to be found alone after dark. Joe Blevins informed us that his wife, Nellie, grew up near Booger Rock and invited us up to meet her. And so we traveled up Beech Mt. Road, known by one and all in the area as Booger Rock Road.

Booger Rock - Where you don't want to be after dark.

Bristol

"A Good Place to Live" states the lighted sign that has marked State Street since 1910. Bristol is a good place to visit as well. Designated as the Birthplace of Country Music by the United States Congress, it lives up to the name with performances somewhere almost nightly, especially during summer months.

You can stand with one foot in Virginia and the other in Tennessee before heading to the Mountain Music Museum and Gift Shop in the Bristol Mall or downtown to the historic district and the Birthplace of Country Music Alliance.

Paramount Center for the Arts on State Street was restored in 1991 to it former glory, but with air conditioning. It's a great place to see a show.

Bristol Rhythm and Roots Reunion Festival lasts three days in September featuring many genres of music at about 15 stages and venues. Featured also are crafts, food, and children's events.

If you're not enthralled with music, you may be in the wrong place. Or racing could be in your blood and the track is just outside of town. The Bristol Motor Speedway and Dragway is billed as the world's fastest half-mile track. There are daily tour opportunities.

"I never ate pumpkin until I made this cheesecake and now it is the ONLY way I will eat pumpkin!!"

Pumpkin Cheesecake
Tammy Martin

2 (8oz.) pkgs. of cream cheese, softened
½ can of pumpkin
½ cup of sugar (Splenda can be used and works wonderfully well)
½ tsp. of vanilla
½ tsp. of ground cinnamon
2 eggs
   dash each of cloves and nutmeg

Crust:

2 cups crushed cinnamon graham crackers (crush in food processor)
6 Tbsps. of melted butter

Mix graham crackers with melted butter in bowl. Spread mixture into a 9-inch pie dish. For batter mix cream cheese, pumpkin, sugar, vanilla and spices at medium speed with electric mixer until well blended. Add eggs; mix until blended. Pour mixture into crust and bake at 350° for 40 minutes or until the center of the cheesecake is almost set. Cool the cheesecake and refrigerate for a least 3 hours or preferably overnight before serving. Garnish as desired.

Environmentally Friendly Window Cleaner

1/2 cup vinegar   *1 qt. water*
1/3 cup ammonia   *Put in spray bottle.*

> A sense of humor is like a needle and thread; It will patch up a great many things.

Refrigerator Ginger Bread
Eleanor Greer

1 cup shortening	4 cups flour
1 cup molasses	4 eggs
1 cup sugar	2 tsps. soda
½ cup raisins	2 tsps. ginger
1 cup buttermilk	2 tsps. cinnamon
1 tsp. salt	½ tsp. allspice

Cream shortening, sugar & eggs together. Add molasses and raisins. Mix flour with spices, salt, and soda. Add dry ingredients and milk alternately a little at a time. Store and bake just the amount you want. For cup cakes bake 20 minutes and for a loaf, bake 30 minutes at 350°.

Sour Dough Bread
Rachel F. Nutter – Glade Spring, VA

Starter (Keep in refrigerator) Feed Starter every 5 – 7 days.

¾ cup sugar	1 cup warm tap water
3 Tbsps. potato flakes	

Feed Starter and leave out of refrigerator 8-10 hours loosely covered before making bread.

Bread

6 cups of bread flour	1 cup of starter
1 Tbsp. salt	1/3 cup of oil
¼ cup sugar	1 ½ cups warm tap water

Mix bread ingredients together and place in large oiled mixing bowl and cover. Let rise 8-10 hours at room temperature (double in bulk). Punch down and divide into three loaves. Place in greased bread pans and let rise until double in bulk. Bake at 350° for 30 minutes.

Strata Milano
Juanita Campany – Abingdon Boarding House - Abingdon, VA

Abingdon Boarding House, built in 1840, is the oldest boarding house still operating in Abingdon. Though modernized, it still retains the charm of an older home that has seen lots of living. Eleanor Roosevelt's father, Elliot, was a frequent boarder. Juanita and Lawrence Company make you feel very welcome with a wonderful breakfast.
www.abingdonboardinghouse.com

6   slices bacon (cooked crisp & crumbled)
3 ¼ cups milk
1   cup ricotta cheese
½   cup feta cheese, crumbled
1   tsp. salt
½   tsp. cayenne pepper
5   eggs
1   cup chopped red onion
1 ¾ cups diced tomato
1 ½ tsps. dried rosemary
1   (16 oz.) loaf sourdough bread
     (1 inch slices, toasted & cubed)
     grated fresh parmesan
     paprika

Whisk eggs, milk, cheeses, salt, and cayenne until well blended. Combine tomato, onion, and rosemary. Arrange half of bread cubes in 9 x 13-inch dish coated with cooking spray. Spoon half of tomato mixture over bread and pour half of milk mixture over tomato mixture. Repeat procedure with remaining bread, tomato and milk mixtures. Sprinkle with paprika and grated parmesan. Cover and refrigerate 8 hours or overnight. Bake at 350° for 45-60 minutes. Crumble bacon on top. Let it set 15 minutes before serving.

Summer Salad
Barbara Faulkner – Abingdon, VA

1 (8 oz.) pkg. cream cheese
1 carton whipped cream
1 can chunk pineapple
1 can fruit cocktail
1 cup powdered sugar

Combine cream cheese and sugar, mix well. Fold in whipped cream & drained fruits. Chill for at least 1 hour and serve.

Moonlite Drive-In

Say you're feeling sorta nostalgic about the good ol' days, remembering days without cell phones or internet, of nickel cokes with nickel peanuts to pour inside, poodle skirts, pop beads, white sidewalls or a white sport coat – and Elvis as king. Since you can't go back there, the next best thing might be motoring down to a drive-in picture show where some good memories linger. For a short but exquisite time, everything could feel right, in a slower world.

You can still spread your blanket on the ground, choose a lawn chair or stay in the car while munching a hot dog, hamburger, or shared popcorn at the Moonlite near Abingdon. It is hanging on, along with a few hundred across the nation, due to the efforts of owner, William Booker, who bought it in 1992. Come 2009, the landmark will celebrate its 60th year, having been in business since 1949.

Only a handful of drive-ins are on the National Historic Registry. The Moonlite is one of them. It is also a State Historic Landmark. But that's rarely why anyone goes. In fact, reasons are quite diverse. Drive-in buffs show up, church youth groups come for a glimpse of yesteryear, old and young still love the casualness of it. Unusual reunions have even taken place, like the "conception" reunion of a few years ago where all the attendees vowed to have been conceived at the Moonlite.

Booker himself has a longstanding love affair with the drive-in. He hid in a trunk with a bunch of friends to sneak in without paying in 1970 – and got caught. He had to pick up trash for two weeks as punishment. And has not gotten over the place, though there's been plenty of work involved in keeping it running. The fence and the marquee both have caught on fire. Speakers started getting stolen. The poles are still there but sound now comes through on the radio.

In recent years, the Moonlite has begun to claim "world famous" status. People from a number of countries have visited including Japan, Australia, Great Britain, and Switzerland. At least two songs have been written about the drive-in and both get played regularly there. And guess what? If you carry a pack of cigarettes in your tee shirt sleeve - or not – it's one of the few places where smoking is still allowed!

**Ah, backseat, back row
Drive-in picture show
Ya got your daddy's car tonight
Eight straight hours of monster movies
At the Moonlite...**

Lyrics of song by Brenda Lee

Swiss Chocolate Cake
Rachel F. Nutter – Glade Spring, VA

1   box Swiss chocolate cake mix
1   small instant vanilla pudding
3   eggs
1   cup oil
1 ½ cups buttermilk

Mix together by hand and bake in 13 x 9-inch pan for 30 minutes at 350°.

Icing

1   (8oz.) cream cheese   1   cup confectioner sugar
½   cup sugar   1   (12 oz.) Cool Whip

Let cream cheese and Cool Whip reach room temperature then mix all ingredients together and ice cake.

*"Teaching them to observe all things whatsoever I have commanded you: and, lo, I am with you always, even unto the end of the world. A-men." **Matthew 28:20***

Taffy
Louise Fortune Hall – Damascus, VA

2   cups sugar
¼   cup water
3   Tbsps. vinegar
    lump of butter size of walnut
3   tsps. vanilla

Prepare in an enamel pan. Put ingredients into pan and boil at low heat, without stirring until hard-crack stage when tested in cold water. Pour into buttered platter and pour the vanilla over syrup and cool until it can be handled with buttered hands. When I say, "cool until it can be handled" it will still be hot. Pull until white and cool – as long as it can be pulled. Stretch into long strip onto table. Cut into 1 ½ inch pieces. Let cool. Wrap each piece in square of wax paper, twisting ends. Keep in refrigerator.

Louise Fortune Hall

She's the go-to person in Damascus when you need to know anything about the town or surrounding areas. Noted and treasured as the area's historian, Louise Hall wrote *A History of Damascus* in 1950 and an addendum in 1978, but states unequivocally, "That's it, I'm not writing the thirty years up to 2008!"

At ninety-six years old, Hall is quick witted and fun to visit. After a phone call that kept extending, she finally said, "Just come on over to see me tomorrow and I'll give you a book to read and tell you more, too. But I'm going out for lunch, don't come until the afternoon."

Louise at her piano.

Upon arrival, a diminutive, vivacious lady who could have easily convinced us that she was seventy something met us at the door. Conversation with Mrs. Hall ranged from Christmases past and present to education to history to making taffy to paw paws and Ginkgo trees to the trails that run through the town where her roots are entrenched, the tunnel, trains, and more.

Louise Fortune was the oldest in a family of five sisters and the only one surviving. Her father, Walter H. Fortune was the first Mayor when Damascus became a town (1904) and Captain W.P. Fortune, her grandfather, was the engineer who completed the railroad bed from Abingdon to Damascus in 1901. An uncle, Robert Fortune became Damascus's first doctor in 1898. Except for the years at school in Maryville and Radford Colleges, all her life has been spent in the town where she was born. The former teacher is a one-woman cheering squad for her corner of the world.

"It was a wonderful place to grow up," exclaims Hall. "My parents had a mini-farm just a block off Main Street with a huge garden, hogs, and two cows. One sister and I had a playhouse over the springhouse and the others had one over the wood house. We were right across the road from where the Old Mill Restaurant is now and our land ran to Beaver Creek. *(continued on next page)*

"Men here had plenty of work and people came from other places to find jobs. The trains were hauling timber out of the mountains daily - huge chestnut and hardwood logs that would be hard to imagine now. The bad thing is they weren't careful about over cutting so the timber boom only lasted about twenty-five years."

"A number of other businesses came to town, often bringing new people in. My husband, George Hall had come to work at the Chemical plant. We married in 1934 and had three children who were raised right in this house."

Mr. and Mrs. Hall were founding members of the Appalachian Trail Club and supporters of whatever bettered the community. It would be much easier to list the civic organizations, boards, and commissions that Louise Hall was *not* involved in than the numerous ones that she has been.

> Bless God for what you have, Trust God for what you need.
> -*Unknown*

Don't like marshmallow cream or sticky fingers, but love chocolate??? Then this recipe is for you!

White Chocolate Rice Krispie Treats
Tammy Martin

7 cups rice krispie cereal
2 bags of white chocolate chips
1 cup of peanut butter

Over a double boiler melt white chocolate chips and stir in peanut butter. Be certain to stir to keep from sticking to pan. Once chips have melted and peanut butter is thoroughly mixed in, pour rice krispie cereal into a large bowl and pour mixture over the cereal. Mix until all cereal is completely covered and pour into a lightly greased 9 x 13 inch Pyrex-type dish. Place in refrigerator to set quickly, but let stand at room temperature before cutting. Delicious!!!

Moonshine Tales

I'll tell you about one of the most honest, hard-working men I ever met in my life. I'm not gonna name any names but he lived on the Tug River and he made moonshine in those mountains where it was extremely difficult to get in and out of. His still was next to impossible to find when he was younger. You had to cross the river from the West Virginia side or go over a mountain that had been stripped in the 40's, down along a creek. No decent road, you mostly walked in there.

If we caught him and he had to stand trial, we could say, 'Be in Grundy at such and such a date and time,' and on that day and at that time, he'd be sitting on the courthouse steps waiting.

Once we served a search warrant for non-tax paid whiskey. He had gotten older by this time. Several officers searched the house and I went out to a little corncrib that stood a short distance away from the house. I could see him in the building as I approached. As I went in the door, I could see a jar lying on it's side with clear liquid running out. By the smell, it was pretty obvious what the contents were. I took a handkerchief and picked the jar up to recap it and asked, 'Is that yours?'

"Yeah, I seed ja coming and thought I'd better pour it out," he replied dryly.

Upon entering I noticed he was putting together a copper coil. Again I questioned him, 'that your coil?'

"No, son, it hain't mine," he answered.

'Well, whose is it?'

"You know I can't tell you that!"

"Okay, but you tell the guy it belongs to that if he wants it, come and see me," I replied.

I spent twenty-one years working for the Bureau of Alcohol, Tobacco, and Firearms (ATF) after ten years as an investigator for the ABC Board in Southwest Virginia. I worked everything this side of the Clinch River. At that time when the ATF was really involved in enforcing non-taxed alcohol, it was a job for a young man. So was the moonshining trade because that is not easy work. They go in with a tremendous load and come out with a load. During the process, there is always the threat of getting caught hanging over their head.

The last time the man I'm speaking of was arrested at moonshine still, I told him, "You're going to have to quit doing this type of work" and spelled out the reasons. "1. You're getting too old. 2. You're leaving too much sign of where you've been. You're making too big a road to the still. 3. You can't hear as well as you used to and 4. You sure can't run fast enough anymore. Why don't you just give it up?"

"Son, let me explain it to where you'll understand it," he said emphatically as he looked me squarely in the face. "See that railroad track over there across the river? I used to work for them. They laid me off twenty-five years or so ago. Now, I don't want none of your damn social security, hain't got no retirement. My job is making liquor. As long as water runs downhill and they sell me sugar, I aim to do just that. Cause that's my job.

Your job is to catch me if you have to. That's the way it is so just do what you have to do. But as long as that water runs downhill and I can buy sugar, making liquor is what I'll do – as long as I can walk."

I had a deep and abiding respect for the man. I respected him for his honesty and his work ethic. He made moonshine whiskey for a living, that was his job. And I was glad when, around this time, the powers that be decided the local and state law enforcement could take care of the illegal whiskey dealings. For me, the mountains had gotten steeper, the violators were faster, and I was not one bit sorry to leave the enforcement of the non-tax paid whiskey business to the state.

Legend: Here's a little story that supposedly happened in the late 1920's, probably during prohibition. It took place in the Camp Creek area near Clintwood and involved a moonshiner named Calvin Swindall. His nickname was "Bear" and that was what everybody knew him by – and most everybody knew him. Some ABC and/or prohibition officers raided a still and everybody ran. Bear took out across a field and reached a fence. As he was going over, one of the officers yelled, "Come on back Bear - hell, everybody knows ya!"

Bear yells back over his shoulder, "Hain't me!" and kept running.
I can't say that's the truth, but it was told on him for years. Don't know if he ever owned up to it or not but he sure took a lot of ribbing about it!   -*as told by Elmer Younce*

Jam sessions are big news these days and cropping up all over. That was not the case over 50 years ago when Gene Boyd began a Thursday morning jam in the Star Barber Shop on West State Street in Bristol. While statistics are not in, his must be one of the longest-running jams in Southwest Virginia.

Nellie Blevins

Nellie Bollinger Blevins grew up on the well-kept hillside farm where her father and mother raised all kinds of plants and doctored their children with home remedies that generally worked well. Her mother had an ulcer on her ankle and used bloodroot to heal it. Bloodroot was also used for boils. Nellie and her siblings had to eat some type of seeds mixed with molasses in the fall to de-worm them. Now she'd love to know the names of the plants her parents used as medicine and is beginning to recognize some. She is also "teaching Joe to be a farmer."

Her brother had an encounter with something near Booger Rock while going to his grandmother's house after dark. He never knew what it was and it didn't grab him but he ran into something that couldn't be explained. Whatever it was terrified him enough that he almost tore his grandmother's door off trying to get in the house quickly.

Joe and Nellie raised their family in Lenoir, NC but have come to the mountains for the summer the past 10 years. Like most farm kids, she has plenty of memories. One is about a mean ol' Dominecker rooster:

"We had this ol' rooster that just loved to flog me and I hated that critter. I dreaded going to feed the cows and milk because he was sure to chase me. One day I went in what we called the cutting room of the barn – where the animal feed was kept – to get feed for the cows. That mean rooster hit me right in the back and that was it for me. I turned on him with murder in my heart and took out after him. He must have felt it because he ran for his life and I stayed behind him. We went around and around that barn until neither of us could barely run. I stumped my toe, which later turned black and blue. About then he slowed and I grabbed him around the neck as I was almost falling. I wrung his neck good, thinking, "You won't never flog me again!" and threw him down the hill before feeling any remorse. Then the milking still had to be done. The consequences began to dawn while doing the milking. "Oh lordy, he's the main rooster. My mom is gonna give me a whipping for this." As I came outside after finishing, still thinking of the punishment that lay in store for sure, something caught my eye. That ol' Dominecker was up, staggering around. But he stayed away from me from then on! In fact, he'd run if he saw me walking toward him."

Until it's demise in 1977, the Virginia Creeper was the highest elevation of any rail line east of the Rockies. The depot at the highest elevation in the eastern United States was Whitetop.

The Old Dasher Churn
Author Unknown – submitted by Gaye Robinson

The old dasher churn that Mother had,
How well I recollect,
The many times unwillingly
With it I did connect.
It didn't seem to offer much
In pleasure, fun or joy,
It only had a dreaded task
For any girl or boy.

That Old wooden churn had a prominent place
–The best place on the floor.
And there it stood defiant like
Inside the kitchen door.
Sometimes the preparation
I glimpsed as I sped
And rather than face the bitter facts
As I passed I turned my head.

At churning time I always wore
A custom odd but clean,
It protected me from splashes,
And a safeguard to the cream.

It was one of Mother's aprons
With the strings tied in a bow,
I resembled the man in our garden
That we called the old scarecrow.

It nearly always happened
And it gave me much concern,
Whenever I had great plans made –
I always had to churn.
Now just to stand and agitate
That sometimes stubborn cream
Was not a job a girl or boy would like,
Twas not a pleasant dream.

But time has made a change in me
And now I am confessing,
The churn that I once hated
Has really been a blessing.
This lesson has been taught to me
Twas hard for me to learn –
If the world has bread and butter
Somebody's got to churn!

White's Mill

    A visit to White's Mill is a trip to an earlier and slower place. It's easy to visualize horses pulling a wooden wagon up to the door loaded with corn or wheat to be ground and neighbors visiting on the porch. The mill has been in the same spot for over two hundred years so there's been much to discuss in all that time.

    Fox and geese games aplenty must have been played to wile away the time, likely on a game board drawn on a cardboard box.

    The Mill has been on the State and National Registries since 1974. The water-powered mill ran until 1989. After being neglected for over a decade, it has been in the process of being restored and operated by the White's Mill Foundation since 2001. A mercantile featuring products from over 100 local artisans, writers, and musicians is located in an old store across the road and should not be missed. Ph. 276-628-2960

Grayson County

Contents

Apple Cinnamon Dip	178
Apple Cobbler	178
Apple Pie	180
Beer Rolls	180
Blackberry Cake	181
Broccoli and Cauliflower Slaw	180
Broccoli Cornbread Casserole	181
Butter Pecan Pound Cake	182
Cabbage Rolls	182
Caesar Salad	183
Chicken Casserole	184
Chicken Salad	184
Chocolate Éclair Cake	185
Cracker Peanut Butter Candy	187
Darlous's Chocolate Gravy	186
Easy Homemade Rolls	187
Fried Cabbage	187
Grandma's Favorite Pumpkin Pie	189
Grandma's Orange Candy Cake	189
Grape Wine	190
Gumdrop Cookies	190
Ham Rolls	193
Hearty Jam Session Soup	194
HoBo Apple Pie Filling	195
Homemade Macaroni and Cheese	196
Hush Puppies	197
Libby's Red Velvet Cake	198
Mom's Real Homemade Mincemeat and Pie	199
Old Fashion Fudge Cake	201
Old-Time Fruit Salad	203
Old Pool Room Hotdog Sauce	203
Potato Salad	206
Pound Cake	206
Rhubarb Cake	209
Rhubarb Strawberry Dessert	209
Riz Biscuits	211
Sliced Dill Pickles	211
Squash Casserole	212
Sugar Free Cherry Jell-O Dessert	212
Tomato Dumplings	213
Venison Roast for Crock-Pot	213
White Fruit Cake	214
Zucchini Fritters	214

**Cabin near entrance to Grayson Highlands State Park:
Photo by: Robert Skeens**

Legend of the Thunder Hole

The next ridge south of Grayson Highlands is a place called Thea's Ridge. Years ago, a fairly thriving community was there, with several log cabins and small houses. Most of the land was open for cattle grazing and gardens and such. Nowadays, the roads that once ran through there are all grown over; mostly just a path can still be followed where the roads were.

This story happened when they were building a road sometime around the turn of the twentieth century. Of course, picks and shovels and maybe horses were being used and it was some hard work. They came to a hollow place in the ground and were trying to figure out what could have caused it. Some thought maybe big trees had been taken out and this was a stump hole. Others held that it was an Indian burial ground and thought there might be artifacts and no telling what in there. The road was built beside the hollow.

A couple of fellows decided to come back sometime and dig further in the hole and see what they could find. So they picked a sunny day when they didn't have anything pressing to do and headed up there. No more had they started digging than thunder started rumbling, the clouds rolled in and rain came down so hard they had to quit.

Doggone if they didn't go back the second time and the same thing happened. They got soaked and stopped by a cabin to get out of the storm. Word spread about a thunderstorm coming up each time the two tried to dig in the hollow.

People started wondering if they were disturbing some kind of spirits, maybe a spell the Native Americans had put on the place. Anyway, it didn't seem that that hole should be disturbed. Of course, at that time, mountain people were pretty superstitious and not highly educated.

But the two buddies did try one more time. Right away the thunder clapped loudly and they took off as the downpour came. Today laurels have grown in the hollow and no one disturbs the thunder hole. I have wondered if it might be good to go and dig in there sometime when we're having a drought. Many times I've walked by the hollow but I just stick to the old path and don't bother the Thunder Hole.   - *Roald Kirby*

Galax, VA is an independent city with ties to both Grayson and Carroll Counties since it sits on the border of both - the county line runs down part of Main Street.

Apple Cinnamon Dip
Regan Delp – Independence, VA

1 (8 oz.) pkg. cream cheese	½ tsp. cinnamon
1 (8 oz.) container vanilla yogurt	½ cup apple sauce
1/3 cup honey	– sweetened
	1 Tbsp. brown sugar

Combine all ingredients. Chill. Serve with sliced apples or fruit of choice.

Apple Cobbler
DeEtte Fine

½   cup (1 stick) butter or margarine
2   cups sugar
2   cups water
1½ cups sifted Martha White self-rising flour
½   cup shortening
1/3 cup milk
2   cups finely chopped apples
1   tsp. cinnamon

Heat oven to 350°. Melt the butter in a 13 x 9 x 2-inch baking dish or sheet cake pan. In a saucepan, heat sugar and water until sugar melts. Cut shortening into flour until particles are like fine crumbs. Add milk and stir with a fork only until dough leaves the side of the bowl. Turn out onto lightly floured board or pastry cloth, knead just until smooth. Roll dough out into a large rectangle about ¼ inches thick. Sprinkle cinnamon over apples; then sprinkle apples evenly over the dough. Roll up dough like a jelly roll. Dampen the edge of the dough with a little water and seal. Slice dough into about 16 slices, ½ inch thick. Place in pan with melted butter. Pour sugar syrup carefully around rolls. (This looks like too much liquid, but the crust will absorb it.) Bake for 55–60 minutes. An all-time favorite, this swirled cobbler is moist and juicy yet flaky on top. This cobbler may be made with other fresh, frozen or canned fruits, such as blackberries, cherries, or peaches. If packed in liquid, drain and substitute for part of the sugar syrup. Always use 2 cups of liquid.

> "Take my yoke upon you, and learn of me; for I am meek and lowly in heart: and ye shall find rest unto your souls. For my yoke is easy, and my burden is light."
> *Matthew 11:29-30*

Debby Stringer – 98.1 WBRF-FM Radio

Debby Stringer was born into radio on New Year's Eve, 1954. Feeding and diaper changes often took place at Station WPAQ (740 AM) in Mt. Airy, NC. Her father, Ralph Epperson, who built the station (the first in Surry County) and began broadcasting there on February 2, 1948 was committed to the people and music of the area. He strongly believed in the beauty and meaning of everyday rural life and because of that, included broadcasting lost pets, gospel music, traditional musicians, and obituaries.

The Merry-Go-Round program, begun by Epperson and now the third oldest live radio program in the United States, takes place every Saturday morning featuring local and traveling musicians. Kelly Epperson is the manager of the station and continues his father's vision of celebrating the culture of the region.

Recordings of numerous regional groups who played live at the station over the years are located at the University of North Carolina in Chapel Hill's Library. Some are also available on a Rounder Records CD. Mr. Epperson's recordings of early Grand Ol' Opry stars who stopped by the station are housed at the Smithsonian Institute and the Library of Congress.

WBRF (98.1 FM), located in Galax, VA, bought in 1985 and managed by Stringer, is also a major supporter of traditional, gospel, and bluegrass music. "We don't want to be a cookie-cutter station. Our announcers are live, down to earth, and present a family type show. My father always said, 'If twelve stations are doing the same programming, why would I want to be number thirteen?'"

The station's broadcasts from the Rex Theater have been immensely popular and now can be heard all over the world, via worldwide web. Daily emails come from people all over the globe, expressing their enjoyment of the music. The Rex has become a tourist destination. The Galax Old-Time Fiddlers Convention can be heard on 98.1, and this year, so can shows from the Blue Ridge Music Center. Gospel music, preaching, teaching, and community service still have a place on the line-up of the Station. Mr. Epperson's vision now beams from a little corner of Virginia into a world badly in need of down to earth family traditions and values.

The restored Rex Theater in Galax hosts many cultural events and shows, the most famous one being "Blue Ridge Backroads," a radio show on Friday nights at 8 o'clock. It is broadcast on WBRF-FM (98.1) year round and features old-time and bluegrass bands.

Apple Pie
Sue Osborne - Mouth of Wilson, VA

4	large tart apples	¾	cup flour
1	cup sugar	1/3	cup butter
1	tsp. cinnamon		

Arrange sliced apples in pie shell. Take ½ cup of sugar and mix with cinnamon. Sprinkle mixture over apples. Sift other ½ cup sugar with flour. Cut butter into flour mixture until crumbly. Sprinkle butter/flour mixture over apples. Bake at 450° for 10 minutes. Bake a 350° for another 40 minutes or until top of pie turns slightly brown.

Troutdale, VA encompasses a one-mile circle around the town's center. Once a lumber boom town and still incorporated, there's no taxes or auto decals. Neither is there a police department.

Beer Rolls
Wilma Testerman – Whitetop, VA

2 cups Bisquick   1 small can beer (approx.)
1 Tbsp. sugar

Mix all ingredients, using enough beer to make the mixture spoonable. Put 1 tsp. oil in each section of a muffin pan. Spoon in mixture filling section 3/4 full. Bake at 425° until brown - about 12 minutes.

Broccoli and Cauliflower Slaw
Lois Smith - Galax, VA

1 head cauliflower   ¼ cup red onion
1 head broccoli   1 cup mozzarella cheese
1 jar bacon bits   1 cup sharp cheddar cheese
1 cup mayonnaise   1 Tbsp. Dijon mustard
1 cup sugar

Place cauliflower in food processor and shred like slaw; empty into large bowl. Shred broccoli in the food processor and add to bowl. Chop onion and add. Mix other ingredients together and pour over broccoli, cauliflower and onion. Blend all together.

*"My wife, Connie, is a **Great** cook and this is one of my very favorite dishes. I like this dish hot out of the oven in a bowl with milk or cream on it. It's so good I included it in a song I wrote. The song is titled "**Country Cooking**" and the third verse is:*

I'm goin' to the country – it's the place for me
Mighty tasty food – you will see.
Country ham, molasses and tea
The blackberry cake will set you free.

Dale Morris
Wolfe Bros.
String Band
Elk Creek, VA
www.geocities.com/
wolfebrothers

Blackberry Cake
Dale Morris – Elk Creek, VA

1 stick melted butter	2 cups flour
1 cup sugar	2½ tsps. baking powder
2 eggs	¼ tsp. salt
1 tsp. vanilla	1 cup milk

Mix all together and beat well.

½ stick butter	
2 cups blackberries	¾ cup brown sugar

Melt butter. Spray a 9 x 13-inch baking dish with non-stick spray and pour butter in baking dish. Spread blackberries over the butter and sprinkle brown sugar over the berries. Pour yellow cake batter over berries and bake at 350° for approx. 30 minutes.

Broccoli Cornbread Casserole
Susan O'Brien

1 box Jiffy cornbread mix	
1 Tbsp. flour	1 (8 oz.) pkg. shredded cheddar cheese
1 box frozen broccoli (thawed and drained)	1 medium onion chopped
2 eggs	2/3 stick margarine, melted

Mix together. Bake 25-30 minutes at 400° in a 8 x 8-inch baking dish.

Butter Pecan Pound Cake
Allen Blevins

1 box butter pecan cake mix	1 cup water
1 can coconut pecan icing	¼ cup powdered sugar
½ cup oil	¼ cup chopped pecans
3 eggs	

Spray bunt cake pan. Put sugar and pecans in bottom of pan. Mix the other five ingredients and beat at medium speed for 2 to 3 minutes. Bake at 325° for 45 to 55 minutes. Let the cake cool in pan, but turn it on the plate and leave the pan over the cake until it cools. It is so moist it seems to squat if you take it from the pan before it cools.

"This recipe was a favorite in our family when I grew up in West Virginia."

Cabbage Rolls
Martha Anderson – Rixey's Market - Independence, VA

1½ lbs. lean ground beef
(half beef and half pork may be substituted)
1 cup uncooked minute rice
1 large onion (diced)
  salt
  pepper
  cabbage leaves
1 quart tomatoes
1 quart sauerkraut

Mix together beef (pork), rice, onion, salt, pepper – set aside. Separate leaves of cabbage and pour boiling water over each to wilt. Leaves <u>must</u> be soft or they will not roll. Form small pups of meat mixture and wrap in leaves. Lay these in large pot or crock-pot. Pour tomatoes and kraut over cabbage rolls. Add enough water to barely cover. I cook mine on medium in crock-pot overnight.

The waxy green leaves of the Galax plant once were shipped to floral shops all over the U.S. by rail. The town of Galax was named for the plant in 1905.

The Davis Bourne Inn

In 1998, the New River was designated the first American Heritage River. It is considered by many to be the second oldest river in the world after the Nile.

Being served dinner cooked by chef Stephen Volinskus on the veranda of Davis Bourne Inn is about as good as it gets. Between the vistas stretching in front and the divine meal that required no effort on your part, well, it's something to write home about. A stay at the inn with Tony and Taphne Volinskus is elegance and down-home combined. I don't know how they accomplish that but it is so nice that they do! Journeys End Restaurant serves dinner and Sunday Brunch. www.davisbourneinn.com

Caesar Salad

Tony & Taphne Volinskus - Davis-Bourne Inn – Independence, VA

- 6 cloves garlic
- 8 filets of anchovy
- 2 Tbsps. Dijon mustard
- ¼ cup sugar
- 1 cup red wine vinegar
- 2 cups olive oil
- ¼ cup fresh lemon juice
- 1 egg

Blend well in the blender and then keep refrigerated.

- 2 heads Romaine
- ½ cup Parmesan cheese
- croutons
- black pepper

Add dressing over lettuce. This recipe can be halved.

Old Fiddler's Convention

Because of an Old Time Fiddler's Convention started in 1935, Galax became known nationally and internationally, and today is noted for preservation of old-time music. What started as a weekend fundraiser by the Galax Moose Lodge now lasts a week, with competitions of various sorts nightly. Wayne Henderson, who has won 1st place on guitar more than a dozen times states, "There's so many talented young people coming now, it gets harder to win. And that's good, cause that's what it's all about. They'll keep the music going."

Chicken Casserole
Geneva C. Higgins – Galax, VA

1 fryer or 5 or 6 chicken breasts
1 pkg. herb stuffing
1 stick margarine
2 cups broth
1 can of cream of chicken soup or cream of mushroom soup or cream of onion soup
1 carton sour cream
   curry powder to taste
   onion powder to taste

Boil chicken until done, then debone. Mix stuffing with melted margarine and 1 ½ cups broth. Line bottom of glass casserole dish with ½ of mixture. Mix together can of soup, sour cream, ½ cup broth, chicken, and curry and onion powder to taste. Pour this mixture over bottom layer and sprinkle remaining stuffing on top. Bake at 350° for 30 minutes.

Chicken Salad
Lois J. Rogers – Galax, VA

3   cups cold, diced chicken
1½   cups chopped celery
¼   cup chopped green peppers
2   hard-boiled eggs
1½   cups mayonnaise

Mix chicken, celery, peppers and eggs. Chill. Before serving, mix with the mayonnaise. Garnish with the whites and yolks of the hard-boiled eggs to look like daisies.

Breakin' Up Christmas

Each year the Rex Theater in Galax hosts a Breakin' Up Christmas party on the first Saturday in January, following a tradition of unknown origins. It seems to have been popular in most of Grayson County, especially the Round Peak area.

Sometimes the celebration lasted about two weeks, going from house to house. It was winter and farm chores were less demanding, so what better chance to have a whingding? Boy, did they know how to throw a party! Furniture was moved into one room or out of the house completely, leaving plenty of room for dancing. Food was plentiful and so were beverages. One lady remembers her mother making one water bucket available to the men. The content was clear like water, but the smell was different.

Women cooked whole country hams, vegetables, biscuits, and pies or cakes. The musicians stood in the doorway so they could be heard in different rooms. Children played or danced, and fell asleep in a corner if the excitement wore them out. There was a Breakin' Up Christmas square dance and a lively song which featured these lyrics:

Santa Claus come, done, and gone.
Breakin' up Christmas right along.

"This is one of the favorite desserts at our New Years Breaking Up Christmas party every year for musicians, neighbors, and Parkway friends. The secret of its goodness is carefully cutting the graham crackers to fit the Pyrex dish and leaving no air spaces between the pudding mixture and crackers and frosting."

Chocolate Éclair Cake

Lois Anderberg Koji – Galax, VA

1   box graham crackers
2   small boxes French vanilla instant pudding
3   cups milk
1   (8 oz.) tub Cool Whip
1   (16 oz.) dark chocolate fudge frosting

Line bottom of a 9 x 13-inch Pyrex dish with graham crackers. Mix pudding, milk, and Cool Whip. Pour half of mixture over crackers and carefully spread. Add another layer of crackers and pudding mixture. Cover with another layer of crackers. Stir frosting and spread on top. Wrap tightly with plastic wrap and refrigerate for 24 hours.

"I am a native of Whitetop, VA, in the western part of Grayson County, VA. Whitetop is the 2nd highest mountain in VA. I attended a one-room school - Mud Creek -grades primary thru 7th grade, 1940 - 1947. We had one teacher, no aid, no electricity, no water and a coal stove. This school (Mud Creek) had a unique ritual about 3 weeks before Christmas. The older guys would climb into school thru the bell tower and nail the door shut! This was called "Shutting the Teacher Out." The teacher came to school, found the doors nailed shut, and then she and the children would make an agreement. She promised a treat for Christmas (usually ½ lb. candy, 2 oranges & nuts). The teacher would go home and the students would go home too. This was a Happy Day for all. Teacher always complied nicely. We loved our teacher (most part) and all respected her. "This was the Good Ole Days" when things were bad, but we didn't know it. We were all in the same boat."

Darlous's Chocolate Gravy

Darlous (Ecky) Blevins Jones – Whitetop, VA

- 6 cups milk or 3 cups of milk & 3 cups of water
- 6 Tbsps. powdered cocoa (more if you like)
- sugar to taste
- 2 drops vanilla
- 2 Tbsps. butter
- flour
- water

Pour milk in pan, let come to a boil then push back on stove. Add cocoa and sugar to taste; mix well. Add vanilla and butter; stir well. Mix flour and water to make thickener (no corn starch then). Pour slowly into mixture as you stir. Get thickness you want then serve with hot biscuits. It is delicious! *"We could hardly sleep when my mother told us she was making this for breakfast. Next morning we'd smell this cooking and it was really an eye opener!"*

"I remember this as a special Sunday morning treat from my Mom. If she wanted us to hurry and get ready for church she just hollered, "Chocolate Gravy!"

-Linda Sharpe

Cracker Peanut Butter Candy
Mary Margaret Pack – Fries, VA

- 1 cup carnation milk or low fat can milk
- 3 cups sugar or diet sugar
- ¾ cup of peanut butter
- 24 saltine crackers (crushed fine)
- 1 tsp. vanilla

Combine sugar and milk in saucepan, stir and boil for 4 minutes. Remove from heat. Add peanut butter and vanilla; then crackers. Stir well. Place in buttered dish and let cool.

Pray for a good harvest, but keep on hoeing.

"Easy" Homemade Rolls
Emma R. Phipps – Mouth of Wilson, VA

- 2 cups warm water
- ½ cup sugar
- ¼ cup shortening
- 2 pkgs. dry yeast
- 2 tsps. salt
- 1 egg, beaten
- 6½ cups to 7 cups plain flour

Put warm water in large mixing bowl. Add yeast, sugar, salt, shortening, beaten egg and mix well. Add about 4 cups flour; mix in with large spoon. Gradually add rest of flour. Mix by hand until mixture is neither sticky nor dry. Cover and allow to rise until doubled in bulk. Punch down, make into rolls, and allow to rise again. Bake at 375° until desired brownness. Makes 18 to 30 rolls.

Fried Cabbage
Alvin Bilbry – Fries, VA

"Fry some fatback to eat with cabbage. Leave 3-4 Tbsps. of drippings in frying pan. Put pot of water on to boil. Chop a cabbage head like kraut or slaw. Dump chopped cabbage into boiling water til wilted (blanched). Dip out into frying pan. Add salt and pepper to taste. Fry about 5 minutes. Eat it with cornbread that you've had baking. I always bake mine at 425° so it'll get good and brown and be tasty!"

Stevie Barr

He plays the banjo like one possessed – and he is – possessed of the talent and knowledge and abandon to make the instrument spring to life in a unique way. His band, *No Speed Limit* has been making waves locally, regionally, and nationally. Barr's songwriting and composing give an added dimension to the already exceptional band.

Stevie Barr "Gettin' down" on his banjo on the street at Galax, VA. Looking on is the publisher of this book.

We visited Stevie in his shop, Barr's Fiddle Shop, on a hectic day. (Maybe every day is hectic.) The phone was ringing, a friend dropped by, customers and lookers wandered in, and he still tried to work in a short interview with us while waiting for students who were expected shortly. He informed us that he has about a hundred students; along with the other irons he has in the fire.

At the Davis-Bourne Inn the night before, we had met two couples from Scotland who were traveling the Crooked Road and came particularly to Galax to visit Barr at the fiddle shop. They had met him on the Scottish Tour of Crooked Road musicians. He tells us he has been to other countries such as Switzerland and France, though he is not bragging. Stevie is quite modest.

Younger looking than his thirty-something age, Barr appears hyperactive. I wondered if, under different circumstances, some pill happy doctor would have put him on Ritalin. But his parents were smart and put him on music instead. Or he just absorbed it, since his parents, Tom and Becky Barr, are musicians who once played with the Whitetop Mountain Band.

Tom Barr is a master fiddle maker, who repaired instruments at home before opening a shop in Galax. He now is semi-retired, leaving the son in charge of Barr's. Since Stevie basically grew up there, it bears the evidence of being left in good hands.

Grandma's Favorite Pumpkin Pie
Leta W. Farmer

1 cup cooked pumpkin (mashed)	2 Tbsps. flour
1 cup milk	1 tsp. cinnamon
1 cup sugar	2 Tbsps. butter
1 or 2 eggs beaten	1 9" piecrust

Bake your crust. Mix ingredients together. Bring to a slow boil, stirring well. Pour into crust. Bake at 350° until brown. Serve with whipped cream.

Grandma's Orange Candy Cake
Barbara Walton – in memory of her grandmother, Marvella Harris

1 cup butter	1 (15 oz.) box golden (white) raisins
2 cups sugar	
6 eggs	1 (16 oz.) bag of orange candy slices
1 Tbsp. vanilla	
4 ¼ cups flour	½ tsp. baking soda
2 (8 oz.) pkgs. Chopped dates	1 tsp. salt
2 cups chopped pecans	¾ cup buttermilk
1 (4 oz.) can shredded coconut	

Cream butter and sugar until fluffy. Beat in eggs one at a time. Add vanilla. Mix dates, pecans, coconut, raisins and chopped candy pieces with ¼ cup flour. Sift together 4 cups flour, baking soda and salt; then alternately fold into creamed mixture with buttermilk. Fold in fruit mixture. Spoon into well greased and floured 10-inch tube pan. Bake at 300° for 2 hours and 30 minutes.

Glaze:

2 tsps. orange rind	¼ cup lemon juice
2 tsps. lemon rind	¼ cup confectionary sugar
¼ cup orange juice	

Mix together and boil to make syrup and then pour on cake to make a glaze.

The first court of newly formed Grayson County was held in 1793 in William Bourne's barn.

Peggy Baldwin grew up near Whitetop Mountain, moved away to the city for 40 years, but came home to retire. She picked up a guitar and plays often, especially at Mount Rogers School and at Chilhowie. She is rightly proud of the rebuilding of Whitetop station, which she worked diligently for. It is now a visitor and community center. Every Friday night the station is host to music, dancing, and good food from 6:30-10:00 PM.

The place to listen or be in a great jam on Tuesday nights is Stringbean Coffee Shop/ Shamrock Tea Room in Galax. It spills onto the street if the weather is warm enough, with two more going inside. There's great food, coffee, tea, and dessert. A Rook game could break out or you could meet old and/or new friends.

Grape Wine
Peggie Baldwin (Guitar player)

1 gallon crushed grapes
water
sugar

To 1 gallon of crushed grapes, put 1 quart of warm water. Cover and stir every day for 9 days. On 9th day strain. To a gallon of juice, put 1 quart of water. Add 2 lbs. of sugar for each gallon of juice. Let it ferment for 2 weeks, stir, and then bottle in dark bottles or store in dark cool place.

Gumdrop Cookies
Glenna Walls (plays banjo)

1 cup margarine	1 cup brown sugar
1 egg	1 tsp. vanilla
½ tsp. baking soda	1½ cups flour
½ tsp. salt	½ tsp. baking powder
1 cup cut-up gumdrops	1 cup quick oats (uncooked)
½ cup chopped nuts	

Cream the margarine and brown sugar. Beat in egg and vanilla. Combine dry ingredients. Gradually add to creamed mixture. Stir in oats, gumdrops and nuts. Drop by teaspoonfuls on ungreased cookie sheet. Bake 12 to 14 minutes at 350°. Makes 5 to 6 dozen cookies.

Emily Spencer

"I believe the kids come out of these classes with a strong sense of self and of their place in the world," states Emily Spencer, speaking of the old-time mountain music program at Mount Rogers Combined School. "They take ownership in the band. Being part of the Albert Hash Memorial Band does so much for each student's self-esteem."

Grades eight through twelve receive academic credit for the string band classes, just as other schools give credits for classes that teach marching band instruments. This was not the case when Albert Hash began volunteering at the school in 1982. He and his daughter, Audrey H. Hamm began teaching and started a student's band. After his passing, Hamm took the work upon herself and Emily volunteered once a week for a number of years. After quite a bit of supplication and some pleading by Spencer, the local school board finally made string band classes part of the curriculum for the 1999-2000 school year.

Though raised in Arlington in northern Virginia, Spencer always felt an affinity for mountain music. Her early training was in violin, but two songs that she liked to play stand out, "Sourwood Mountain" and "Irish Washer Woman." Heading south to college at Wise, VA as soon as possible, she felt right at home and continued to learn more about mountain music. Jont Blevins, who was born in 1900, taught her a great deal about playing claw hammer banjo in a style dating back to the Civil War. Her instruments of choice are guitar and banjo, though she can pick a tune from anything with a string on it – and maybe some without.

Spencer and her husband, Thornton, who is a master fiddle player, are part of the Whitetop Mountain Band, begun by Albert Hash in the 1940's. This band has had a number of great musicians through the years who have done much to preserve the Whitetop region's style of playing, especially on fiddle and banjo. Their daughter, Martha, is part of the band; rounding it out is Debbie Bramer, Jackson Cunningham and Spencer Pennington. The band has been called the most celebrated string band from the Blue Ridge – high praise for an area that breeds outstanding musicians like rabbits.

It's an amazing thing to watch Emily Spencer teach music. We didn't sit in on her school classes, but went to the Community Music Program that is held on Tuesday nights at the school and includes all ages. Young and old hit licks together and cheered each other on. She played along with the students, stopping occasionally to make a suggestion to someone about a method of making their sound smoother. Everyone is encouraged to play by ear and to switch among instruments, which she does frequently, from banjo to

Emily Spencer at work, teaching banjo lessons.

guitar to fiddle, whatever the student is playing. Even the young students change instruments quicker than most of us can change from flip-flops to lace-ups. Everyone was immersed in the music, learning from each other as well as the teacher.

Some school students stopped by, along with a couple who had already graduated. "We can't keep them from coming back even after they graduate," Emily laughs. "They're always dropping by because we're like family here."

A considerable amount of recognition has come their way since the inception of what is now called the Albert Hash Memorial Band. Performances have been given at many venues across the United States, television and radio have done features, and magazine and newspaper articles have been written.

"We are like a sports team, though, because we loose players each year and have to rebuild," explains Spencer.

While that's true, Grayson County has a magnificent heritage of music; young musicians are easier to come by than in most places. While ability appears to float through the air or be imbedded in DNA, and it certainly stands out in some bloodlines, there's an added explanation for the seemingly endless talent. Older musicians will help anyone with a desire and a willingness to learn. It's tradition and has been that way through the ages. That's why old-time is still around and will be – because the talented play for the joy and the love of it and want to pass it on- and the band is part of that connection.

"Our little school is a special place," says Emily Spencer. "It is rare in today's world to have a place like this. My hope is that people will appreciate the uniqueness and let us continue the program as it is."

Grayson Highlands State Park

"Wild Pony" of Grayson Highlands going after a hemp necklace.

If you have not been an outdoor enthusiast in the past, a trip to Grayson Highlands might turn you into one. The loftiest state park in Virginia offers fantastic views, alpine meadows, camping, and hiking. Horse trails in the park lead to longer trails in the Jefferson National Forest and the Appalachian Trail footpath can easily be accessed. There are trout streams for fishing, wild ponies, and a great picnic area. On the third Saturday in June, the picnic area echoes with the picking and singing of the Wayne Henderson Music Festival and Guitar Competition. A two-day Fall Festival held the last full weekend in September winds up the season with a bang.

Ham Rolls
Pattie Fields

1 package of Carl Budding Ham
   low fat cream cheese
   green onions
   ranch dressing, dry
   whole-wheat Tortilla shells

Chop ham into small pieces. Chop green part of onion. Add cream cheese and ranch dressing together. Spread on Tortilla shell about ¼ inch from sides. Roll. Chill and cut however you want, and serve.

"I like to have friends over for soup on winter evenings before the Tuesday night jam session at Stringbean in Galax. A stick-to-your-ribs soup fortifies everyone to face the cold and dark, bundled up and carrying instruments. Here's a favorite that's also wonderful to take to any friends who are feeling under the weather. It tastes great and it's full of things that are good for you!"

Hearty Jam Session Soup

Amy and Rick Boucher – Independence, VA

¼ cup olive oil
4 cloves minced garlic
1 cup chopped onion
½ cup chopped celery
1/3 cup flour
1 large stalk broccoli, chopped (peeled stalk and tops)
4 cups potatoes cut in bite-size pieces
3 cups chicken bouillon
3 cups milk
6-8 skinless chicken tenders, cut in small bite-size pieces (or cut up skinless, boneless chicken breasts)
salt and pepper
1½ cups grated or chopped Mountaineer cheese from Meadow Creek Dairy in Galax (their cheese is available via the Internet, www.meadowcreekdairy.com. If you cannot get Mountaineer, you may substitute Swiss or medium cheddar.)

In large kettle sauté onion, garlic and celery in olive oil. Add flour and blend. (This is your thickener.) Add bouillon and milk. Bring to a simmer and add the broccoli. Simmer 15 minutes. (Eventually, the broccoli mostly dissolves into the soup.) Add the potatoes. Simmer till the potatoes are just cooked (firm and not mushy – this will depend on the variety of potato you're using. Test frequently with a fork for doneness). Add the chicken and cook until the chicken is done, only about five minutes more. Turn the soup down and gradually add the cheese until it blends in. Season with freshly ground pepper and salt to taste.

Serve with the bread and salad that your guitar-playing friend brings. Cut the recipe in half for smaller groups. It does not freeze well and is best straight from the stove, but keeps fine in the fridge for a couple of days. It's so yummy that odds are you'll only get leftovers once.

Pauline Lemons

Her smile lights up the room. "I love everything I do here," she exclaims, referring to her job at Rooftop of Virginia. "And I love all the people." She helps with programs for the seniors, serving food, and does a good deal of paper shredding. It doesn't matter what the job, she approaches any with a positive attitude.

"We couldn't do without Miss Pauline," laughs Terri Gillespie, Public Relations Manager/Planner. "She keeps us straight. There's no one like her."

Miss Pauline came to Galax as an eight-year-old from North Carolina with her family. Their belongings were packed in a wagon pulled by horses and they drove across the frozen river to get to their new home.

Walking to school was a given at that time. But Lemons has spent much of her life walking: to work at a cotton mill and a hosiery mill. Later she walked to Galax Hospital and eventually to Twin County Hospital, where she retired. Anyone who has ever driven up the hill to Twin County can appreciate that walk. Of course, she didn't walk every day; sometimes someone gave her a lift, as she is quick to say.

Along the way, Miss Pauline raised 8 children and 2 grandchildren. Neither she nor her husband ever drove. Perhaps that is why she is spry today. Or maybe people were made tougher back in August 1914, when she came along. One thing is for sure, if attitude is everything, then at 94 Miss Pauline Lemons has it all.

Hobo Apple Pie Filling

Martha Hall – Mouth of Wilson, VA

3 gallons apples (sliced thin)
4 lbs. sugar
1 cup corn starch
1 cup tapioca
1 Tbsp. apple pie spice
1 tsp. nutmeg

Mix all together in container and let set for 3 or 4 hours. Then pack in jars and process in hot water bath for 50 minutes. We cook it on the stove until thick and can it hot. It always seals.

Hobo pies keep several workers busy, preparing and cooking them over a fire at the Grayson Highlands Fall Festival. They are a hit with the crowds every year.

"For as long as I can remember, this dish was made by my mother, Beulah Crockett Youngblood. It was one of those recipes that were <u>never</u> written down – you <u>just</u> made it! Everyone loved this dish of Mama's and of course, I learned to make it. It has always been a staple at all our family gatherings and it has become a favorite of everyone who tries it. I had to finally make a written version of the recipe for my children when they married and for so many others who have wanted the recipe.

Our family was a very musical family and at every gathering, after we ate, there was always singing. Daddy (Norris Youngblood) played the guitar and my sister and I played the piano. Daddy and all my brothers, sisters, and cousins would sing and harmonize. The delicious home cooking and singing were a part of every family get-together. Wonderful Memories!"

'Homemade' Macaroni & Cheese
Pat Youngblood Cox – Galax, VA

salt water	1 cup shredded sharp cheddar cheese
2 cups elbow macaroni	squeeze butter
1 tsp. salt	1 can evaporated milk
chunks of Velveeta cheese (or Kroger's Nice N' Cheesy)	coarse black pepper to taste

Put water in a medium – sized kettle, add a little salt and bring to a boil. Add 2 cups of elbow macaroni to the boiling water. Stir often. Cook for about 10 minutes, until macaroni is swollen and soft. Keep enough of the water with the macaroni to just barely see it (almost to the top of the macaroni). Pour ½ of the macaroni & water into a casserole dish. Sprinkle with ½ tsp. salt. Cut chunks of Velveeta cheese (or Kroger's Nice N' Cheesy) and put it in the macaroni. Then sprinkle with about ½ cup shredded sharp cheddar cheese. Squirt a little bit of squeeze butter onto the macaroni & cheese. Pour the rest of the macaroni in the dish and again salt it as before. Repeat the cheeses. No need for more butter. Use can evaporated milk to fill up the casserole (about to the top of the macaroni). This milk makes the macaroni and cheese real creamy & delicious. Before baking, sprinkle coarse black pepper on top. Bake at 350° - covered for 15 minutes, uncovered for 10 minutes. Delicious!!

Rooftop of Virginia CAP Craft Center

The First Baptist Church building in Galax celebrated its 100th birthday in 2007. The cathedral-type building is not a church these days, but a community action agency. Various assistance programs are housed here for the citizens of Grayson and Carroll Counties, as well as the city of Galax. Rooftop was formed in 1965 as a result of the enactment of the Economic Opportunity Act of 1964 to help low-income citizens. The Craft Center, the most widely known of their agencies, has been operating for 40 years, offering a wide variety of authentic handmade crafts from local artisans, as well as books and CDs. Rooftop also has a satellite summer location in Grayson Highlands State Park.

Place a layer of marshmallows in the bottom of a pumpkin pie, and then add the filling. You will have a nice topping because the marshmallows rise to the top as it bakes.

"Hush Puppies"
Peggie Baldwin (guitar player)

½ cup sifted flour
2   tsps. sugar   1   egg
½   tsp. salt   ¾   cup milk
1½ cups yellow corn meal   chopped onion (optional)

Into corn meal add flour, sugar, salt, egg, and milk, stirring lightly. Chopped onion may be added if desired. Drop a full tsp. for each puppy into deep hot fat (oil). Fry a few at a time, do not crowd. Drain on paper towel. (Serve hot)

Ward Manor at Buck Mountain is situated on 280 acres of loveliness. The Bicentennial Farm has been in the family since 1777 with a grant from the Commonwealth to Nathan Ward. The house was built in 1915. The current owner heard his grandmother, Rose Ward Jenkins say of her 1st cousin, Wade Ward, renowned banjo player. "He just hung out in bars and music halls playing that music all the time. He never did get out and work in the fields like other folks."   www.wardmanor.com

You don't stop laughing because you grow old. You grow old because you stop laughing.

*"We take call in orders. We do birthday and wedding cakes. Our specialty is our sour dough breads. We are also getting ready to start good country cookin'. Our name will be changed to: **Grandmama's Bakery and Country Kitchen**."*

Libby's Red Velvet Cake
Pauline A. Phipps – Grandmama's Bakery – Independence, VA

1½ cups sugar	2 Tbsps. cocoa
2 eggs	¼ tsp. salt
2¾ cups cake flour	1 tsp. baking soda
2 cups cooking oil	1 tsp. vinegar
1 cup buttermilk	red food coloring
1 tsp. vanilla	

Cream together oil, sugar and vanilla. Add eggs one at a time, beating after each addition. Add red food coloring and vinegar. In a separate bowl, mix together flour, baking soda, salt, and cocoa. Sift flour mixture and add to batter alternately with buttermilk. Pour batter into three 8-inch round cake pans and bake for 30 minutes at 350°. Remove from oven and let cool before icing.

Icing:
- 1 box powdered sugar
- 1 stick margarine
- 1 tsp. vanilla
- 1 (8 oz.) cream cheese
- 1 cup chopped pecans

Cream together softened cream cheese and margarine. Mix well. Add powdered sugar and vanilla, blending until smooth. Fold in chopped pecans before frosting the cooled cake.

Mom's Real Homemade Mincemeat and Pie

Farm recipe of Mary Jane Johnson submitted by Joyce Johnson Rouse – Independence, VA

- 3 cups cooked, then ground meat (usually beef, but venison works great too)
- 1 quart applesauce or 12 chopped apples
- ½ pound seedless raisins
- ½ cup of cider vinegar
- ¼ cup water
- 3 cups sugar (or substitute honey and molasses combination)
- ½ tsp. allspice
- ¼ tsp. ground cloves
- ¾ tsp. salt
- ¾ tsp. nutmeg
- 1 heaping tsp. cinnamon
- 2 Tbsps. brown sugar
- ¼-½ cup brandy or rum (optional) be sure to put it in the cooking pot, not the cook!

Mix all together and heat while stirring until it begins to bubble, reduce heat and simmer gently for 15 minutes. Makes 3 pies. I freeze mincemeat in 3 containers until needed. Fill unbaked pie shell with 1/3 of mixture. If deep dish, add 2 peeled, sliced apples on top and cover with top crust or cobbler topping. Bake at 375° for about 40-45 minutes. Top with ice cream or whipped cream. Have cholesterol checked after eating 3 pieces with ice cream!

The New River Trail State Park extends 57 miles, from Galax to Pulaski, VA, including a 5-mile spur into Fries. The trail parallels the New River for 39 miles and Chestnut Creek for 12 miles.

Joyce Johnson Rouse – Earth Mama

The earth could use more mamas like Joyce, who is dedicated to making it a better place. Not only is she concerned with the renewing of natural resources, the healing of each individual's spirits are addressed through her music. The energy field around Rouse fairly crackles with enthusiasm for life and the work she does.

The day we met, Joyce told us of a song she'd written, *Virginia Beauty*, and then she said, "Come on over to the courthouse where

Earth Mama Joyce Johnson Rouse catches a sunbeam in her window.

> Be thankful for dirty dishes; they have a tale to tell, while others are starving, we're eating very well.

there's a piano and I'll sing it for you."

And so we followed across the street and up the twisting stairs to the top floor of the 1908 Courthouse in Independence for a private concert. The beauty of her voice blew us away. The lyrics are lovely, but are brought to life by Rouse's singing of them. Now we understand how one can "heal the earth one song at a time."

Virginia Beauty

Used by permission of Joyce Johnson Rouse 2007 Rouse House Music (ASCAP)
Earth Mama Music – www.earthmama.org   all rights reserved.

> I never tire of the beauty of Virginia,
> From the mountains to the Chesapeake.
> I lift my eyes to the wonder of the skyline.
> It takes my breath and I can hardly speak.
>
> Virginia Beauty is always with me
> Everywhere I go. Until I can get home
> To Virginia Beauty singing out to me,
> There is nowhere that I'd rather be.
>
> I walk inspired by the beauty of Virginia,
> Cardinals whistling and pretty dogwood days,
> I lift my hands to preserve her pristine beauty,
> From the coal ridges eastward to the Bay.

Chorus

I am inclined to be always in Virginia—
Tidewater breeze to the Appalachian Trail.
I love the song of a Blue Ridge summer evening—
The city lights and the country lanes.

Chorus

Bridge: Celebrate the miner, farmer, artist and the scholar,
Presidents and teachers, from the Piedmont to the cool, shady hollers.
Travel 'Round the Mountain or down the Crooked Road,
Expressions of the heart are everywhere you go.
Rappahannock and Elizabeth, the Clinch and the New and O
    Shenandoah.

I can rest my eyes on springtime in Virginia,
Apple Blossom and Maple Sugar Days,
The Blue and Gray resting peaceful on the hillside
Where together now their grandchildren play.

Chorus

Kate Irwin, a graphic designer who owns Duck Roost Inn (www.duckroostinn.com) utilizes the old chicken house on her place in a novel way - as her office. If she happens to be in the kitchen baking, as she was when we visited, the wonderful aroma makes you feel like you're going to visit grandma.

Old Fashioned Fudge Cake
Inez McRoberts – Galax, VA

2 cups self rising flour	2 eggs
2 cups sugar	1 cup milk
5 Tbsps. cocoa	2 tsps. vanilla
¾ cup oil	¾ cup hot water

Combine flour, sugar and cocoa. Add oil, eggs, milk, and vanilla. Mix well for 1 minute. Lastly, add hot water and beat. Bake in greased 9 x 13-inch pan at 350° for 30-35 minutes. Cool and frost with Chocolate Butter Cream icing.

Rixey's Market

I didn't notice a checkerboard. That is not to say one isn't there; in fact, it would be surprising if one wasn't around somewhere. A pot-bellied stove was nowhere in sight either, but must have been part of the décor in earlier days. Otherwise, Rixey's Market feels and looks and even smells like a traditional general store – with modern amenities.

Perhaps there were many things I didn't notice; the ambience of the place set me back in time to country stores of my childhood, particularly to Vesta Supply, owned by my father, Sparrell Dalton and his partner, Coy Vipperman, for many years. The feeling was so similar somehow, items for every need and little surprises hanging on the walls or on shelves. Ricky Anderson tells me they sold and changed tires at one time, as did my father.

Rixey and Norine Anderson opened the store in 1957 when their son, Ricky was ten years old and in the fourth grade. Ricky and his wife, Martha, celebrated the fiftieth year of the store's service to the community in 2007. And "service" is not an old-fashioned word here, he is proud to offer great variety and great service to neighbors and travelers alike.

Farm supplies - including vegetable and flower plants in the spring, handyman needs, groceries, hunting and fishing supplies, products for livestock and pets, fresh produce, and groceries can easily be found in the store. During hunting season, animals can be checked in here while the hunter grabs a hot dog for lunch and catches up on who's turned in the biggest deer or best antlers. Fishermen can pick up supplies and a license if it's needed. Hey, they can buy a lottery ticket or have a key made or get some cash from the ATM, too! As a bonus, Rixey's carries private label gourmet preserves, pickles, relishes, and sauces, along with local honey. And they encourage browsers.

Though Anderson went to college to be a teacher, the family store appealed to him more. His wife, Martha, has been the educator in the family, working thirty-one years with the Grayson County School system. She and their son, Andy, have been part of the family owned business through the years, helping out as needed.

Seven employees and Anderson keep the store open ten hours daily, from 8 AM – 6 PM. But they follow a custom of older days by closing on Sundays. Another flashback, remembering my father saying, "If I can't make a living in six days, probably wouldn't by working the seventh, either."

A tip of the hat to Rixey's, a marvelous blending of vintage and up-to-the-minute!

Old-Time Fruit Salad

Martha Anderson – Independence, VA

- 3 beaten eggs
- ¾ cup sugar
- 3 Tbsps. butter, softened
- ½ cup lemon juice
- 3 Golden Delicious apples, peeled and chopped
- 1 bunch seedless green grapes
- 1 bunch seedless red grapes
- 1 (20 oz.) can pineapple tidbits, drained
- ½ cup chopped pecans or walnuts
- 1½ cups mini marshmallows

Combine eggs, sugar and butter in saucepan; stir in lemon juice. Cook over medium heat until thickened, stirring constantly. It will thicken quickly. Refrigerate until cool. In a large serving bowl, place fruit, nuts and marshmallows. Pour dressing over mixture, and mix well. (To retain natural color of apples toss a little lemon juice on them). This is great for church picnics!

"But seek ye first the kingdom of God, and his righteousness; and all these things shall to added unto you."
Matthew 6:33

"I was 90 years old on 12/5/07. I used this recipe in my lunchroom called East End Lunch & Pool Hall in Proctorville, Ohio for many years. We sold lots of hot dogs and at that time we sold them for $1.00 a dog and made money!!! Try it."

Old Pool Room Hot Dog Sauce

Selma Bellville – Fries, VA

- 3 lbs. hamburger
- 3 onions – chopped
- 1 (46 oz.) tomato juice
- ½ large bottle catsup
- 2 Tbsps. garlic
- 2 Tbsps. chili powder
- 1 Tbsp. paprika
- 1 Tbsp. pepper (black)
- 1 Tbsp. hot sauce
- 1 Tbsp. A-1 sauce
- 1 Tbsp. Worcestershire sauce
- 2 Tbsps. sugar
- salt to taste
- cummin (plenty!)

Brown hamburger, add the rest of the ingredients and cook slow.

Blue Ridge Music Center

Over twenty years ago, when heritage tourism was unheard of, the city of Galax, VA donated over 1,000 acres of land at Fishers Peak to the Blue Ridge Parkway for the purpose of constructing a venue for travelers to experience and learn about traditional music. Though Congress established the area in 1985 to celebrate a living music culture and commemorate the roots of American music, the actual Center was a long time in coming.

Piedmont Blues artist Phil Wiggins on harmonica and John Cephas on guitar. They are well known Blues singers who perform as Cephas & Wiggins.

Joe Wilson, former Director of the National Council for the Traditional Arts, recounts how he came on board with the planning for the Center. Parkway Superintendent, Gary Everhart, approached Wilson with a request to put together a celebration for the 50th anniversary of the parkway. "We had a great day at Cumberland Knob with a crowd listening to groups from the area playing real mountain music."

"At breakfast the next morning, I told Gary, 'Sure was nice to listen to Appalachian music played by people from Appalachia. You guys usually have somebody from Connecticut or somewhere strumming."

He came right back with, "Well, when are you going to get a place built for traditional music to be played?"

Funding was a problem from the beginning. Rick Boucher, ninth district congressman from Abingdon became a champion of the Center. Obtaining money for the project became "kind of a career" as he worked tirelessly to see the completion of the $13 million undertaking. Many setbacks and years later, in 2001, the amphitheater began operation and was completed in 2005 with the opening of the 17,000 square foot Interpretive Center. It is now operated by a partnership between the National Park Service and the National Council for the Traditional Arts.

World-class interactive exhibits are planned as a permanent fixture inside the center but, presently, temporary displays highlight early pioneers of traditional music. There is a space for traveling exhibits as well. A luthiers shop shows how instruments are made by hand. The center houses a 100-seat auditorium, classrooms, meeting space, and a sales area. Volunteers have developed thirteen miles of hiking trails for those whose feet were made for walking instead of dancing.

The amphitheater, near the base of the hillside, can be reached by parking in the lot in front of the state-of-the-art interpretive center and walking across a bridge. From that stage, it is not unusual to hear songs that have existed so long their origins are unknown, with titles that you may or may not ever have heard of - *Pretty Polly, Honeysuckle Blues, Old Joe Clark, or Whoa Mule* could pop up any ol' time.

National Heritage Fellowship Award winners with names like Doc Watson, Etta Baker, Ralph Stanley, and Wayne Henderson have graced the stage of the amphitheater during the years it has been operating. Ricky Skaggs, the AltaKai Throat Singers from Central Asia, Del McCoury, and Roni Stoneman of Hee-Haw fame - whose family originally hailed from nearby Fries, VA – have performed on the same boards. But there are hundreds of local and regionally known (and not so known) bands that pick and sing here as well. In fact, the Center is much more concerned with presenting good music that reflects the historical traditions of these mountains than with big-name stars. One thing can be counted on; exceptional musicians will be on that stage.

Program Director, Debbie Robinson, has a different resident artist scheduled on site each day except Saturday for the 2008 season. You may see old-time musicians, storytellers, a pencil artist, or an instrument maker demonstrating his craft.

Jam sessions are welcomed and encouraged any day of the week, from May to November 2, and might break out any time two instrument- bearing musicians show up. "First Saturday" square dances will be featured this season. Free group lessons will be given from 4:30 – 5:30 and the square dance will begin at 6:00 on each first Saturday from June to September.

Continuing the heritage of mountain music is the goal of the Junior Appalachian Musicians Program that began in the fall of 2007. In that same spirit, a Youth Competition – guitar, fiddle, banjo, and mandolin - is held in July each year.

For the 6:00 PM program, a $3.00 donation is appreciated and a few special shows require as much as a $10.00 fee. Children under eleven are free.

Good picking at one of the main venues of the Crooked Road Heritage Music Trails, lovely scenery, interesting exhibits – what more is needed for a good time in the mountains? Well, perhaps a jacket, (even in July) an umbrella, and a chair!

Potato Salad
Leah Halsey – Mouth of Wilson, VA

5 cups boiled potatoes, chopped	½ cup sweet pickle, chopped
3 boiled eggs, chopped	¼ cup celery, chopped
½ cup onion, chopped	¼ cup green pepper, chopped

Place in large bowl and mix together.

Dressing:

2 eggs (lightly beaten)	9 Tbsps. cream or ½ cup milk and 2 Tbsps. margarine
4 Tbsps. sugar	salt and pepper to taste
6 Tbsps. vinegar	paprika

Mix in saucepan and place on medium heat. Bring to boiling point, stirring all the time. Remove from heat and cool. Pour over potato mixture. Sprinkle with paprika.

"This is one of my favorites from a collection of recipes gathered by women of the Galax community in 1956."

Potato Burn Relief
Janet Phipps – Galax, VA

If you receive any kind of burn, immediately cut an Irish potato, scrape the white flesh with a dull (butter) knife and pack the resulting pulp onto the burn. Repeat as often as necessary until the heat is gone. May be wrapped into place with a cloth. Guaranteed to keep burn from blistering!

Pound Cake
Lois J. Rogers – Galax, VA

1 cup butter	½ tsp. soda
3 cups sugar	½ tsp. cream of tartar
8 eggs, beaten separately	½ cup sour cream or buttermilk
4 cups flour	

Cream butter and sugar together. Add egg yolks. Alternate mixing the flour and the egg whites to the mixture. Just before putting it in the oven, dissolve soda, cream of tartar, and sour cream or buttermilk and add to other ingredients. Bake at 375° for 2 hours.

Audrey Hash Hamm

Her earliest memory is listening to E.C. and Orna Ball pick and sing with her father, a fine fiddler, while being rocked to sleep by her mother. A comforting sound and one that foretold the course of her life. While their names meant little to the child, all three are remembered today as pioneers and keepers of mountain music.

Another memory was of learning two songs from her uncle, Thorton Spencer, when she was about three years old - *Amazing Grace* and *Too Old to Cut the Mustard*. One day the preacher stopped by and her proud mother requested that Audrey sing for him. Much to her mother's chagrin, she burst into *Too Old to Cut the Mustard*, singing it through. "Well, I didn't know the difference," she laughs.

Her parent's home was always filled with music. People dropped by often and Hamm remembers a special quality of her mother's - who wasn't a musician but strongly supported her father. "No matter how many showed up, she always was able to put enough in the pot to feed everybody. She'd tell everybody they were welcome to eat and play music and visit but when it got bedtime, they needed to go home. That's a pretty good way to work things, isn't it?"

Albert Hash, Audrey's father, is one of the most revered names in Grayson County, especially when it comes to old-time music and craftsmanship of fiddles. Not only were his fiddles intricately carved in beautiful wood, the sound produced by those fiddles was renowned. His daughter remembers his wonderful sense of humor and how he read to educate himself. Early on he worked to better the community and pass on the traditional music.

"My father graduated from Mount Rogers when it was just the rock school," says Audrey. "When it became clear that a bigger school was needed, he told us he walked all over Grayson County getting a petition signed to expand the school. Only one person refused to sign it."

"Though he was still a teenager, he went to Independence to the School Board Office with a man Dad described as a big lumberjack. The big fellow walked into the office, sat down in a chair, propped his feet on the official's desk and stated bluntly, 'We've come after a school.' They got one, too," she laughs.

Audrey inherited her father's love of instrument building and worked with him for years. She also assisted him with the old-time lessons he initiated at the volunteer fire department. When he heard that Mount Rogers had failed for the second time to get a band director, he took action.

"If we can't be bigger or better, why can't we be different?" Hash asked, and began working to voluntarily start string music lessons at the school.

Audrey Hash Hamm

Albert and Audrey had to go before the school board to get the plan approved because it would take class time. When the chairman called Mr. Hash's name, he said aloud, "Go ahead, Audrey, and tell them what you want to do."

"Well, I *had* put on a dress but thought I was going to support him. I somehow stood up and explained our plan, just before my knees buckled out from under me. And the board approved it!"

They repaired old instruments so everyone would have something to play. Sadly, her father died early the next year, leaving Hamm to carry on the classes. With other volunteers, she managed for thirteen years. Seeing the effort that teachers put forth at the school for each student gave her an appreciation for the "big family" feel of Mount Rogers. While it may not be feasible to keep the school open, she hopes that it can at least become a cultural center or something to benefit the community.

"I guess the thing I am most proud of in my whole life is the year we got invited to bring our little band to Florida," she says. "We needed $10,000 dollars to go and I had no idea how we'd raise it, but we did."

A teacher (librarian, drivers ed, coach,) at Mount Rogers, Teena Moorefield, convinced Hamm it could be done. With Moorefield's help, they held yard sales, raffles, and dug up rhododendron to sell at a festival. Many people pitched in and they managed to take 22 kids and 8 adults to Cyprus Gardens to perform. They wore white jeans and t-shirts made up with a logo. Most of the kids had never stayed in a motel before. "I was so proud of them," she says. "And Emily (Spencer) has done amazing things with those kids since she's been doing credit classes. She is wonderful with the kids."

Today Hamm carries on tradition by teaching and building fiddles. One of her apprentices was 72 years old but usually they're much younger. "If someone really wants to learn, I'll hand them a block of wood and tell them to go build a fiddle. You learn by doing," she explains.

It is hard, grubby work, not at all glamorous as some might think, according to Audrey, who builds fiddles, but plays a guitar. "By the time you get down to the detail part, you begin to take pride in it and think maybe it was worth the rough work."

Rhubarb Cake
Audrey Hash Hamm

1 ½	cups rhubarb	½	cup milk
1	cup sugar	1	tsp. baking powder
1	egg	2	Tbsps. butter
2	Tbsps. flour		pinch of salt
1	cup flour (plain)		

Wash rhubarb and cut into pieces. Mix together: sugar, flour and egg. Place in well-buttered baking dish. Can use cake mix for top layer or mix flour, milk, butter, baking powder, and salt. Pour on top of rhubarb mixture. Bake at 350 ° about 30 to 45 minutes. Serve with whipped cream.

Home Remedy for Ants!

2 parts molasses
1 part sugar
1 part yeast
Mix together.
Place on plastic near where ants are.

Rhubarb/Strawberry Dessert
Janet Phipps – Galax, VA

4 cups rhubarb
1 cup sugar
1 (3 oz.) pkg. strawberry Jell-O (dry)
1 Jiffy yellow cake mix (or ½ regular cake mix)
1 cup water
1/3 cup melted butter

Spread chopped rhubarb in buttered 9x13-inch cake pan. Mix sugar, Jell-O, and cake mix together and sprinkle over rhubarb. Pour water and melted butter on top. Bake 50 minutes at 350°. Serve warm with whipped cream/topping or ice cream.

Wayne Henderson

Wayne Henderson is well known as a luthier and guitar picker. Grayson Highlands State Park hosts a festival named after the National Heritage Fellowship Award winner that has become the place to be on the third Saturday in June. He is generous in supporting fundraisers for worthy causes or for educational programs. But lesser known are his cooking skills.

In fact, Henderson was quite surprised to get to Washington, DC in 2007 and find that he was scheduled to give a cooking demonstration at the Smithsonian Folk Life Festival, along with instrument making. "Somebody decided that I could cook. I wasn't sure whether they were playing a joke on me or not."

But there was a stove and nice cooking area set up, featuring a mirror over the stove to reflect the skill of the chef. "Well," he said, deciding to have some fun, "I might be able to cook up some squirrel heads and gravy. These little ol' squirrels running around here are really friendly, so they shouldn't be too hard to catch."

The ladies who were assigned to assist each chef were aghast. "Oh, I don't think the Park Service would let anybody cook one of these squirrels. You'll get us all thrown out of here if you catch one."

On Saturday morning, Henderson showed up at the cooking site with a covered bucket, still wondering who got him into this. "Here's the three squirrels that James killed," he told the assistants, who stood ready to help prepare whatever was needed. "Can you all clean them?" (James Crumpler, a wood craftsman, was demonstrating rail splitting.)

The expressions on their faces were priceless. The cooking show turned out quite successful, between his badgering of the assistants, storytelling, music, and finally the cooking of the… well, the omelet.

(Though there was nothing in Wayne's bucket, he has eaten his share of squirrel heads and gravy, as have large numbers of mountain folk. "We used to dig around in the gravy with a big spoon to find the little heads. Just tap them with a teaspoon

to crack them open. The brains were a delicacy."

Lane Rakes of Shooting Creek in Franklin County used to can the squirrel heads, but not anymore due to the rabies outbreak.

It appears the song "Squirrel Heads and Gravy" sprang more from food on the table than imagination.)

Riz Biscuits
Bytha Lynn Moxley – Independence, VA

- 2½ cups all purpose flour
- ¼ tsp. soda
- 1 tsp. salt
- 3 Tbsps. sugar
- 1 cake yeast
- 1 cup warm buttermilk
- 1/3 cup shortening

Sift flour, soda, salt, and sugar. Dissolve yeast in warm buttermilk. Cut shortening into flour. Mix all together. Turn out on board. Knead until smooth. Roll ¼ inch thick. Brush tops with melted butter. Placed one biscuit on tops of another-making double biscuits. Cover, place in warm place to rise until double (about 1 hour). Bake 375° for 12 to 15 minutes. Makes about 1 ½ dozen.

The best things in life must come by effort from within... not by gifts from without.

Sliced Dill Pickles
Wilma Testerman – Whitetop, VA

- 1 gallon dill pickle chips
- 5 lbs. sugar
- 3 cloves garlic (chopped)
- 1 small bottle Texas Pete sauce

Drain pickles in colander. Put layer of sugar, a layer of pickles, a drop of sauce and some chopped garlic pieces into pickle jar. Continue layering until it is all in jar. You will have to apply pressure, packing each layer firmly. Replace lid and turn jar upside down for two days, making sure sugar is dissolved. Does not have to be refrigerated.

Squash Casserole
Glenna Walls (plays banjo)

6	cups yellow or zucchini squash or half of each	1	cup shredded carrots
¼	cup chopped onion	1	(8 oz.) pkg. herb stuffing mix
1	can cream of chicken soup	½	cup melted margarine
1	cup sour cream		

Heat oven to 350°. Cook squash and onion in boiling salted water for 5 minutes, drain. Mix soup and sour cream. Stir in the carrots; fold in the squash and onion. Combine stuffing mix and butter. Spread half stuffing mix in lightly butter 12 x 7.5-inch baking dish, spoon vegetable mixture over stuffing. Sprinkle remaining stuffing mixture over vegetables. Bake at 350° for 25 to 30 minutes until heated thoroughly and top is bubbly and light golden brown. Yields: 6 to 8 servings. (I do not add the shredded carrots.)

Garlic, cloves, and pepper flavors get stronger when they are frozen. Onion, sage, and salt get milder. Green pepper may change the flavor of frozen casserole.

Sugar Free Cherry Jell-O Dessert
Tricia R. Moore – Serendipity Antiques & Accents – Galax, VA

- 1 regular size pkg. sugar free cherry Jell-O
- 1 regular size pkg. sugar free cranberry Jell-O
- 1 (15 oz.) can no sugar added crushed pineapple
- 1 (14 oz.) pkg. fresh or frozen strawberries
- 1 ½ cups of chopped pecans
- Splenda

Slice strawberries and sweeten with Splenda. Drain pineapple and add enough water to juice to make 1 cup. Bring juice/water to a boil and dissolve Jell-O. Mix remaining ingredients. Pour half of mixture into square dish and refrigerate until set. Save other half to use as last layer. Mix the following and spread on set Jell-O mixture:

- 1 (8 oz.) pkg. cream cheese, softened
- 1 small carton lite Cool Whip, thawed
- ½ cup splenda

Tomato Dumplings
Linda J. Sharpe

1 quart tomatoes	sugar
salt	1½ cups Bisquick mix
pepper	milk

Place tomatoes in 2 to 3 quart sauce pan and add salt, sugar and pepper to desired taste. Bring the tomatoes to a rolling boil. Make dumplings with Bisquick mix and enough milk to make a stiff dough. Drop by spoonfuls into tomatoes; let them cook uncovered for approximately 8 to 10 minutes. Gently stir, turn heat off and cover pan and let set for 10 to 15 minutes.

The freshness of eggs can be determined easily. Place them in a bowl of water; if they float, throw them away. If they rise a bit in the water, use them quickly for baking!

"I'm the great niece of Uncle Charlie Higgins (Many times 1st place winner in Fiddle competition at The Galax Oldtime Fiddler's Convention.")

Venison Roast for Crock-Pot
Karen Higgins – Galax, VA

2-2½ lbs. venison roast	1 (6 oz.) can tomato paste
1 Tbsp. oil	1 Tbsp. brown sugar
2 stalks celery, sliced	½ Tbsp. Worcestershire sauce
1 medium onion, sliced	1 tsp. salt
1 (15 oz.) can tomato sauce	pepper to taste

In skillet, brown roast on all sides in hot oil. Place celery and onion in bottom of crock-pot. Place roast on top. In bowl, combine tomato sauce, tomato paste, brown sugar, Worcestershire sauce, pepper and salt. Mix well and pour over roast. Cover and cook on low heat 10 to 12 hours or until meat is tender. I use a quart of tomatoes instead of tomato sauce and tomato paste.

Southerners know how many fresh vegetables, fish, etc. constitutes a "mess." It's enough to feed the number of people in the intended household. Mountain folks add a little extra in case somebody drops in.

"This recipe is submitted in memory of my mother, Hessie Parks Wingfield. I have used this recipe often during my life time."

White Fruit Cake

Mary Jane Hollingsworth – Troutdale, VA

1½	cups sugar
½	lb. butter, softened
5	egg yokes, beaten
1	cup milk
3	cups flour
2½	tsps. baking powder
¼	tsp. salt
2	egg whites, unbeaten
1	tsp. lemon or almond flavoring, or both
1	lb. white raisins
½	lb. pineapple (glazed)
¼	lb. citron (optional) (glazed)
¼	lb. glazed cherries
1	lb. mixed nuts

Mix together. Grease pan lightly. Bake at 250° for 2 – 3 hours. You can test with toothpick and tell when done.

Zucchini Fritters

Janet Phipps – Galax, VA

3	cups shredded zucchini	1	egg, beaten
½	cup grated cheddar cheese	1	tsp. salt
3	Tbsps. minced parsley		dash of pepper
1	clove garlic, minced	1	cup Bisquick

Mix well and drop spoonfuls into heated oil in skillet turning until golden brown.

Mount Rogers Combined School

Eight caps and gowns were required for the 2008 graduating class of Mount Rogers Combined School, three more than was needed the year before. The entire student body consisted of ninety-three students in pre-kindergarten through twelfth grade. Numbers, however, can't begin to show the impact of the school on the community or the young people who pass through the doors daily.

In 1932, a small rock school was built with the hands, tools, and horses of local parents to educate the children who live in the foothills of Mount Rogers (elev. 5,729 ft.) and Whitetop (elev. 5,520 ft.) mountains, where the weather is temperamental, often changing in a matter of minutes. Ten miles away rain may fall, while at Whitetop the roads rapidly turn treacherous with ice or snow. Living on the "Rooftop of Virginia" (both mountains are well over 5,000 ft. high) has its highs and lows.

Nature has been very generous here. The beauty and diversity of the area is impressive. Being somewhat isolated has created a close-knit community, a place where neighbors look after each other and take pride in their school. Many of the parents and grandparents of today's students attended the school in their day. They know first hand that smaller classes mean more individual attention and that the teachers are interested in each child's performance.

Personal attention is also what principal, Judy Greer, thinks is the best thing about the school. "There are challenges for high school grades, though," she explains. "It's hard to offer all the classes needed. We have to use some on-line classes."

Josh Testerman, a member of the graduating class was adamant, "I wouldn't want to go anywhere else to school, especially around here. There's a big rivalry between us and the other high schools." But he admits, "It's bad to feel the way we do, though, I guess."

Mrs. Wilma Testerman started first grade there at six years old. She graduated and went away to college, came back as a teacher, and was principal for twenty years – retiring in 1999. "It was great attending school here," she says. "We had time for fun. So much of the fun has been taken out of the classrooms now."

It's been said that she ran a tight ship always expecting the best from each child. "I know you can do better," she'd tell a child having problems, and then proceed to help them do better. Testerman is proud of the students who needed help and got it at Mount Rogers. "Several students came to us who were not doing well in their former schools. Some were sad cases because they didn't feel part of anything. With help and success in even one area, they straightened up and walked proud. That made a difference in every part of their lives."

In 1982 Albert Hash, a local instrument maker and musician, and his daughter, Audrey, volunteered to start a string music band at the school. After he died unexpectedly, she carried on the program for about thirteen years. The band only met once a week and received no academic credit for the class, but they soon began playing at some local events. After all, this music was part of their culture and heritage, "almost innate," says Judy Greer. Many arts and cultural organizations, as well as the media became interested and the Albert Hash Memorial Band has carried old-time string music all over the United States.

"The band was well accepted everywhere they went, and have become highly acclaimed," states Wilma Testerman. "Through them, several grants have been given toward the program. Their performances have brought tourist into the area to hear more mountain music."

Mount Rogers School has lived on borrowed time for several years. Now Judy Greer understands that they may have one or two more years before a new school is completed about seventeen miles away. "I realize change is important. Transporting these children will be a nightmare because the weather is an issue here. I was raised a few miles away but really didn't understand it until I've drove up here the past two years to work."

"I want what's best for the children," says Mrs. Testerman, who lives near the school. "Those pre-school and kindergarten will be riding about an hour to get to school. In the winter, it will be still be dark when they're picked up. It will be a long, hard day for such young ones. Slick roads are a concern because it's a different world up here."

She once had to teach by demonstration the difference between Whitetop's road conditions versus Independence. Some curious flatland (compared to Whitetop) newsmen from Roanoke became intrigued because Mount Rogers was closed while the other county schools operated. They drove up one day, following Rt. 58 from Volney. Upon arrival, they proceeded to tell her that while the road was somewhat slippery, it didn't appear *that* much worse than the lower elevations.

"Try the road behind the school," she replied, knowing it was in bad shape. "Come back and tell me what you think."

They took off and were gone quite a while. Most of that time was spent getting out of the ditch they slid into. When the media returned, she politely ("I'm always very polite when I'm up to something!") told them there were a couple more roads they should try, Upper Helton and Mud Creek.

"Oh, we've seen enough for today," they said as they headed for the door.

"Did you send them back to interstate 81 across Whitetop and through Damascus?" I laughingly ask.

"Well, no, I didn't. It would have been a good lesson, but I really didn't want to get them killed. I just wanted them to have a good taste of road conditions here."

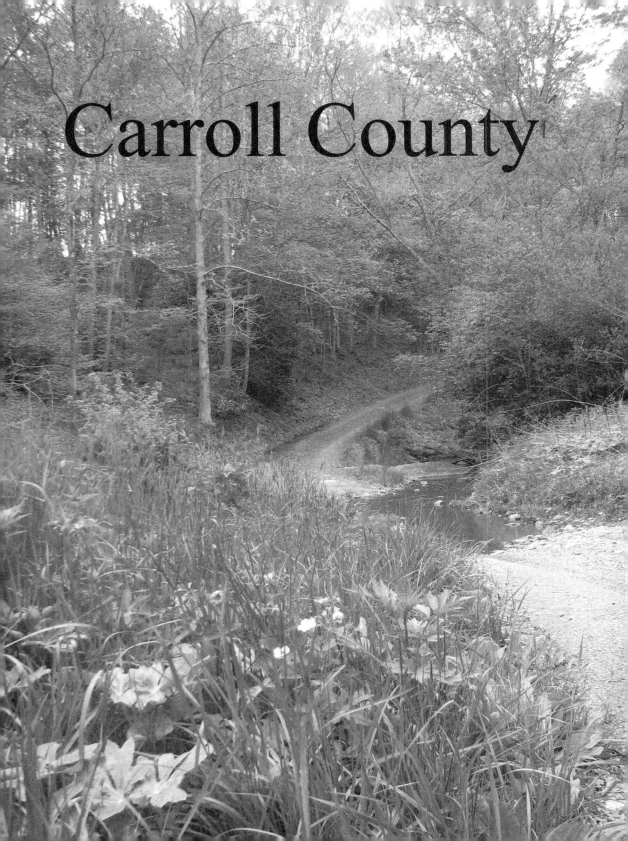

Carroll County

Contents

Aunt Robertha's Dilly Beans...............220
Barbeque Beef Tips............................220
Beans..221
Best Fried Apple Pie..........................222
Broccoli Casserole.............................221
Buckwheat Cakes..............................223
Buttermilk Pound Cake.....................222
Chocolate No-Bake Cookie Bars.....224
Corn Bread Salad..............................224
Corn Pudding....................................225
Fresh Apple Cake..............................225
Fresh Apple Cake..............................227
Garbanzo Salad.................................227
Gingerbread with Orange Sauce........228
Grits and Cheese Casserole...............228
Ground Cherry Preserves..................231
Hospitality Pie..................................232
Houston's Favorite Apple Pie............233
Hummingbird Cake...........................235
Key Lime Cake..................................236
Mama's Coconut Pie.........................237
Melt in Your Mouth Chicken Pie.....238
Molasses Stack Cake 239
Mom's No-Bake Blueberry Dessert..240
Mountain Breakfast Bake................241
Mountain Chow-Chow....................242
Never Fail Egg Custard Pie............242
No-Egg Cake 243
Old Timey Potato Soup...................243
Peanut Butter Fudge........................247
Pork Chop and Potatoes..................246
Rave Review Coconut Cake...........247
Red Cabbage Kraut.........................248
Refrigerator Pickles 248
Sausage Gravy.................................250
Sweet Pepper Relish........................251
Sweet Potato Biscuits......................251
Taco Soup..252
Tupelo Fruit Salad...........................252
Zucchini Relish...............................256

Peaceful winding lane along the Crooked Road.
Photo by Betty Skeens

Willard Gayheart and Bobby Patterson

Captured in pencil, this is one of Willard's remembrances with his pickin' partner, Bobby Patterson.

On Tuesdays during the summer, the two buddies can be seen picking, singing, and grinning at the Blue Ridge Music Center. Both are genial and knowledgeable, as well as fine musicians, therefore, a great introduction to visitors who may not be familiar with the music of the mountains. At first glance, one might think them two retired cronies with plenty of time and not much to do. That would be dead wrong.

Patterson is owner of the Heritage Shoppe which sells an almost perplexing array of items: instruments, CD's, cake decorating supplies, special occasion needs and who knows what else? It is the "store that has something everyone can enjoy." He is involved in the Galax Moose Lodge, which handles the Fiddlers Convention, along with other community organizations, and with his family.

Gayheart is an exceptional pencil artist whose work "conveys a message." "All my prints are real people and have a story associated with them," he says. He owns the Front Porch Gallery next door to the Heritage Shoppe in Woodlawn. His family also is involved with his endeavors.

Willard and Bobby have played with different bands through the years. Both are songwriters and often perform as a Duo, but for many years have been with a band they founded in 1972 called the Highlanders. The Highlanders are a crowd favorite wherever they appear.

So they may qualify for a senior discount but seem to have the energy of the proverbial spring chickens. With schedules that would tax people half their age, they appear relaxed and at ease with the busy lives they lead. And they very well fit the description of a friend, Joyce Rouse, who called them, "two little boys in older men's bodies."

Aunt Robertha's Dilly Beans
Tess Caldwell

    green beans (stringless, tender)
½ tsp. red cayenne pepper (each jar)
1 sprig fresh dill (each jar)
1 clove garlic (each jar)
2 cups vinegar (dark)
2 cups water
¼ cup pickling salt

Wash pint jars or quart jars if beans are really long. Place ½ tsp. red pepper, sprig of fresh dill and 1 clove garlic in each jar (double if using quarts). Wash and string beans, don't break. Boil beans about 10 minutes until barely tender. Drain. Pack beans on ends (straight up and down) in jars. Boil vinegar, water and salt and pour over beans. Additional batches of vinegar mix may be boiled as needed.

Barbeque Beef Tips
Nelson Lundy

¾	cup chopped onion	3	dashes Worcestershire sauce
½	cup butter	2	Tbsps. mustard
¾	cup ketchup	2	tsps. salt
1	cup water	½	tsp. black pepper
1/3	cup lemon juice	1/8	tsp. red pepper
3	Tbsps. sugar	3	cups lean chuck

Cook onion in butter until soft. Add remaining ingredients except meat and simmer for 10 minutes. Boil Chuck roast until tender in covered saucepan. When cool chop and place in casserole dish. Cover with barbecue sauce. Bake at 200° for 1 hour. Yields: 6 servings. Sauce may be used over hamburgers, chicken or wild game.

"Winter is a good time for a jam session at home. This recipe will feed about as many people as you can fit in your living room. Serve with cornbread, chopped onions and hot peppers. Get your friends to bring some side dishes. If they aren't apt to do this, I'll make some slaw, maybe fresh salsa, and some redskin potatoes. Scrub the potatoes and cut them in 2 or 3 pieces. Boil them until nearly tender, and then put them in an open pan in a medium oven with salt, pepper, and bacon strips on top. All of this can be done ahead and can set for quite a while until people want to eat. We started the bean parties so we could have the older musicians over on a Sunday afternoon and not have them feel obligated to cook. One of our fiddler friends always brought a package of beans "for the next party."

Beans
Melvin & Dea Felts – Mountain Ivy Band – Galax, VA

3	lbs. dry beans (I recommend half pintos and half great northerns)	salt water
½	lb. bacon cut in pieces	

Soak the beans overnight in plenty of water; in the morning, rinse them several times. Put them in a big pot along with the bacon. Keep them covered with water, and simmer them 3 hours. At the last hour, add a handful of salt. Do not add salt until the beans are pretty well done.

Broccoli Casserole
Pat Davis

2   pkgs. frozen broccoli in cheese sauce (cut in pieces)
1/3 cup mayonnaise   1   small onion chopped fine
     salt and pepper to taste   1   can mushroom drained
2   beaten eggs   ½   pkg. Pepperidge Farm Herb Stuffing
1   can cream of mushroom soup   2/3 stick melted margarine

Combine the broccoli, mayonnaise, salt & pepper, eggs, mushroom soup, onion, and mushrooms and mix well. Pour into greased casserole dish. Mix the stuffing and the melted margarine and place on top of the broccoli mixture. Bake at 350° for 45 minutes uncovered.

Best Fried Apple Pies
Ruth W. Turner – Woodlawn, VA

½ lb. bag dried apples
½ cup sugar (or sweetened to taste)
2 Tbsps. flour
½ tsp. cinnamon
½ tsp. nutmeg
¼ tsp. cloves
¼ stick butter
¾ cup evaporated milk

Wash dried apples, place in large pot and cover with water. Cook until done on medium heat, stirring several times. Watch carefully. They swell up and boil over if not stirred down. When apples are well cooked, mash with a potato masher. Mix flour with sugar and add ingredients in order. Stir well. Make desired amount of pastry using Jiffy mix and very little ice water, just to make a stiff dough. Pinch off egg size balls of dough and knead on a floured surface. Roll out wafer thin. Place large tablespoon of apple mixture on wafer circle (on one side) fold other side over and pinch edges together. Fry in hot canola oil until done and brown on each side. Stack in plate, cool and enjoy!

"Fried Apple Pies were always a treat for our family in Carroll County. Uncooked pies may be frozen, then thawed and fried."

Fried Apple Pie Pastry
Janice McCraw

4 cups self-rising flour
1 cup butter, softened
¾ cup water

Combine ingredients, mixing well. Refrigerate overnight. Yield: enough for about 3 dozen 4-inch pies.

Buttermilk Pound Cake
Lacie H. Kemp – Dugspur, VA

1 cup Crisco
3 cups sugar
6 eggs, separated
3 cups flour (don't bother to sift)
½ tsp. soda
½ tsp. salt
1 tsp. vanilla
1 cup buttermilk (not the fat free)

Cream sugar and Crisco. Add egg yolks one at a time, beating after each one. Beat egg whites until stiff and set aside. Combine flour, salt, and soda in separate bowl. Add flour mixture to creamed mixture alternately with buttermilk starting and ending with buttermilk. Add vanilla. Fold egg whites into batter. Bake in a large bundt or tube pan, greased with Crisco then floured. Bake at 350° for 1 hour or until done. Cool 10 minutes then remove from pan.

"My mother made up buckwheat batter and left it on the back of the wood stove all winter. She added buckwheat flour, soda, and hot water or milk on the mornings that she fried them for us. That was often because eggs were scarcer in cold weather. And she sold eggs, so we didn't get to eat them anytime we wanted to. Easter was the exception; our treat for that holiday was all the eggs we wanted to eat. Chickens used to roam and would sometimes make a hidden nest to lay their eggs. My younger brother, Garnie, and I (sometimes my twin sister) used to hunt for nests where the chickens were laying and sneak eggs out. If none could be found, we probably snitched a few from the henhouse. We'd gather rocks and make a little fire pit to build a fire and boil them in a bucket. Of course, a little salt had to be snuck out, with maybe a smidgen of butter. They were delicious! Best eggs I ever had in my life - maybe because we sneaked around to do it.

They killed hogs so we had meat to eat with the buckwheat cakes. Gravy is what you slosh on to make them good, and maybe one with syrup or molasses or apple butter to top it off. With seven children to feed, my parents bought Karo Syrup in a gallon tin bucket with a metal handle on it. They probably could have got by with a half-gallon except for my brother, Orby, who could eat more buckwheat cakes (12-15 at a sitting) and syrup than two or three other people. He was long and skinny and stayed that way all his life."

"Trust in the LORD with all thine heart; and lean not unto thine own understanding. In all thy ways acknowledge him, and he shall direct thy paths." ***Proverbs 3:5-6***

Buckwheat Cakes

Luvina Dalton – Laurel Fork, VA

1	cup sweet milk	1	tsp. soda
1	cup buttermilk	1	tsp. salt
1	cup hot water	½	cup self-rising flour
2	Tbsps. baking powder	2	cups buckwheat flour

Mix dry ingredients with buckwheat flour in bowl. Add liquids and stir, adding more buckwheat flour if needed. Batter should be good pouring consistency, a bit thinner than regular pancake batter. Skillet or grill needs to be hot and greased. The old-timey way was to rub a square of fatback meat over the pan before each batch. Note: For a slightly sour flavor, leave sitting out overnight.

Folk Remedy – Cure a Cough

"This was given to my sister who had whooping cough. She had coughed for about a year. Mama fixed this tea and she quit coughing and is now 82 years old."
—Barbara Caldwell

Gather these herbs from the woods:
Star Root
Rats Vein
Black Snake Root
Colts Foot
Ginseng
Mt. Tea (Tea-berries)

Boil in pot to make a tea. Sweeten with rock candy. Add moonshine according to age of sick person.

Chocolate No-Bake Cookie Bars

Tootsie Barr - Rhudy's Restaurant – Crooked Oak, VA

2	Tbsps. Hershey's cocoa
2	cups of sugar
1	stick of butter
½	cup milk
1	cup of peanut butter
2½	cups of 1 minute oatmeal
1	tsp. vanilla flavoring

Grease an 8 x 8-inch square pan with butter. In a large pot mix the cocoa, sugar, butter and milk together and boil on medium heat for 5 minutes. Remove from heat and add peanut butter, oatmeal and vanilla. Mix well then pour into greased pan. Let set for 1 hour before cutting into squares.

Corn Bread Salad

Debra Bramer – Bass player with Whitetop Mountain Band

1	(8.5 oz.) box corn bread muffin mix
1	medium bell pepper, chopped
1	medium onion, chopped
3-5	tomatoes, chopped
1	lb. bacon, fried and crumbled
1½	to 2 cups mayonnaise
1	tsp. sugar
¼	cup salad pickles (relish)

Make corn bread according to box directions. Crumble ½ of the corn bread in bottom of a 9 x 13-inch casserole dish. Layer vegetables and bacon in order, saving enough bacon to put on top. Mix mayonnaise, sugar, and salad pickles. Spread on top of the vegetables. Cover with the remaining ½ of corn bread and sprinkle with bacon.

Corn Pudding
Lacie H. Kemp – Dugspur, VA

2	cups water
½	tsp. salt
½	cup grits
1	tsp. butter
1	(17 oz.) can cream style corn
2	large eggs, beaten
2	large whites of eggs, beaten
1	cup cheese (Monterey Jack)
1	(4 oz.) can chili peppers
¼	cup milk
¼	tsp. ground red pepper

Bring water and salt to a boil gradually stirring in grits. Cook 15 to 20 minutes. Remove from heat and add butter and cheese, let set 2 minutes. Preheat oven 350°. Lightly grease 1½-quart dish. Stir in remaining ingredients. Pour in prepared dish and bake for 1 hour and 15 minutes.

"Ask, and it shall be given you; seek, and ye shall find; knock, and it shall be opened unto you:"
Matthew 7:7

Fresh Apple Cake
Judy Lundy

2	cups sugar	2	tsps. baking powder
1	cup Wesson oil	1	tsp. vanilla
2	large eggs	2½	cups plain flour
1	tsp. soda	1	cup chopped pecans
1	tsp. salt	3	cups chopped raw apples

Mix this recipe by hand. Prepare apples and set aside. Measure oil into bowl. Add sugar and eggs and mix well. Sift flour into bowl; add salt, soda, and baking powder, mix well. Add flour mixture to creamy mixture and mix well. Add vanilla. Fold in chopped nuts and apples. Bake at 350° for about 55 to 60 minutes in tube pan.

Family Shoe Store

Glen and Avenel Jackson

Glen Jackson found his life's work in part because his feet hurt. Since he had a tough time finding shoes to fit, he thought that other people might have the same problem. While working in the Commissioners office in the late 1940's, he and a friend, Allen Easter, decided to enter into a partnership in the shoe store business. The door of the Family Shoe Store opened in 1950.

The first years were lean. But they were able to get a credit manager of a company to extend credit and even a discount although they couldn't pay right away. "It used to be that you could get acquainted with manufacturers and build a working relationship. Salesman would come by and could often advise you on buying and understanding how the shoes were made. That's not possible now."

Jackson also credits the customers with helping train them. The customers explained problem feet and shoes that wore well, etc. Through the years, the store has been noted for carrying odd and large sizes, as well as quality shoes and service.

The building they're in used to house a hospital upstairs, run by Dr. Glenn Cox. Avenel Jackson worked in the shoe store with her husband while pregnant with their children, as she still does today. "When our son was born, I was in the store all day, then went on upstairs and had him that night," she laughs.

While the shoe business can be hard work, Glen Jackson has worked harder for much less money. "I made 25 cents a day hoeing corn as a kid," he recalls. Somebody decided to build a dam on Big Reed Island Creek to start a mill and paid him 50 cents a day to work. "I got rich enough to buy me a gun," he laughs.

Before serving in WWII, Jackson farmed and hauled coal from a pony mine. He paid $25 a load and hauled it back and unloaded it by hand for the customer and charged $50. At the time, gasoline was 20 cents a gallon.

A natural storyteller, Glen has a wealth of knowledge about Carroll County. One amusing story was learned when he worked in the Commissioners office in the historic courthouse next door. It seems when bathrooms were first installed in the courthouse, farmers were not familiar with the workings of the new-fangled commodes. Their habit of carrying corncobs in overall pockets around the farm and to the outhouse for the finish work persisted in the new bathrooms. It took some convincing before they quit stopping up the plumbing with corncobs!

How long will Glen and Avenel, with help from their sons, keep the store running? At 85, Jackson plans to keep on as long as possible. "We can't quit. Our money is tied up in these shoe boxes and we can't eat them," he says.

Even a watch that won't run is right twice a day.

Fresh Apple Cake
Avenelle Jackson – Laurel Fork, VA

3	eggs	3	cups plain flour
1½	cups Wesson oil	1	tsp. salt
3	cups apples, chop fine (Golden Delicious)	2	tsps. vanilla
1	tsp. soda	1	cup pecans, chopped (or black walnuts)
2	cups sugar		

Mix sugar, oil, add eggs one at a time and beat well, (sift flour, soda and salt), and add dry ingredients, then vanilla, apples and nuts. Pour into greased, floured tube pan and bake at 350° for one hour – more if needed.

Garbanzo Salad
Marcella Taylor

1	head lettuce	1	can garbanzo beans, drained
2-3	tomatoes diced	1	(8 oz.) pkg. shredded cheese
1	onion diced		
1	can kidney beans, drained and rinsed		

Layer these ingredients in large bowl. Cover these layers with 16 oz. bottle of ranch dressing. Can cover and refrigerate overnight if needed. When ready to serve, add 1 bag of crushed Doritos. Mix well.

Gingerbread with Orange Sauce
Lacie H. Kemp – Dugspur, VA

> What you are is God's gift to you. What you make of yourself is your gift to God.

1	cup sugar	½	tsp. cloves
1	cup Wesson oil	3	eggs
1	cup molasses	1	cup hot water
2	cups flour	½	tsp. salt
1	tsp. ginger	2	tsps. soda
2	tsps. cinnamon		

Sift flour with soda, salt and spices. Mix oil and sugar. Add beaten eggs and molasses. Add sifted dry ingredients and hot water alternately. Beat until smooth. Pour into well greased and floured pan. Bake in a 9 x 13 inch pan at 350° for 40 to 45 minutes.

Orange Sauce:

1	cup sugar	2	Tbsps. flour
1	cup orange juice	¼	tsp. salt
½	cup water	1	Tbsp. butter

Put orange juice into small saucepan. Mix sugar, flour, water, salt, and melted butter together and add to cold orange juice. Cook over medium heat until it becomes thick. Remove from flame and allow to cool, slightly. Pour over gingerbread and serve warm or cold.

Grits and Cheese Casserole
Lacie H. Kemp – Dugspur, VA

4	cups boiling water	1	cup milk
1	cup grits	½	cup butter
4	eggs beaten	2	Tbsps. chopped onions (optional)
1	cup cracker barrel sharp cheese, grated		few grains cayenne pepper

Stir grits slowly into boiling water. Cook 4 to 5 minutes, stirring constantly. Remove from heat and stir in eggs, cheese; milk, butter and pepper. Pour into greased casserole dish. Sprinkle top with grated cheese. Bake at 350° for 1 hour.

Big Meetings in the Blue Ridge

Twilight gathered as two teenage girls hurried down a dusty road, dressed in their best. During the five-mile-plus journey, they cut through fields; taking all the shortcuts they knew to spare their already tired feet. The day had been exciting and tomorrow would be even better, but first the twins had to make it to their sister's house.

The association at Connors Grove Primitive Baptist Church had taken place that Saturday - with horses, buggies, cars, and flocks of people lining the road outside the church. Laurel Fork Primitive Baptist's Big August Meeting would be the next day and seeing that many people in one weekend would be something to talk about for months – especially the boys who were sure to show up, knowing girls would be there.

Every Primitive Baptist church has a specific day set aside to conduct a yearly Communion and foot-washing event, usually during an annual Association meeting. The preaching day of the "soshciation" with dinner on the grounds, though no one can say exactly when or why, became a festival for the whole countryside. A holiday spirit filled the air and the dirt roads were jammed with people who came - in the early days - on foot, horseback, and in buggies or carts. Cars were scarce. Inside the Lord's house the congregation sang, listened to preaching, took communion, and conducted business. Outside was happy bedlam, a country fair.

Why would a special religious day for the Primitive Baptist Church become a phenomenal draw for the whole countryside? Early twentieth century Blue Ridge Mountains dwellers were fairly isolated, particularly the area where Floyd, Patrick, and Carroll counties stretch to connect. Families worked long hours and visits were infrequent. They craved interaction and some excitement. Churches provided a social outlet and extended open invitations, though it seems highly unlikely the assemblage expected the throngs that eventually showed up.

The Elders and congregation practiced Biblical and practical tolerance, however. Willadean Nester, of Laurel Fork explained why, "Almost everybody outside was a neighbor or kin. The church members' children were likely out walking up and down the road for the biggest part of the day."

Callie Handy, born in 1900, reminisced at 106 years old about riding a horse to Connors Grove for the meeting at fifteen or sixteen. "A boy on the road wanted to race my horse. I was a show-out and wasn't about to let him beat me. A big mud-hole didn't stop us, but I splashed mud all over my new blouse. I went on to church, didn't aim to miss it, but don't you know I looked a mess?" she giggled.

By the 1930's, hucksters were setting up stands with colorful displays of merchandise and snacks along the road, and a big truck brought watermelons. "It was the only time we ever saw a watermelon," states Sadie Goad. "Big Meeting was the most exciting thing that happened during the year when I was a kid."

Ice cream and soda pop became possible with the use of dry ice. Wooden stands, only used once a year, were built along the dirt roads to some churches, selling hot dogs and more food items. A "cameraman" named Montgomery sometimes showed up to photograph normally gregarious people who sat stiff and solemn for their picture. The eagerly anticipated day was almost overwhelming to mountain youngsters unaccustomed to such novelties.

Adolescents practiced an early form of cruising, albeit on foot. They flirted and formed alliances, many of which didn't last the day; a few relationships became lifetime commitments. Neighbors and friends visited and caught up on the news, sometimes for the past year. Children had free rein to run and play. Men gathered under trees to talk crops and general business, sometimes discretely passing around a canning jar or flask. (Outside folks, not the church members)

Families picnicked on the ground or sat on logs. As time went on, the churches built tables and the food was served communally to all who cared to eat. Imogene Martin, who grew up in Bell Spur Church, has memories of making mounds of peanut butter and crackers, an easy item to eat without utensils. Elder Raymond Sumner of Woodlawn recollected, too, enjoying the same treat in churches near Hillsville, the only time he got peanut butter.

Hallie Stanley, a life-long member of Maple Shade Primitive Baptist, recalls the crowds stretching at least a mile in each direction of the vendor-lined road in front of the church on Big Meeting day during the 1930's. "Of course, I was right there walking up and down the road with all the other young people. I spent most of the day changing boyfriends. One big meeting day, I traded about four times. A present, especially the little cellophane dolls on a cane, from one of the stands would turn my head," she laughingly recalls.

Because the congregation overflowed the small church on that day, a permanent wooden platform was built outdoors for the speaker while the faithful sat on boards laid across tree stumps. The less-than-faithful enjoyed their holiday along the dirt road in much the same way as visitors to all the annual business meetings of Primitive Baptist churches in that tri-county area of the Blue Ridge Mountains did.

Concord Primitive Baptist sits less than a mile from the Parkway overpass in Meadows of Dan. Arlie Burnette was raised in sight of the building and will never forget the stir caused by an Association Meeting in 1927. "Concord attracted huge crowds outside, but I can't remember any stands being set up," he says. "My grandparents and neighbors prepared all week for it. They killed and plucked chickens and slaughtered a beef cow to help feed the guests who traveled miles to attend. Every house in the community overflowed with relatives and friends coming for the three-day meeting."

New Hope, commonly called The Bridge, near Hillsville was a huge affair akin to the Laurel Fork Meeting in popularity. These two churches (and possibly others) continued to attract people into the early 1960's, even teenage drivers who created clouds of dust as they drove through to see and be seen. But Vendors had dwindled and change was in the air. Due in part to the influence of cars, a way of life came to an end. Other opportunities for entertainment became easily accessible. Vietnam sucked up young men, teenagers rebelled, some married and moved away, and an era ended with no one understanding the extent of what was being given up. Chance meetings at Wal-Mart – however pleasant – just can't generate the same feeling of fellowship as those old-time meetings.

And what of the twins who walked all day in their good shoes? Viola succumbed to tuberculosis at age nineteen and the other, Luvina, survived to spend a week's salary ($2.00) on a pair of high-heeled sandals to attend "Big Meeting" with her boyfriend. They married and produced three daughters. We all call her Mom.

Ground Cherry Preserves
Luvina Dalton – Laurel Fork, VA

6   **cups sugar**
3   **cups water**
3   **cups ground cherries**
1/3 **cup vinegar or lemon juice**

Boil sugar & water until well dissolved. Add lemon juice or vinegar and cook until clear about 5 minutes. Drop in whole ground cherries and cook until thickened – maybe 5 more minutes. Remove from heat and immediately pour into hot, sterilized glass jars, seal at once.

Ground Cherries

"I am thankful for the old-time country music and that we are keeping it going as part of our culture. In 1940, I was 6 years old when Charlie Monroe's band played at the school I attended. My father took me to see them. The only thing I remember was Charlie singing "I Traced Her Footprints in the Snow." That song was so real to me I could see the snow and feel being lost out in it. I got up early the next morning and while my mother cooked breakfast on a wood cook stove, I sat in my father's lap and he sang " I Traced Her Footprints in the Snow" until I knew every word of the song. I'll never forget that and it made me always love country music- even though I can't play or sing!" - Gaye B. Robinson

Now some folks like the summertime when they can walk about
Strolling through the meadow green it's pleasant there's no doubt
But give me the wintertime when the snow is on the ground
For I found her when the snow was on the ground.

Life is a coin. You can spend it any way you wish, but you can only spend it once.

Hospitality Pie
Gaye Robinson – Cana, VA

3   pie shells baked and cooled
1   cup sliced almonds
1   stick margarine
2   cups coconut
1   (14.5 oz.) can sweetened condensed milk
1   (8 oz.) pkg. cream cheese (softened)
1   (16 oz.) container of whipped topping, thawed
1   jar of caramel or butterscotch ice cream topping

Bake 3 pie shells and let cool. Mix the almonds, margarine, and coconut in shallow baking pan. Toast, stirring in a 350° oven until golden brown; watch to prevent burning. Remove from oven and cool. Combine and blend together condensed milk and cream cheese, fold in whipped topping. Put half of the cream cheese mixture into 3 pie shells, dividing evenly. Sprinkle with coconut mixture. Drizzle with ice cream topping. Repeat with remaining cream cheese mixture, coconut mixture, and topping. Keep refrigerated. Freezes well.

"I started making this pie for my grandson, Houston, about 2 years ago when he asked me "Grandma can you make an apple pie?" I worked with 3 different pie recipes but basically I used the recipe for a French apple pie found on the inside box of great value piecrust. I altered my pie by adding juice of one lemon and adjusted the cornstarch to the amount of juice and the type of apple you are using. Adjust spices to your taste."

Houston's Favorite Apple Pie
Barbara Caldwell

1   unbaked piecrust
1   cup white sugar
¼   cup cornstarch
1   tsp. ground nutmeg
¼   tsp. ground cinnamon
½   tsp. allspice
    pinch of salt
6   cups thinly sliced tart baking apple (preferably Granny Smith)
1   cup all purpose flour
½   cup butter
¾   cup firmly packed brown sugar
    juice of 1 lemon (optional)

Houston is the 15-year-old son of Kenneth and Tess Caldwell and grandson of Barbara Caldwell. Houston's favorite food is Apple Pie. He is presently playing the banjo with the bluegrass band ***Brokenwire.***

Preheat oven to 350°. Mix sugar, cornstarch, spices and salt into bowl. Stir in apples and juice of 1 lemon. Pour all this into pie pan. Mix all-purpose flour with brown sugar and butter. Mix until crumbly and sprinkle over top of pie. Bake for 1 hour and 30 minutes.

"For I am persuaded, that neither death, nor life, nor angels, nor principalities, nor powers, nor things present, nor things to come, nor height, nor depth, nor any other creature, shall be able to separate us from the love of God, which is in Christ Jesus our Lord." **Romans 8:38-39**

Gilbert and Betty Fortner

"Gilbert and I celebrated our 57th wedding anniversary December 23, 2007. Each month we count our blessings for another month together. He is 80 and I am 74 and we sing mostly as a duet now. He is a guitar picker who fools around a little with a banjo. He plays piano for our small Methodist Congregation each Sunday.

Our quartet partners have passed away. We sang with Cone Pierce and Marion Cooper for many years. Gilbert played the guitar and our daughter played the piano when she could be with us. Sometimes she substituted for me as altoist.

In 1968, we entered the old-time Fiddlers convention sponsored by the Low Gap Ruritan Club and won first place in the gospel-singing category. It was the first and only time we ever entered a contest. Gilbert and I still have the ribbon.

We first started singing with my father, Samuel Jones, a wonderful bass singer, my mother, Effie, a soprano, and our daughter, Phyllis, who was eleven years old at the time. We followed the Grayson County monthly singing convention all over Grayson and Carroll counties for years. E.C. Ball, better known as Slim, was the M.C. and leader of these conventions. It was mostly Baptist churches but we also sang in many other denominations.

Gilbert, Marion, and Cone went with Slim and Orna Ball up to Pennsylvania to a festival in a park. (He doesn't remember the name of the town.) Slim was invited because of his unique finger picking.

Our son-in-law, Kenneth, is a minister. When he was pastoring at Hiltons, VA, we used to go to the Carter Fold. Jeanette Carter was a member of the church he pastored. She liked to hear Kenneth, Phyllis, Gilbert and I sing. One Christmas season we were at the Carter Fold Christmas show and we were invited to come up and sing impromptu. Gilbert borrowed a guitar and the whole family – Aaron, Angie, Emily, Kenneth, Phyllis, Gilbert, and I sang, "I'm so Glad I Know Who Jesus Is." Later, Ken and Phyllis and their family recorded a cassette because so many people wanted their music and we sang that song with them as a quartet on the tape.

We met Ken Childress when Kenneth and Phyllis went to Clintwood to pastor at the Clintwood United Methodist Church. We fell in love with the people there, and especially Ken. We love his gospel music, his ballads, and country singing. The church sponsored some stringed instrument jams and we tried to be at most of them. We would also get together with Ken's friends at the parsonage and have real free for all sessions that would last for hours.

Jamming sessions are picking up in popularity in churches, coffee houses, and home meetings again. We don't get to too many of them because of our age and health. This is an old recipe and my married children want me to bake this cake when they come home for Thanksgiving." -Betty Fortner

Hummingbird Cake

Betty Fortner – City of Galax, VA

3	cups flour	3	eggs, well beaten
2	cups sugar	1 ½	cups vegetable oil
1	tsp. salt	1	cup nuts (usually pecans)
1	tsp. soda	1	(8 oz.) can crushed pineapple undrained
1 ½	tsp. vanilla		
1	tsp. cinnamon	2	cups bananas, mashed

Mix dry ingredients; add eggs and oil. Stir until moist. Stir in vanilla, pineapple and nuts. Add bananas. Bake at 350° for 25-30 minutes. (Do not use mixer on cake). I bake my cake in two 9-inch layer cake pans.

Frosting:

1	(8 oz.) cream cheese (softened)	1	tsp. vanilla
½	stick margarine (softened)	½	cup chopped nuts
1	box powdered sugar		

Beat the cream cheese and margarine until smooth. Add the sugar, vanilla and nuts. Spread on cake.

One of three fee-fishing, stocked trout streams in Virginia is located in Woodlawn. Five miles of fishing are available, along with picnic tables and a concession stand. It is handicapped accessible.

The scenic Blue Ridge Parkway travels the crest of the Blue Ridge Mountains through a part of four counties involved with the Crooked Road Music Trail. They are Floyd, Patrick, Carroll, and Grayson. The Twin Counties of Carroll and Grayson, and the city of Galax host the Blue Ridge Music Center.

Buddy Crisp at Arthur Smith Show

Buddy Crisp-Carl Hunt and the Lucky Five appearing on the Arthur Smith Show. (L to R) Lawrence Prevette, Ronnie Prevette, Carl Christy, Arthur Smith, Buddy Crisp and Carl Hunt.

Hillsville is the only incorporated town in Carroll County. It was first incorporated in 1878 and repealed ten years later. In 1900, the town was incorporated again, though it was still an unpopular action. An election was held for a Board of Trustees, and those elected pledged not to qualify and not to serve, leaving the town essentially with no formal government for twenty more years.

Key Lime Cake
Joyce Harris – Meadows of Dan, VA

1 lemon supreme cake mix
1 large lime Jell-O
1 cup orange juice
5 eggs
1 cup oil

Mix orange juice and oil together. Add one egg at a time beating after each egg. Then add dry ingredients and mix until smooth. Grease and flour 3 cake pans and bake at 325° for 25-30 minutes. Cool and ice:

1 (8 oz.) cream cheese
½ cup butter
1 box confectioner's sugar
1 tsp. vanilla

Combine cream cheese and butter. Beat in sugar and vanilla till creamy.

"I started making this pie at age 12 because my older brother said I could make a pie as good as our mother. When we lived at home I made pies with country milk and butter. So one year after I moved away from home we were having a family reunion, my brother said my pies were too white from using store bought eggs. This is when I started using ¼ tsp. of food coloring to make the pie look richer. He never knew the difference. Over the years as I took these same pies he began to tell that no one but me could make pies like our mother."

Mama's Coconut Pie
Barbara Caldwell

1 ½ cups sugar
4 eggs
vanilla flavoring
coconut flavoring
pinch of salt
¾ cup of flour
½ gallon whole milk
¼ tsp. yellow food coloring (optional)
1 large can sweetened coconut
2 baked 9-inch pie shells

Beat eggs and put maybe 2 cups of milk, flour and sugar in a bowl, mixing thoroughly. Pour into pot; add rest of milk (I usually have almost a pint left). Add flavoring to taste and more sugar if needed. Taste and add accordingly. Boil mixture until it thickens. Stir almost entire can of coconut (leaving some for topping). Pour into baked pie shells.

Topping:
1 pint of heavy whipping cream (cold)
coconut flavoring
vanilla flavoring
pinch of salt
¼ white sugar
4 Tbsps. powdered sugar

Have whipped cream cold and beat until partially thick. Add flavorings, sugar and salt and beat until thick. Put onto cold pies and sprinkle with remaining coconut.

This same recipe can be made using different flavors for butterscotch or chocolate pie. With butterscotch, use brown sugar and about ¾ bag melted butterscotch morsels. For chocolate pie use melted chocolate morsels or a large chocolate bar.

"My husband, Buddy Crisp, played bluegrass in a band "The Blue Ridge Boys." The members were Buddy Crisp, Red Barker, Jim Holder, Cub McGee, Larry Richardson and Coy Revels. They played local fiddlers conventions and private shows and traveled on weekends. They had full time jobs to support their families, but they loved their music. He also played with "The Blue Mountain Boys" and "Buddy Crisp and The Lucky Five." The last band he played with was "The Oak Island Boys." In later years he sung country music. He is now retired, but still loves music and plays when he can find others to jam with. In his travels we met some big stars; he has opened shows for Loretta Lynn, Dolly Parton, The Osborne Brothers (Sonny and Bob) to name a few. Needless to say we really had a good time and met good friends all around the country."

Folk Remedy:
Good for hangnails and ingrown toenails, pour 1 cup of vinegar in pan of hot water and soak.
— *Marie Crisp*

Melt In Your Mouth Chicken Pie
Marie Crisp – Fancy Gap, VA

3   lbs. whole chicken (or 3 large breast pieces)
2   cups of chicken broth, reserved
1   can cream of chicken soup, condensed
1   cup self-rising flour
1   tsp. salt
½   tsp. pepper
1   cup buttermilk
1   stick butter (or margarine) melted

Cook chicken until tender. Remove meat from bones. Remove any skin. Cut chicken into small pieces and place in 13 x 9-inch baking pan. In a saucepan, mix and bring to a boil chicken broth and soup. Pour over chicken. In small bowl, combine butter, flour, salt, pepper, and buttermilk. Mix well and pour or spoon on top of chicken mixture. Bake at 425° for 25-30 minutes until browned.

The 250-acre Devil's Den nature preserve at Fancy Gap features walking trails, picnic areas and a cave that was a major tourist attraction in the 1920's due to it's part in the Sidna Allen courthouse shooting. It's said the cave was used as a hideout for the Allens.

Molasses Stack Cake

Hallie Stanley - Laurel Fork, VA

1 cup sugar
1 cup shortening
1 cup molasses
1 tsp. soda (mix with molasses)
½ cup buttermilk
2 eggs
4 cups flour
½ tsp. each of cinnamon, cloves, ginger, & salt

Combine and beat sugar, shortening, and eggs. Add buttermilk, molasses, spices and salt; mix well. Beat in flour a cup at a time until just blended. More flour may have to be added to make dough consistency to roll out like biscuits, only quite thin. Cut out into desired size and bake on cookie sheet or put in cake pans. Bake at 350° for 8-10 minutes according to oven. Don't over bake. Put apple butter between layers and on top. Store in cool place for a few days before cutting.

For an infection, dissolve ½ cup Epsom salts in a cup of hot water. Dip cloth in, wring excess water out, and place poultice on infected area 2 or 3 times a day for about ½ hour. — *Hallie Stanley*

Old man winter is not always informed about global warming along the crest of the Blue Ridge Mountains

"This recipe was one of my Mom's favorites. It's so rich! I couldn't resist saying that I took out all the calories. It's impossible – too mouth watering and melt in your mouth good. If Lay's had not come up with "Bet you can't eat just one: I'd have to say it about this dessert. One piece isn't enough!"

Mom's No-Bake Blueberry Dessert
Don Foster – The Inn at Orchard Gap – Fancy Gap, VA

- 2 (12 oz.) cans blueberry pie filling
- 1 box vanilla wafers
- 1 stick butter
- 2 eggs
- 2 cups of powdered sugar
- 2 pkgs. Dream Whip – 3 oz. total
- 1 cup milk
- 1 tsp. vanilla flavoring

Use a 9 x 13-inch glass dish. Crush most of the vanilla wafers to cover the bottom of the pan saving some for covering the top with a thin layer. Save approximately (28) wafers for lining the edge of the pan. Mix the butter, powdered sugar, and eggs to a soft consistency and spoon over the crushed vanilla wafers. Then cover this mixture with the 2 cans of blueberry pie filling. The topping is a mix of 1 cup milk with the Dream Whip and the vanilla flavoring. Beat until the Dream Whip sets up. Cover the blueberry pie filling with the whip and then sprinkle the last of the vanilla wafer crumbs on top. Set in the refrigerator overnight. Ready to serve. Other pie fillings may be substitute

It's easy enough to be pleasant, When life flows by like a song; But th' man worthwhile Is the man with a smile, When ever'thing goes dead wrong.

In 1956, Minnie Jessup delivered a beautiful baby girl named Joan at the Hillsville Hospital, located over the Family Shoe Store in Hillsville. The cost for her seven-day stay was as follows: Professional services - $65.00 (this included pre-natal care, as well as delivery; Room-$12.00 per day (included meals from Diner); Operating room - $ 12.50; Lab - $8.00; Anesthetic - $10.00; Nursery- $14.00 (the new member of the family wasn't covered by insurance so the parents had to pay the $14.) She remembers having really good care from Dr. J.H. Early, who would come over to check on her several times a day. Dr. Glenn Cox started the hospital and Dr. Moir Martin worked there as well.

"This is one of the favorite bakes that we do here at the Inn. We get lots of request from repeat customers for this bake- both veggie and meat."

Mountain Breakfast Bake

Don & Sherry Foster – Inn at Orchard Gap – Fancy Gap, VA, info@innatorchardgap.com

1	box puff pastries (2 sheets)
1	lb. crumbled sausage
15	slices crumbled bacon
1-2	tsps. dried onion flakes
1	cup fresh mushrooms, sliced
1	pkg. chopped broccoli (asparagus may be substituted)
10	large eggs
	butter
½	cup half and half
2	cups of fiesta shredded cheese
1	(28 oz.) pkg. of Potatoes O'Brien
	sliced fresh tomatoes
	sour cream

Follow package directions for puff pastry. Spray a 9 x 13-inch baking dish with nonstick cooking spray. Roll out puff pastry and line pan making sure it is 1 inch up on all sides. Brown sausage and cook bacon (if you are adding meat to you bake.). Bacon and sausage should be crumbled for spreading.

Place package of Potatoes O'Brien in large skillet with 2 tsps. of butter and cook until almost done. In a large bowl beat eggs and half and half. Cook broccoli and mushrooms in butter until tender. Spread potatoes in baking pan first, followed by bacon and/or sausage. Add veggie mixture next, followed by egg/milk mixture. Sprinkle liberally with shredded cheese and place in the oven at 350°. Bake approximately 45 minutes until golden brown. Serve with fresh tomatoes and a dollop of sour cream for taste. You can refrigerate and let set overnight to save clean up and preparation time in the morning. Allow an extra 15 minutes cooking time if refrigerated. Serve fresh fruit as an addition, and you have a wonderful meal. Enjoy!

The first circulating school library in the state was begun in Carroll county in the 1930's.

"My mother, Vivian Amburn Morris, of Carroll County, VA made this every summer. It's a must for pinto beans and cornbread – which we ate on a regular basis while I was growing up. "Soup Beans," cornbread, and fried potatoes – all cooked on Mother's wood burning cook stove fed us year round, and this meal is still a favorite."

Mountain Chow–Chow
Dale Morris – Wolfe Bros. String Band

Chop up the following:
- 2 gallons of green tomatoes
- 12 large onions
- 3 heads of cabbage
- 2 gallons sweet green peppers
- 5 big cucumbers

"For by grace are ye saved through faith; and that not of yourselves: It is the gift of God."
-*Ephesians 2:8*

Salt the above mixture to taste. Let it set for 8 to 24 hours then drain.

Bring to a boil the following ingredients:
- 1 quart of vinegar
- 1 quart of sugar
- 1 (1¼ ozs.) of mustard seed
- 1 box (1¼ ozs.) of celery seed
- 2 tsps. of ground turmeric

Pour this mixture over the chopped vegetables in a large container. Bring to a boil for 20 minutes. Put in your jars – can and seal – process pints 10 to 15 minutes in water bath. This recipe makes 15 to 18 pints.

"Our Dad's favorite pie was Mom's Never Fail Egg Custard Pie. He enjoyed it so much."

Never Fail Egg Custard Pie
Sandra Cockerham – Hillsville, VA

- 3 cups milk
- 5 eggs beaten
- 1 cup sugar
- ½ tsp. nutmeg
- 1 tsp. vanilla
- pinch salt

Mix together and pour in unbaked piecrust slowly. Bake 400° until filling is firm and slightly brown.

"This recipe came from Grandma Ogle's cookbook, early 1900's. My mom, Zella Mae Ogle White, made this. Chickens weren't laying!"

No Egg Cake
Erselle Williams

2	cups sugar	3	cups flour
¼	cup lard or butter	2	heaping tsps. baking powder
1	cup sweet cream	½	tsp. vanilla flavoring
1	cup sweet milk		

Cream lard and sugar; beat well. Add vanilla. Sift dry ingredients together. Add dry ingredients alternately with the milk. Mix well. Add sweet cream and mix well. Pour in a greased 8-inch pan, and bake in 350° oven for 30-40 minutes.

"This recipe is from our mom, Bertie White. Times could be hard in the old days, but if a cow was in the barnyard and potatoes and onions stored in the root cellar, then a hearty soup supper was always possible. Served with cornbread and a dish of home canned fruit, this supper was a long winter favorite of ours in the mountains."

Old Timey Potato Soup
Sandra Cockerham –Hillsville, VA

1	medium onion, minced	4	cups milk
¼	cup butter		few dashes celery seed
4	cups diced raw potatoes		salt and pepper to taste
2	cups water	4	slices bacon cooked and
1	tsp. salt		crumbled if desired

Sauté onion in butter until translucent. Add potatoes, water and salt and cook until tender. Add milk and season with celery seed, salt and pepper to taste. Add bacon if desired. Simmer a few minutes before serving.

Drain Cleaner

1 cup salt
1 cup soda
¼ cup cream of tartar

Mix together. Put ¼ cup in sink and pour 2 cups boiling water after it.

Glen Jackson and the Labor Day Gun Show and Flea Market

The small town of Hillsville, VA (pop.2, 607) operates at a leisurely pace most of the year; however, a drastic change occurs each Labor Day weekend when the flea market descends. Considered the largest event of its kind on the east coast, the four- day Gun Show and Flea Market has the town bulging and scrambling to hold upwards to a million people. They come from all over America and even foreign countries to sell, trade, browse, socialize, or snap up that special treasure.

The collective efforts of many volunteers keep the show going, but one man's resolution in the beginning got the whole thing off the ground. That man is Glen Jackson, owner of Family Shoe Store and member of VFW Grover King Post 1115, the group that sponsors the event.

It all started in 1967 when the post was in dire need of funds to pay for a new building. A friend from Florida told Glen about Gun Shows, which were popular in several southern states. Jackson gained the support of Gene Pack, the Hillsville Police Chief, who happened to be an avid gun trader. With that, a proposal was made to the Post to host a trade show for guns, knives, coins and Indian relics. Though there were qualms, the event was approved with Jackson as the promoter.

"I had never been to a gun show and didn't know a thing in the world about one," Jackson laughs. "I drove hours in every direction, putting up posters on poles and vacant buildings and wherever businesses allowed them." He also wrote to newspapers, radio and TV stations, gun and coin shops, and sporting goods stores.

The first snag appeared in the form of a $200.00 "Itinerant Vendor's License" and a $5.00 certificate that state law required of each vendor to collect state taxes. It was then learned that potential shows in Virginia had been shut down due to these fees.

Mild mannered Glen Jackson is no quitter. He is a gentle persuader with steely resolve who figures there's a way if you find the right approach to the problem. He headed to Richmond and convinced tax officials to allow the gun show to operate under one license issued to the VFW Post. Next year - another trip to Richmond. By the third year, the assistant tax commissioner remembered him and was friendly but unreceptive to stretching the law again.

"But I knew about a big gun show that had been allowed in Hampton and I asked him if they were trying to discriminate against our little mountain VFW Post. He called the Attorney General's office and convinced them to give us one more year if I'd promise to help get the legislature to amend the law. I did – with the aid of Jerry Geisler, our representative from Carroll County."

The first year, Jackson advised a dubious kitchen committee to prepare for 2,000 customers. When one hundred vendors and 5,000 visitors showed up, members scurried to stores in surrounding areas in search of enough food and drinks for the crowd.

The second year, a vendor showed up with glassware to sell. "The gun dealers didn't want him inside the building," says Glen, "so I allowed him to set up outside" – and thus a tradition was born.

Glen with customer, Sadie Goad.

Thousands now offer their wares inside the VFW lot and in yards and fields along Stuart Drive (Rt. 58). (In the beginning, cows were removed from the fields just prior to being rented to sellers, who did some serious sidestepping to avoid the often-fresh evidence left behind.) Other than the sale of pets, one would be hard-pressed to imagine an item – collectible, antique, or junk - *not* for sale somewhere in the town. Time and stamina are the criteria required to locate the desired item.

The whole Jackson family was involved in promoting the gun show during the early years. They traveled to other gun shows on the east coast and westward – distributing flyers and talking to people. "We couldn't go anywhere without putting up posters," laughs his wife, Avenel.

Glen still works the show but not the two months he used to spend each year working on the event. "I advertised hard for a reason," he smilingly explains. "I financed the publicity for the first two years and they needed to be successful to pay me back."

In recent years, Jackson has received publicity himself, something he doesn't covet. His method is more a behind the scenes worker. Without fanfare at 85 years old, he goes about the business of selling shoes and doing small acts of kindness, things he and Avenel consider just being neighborly.

Just when you think you've captured the calm essence of the small town businessman, he tells you about his hobby, which came about as a by-product of the travels to gun shows and which health has restrained: Rattlesnake hunting. "It's the most interesting hunting I've ever done. It seems like the snake has more of a chance than a rabbit or squirrel that you hunt with a gun. You have to grab him right behind the head with this little gizmo and hold him steady, then pull his tail up and make a loop and throw him in a sack." Right…

Avenel, who prefers to read, states, "I could always tell when he had caught snakes by the way he carried the bag out in front or to the side. Some of the hunters sling them over their shoulder."

When asked whether he is pleased with the way the gun show has expanded through the years, Jackson replies, "Well, I still believe it's a good thing. It has generated a lot of greed and I don't like that. But it gives people a market and there are mostly quality dealers who come. A lot of quality buyers, too. You can get honest appraisals down there. The Post makes money that we use for the community all year."

And is the event good for the shoe business? With a chuckle he replies, "It kills the shoe business. Nobody comes uptown."

The New

Majestically runs
The second oldest river
Full of life, it flows.
Haiku - Betty Skeens

Pork Chops and Potatoes
Lacie H. Kemp – Dugspur, VA

6   (½ inch thick) boneless pork chops
6   medium red potatoes – thinly sliced
1   medium onion – thinly sliced
2   tsps. dried thyme
1   tsp. salt
1   tsp. pepper
¼   cup butter or margarine
1   beef bouillon cube
1   cup hot water
2   Tbsps. all-purpose flour
¼   cup water
    garnish fresh thyme sprigs

Brown pork chops in vegetable cooking spray on each side. Layer half of potatoes and onions in 13 x 9-inch baking dish. Sprinkle with half each thyme, salt, and pepper. Dot with 2 Tbsps. butter. Top with pork chops. Repeat with remaining potatoes, onions, seasonings and butter. Dissolve bouillon cube in 1 cup hot water. Pour over potatoes. Bake covered at 350° for 1 hour. Remove pork chops with potatoes with a slotted spoon. Pour drippings into skillet, whisk all-purpose flour and ¼ cup water until smooth. Cook in drippings until thick and bubbly. Serve over pork chops and potatoes.

Peanut Butter Fudge
Tricia Chandler

- 4 cups sugar
- 1 cup evaporated canned milk
- 1 stick butter
- 1 Tbsp. vinegar
- 1 (12 oz.) jar marshmallow cream
- 1 (12 oz.) jar peanut butter

Mix sugar, milk, butter and vinegar. Boil for 6 minutes. Take off stove and stir in marshmallow cream and peanut butter. Mix well and pour into lightly greased pan. Cool completely before cutting.

To keep hot oil from splattering, Sprinkle a little flour or salt in the pan before frying.

Rave Review Coconut Cake
Sue Lundy

- 1 pkg. yellow cake mix
- 1 pkg. (4 serving size) instant Jell-O vanilla pudding & pie filling
- 1 1/3 cups water
- 4 eggs
- ¼ cup oil
- 2 cups Bakers angel flake coconut
- 1 cup chopped pecans or walnuts

Blend cake mix, pudding mix, water, eggs and oil in large mixing bowl. Beat medium speed 4 minutes. Stir in coconut and nuts. Pour into 3 greased and floured 9-inch cake pans. Bake at 350° for 30 to 35 minutes. Remove and cool on rack. Frost:

Coconut Cream Cheese Frosting

- 4 Tbsps. butter or margarine
- 2 cups Bakers angel flake coconut
- 1 (8 oz.) pkg. cream cheese
- 2 tsps. milk
- 3 ½ cups confectionary sugar sifted
- 1 tsp. vanilla

Melt 2 Tbsps. butter in skillet. Add coconut and stir constantly over low heat until golden brown. Spread coconut on was paper to cool. Cream cheese, add milk and sugar alternately beating well. Add vanilla. Stir in 1 ¾ cups coconut. Spread on top and sides of cake layers. Sprinkle with remaining coconut.

Red Cabbage Kraut
Lacie H. Kemp – Dugspur, VA

2-3	lbs. red cabbage (head of cabbage)
2-3	Tbsps. butter, lard, or bacon grease
	minced bacon
1	Tbsp. sugar
1	large apple, chopped
1	onion, minced
4	Tbsps. white or wine vinegar
	salt
1-2	cups water or stock as needed
¼	cup red currant jelly
	Cornstarch to thicken

Shred cabbage, discard core and tough ribs. Heat fat in fry pan. Add sugar, heat slowly until brown. Add apple and onion. Cover and heat slowly for 3-4 minutes. Add cabbage and toss until coated with fat. Pour vinegar over kraut. Cover pot and cook 10 minutes until cabbage turn blue or bright purple. Sprinkle with salt. Add 1 cup water, cover and cook slowly 1 ½ to 2 hrs. Add jelly and thickening.

Refrigerator Pickles
Gaye Robinson – Cana

7	cups sliced, unpeeled cucumbers
1	cup sliced onions
1	tsp. celery seed
2	Tbsps. salt
1	cup white vinegar
2	cups sugar

Sprinkle cukes and onions with salt and let set 1 hour. (I sometimes set in refrigerator over night). Drain well. In kettle mix sugar, vinegar, and celery seed. Heat until sugar dissolves. Pack cukes in jars. Pour mixture over them and put lids on tight, do not have to seal. Store in refrigerator up to six months. Keep lids on tight is the secret.

Hillsville Diner

"Mac" McPeak at Hillsville Diner

The oldest continuously operating diner in Virginia sits beside the Family Shoe Store where it has quietly and efficiently served the town of Hillsville and surrounding communities since 1946. Grandchildren and great-grandchildren of some early "regulars" now stop in for breakfast or meat/vegetables plates that were a staple when factory workers dashed in for their thirty-minute lunches.

A member of the McPeak family has operated the Diner since the early fifties, beginning with "Uncle Roy" who sold out to current owner, "Mac" McPeak's father, Dempsey, in 1966. Mac worked there with his father and mother while in high school and is currently in his twenty-fifth year of ownership.

"I enjoy it more now than I ever did," he states. "I was 28 years old when I took over and getting up at 1:00 AM was rough. Still is. I come in and do the prep work every morning, including Saturdays."

They pride themselves on service and quality food at a decent price. That, and a welcoming atmosphere have kept locals coming in for over sixty years to trade news, quips, and just greet neighbors and the McPeaks. Nostalgia plays a part these days, also." We've seen lots of changes," Mac says. "The factories are gone. But the novelty of the place has grown in the last ten years or so and we get people from everywhere. They come off the interstate looking for hometown places."

And the grills and other equipment in the Jerry O'Mahoney diner that was built in the 1930's and considered the "Cadillac" of its day? Still working…

NOTES:

"Our church, Glenwood United Methodist on Coal Creek Road, Galax, VA has a breakfast twice a year to raise funds and share in a community gathering. We serve sausage gravy on homemade biscuits. This is my recipe and we have had comments; "This is the best sausage gravy I've ever had." Hope you enjoy it too."

Sausage Gravy
Ruth Shropshire – Galax, VA

| ½ | lb. Neese's sausage | 2 cups milk |
| ¼ | cup flour | salt & pepper to taste |

Take ½ lb. of Neese's sausage and crumble into 10" iron skillet. Fry at medium heat until cooked and slightly browned. Add ¼ cup flour and stir in and let cook for a few minutes. Add 2 cups milk (we use 1 cup evaporated milk mixed with 1 cup water) and stir until thickens into creamy gravy. Add salt & pepper to taste. Serve over split biscuits hot from the oven. Enjoy! One batch serves 3-4 people depending on how hungry they are.

"I grew up in the southern part of Carroll County (Cana). My father passed away at a young age, which left mother to raise seven children. Life was hard for her because she never had a driver's license so she had to depend on rides from others. We lived a good mile off the state road which meant we walked to meet the bus and Mama walked to meet a ride to work. We had no running water or indoor heat. We cooked and heated the house with wood stoves. To make life easier Mama's dad gave her some land to build a house where it would be closer to the bus stop, church, and a community store. A cousin picked us up for church on Sundays and while they were working on the house he would take us by to check out the progress. My brother was three years

old at the time and had never seen a bathtub. He saw the tub and said; "look we already have a bed." Of course the rest of us laughed at him and still pick at him from time to time. Life became easier once the house was finished. We now had oil heat, running water, and an indoor bathroom complete with a bathtub, which was better than the washtub we were used to bathing in. This recipe was passed on to me from my mother-in-law, Thelma Johnson McCraw. It is my husband's favorite with pinto's or potatoes."

Sweet Pepper Relish
Janice McCraw – Cana, VA

12	green peppers	2	cups sugar
12	red peppers	1	Tbsp. salt
3	onions	1	quart vinegar

Remove seeds from peppers and grind them along with onions. (I use a meat grinder.) Cover with boiling water, bring to another boil and let stand 10 minutes. Drain as dry as possible; add remaining ingredients and bring to a boil. Simmer 15 minutes and put in hot sterile jars. Throw a towel over cans until they seal and get cold.

Marinate meat in a plastic bag for convenience and good results. Clean up is a cinch - just toss the bag!

Sweet Potato Biscuits
Linda Dawson

2	cups self-rising flour	1	cup cooked, mashed sweet potatoes
1	Tbsp. sugar		
1/3	cup shortening	¾	cup buttermilk

In a large bowl sift together flour and sugar. Cut in shortening and add sweet potatoes. Stir in enough buttermilk to make a stiff dough. Place dough on floured board and knead lightly. Roll out to ½ inch thickness. Cut with cutter. Bake in 450° oven until brown. Makes 12-15 biscuits.

"We have lived along the Crooked Road for approximately 15 years. We now live on the Blue Ridge Parkway at Fancy Gap about 10 miles from the Music Park. We visit there as often as possible, as we love the music and the beautiful park. My recipe is for "Taco Soup" which is delightful on a cold wintry day. Also good for gatherings.

Taco Soup
Peggy Underwood – Fancy Gap, VA

- 1 lb. hamburger browned and drained
- 1 medium onion cooked with hamburger
- 2 cans beans (black, pinto, or ranch)
- 1 can Mexi corn
- 1 can hominy
- 1 can diced tomatoes
- 1 can Rotel tomatoes with chilies (I use mild)
- 1 pkg. Taco seasoning mix
- 1 can tomato sauce (small can)

Mix all ingredients together. I use a crock pot ant let it simmer on low. Cook 3 – 4 hours. It doesn't take all day as everything is already cooked. Great served with cornbread and cheese.

> Just about the time you can make ends meet, somebody moves the ends.

Tupelo Fruit Salad
Joanne M. Villees – Blacksnake Meadery – Dugspur, VA

assorted berries
apples
cantaloupe
Honeydew

Blacksnake Tupelo Honey Wine
cinnamon sticks
orange peel

Combine 2 cups of mead (honey wine) with 1 cinnamon stick and a Tbsp. of orange zest. Heat for 10 minutes and set aside to cool. Cut up fruit. Proportions depend on your preference. Mix fruit together in a large bowl. Pour cooled mead mixture through a strainer. Add strained mulled mead to fruit.

Sylvatus Born

I guess the very earliest event I can remember was the night James Mondes (Sonny) was born. We lived at Grandpa Ogle's house and it was a very cold night, December 2, 1936. Dad got Pearl Chitwood to come and be with mama, and sometime during the night I crept to the top of the steps. I can remember hugging the big post and how cold it was. I suppose after being told to stay upstairs, I was wondering why I couldn't go down. Dad saw me and told me to go back to bed but Pearl told him to let me come on down. Mom was in bed and Pearl sat in a rocking chair in front of the fireplace. She took me on her lap and showed me a gauze box and said that was what my brother came in.

Mom went to State Teachers College in Radford before she married, then taught school and took classes by mail. She went to Hillsville, VA to take her exams. She went back to Radford when I was a few months old and we moved there. I was five years old, and turned six, the last year she taught at Elk Spur School, in Fancy Gap, VA. Elk Spur, a one-room school in a church, had seven grades. She was my first grade teacher.

We had a wood heater to keep us warm in the winter. Children took turns carrying water from the spring. Two smaller children would go to the spring together and put a stick through the bail so it wouldn't be too heavy.

We moved over in the hollow behind my grandparents in the Will Smith House. The Will Smith House had quite a history. A one-room log cabin, it was a saloon in the days that Sylvatus was a mining town. When it became illegal to make whisky, pipes were run from the still under the floor for service to the customers, according to legend.

Grandpa White came to see us in his older years. I remember him sitting on the front porch over in the hollow in a straight-backed chair, tilted back against the wall. He loved white sweet apples. We got him some off the tree and he peeled them and scrapped them because he didn't have any teeth. While he was eating the apples he told us that there used to be a still just over the hill behind our corn crib. We had corn in that field but I always wondered just where it had been.

I couldn't have been very old because I was about ten when he died. I know I was a flower girl. I like that custom. They don't do it any more.

At this time there was two general stores, Charley and Emlie Linsey's and Teeb Dalton's, a Post Office, and Mrs. Smith's Lunch Room, in Sylvatus. If Mom sent one of us to the stores, a neighbor in the yard or on the porch would sometimes give us special news to "be sure to tell your mom", such as - someone getting married, a new baby on the way, or someone being sick. Our beautiful Sylvatus High School, sat on a hill overlooking the village below. A highway, Route 100, ran a few hundred feet below our school; a few places of business were in the valley alongside the road. A small creek run behind the businesses then another higher hill loomed upward just behind the creek, along which run a railroad track and houses were scattered along the hillside.

A freight train called "The Betty Baker", used to run those tracks and haul ore from The Betty Baker Mine, which was east of our school. I don't know when the tracks were built but when I was in grade school those tracks were torn up to use for scrap metal because of the war. We had scrap metal drives and carried every piece we could find that could be taken on the school bus and piled up between the school and ball field. Then a big truck would pick it up and haul it away.

Whenever mom had a few eggs to sell or she needed to sell a hen or two we also took them on the school bus and got off just before going on the school grounds at Mr. Marshall's Barber Shop. Mr. Marshall was not only the barber but also he bought and sold items the farmers had to sell. In the summer after mom and grandma canned all the blackberries they needed, we picked and sold them to Mr. Marshall for winemakers. He paid us eleven cents per pound. I sold almost $50 dollars worth one summer and my sister about $70. I wore the pages out in our Montgomery Ward catalog deciding what to spend my money on. I finally ordered a blue two-piece dress that felt special to me.

While in the third grade we read a story about a boy who had bought a kite. There was a picture of the kite on one page and a picture of the boy flying the kite on the next page. I wanted a kite so bad but we never got many store bought things and I really had never seen one so I doubt if the stores at home even carried them. Anyway, we never asked for anything except at Christmas when we all got a toy, clothes or maybe material to make a dress, and we always asked for oranges and a box of raisins.

One weekend I got some wood strips, brown paper bags, a hammer, and nails and worked hard making me a kite. I built the frame, covered it with paper and made a tail with bows down it. I was so proud of it. The March wind was blowing hard so I took the kite up a hill and ran down as fast as I could. All it would do was bounce on the ground. I went back up the hill and ran down many, many, times, but I never could get that kite off the ground. Daddy came home about the time I was giving up. He just looked at it, grinned, and said "I believe it's a little heavy, ain't it Ersie?"

After moving to Martinsville, I got a job at Eagles 5 & 10, my first real job. Guess what I sold on my counter? Kites! And I couldn't believe how light and fragile they were. I smiled all day thinking about the kite I had made.

Our neighbors Norm and Callie - I cannot remember their last names - asked us to come visit them and listen to their radio. This was in about 1938 or '39. They lived in a one-room log cabin that had been a school called "The Buckwheat College."

I loved music and I will never forget listening to Lula Bell and Scottie sing, "Put on Your Old Grey Bonnet." I sang what I could remember for weeks to come. This probably started dad to thinking of getting us a radio.

Dad worked swing shifts in the mines at Austinsville, VA. One night he got home and woke us all up about 12:30 am. He had bought a Philco battery powered radio. (The battery felt like it weighed about 25 pounds when Mom ordered one and I had to carry it home.) He tied the aerial wire to the back of the car bumper, I think, and we all listened to Wheeling, West Virginia. The music was beautiful and we were all happier than we were with a new pair of shoes. Every Saturday night Emory and Tiny (Mary Elizabeth) Ogle, our cousins, would come over and we'd all listen to The Grand Old Opry.

I wanted to learn to play the piano. I tried to pick out tunes on grandma's piano, the hunt and peck system. When I finally could play a tune, I would try to play every chance I got, even on the coldest winter days. There was no heat in the living room so I had a coat and gloves on. Mama knew how to read notes and showed me how to play *Lord, I'm Coming Home* and *Beautiful Isle of Somewhere*. I picked out other songs from that. I would pretend I was playing in Carnegie Hall and I couldn't make a mistake. I didn't know where this Hall was but I heard only the best musicians could play there.

I was in the lower grade school when Mr. Ralph Arbaugh, a high school teacher and a missionary, asked all who attended school to memorize a Bible verse. Then we would climb the high hill in Sylvatus to sing some songs, and recite our verses. On the appointed day, after school, all who could go climbed that high hill. Mr. Arbaugh played the accordion and his friend played a trumpet. The music from those instruments rang out all over the village of Sylvatus as they played," Jesus Saves, Jesus Saves." This was one of my most memorable evenings. He gave all who recited a Bible verse a small blue New Testament, which I still have.

Our summers were always busy. The whole family worked in the garden, picked cherries and blackberries, wild blueberries and strawberries. We canned all the fruits and vegetables. We grew our broomcorn to make brooms also. Grandma put the broomcorn in a bunch and soaked the stalks in hot water until they were soft. Grandpa cut slender, straight sticks to go in the center of the handle. Then she tied a piece of binder twine just above the sweeping part of the broomcorn and put her foot on the stalks as she pulled the twine around and around the stalks drawing it tight then tied it off. When the broom stalks dried it was a very good broom and the tied stalks made a good handle. She made small ones for the children and larger ones for adults.

In the evenings, after a hard day's work, my grandfather would get his homemade banjo out and pick while sitting on the porch. It was made from some animal's hide. Grandma sat too, but her fingers were always busy stringing beans or shelling peas.

Mama made the best grape juice. She would fill a half gallon jar about half full of grapes and finish the jar with water then add sugar, and process it about 2 or more hours in a hot water bath. One winter night Gertrude McGrady came home with Sara to spend the night. We had what you would call today a pajama party. We popped popcorn in a wire popper over the fireplace and opened a jar of that good cold grape juice. I guess that grape juice had not sealed properly and it had got a little hard. We giggled and talked most of the night and didn't know why we were so giddy.

One summer a neighbor came out to buy a bushel of green beans. Grandpa told me to go pick the beans for Mr. Kemp. I took the bushel basket and headed for the meadow. It was late afternoon and had been a very hot day and I was already tired. It seamed I would never get the basket full. Finally it was full and I lugged it to the house. Mr. Kemp paid grandpa two dollars for the beans and went out on the porch to get them. I was so embarrassed when Grandpa said "Ersie, when some one buys a bushel of beans he wants a bushel of beans." The beans had settled. Grandpa gave me a peck basket and sent me back to the bean patch. When I returned he said "now pack them down and round it high." He didn't say any more about the beans but I would never forget the lesson I learned that day. I decided this was like the farmers dozen, when someone bought a dozen eggs he always gave them thirteen. —*Erselle White Williams*

Zucchini Relish
Mallie V. Roberts – Galax, VA

10 cups zucchini	1/3 cup salt	1 tsp celery seed
2 green peppers	1 tsp. turmeric	½ tsp. black pepper
2 red peppers	1 Tbsp. cornstarch	2½ cups vinegar
4 cups onions	1 tsp. nutmeg	4½ cups sugar

Using a glass bowl, mix the zucchini, green and red peppers, onions, and salt together. Set in refrigerator over night. Next morning drain well. In a separate pan mix the turmeric, cornstarch, nutmeg, celery seed, black pepper, vinegar and sugar. Stir well and bring to a boil. Boil for 20 minutes. Pour this over the vegetable mixture. Pack in pint jars, seal, and water-bath for 25 minutes.

Patrick County

Contents

Bean Soup with Bam...................259	Killer Meatloaf..............................276
Becky's Cranberry Salad..............260	LaNita's Bread Pudding................277
Beef and Macaroni Casserole........261	Mama's Old Fashion Fried Cabbage...278
Beef Stew.....................................261	Meatloaf......................................279
Bourbon Balls..............................262	Merry Cherry Cheesecake Bars.........281
Bundt Calzone.............................262	MJ's Best Red Dressing................280
Chocolate Pie..............................265	Molasses Cookies.......................284
Chocolate Pie..............................266	Oatmeal Pie.................................286
Circle the Wagon Breakfast Pie.....268	Peanut Butter Frosts.....................285
Coconut Caramel Pie....................265	Potato Candy...............................286
Corn Cobb Jelly...........................269	Rice and Bean Spanish Dish.........288
Crocked Road Mud Cake.............269	Rum Cake....................................288
Crusty Beef Casserole..................270	Scalloped Potatoes......................294
Danish Potato Salad.....................270	Simple Grilled Striped Bass..........293
Date Nut Bars..............................272	Spinach Casserole.......................294
Deviled Eggs...............................273	Squirrel Pot Pie............................295
Fire and Ice Tomatoes..................273	Sweet Broccoli Slaw....................296
Fried Mud Turtle.........................275	Sweet Potato Balls.......................296
Green Pea Casserole....................275	Sweet Potato Dumplings..............297
Homemade Fresh Salsa................276	Turkey Hash.................................298
Indian Ash Cake..........................276	Whitt Farm Grape Salad...............299

Photo: porch of Reynolds Homestead

Built in 1843, the Reynolds Homestead is an outreach facility of VA Tech. Several yearly events, programs, and classes are part of their Continuing Education Program. The old homeplace of R.J. Reynolds, founder of the tobacco company of the same name, has been restored to its 19th century state.

The Stuff of Life

I'd always heard bread was the staff of life. I never questioned that old aphorism until 1988 when I moved to a cleavage in the bosom of the Blue Ridge. One afternoon, I was visiting a neighbor when her teen-aged son arrived home from school. He proceeded to dish up a bowl of something from a huge pot that had been simmering on the kitchen stove. Beans! Pinto beans, to be exact. Never heard of 'em! I declined the offer to share his snack.

A few weeks later, I was introduced to a local ritual – the annual agricultural fair. What a great chance to sample some local fare! The first thing I came to was a pinto bean booth. Pinto beans with cornbread, with onions, with hot sauce, or all of the above. I passed on it.

I next encountered the ubiquitous vegetable at a "fiddling" in a friend's barn. The centerpiece in a monumental spread of food was a huge black iron pot full of - guess what- suspended over an open fire. Rude not to try some! Doctored with hot sauce and chopped onions and mopped up with cornbread, the pinto beans tasted like more.

I never saw pintos on the menu of our favorite restaurant but noticed them being served to another patron. "Oh, everybody knows we always have a pot going," was the explanation.

Twenty years later, I no longer question this omni-present "musical fruit" and have come to appreciate its connection with the longevity (and frugality) of our citizens. If you can't beat 'em, join 'em! Around here, beans are the *stuff* of life. *–Gwen S. Clarke*

Bean Soup with BAM!
Gwen Clarke – Stuart, VA

2	cups beans (pinto, navy or whatever)	1	clove of garlic, minced
	ham hock	1	cup crushed tomatoes in puree
1	large onion, diced	1	can of Rotel tomatoes with green chiles
¼	cup chopped celery leaves		
2	Tbsps. lemon juice	2	cans of beef or chicken broth
			salt to taste

Rinse beans and soak overnight. Drain and simmer with a ham hock for 2 to 3 hours in 2 quarts of water. Remove ham hock, and when cool enough to handle, cut off the meat and add to the pot with 1 diced onion, chopped celery leaves, lemon juice, garlic, tomatoes in puree, Rotel tomatoes with green chiles, and beef or chicken broth.
Salt to taste only after beans are tender.

Becky's Cranberry Salad

Becky Noonkester – Willis Gap Community Center - Ararat, VA

2   pkgs. raspberry or grape Jell-O
1   tall can pineapple-drained
2   cans cranberry sauce-whole berries
2   stalks celery-cut in small pieces
1   orange-cut in chunks
1   firm apple-cut in small chunks
1   cup pecan pieces
2   cups or less boiling water

Mix Jell-O in boiling water and stir until dissolved. Add pineapple, cranberry sauce, celery, oranges, apples, and pecan pieces. Mix well. Refrigerate about 1½ hours. Good at Thanksgiving, Christmas, or just anytime.

Willis Gap Community Center Jam session has been keeping people dancing or just enjoying the music on Friday nights for the past five years, due to the efforts of Becky Noonkester and Mr. and Mrs. Otto Hiatt. Everyone who comes to pick gets a turn and the whole community has a fine time. They welcome visitors and jammers!
276-694-8367

Willis Gap Community Center Jam

Beef and Macaroni Casserole
Mozelle Holt

1   lb. ground beef or turkey
1   lb. macaroni
1   can tomatoes
1   small onion
1   green pepper
1   tsp. salt
1   cup grated cheese
    black pepper

Lightly sauté onion and peppers in saucepan. Add beef or turkey and cook until brown. Cook macaroni until done and add to mixture. Add tomatoes, salt and pepper; simmer for 30 minutes. Place in baking dish, add cheese and bake in 350° oven until melted.

Calorie free club soda adds sparkle to fruit juice. It also reduces calories and makes the juice go farther.

"This is a recipe of my late husband, William R. Willard."

Beef Stew
Rosie H. Willard – Stuart, VA

3   lbs. chuck roast (cut up)
1   large can tomato paste
4-5   carrots
4-5   onions
4-5   stalks celery
10-12 potatoes
       sugar (optional)

Bring beef to a boil. Salt and pepper meat. Let cook about 40 minutes; add tomato paste, carrots, onions, and celery. Cook 1 hour and add potatoes and salt. Cook 1 hour and 15 minutes, stirring occasionally during cooking. Bring to a full boil and cut off.

Bourbon Balls
Marjie Haden – Stuart, VA

¼ cup soft butter
1/3 cup Kentucky Gentlemen Bourbon
1 lb. powdered sugar
3 cups large pecan halves
1 (12 oz.) pkg. semi-sweet chocolate chips
½ block household paraffin

Mix the butter, bourbon, and powdered sugar together for filling. Heat chocolate chips and paraffin in double boiler until melted. Place filling between 2 pecan halves and dip in chocolate. Cover completely or partially with chocolate.

> "Fear thou not; for I am with thee: be not dismayed; for I am thy God: I will strengthen thee; yea, I will help thee; yea, I will uphold thee with the right hand of my righteousness."
> *Isaiah 41:10*

Bundt Calzone
Margaret Noonkester

2 Tbsps. grated Parmesan cheese
1 (1 lb.) loaf frozen bread dough, thawed
½ cup prepared pizza sauce
2 tsps. chopped garlic
1 cup (4 oz.) shredded mozzarella cheese
½ cup sliced fresh mushrooms
2 Tbsps. chopped onion
½ cup (about 4 oz.) pepperoni, chopped

Heat oven to 400°. Grease 10 or 12 cup bundt pan; sprinkle with Parmesan cheese. On lightly floured surface, roll dough into a 10 x 20 inch rectangle. Spread dough with pizza sauce; sprinkle with garlic. Layer remaining ingredients as listed. Starting at long edge, tightly roll up dough; pinching edges to seal. Place seam side down; pinch ends to seal and put in Bundt pan. Cover; let rise in warm place 25 to 30 minutes or until almost double in size. Bake at 400° for 25 to 30 minutes or until golden brown. Let stand 5 minutes. Invert onto serving plate.

With Love ~ To the Meadows of Dan

I have lived in Meadows of Dan all my life, as did all my people since the times of the earliest settlers. I love this place for its simple beauty, the wildlife, the people, the culture and history. Unlike many people these days, I have a sense of home and community. I am deeply rooted and feel nourished and renewed by living close to the land. Each morning whether rain or shine, I have to venture out to feed the horses, ducks, chickens and a wide array of various strays that end up living here with me. One of the strays, a very special mule named Otis, was saved from a certain destiny in a glue factory. I look forward to seeing him everyday and he looks forward to seeing me.

I own a country store called Poor Farmer's Market. The name started out as sort of a joke although we were most definitely poor farmers at the time. The name stuck and I have been working there my entire adult life. I think I inherited entrepreneurship from my grandmother, Gracie Brunette Keith Cockram. Her first husband died leaving her with six small children. She married again and had three more children and then her second husband died. I remember well her plowing the fields behind an old workhorse, me up on it's back holding on to the harnesses for dear life. My parents went to work in the factory in Stuart so I stayed with my grandmother mostly. I can see her face now, even though I was not much more than a toddler, sweat pouring down as she held on tight and strong to that plow. She grew vegetables and made chow-chow and all kinds of canned goods and soap and since she didn't drive, she would have someone, usually my father, drive us out on the side of the road at Lover's Leap to sell our produce to the tourists who were headed to the Blue Ridge Parkway.

She had so many old tales, ghost stories, and stories of witches that would cause the cows to go dry. I remember a tale she told about how there was a cemetery that was said to be haunted and everyone believed it was true. There was a frolic going on one night in somebody's house, a little moonshine passed around, and a dare was made that none of the men would go up on top of the hill to that "hainted" cemetery and leave a pitchfork for proof. One particular man took the bet. He never came back down. Of course everyone else was too afraid to go up there to look for him. When morning light came a group headed on up the hill. They found the man's body there half way over the fence. As he was crossing he put the pitchfork down on the other side and caught his long coattail in it and there he died of a heart attack.

Outside Poor Farmer's Market at Meadows of Dan.

My dad, Mike Shelor, was a moonshiner tried and true until he met my mama and she put an end to all that and made him take a respectable job in the factory. He has tales of his moonshining days, but the story of his life that has always stood out most in my mind is about how when he was a little boy the family was very, very poor. There was a time when they were all hungry and the only thing they had to eat was a pone of warm cornbread his mama just made and some cold milk that was out in the springhouse. He told how she sent him, a barefooted skinny little boy, for the milk, and in his hunger and excitement to get to eat, he was running so fast with it he stumbled and the glass jar shattered. Obviously the only thing the family of eight had then was cornbread and water. He felt so bad about that but they made it. His house had a dirt floor.

One of the things I love most here are the old country churches where people still actually attend regularly. I love the old gospel songs I was raised on. I can hear my grandmother singing "Amazing Grace" even now and the simple clear voices in the Primitive Baptist church singing "Are You Washed in the Blood of the Lamb?" For me the simple and pure sounds of voices in harmony, without overwhelming instruments like drums and electric guitars, meet my deeper spiritual needs. Just thinking of sitting in an old church with those bright-eyed, good-hearted country people singing "Shall We Gather at the River?" almost brings the tears. — *Felicia Shelor*

Chocolate Pie

Nellie Hiatt – plays the guitar at Willis Gap Jam

1½ cups sugar	1 cup milk
1/3 cup cocoa	2 egg yolks
5 Tbsps. flour	1 stick butter
pinch of salt	1 tsp. vanilla

Sift the sugar, cocoa, flour and salt together. Add the milk and 2 egg yolks and mix well. Cook in the microwave on high 12 or 14 minutes or until thick. Take out of microwave and add butter and vanilla. Pour into baked piecrust.

Meringue

1 Tbsp. cornstarch	2 egg whites
1 Tbsp. water	6 Tbsps. sugar
1 cup boiling water	1 tsp. vanilla

Mix the cornstarch and water together and add to boiling water. Cook until thick. Cool completely. Beat egg whites until stiff. Fold the sugar and vanilla into egg whites. Add the cornstarch mixture and beat until completely blended. Place on top of pie and cook at 350° until brown.

> Jest be shore yore brain is in gear 'fore you let out the clutch on yore mouth.
> —*Unknown*

Coconut Caramel Pie

Maxine Smith

2 (8 inch) pie shells or graham cracker shells	1 (8 oz.) softened cream cheese
7 ozs. coconut	1 can sweetened condensed milk
¼ cup margarine	16 ozs. Cool Whip
½ cup chopped pecans or English walnuts	1 Tbsp. lemon juice
	caramel topping

Bake the pie shells and let cool. Brown coconut, margarine, and nuts in skillet. Let cool. Beat together cream cheese and sweetened condensed milk. Fold in the Cool Whip and lemon juice. Layer in pie shell: ½ cream cheese mixture, ½ coconut mixture. Drizzle with caramel topping. Freeze.

Chocolate Pie
June S. Martin

- ¾ cup plain flour
- 2 cups sugar
- 2 Tbsps. cocoa
- 5 eggs, separated
- 4 cups milk
- ½ stick butter
- 1 tsp. vanilla flavoring
- pinch of salt
- 2 deep-dish pie shells

Garlic doesn't have to be peeled before being minced in a garlic press. When you squeeze the clove flesh through the holes, the skin will stay behind in the press.

Mix flour, cocoa, sugar and salt. Whisk in milk until mixture is moistened. Add egg yolks and remainder of milk. Mix well. Cook in microwave until thick. Start with five minutes, whisk. Then cook at 3-minute intervals until you get the right thickness. Do not overcook. Remove from microwave and add butter and flavoring. Whisk until smooth. Pour into 2 deep-dish baked pie shells. Top with meringue:

- 5 egg whites
- 2/3 cup of sugar

Beat egg whites until they start to thicken. Then add sugar and continue to beat on high until thick. Bake in 350° oven until light brown.

Note: To make butterscotch pies, substitute brown sugar for white, omit cocoa, and use maple flavoring instead of vanilla. For coconut pies, omit cocoa. Add one cup of coconut, flavoring, and butter to the filling after it is cooked. You may use vanilla or coconut flavoring or both. Sprinkle coconut on top of meringue before baking.

Bull Mountain Arts is a cooperative gallery for local artisans and member of 'Round the Mountain – Southwest Virginia's Artisan Network. You can find exceptional treasures here! Open most days beside the Star Theater in Stuart. **276-694-6850**

Matt Burnette and Ella Smith Burnette
Submitted by Linda Fain, granddaughter

Madison Lee "Matt" Burnette and Ella Smith were married November 27, 1926. During his courtship visits, he would tie his horse to an apple tree in her front yard. The horse would paw the ground beneath the tree while he waited. Ella's father finally asked him to tie his horse somewhere else because the hole where the horse had pawed was getting so deep that Mr. Smith was afraid the apple tree roots would be weakened and the tree might fall over.

Matt was the whistler, singer, carver, toy maker, storyteller, jokester, auctioneer, farmer, and family man. Early on, he worked on his Meadows of Dan farm and on the construction of the Blue Ridge Parkway. He helped with the construction of 20 miles of the Parkway and was paid 30 cents an hour.

At the age of eleven he auctioned off the logs that were cut while clearing the site of the Concord Primitive Baptist Church. He used to say that auctioneering was as natural as talking; he felt that he was born to be an auctioneer. Possessed of a beautiful bass voice, Matt sang at funerals and made a couple of records. In later years he was employed as custodian at the Meadows of Dan School.

After retiring, much time was spent whittling Appalachian style toys like popguns, slingshots and puzzle games –whistling or singing all the while. When seen in the community, Matt often was carrying a walking cane hand fashioned out of an oddly shaped sapling he had found in the woods or someone brought to him. A collection of his toys is housed at the Library of Congress in the Folklife Division.

With great pleasure, he demonstrated his toys, told yarns, and entertained visitors. His repertoire for visitors was unlimited and included old-time remedies, sleight of hand tricks, singing of hymns, and ghost stories.

One of Matt's favorite stories was about a piece of old inner tube a man gave him as a child. He told how he carried it home and how his mother wrapped it in paper and put it in an old trunk so sunlight couldn't deteriorate it. He would go to that trunk and take out the piece of old inner tube and cut off just enough for a new slingshot and then carefully wrap the remainder back up and store it away.

Ella Smith Burnette was born August 6, 1908, in Carroll County, Virginia. Most of her married life was spent as a homemaker, mother, and grandmother and was a charter member of the Meadows of Dan Home Demonstration Club. She assisted and supported Matt in his projects while raising their three sons. During the construction of the

City of Danville Dam (Pinnacles) and the Blue Ridge Parkway, many people boarded at the Burnette's home where they enjoyed the delicious homemade meals prepared by Ella. No one who visited ever left without being offered food. Some of Ella's other talents were sewing, quilting and crocheting. She made old-fashioned Colonial style bonnets that she sold locally. Her friends and relatives still have crocheted ponchos, shawls, afghans, handbags, hats, and other items that Ella crafted, as well as beautiful quilts in which she took great pride.

Matt was intensely proud of the community where his entire life was lived, within 1/2 mile of his birthplace. He and Ella were married 60 years. Presently they rest side by side at the Meadows of Dan Baptist Church Cemetery, which adjoins the land they owned before the building of the Blue Ridge Parkway. - *Originally written by Joyce Webb*

Circle the Wagons Breakfast Pie
Gary & Cindy Hoback – Wolf Creek Farm – Ararat, VA

3   cups frozen Potatoes O'Brien
¼   cup chopped green onion
½   cup shredded cheddar cheese
¼   cup melted butter
6   ozs. softened cream cheese
2   Tbsps. milk
     salt & pepper to taste
¼   tsp. Greek all-purpose seasoning
1   can corned beef hash

Batter:
¾   cup biscuit mix
2   eggs
1/3 cup milk

Preheat oven to 375°. Grease a casserole dish. Spread potatoes in dish; cover with melted butter, then shredded cheese. Mix onion, milk, cream cheese, salt, pepper, and seasoning. Spread over potato mixture. Slice corned beef hash in small half-circle slices. Arrange on top of potato mixture in a circular fashion. Beat together batter ingredients and pour around the hash slices. Bake 25-30 minutes until lightly browned. Serves 8.

Corn Cob Jelly
Recipe of Ella S. Burnette – Meadows of Dan, VA - submitted by Linda Fain

NOTES:

- 12 medium red corncobs
- 2 quarts water
- 1 (1¼ oz.) pkg. powdered pectin
- 3 cups sugar

Wash the corncobs and cut in 4-inch lengths. Put in saucepan; add 2 quarts water and bring to boil. Reduce heat and simmer for 35-40 minutes. Strain the juice. Measure 3 cups juice into large container. Add the powdered pectin and bring to boil. Add sugar and boil 5 minutes. Skim and pour into hot, sterilized glasses or jars, and seal.

"Crooked Road" Mud Cake
Edna W. Harold

- 2 sticks margarine
- 2 cups sugar
- ½ cup cocoa
- 5 eggs (one at a time)
- 1½ cups plain flour
- 1 tsp. baking powder
- ½ tsp. salt
- ½ cup milk
- ½ tsp. vanilla

Sift the flour, baking powder, and salt together and set aside. Mix all ingredients in order listed. Bake in greased and floured 9 x 13 inch pan at 350° for 30 minutes. Take out of oven and pour 1 jar of marshmallow crème on top. Let cool. Mix the following ingredients together to make an icing and spread on cake:

- 1 stick margarine (melted)
- ¼ cup cocoa
- 1 box powdered sugar
- 5 Tbsps. milk
- 1 tsp. vanilla

Crusty Beef Casserole
Linda Bryant – Stuart, VA

2 Tbsps. vegetable oil
1 onion, chopped
2 lbs. ground beef
4 (10½ oz.) cans meatless mushroom spaghetti sauce
½ lb. fine noodles, cooked and drained
1 (8 oz.) extra sharp cheddar cheese, 1st layer
1 (8 oz.) sharp cheddar, 2nd layer

Heat oil, add onion, and cook until golden brown. Add meat; cook until meat loses red color. Drain off fat. Add spaghetti sauce (you can use different flavors of sauce if you so desire) and heat. Arrange ½ noodles, ½ sauce, and cheese in a 13 x 9 inch baking dish. Make another layer. Top with cheese. Bake 1 hour at 350°. Place a piece of Reynolds wrap on top until it is just about done to keep it from being hard on top.

> Life is 10 percent what you make it and 90 percent how you take it.

Danish Potato Salad
Brenda Troutt

¼ cup vinegar
¼ cup water
¼ cup sugar
¼ tsp. salt
   dash of pepper
1 tsp. prepared mustard
2 eggs, well beaten
1 cup mayonnaise
4 cups cooked potatoes
2 hard cooked eggs, chopped
½ cup sweet pickle relish
1 tsp. minced onion

Combine first six ingredients. Bring to a boil. Reduce heat, gradually add in well-beaten eggs. Cook, stirring constantly, until thickened, about 5 minutes. Beat in mayonnaise. Mix together remaining ingredients. Pour on dressing and toss gently.

A two-day Civil War Reenactment takes place each October on the grounds of Laurel Hill in Ararat, Virginia, featuring period activities such as church services, the field hospital, a fashion show, lectures, etc.

Tom Perry

Laurel Hill Farm in Ararat, VA, the birthplace of James Ewell Brown (Jeb) Stuart, is on Virginia's State Historic Landmarks Register and the National Register of Historic Places, although none of the original buildings are still standing. The preservation of the 75-acre tract is due to the efforts of author and historian Thomas David (Tom) Perry who started the J.E.B. Stuart Birthplace Preservation Trust in 1990. Perry speaks extensively on the Civil War in Southwest Virginia and the life of Jeb Stuart. Along with the eight interpretative signs at Laurel Hill and other historical markers, he has written three books about J.E.B. Stuart and two about Patrick County. His latest book is *"God's Will Be Done: The Christian Life of Jeb Stuart."*   www.freestateofpatrick.com

> *"Peace I leave with you, my peace I give unto you: not as the world giveth, give I unto you. Le not your heart be troubled, neither let it be afraid."* **John 14:27**

Date Nut Bars
Betty Perry – Ararat, VA

¾ cup self rising flour
1 cup sugar
½ cup Mazola oil
2 eggs
½ tsp. vanilla
1 cup dates (8oz pkg) finely cut
1 cup chopped pecans

Mix flour and sugar. Make a well and add in order - Mazola oil, eggs, and vanilla. Beat until smooth. Add dates and nuts, mix well. Turn into greased 12 x 17 x 2-inch baking dish. Bake at 350° for 20 to 25 minutes. Cut into bars while warm.

Scaling a fish is easier if vinegar is rubbed on the scales first.

Roy and Reba Stoffel create hand built clay pottery. One of his bowls was presented to Governor Kaine on the occasion of a GED graduation at Reynolds Homestead in June, 2007. "Hillbillies" are one of his specialties.

Deviled Eggs
Recipe from old handwritten cookbook – Submitted by Roy Stoffel – Stuart, VA

Eggs
Salt & pepper
Butter
Mustard
Vinegar
Minced potted ham
Mayonnaise

Hard boil eggs. Cut cooked eggs in half, either lengthwise or crosswise. Mash yolks, season with pepper and salt, butter, a little mustard and vinegar. Minced potted ham may be added to yolks or mix with mayonnaise. Refill whites with mixture, put 2 halves together, and wrap each egg in square of waxed paper. Ideal for picnic lunch.

Fire and Ice Tomatoes
Claudette Smith

6   large tomatoes, sliced
1   large bell pepper, sliced
1   large onion, sliced

Place the vegetables in a bowl. Mix the following and boil together for 1 minute and then pour over vegetables. Chill for 24 hours and serve.

¾   cup vinegar
2   tsps. salt
4½ tsps. sugar
¼   cup water

> In every walk with nature, one receives far more than he seeks.
> -*John Muir*

Mayberry Trading Post has long been a favorite stop along the Blue Ridge Parkway between milepost 180-181. The historical building (circa 1892) that was once a post office and general store, now is a general store. Nearby is Mayberry Presbyterian Church, one of the rock churches immortalized in the book, "The Man Who Moved a Mountain."

The First Recipe

    Clip, Clop, Clippity, Clop – Sam and Pete, two frisky Belgium horses, pulled the handcrafted cherry wagon toward the Bob White Covered Bridge in Woolwine, VA. The morning air was pleasant with the promise of the day. It was the second trip for the pair and they were more than up to the task. Libby and I felt lucky to be the only passengers, riding with William, the driver, and Bradley, his grandson and sidekick. Clippity, clop - went the horse's hooves on the sturdy old wooden boards as we entered the weathered structure; the timbers responded with welcoming creaks as though happy to be of use again. For a brief moment in the coolness of the bridge, we glimpsed a bit of life gone by. It was lovely. All too quickly, we exited the other side of the bridge and continued up the gravel road to the pavement. Clip, clip, clop, - the staccato was louder here.

    People waved from passing automobiles and from their yards. We all waved back. After we complimented the wagon, William explained how his son-in-law had cut trees and sawed the lumber – then he and another son-in-law constructed it. Soon the conversation turned to food. William told us how he made sausage gravy, Bradley's favorite. (He mixes the flour and milk together before adding it to the sausage drippings.) Then he added, "Mud turtle is a favorite with my whole family," and proceeded to explain how to trap and shoot the soon-to-be meal.

    The clippity - clopping of the horse's hooves and the image of cleaning and cooking the mud turtle had woven a spell about us. Houses and people passed unnoticed as we followed the cooking process. After a bit, we exited the paved road into a meadow that wound past two more covered bridges. The ride was one that our ancestors might have felt very comfortable taking – especially in those cushy seats. They would be flabbergasted! For all William's authenticity in building the wagon, he cut loose from tradition and installed automobile seats to ride on and modern tires in place of wooden wheels. We were right glad that he did.

William's Recipe for Fried Mud Turtle

William Collins - Patrick Spring, VA

Have water boiling in large pot. Drop whole turtle (dead) into water for a few minutes, which will loosen dark skin. Peel quickly. With sharp knife, cut between meat and top shell, and then bottom shell. To separate into pieces, cut up near joints. Soak in salt water until next day.
Boil until tender. Takes a while.

Prepare a batter: 1   egg
   Equal amounts of flour and cornmeal
   Milk as needed
   Pepper and Salt

Heat homemade lard. Dip pieces into batter until well coated. Drop battered turtle into hot grease and cook until browned. Serve warm. (In lieu of homemade lard, shortening or oil may be used.)

Mothers, as well as fools, sometimes walk where angels fear to tread.

Green Pea Casserole

Margie E. Fleming

1	onion, chopped
½	green bell pepper, chopped
4	ribs of celery, chopped
1	stick margarine
1	(4 oz.) can mushrooms, chopped
1	can cream mushroom soup
1	jar pimentos, chopped
2	cans green peas, drained (reserve 1 cup juice)
1	cup fine, dry breadcrumbs

Sauté onion, pepper, and celery in ½ stick of margarine. Mix mushrooms, soup, pimentos and the pea liquid together. Combine all ingredients except breadcrumbs and margarine in a large greased casserole dish. Top with breadcrumbs and dot with remaining margarine. Bake for 30 minutes at 350°.

Homemade Fresh Salsa
Vickie Wasoski – EFNEP Program Assistant

Wolf Creek Cherokee Tribe of Stuart operates a lovely Museum on Blue Ridge St. Stop by and see Chief and Littlewolf who know the stories. www.wolfcreek cherokeetribe.com

3	large tomatoes	½	tsp. sugar
1	green bell pepper	1	Tbsp. cilantro
1	red bell pepper	1	can black beans
1	jalapeno pepper (small)		(drained and rinsed)
1	medium onion	1	small can corn
2	garlic cloves (2sections)		(drained) optional
1	tsp. cumin		
½	tsp. salt		

Chop all ingredients very small. Stir together and refrigerate for at least one hour so flavors blend together. Stir and serve with chips.

Indian Ash Cake
Littlewolf Griffith – Wolf Creek Cherokee Tribe – Stuart, VA

Make a stiff dough of self-rising white flour and warm water (can be made of Corn meal)
Rake ashes back, then spread oak leaves on hot stones at the bottom of the fireplace or a pot belled stove. Lay on pone of dough. Cover with more oak leaves and pile on red-hot ashes. Remove pone of bread when done and eat as bread with homemade butter.

Killer Meat Loaf
Jack TeBo – Meadows of Dan, VA

Jack is author of the action thriller book, *"The Danger Within."*

2	lbs. 80% ground beef	2	large eggs
¼	cup diced green pepper	1	can onion soup
¼	cup diced onions	1	small can tomato sauce

Hand-mix the ground beef, green pepper, dried onions, and eggs. Add and mix the onion soup. Cook at 350° until top crusts over. Pour on tomato sauce. Bake for 10 minutes.

"LaNita Howell was born in Meadows of Dan, the daughter of Ruby Underwood Howell and William Cruise Howell. She has lived near Meadows of Dan most of her life and worked until her retirement in the Patrick County School System. She has always been active in her church and spent many years playing piano and organ for services. She was a member of Robert Childress's congregation at Slate Mountain Church in her youth. She now works occasionally as a guide for a bus tour of the Childress rock churches. Since her retirement she spends time in community service, helping with the local "Meals on Wheels" and other activities. She and her husband, Wendell Harris, also enjoy the many musical events along the Crooked Road in Patrick County.

LaNita comes from a musical family. Her father, William Cruise Howell, was well known locally as a banjo player and in his later years crafted musical instruments, especially banjos. LaNita's son is Sammy Shelor, multiple winner of IBMA's Banjo Player of the Year and the talented leader of the bluegrass band, **Lonesome River Band**." -Leslie Shelor

Lemon juice rubbed on a fish before cooking will enhance the flavor and help maintain a good color.

LaNita's Bread Pudding
LaNita Howell Harris – Meadows of Dan, VA

5   leftover biscuits
    milk
2   large eggs, beaten
2/3 cup sugar
½   cup raisins
1   tsp. vanilla flavoring
2   tsps. melted margarine

Crumble biscuits into medium casserole dish. Add milk to cover well and let sit for 15 minutes to soften crumbs. Stir in beaten eggs, sugar, and raisins. Mix in vanilla flavoring. Add melted margarine to mixture. Stir all ingredients well. Bake in pre-heated 350° oven for about 35 minutes or until lightly browned.

Rubbing alcohol will remove ballpoint ink marks. So will hairspray - cheaper works best.

"Myrtle Inscore's fried cabbage is the requested dish at any gathering and she always brings home an empty bowl. She was born on a farm in Claudville, VA on the banks of the Little Dan River, one of 12 children of Jim and Shuggie Bowman Hall. In January 2008, only she and her brother, Willie Hall are still living. She and her husband Russell Inscore operated Inscore's Grocery for many years on the Willis Gap Road in Ararat. He passed away in May 1998. At age 89, Myrtle continues to mow her own yard and to have a showcase yard filled with flowers all summer. One of her latest projects has been to paint her bedroom all by herself. She is an amazing woman who still cooks in the old-timey way and who still makes a mean pot of chicken and dumplings."

Mama's Old Fashioned Fried Cabbage
Recipe of Myrtle Hall Inscore – Ararat, VA – submitted by her three daughters

1 cabbage head, chopped
   salt & sugar to taste
   canola oil or couple of pieces of fatback

Chop cabbage very fine in a large bowl. Add salt and sugar to taste, mix it with your hands. Begin with ½ cup sugar and then experiment (I use enough sugar to make the cabbage very sweet.)
Heat canola oil for the healthy version; otherwise fry a couple of pieces of fatback to get a good amount of grease and when hot (not warm), add the cabbage. Begin stirring the cabbage mixture immediately and stir until it is hot and has started to turn color. Put the lid on the pot and cut the stove eye off. Leave on the stove eye for several minutes and the cabbage will continue the cooking process. DO NOT ADD ANY WATER.

"I was a tomboy growing up. My brother and I played cowboys and used my baby carriage as a stagecoach. We both had little cap guns. They were a lot more fun than playing dolls.

Mama and Daddy raised everything you could think of where we lived out in the Five Forks area. There was an apple orchard, tobacco, gardens, cows, horses, pigs – you name it. We didn't suffer during the depression because of having plenty of food and wonderful neighbors. Daddy repaired our shoes, pulled teeth with little pliers, and could fix about anything.

There were bad times. My oldest sister caught on fire trying to put wood in the stove when mama went outside for something. They rolled her in a rug to put out the fire but she died. Today she could have been saved but not then. All three of my brothers went into service in World War II and that was a rough time.

After I was grown, my father, who played the organ and piano, ended up being a preacher. My grandfather, John Henry (Pet) Mitchell, would come on Sunday afternoons and play the fiddle. People would stop by to listen to the music." -Barbara Hopkins

Meat Loaf

Barbara Hopkins – Stuart, VA

1	lb. hamburger	1/3	cup oatmeal
½	cup water	1	onion, chopped
¼	cup tomato ketchup	¼	cup green pepper (optional)
1	tsp. salt	¼	tsp. pepper

Combine all ingredients. Shape loaf in baking dish. Cook 10 minutes while making sauce. Combine the following and spoon sauce over meat loaf. Bake 50 minutes at 350°.

1	Tbsp. vinegar	½	cup ketchup
¼	cup water	1	Tbsp. Worcestershire sauce
1	tsp. sugar		

Home Remedy for Poison Oak
Gurney Royall

Take 3 bloodroots (or coon root) the size of your little finger and put in pint of clear liquor. Let it set for approximately 3 days. Take 1 tsp. 2 times a day for 7 days. Don't drink Dr. Pepper or other soft drink after dosage. Milk is a better choice. If you are allergic to sulfur, don't take. You can mix with rubbing alcohol to rub on your poison oak. Also works for shingles.

Jasmine and lighter-bodied teas like Formosa oolong, have a natural sweetness, reducing the need for sugars or sweetners. They make a great iced tea as well.

"Charlie and I are both avid gardeners – as well as musicians! We love to eat goodies fresh out of the garden round here in Patrick County! We always grow lots of salad greens, lettuce and romaine as well as beet greens and Arugula. This dressing never fails to get the ...mmm... response! This recipe comes from The Inn at Cedar Falls in southern Ohio but the moment I tasted it, I remembered my mother's homemade French dressing! It has never failed to elicit raves from salad eaters... We have been performing and recording in the acoustic music industry for a combined total of more than forty years, traveling internationally as well as throughout the United States. We spent over fifteen years as the "rhythm core" of the Dry Branch Fire Squad bluegrass band and recorded many projects on niche super-label, Rounder Records. We have recently recorded four independent music projects: find them at www.Geobuilt.com Working as a duet or in concert with fine musicians, we enjoy sharing American Acoustic Music with the live audience! In 2006, we moved to Patrick Springs, VA, on "The Crooked Road: Virginia's Heritage Music Trail!"

MJ's Best Red Dressing
Mary Jo and Charlie Leet – Patrick Springs, VA

1/3 cup sugar
1   tsp. paprika
1   tsp. salt
1/3 cup cider vinegar
1   cup vegetable oil, 1/3 cup at a time
1/3 cup ketchup

In a pint jar, combine the sugar, paprika, and salt. Add the cider vinegar and shake, shake, shake! Add the oil 1/3 cup at a time and shake after each addition. Add the ketchup and shake, shake, shake! I "lighten" the recipe by making the last "1/3 cup oil" addition be "water" and I have never had a complaint. Of course, the fresher the paprika, the better, and spicy paprika is wonderful! The gals at the Inn insisted this needs to be shaken in a jar. I didn't ask why and haven't tried it any other way!!

Merry Cherry Cheesecake Bars

Ann A. Steekler- Stuart, VA

1¼ cups all-purpose flour
½ cup packed brown sugar
¼ cup margarine
1 (8 oz.) pkg. cream cheese
1/3 cup sugar
1 egg
2 Tbsps. lemon juice
½ cup red cherries
½ cup green cherries

Mix the flour, brown sugar and margarine to make crust. Reserve ½ cup crumbs from this mixture. Heat oven to 350°. Press remainder of crumbs in 13 x 9-inch pan. Beat cream cheese, sugar and egg until mixed. Add cherries and lemon juice. Spread over crust. Sprinkle with reserved crumbs. Bake for 20 minutes or until lightly browned. Cool and cut into bars. Keep refrigerated.

Smith River Church of the Brethren

Love Feast and Communion Service

He riseth from supper, and laid aside his garments; and took a towel, and girded himself. After that he poureth water into a basin, and began to wash the disciples' feet, and to wipe them with the towel wherewith he was girded. John 13:4-5

    The first small step toward compiling a cookbook/storybook was taken in June 2007, when we attended the Covered Bridge Festival in Patrick County. We were excited but unsure, testing the waters, learning as we went. So many people we met that day received our idea positively and gave great encouragement for the project, including then Tourism Director, Jeannie Frisco.

    A vital part of the festival is the lovely white church built by, and named for, the waters of the Smith River in 1892. After all, the Bob White Covered Bridge was built to connect the church to the main road in 1921 and was used many years. That day we met some of the fetching ladies of the church, Carol Ann Turner, Barbara Harbour, Joan Turner, Brenda Troutt, and Linda Bryant.

    After expressing admiration for their neat and well-kept church, Carol Ann asked if we would like to see the inside, so she and Linda gave us a tour. As we rambled, she explained how they cooked beef for the semi-annual Love Feast and Communion Service. This special commemoration includes washing each other's feet to symbolize the

way in which Jesus showed servitude by washing the disciple's feet during his last Passover meal with them. She invited us to the next service, to be held in October.

On the appointed day in October, it was hot, dry, and dusty. My husband and I went to Lynchburg for our grandson's football game and Libby had a trip also. But we managed to clean our feet especially well, get together, and motor into the parking lot in Woolwine at the proper time.

Apprehension set in the minute we parked the car and noticed some women walking toward the church in dresses or skirts and with a covering on their heads. Oh, boy, we had worn pants. We sat for a few minutes, gathering courage, when another car parked and two ladies got out with pants on. Whew! But they still had the same neat little head covering. Well, we couldn't sit in the car; people were beginning to look at us. They knew we were visitors, we reasoned, so would not expect us to own the headpiece.

As we approached the door, members expressed friendly greetings. Happy day, there stood Carol Ann, our angel, with two headpieces (prayer caps) in her hands. She placed a prayer cap on each of our heads and led us down the aisle to sit with her and other friends.

The men occupied one side of the aisle and women the other. She pointed out her own family members, explaining that it was tradition during this service for the women to wash each other's feet and the men to do likewise. It seemed a very practical method to me. We were introduced to several congregants and Carol continued to explain different things about the church, such as the little wooden ledge attached to the back of the pew in front of us which held the beef for the fellowship meal and communion cup.

A heavenly smell permeated the sanctuary. It is no exaggeration to say I had never smelled such an extraordinary beef aroma. Our angel had cooked that, too, and here is what she did: Soaked it overnight in water that was drained off in the morning. The beef was slowly cooked all day, until it fell into small shreds, with salt and some butter added in the afternoon. That was it. Other than perhaps a blessing.

Opening remarks by the pastor, songs of joy, and a period of silent as well as verbal prayer prepare hearts for the holy service. Scriptures were read. Foot washing came next. The way it was done was so practical and so reverent at the same time; both Libby and I were awestruck.

The lady in the pew in front of Carol Ann stepped back and a towel/apron was tied around her waist with another placed across her shoulder. Carol Ann removed her shoes and the lady simply and gently washed her feet and dried them. She then tied the apron around Carol Ann, placed the towel across her shoulder and hugged her. The pastor, Mr. Troutt, had suggested telling the person whose feet you washed, "I Love You."

A cappella singing began, voices softly filling all the spaces in the room with an intimate, soulful beauty. Somehow the sound dispelled any awkwardness, leaving only reverence. Betty Jane Holt lead the congregation in *"Father's have a home, sweet home,"* that continues with a verse each for Mother's, Sisters, and Brothers.

It was my turn. Carol Ann washed with quiet dignity my less than pretty feet. The water was warm but would not have mattered had it been cold. With the washing and drying came a feeling of connection, of being involved in something beyond ourselves. When she finished drying my feet and tied the apron on me with a hug, I felt loved as a fellow human being and a child of God.

As the singing continued, so did the pan of water. We slid it on the floor to the next person on the pew and there was plenty of room. I washed and dried Libby's feet, tied the apron, and hugged her. She continued the process with the person beside her. I can think of no way to describe it except as a joyous and humbling experience. Though singing was part of the ritual, in respect to the people around me I did not burst into out-of-key song. But I really wished my voice could carry a tune.

Men of the church read more scripture. Thanks were returned for the food about to be received. We began eating the meal of fellowship - beef and beef sop on bread – every bit as wonderful as it smelled. Once again came the feeling of receiving a blessing along with the folded sandwich.

"At the Cross" was the next song, a reminder of where the night ended for Jesus. After the reading of the prophecy (Isaiah 53) and the fulfillment (John 19:1-30) came the sacrament of communion. The service ended with a closing prayer and a song, *God Be With You*. No further benediction was given and we left quietly. With hearts so full, nothing needed to be said.

Marvin and Helen Cockram have been members of the Highlanders Band for many years.

"I grew up on a farm and as a small child I would be at my grandparents when molasses boiling time came. I enjoyed all that went along with it – popping corn, making taffy, eating cookies, apples, melons and sopping the boiler. After a few years, their health kept them from doing any hard work and they had to give up boiling molasses.

I married Marvin Cockram when I was 18 and he was 20. We helped my parents on the farm and also worked jobs. Every year about time to boil molasses I would ask them when we would grow cane and boil molasses. They finally gave in about 1973 and we kept it going until about 1998. I am hoping that our grandchildren will start growing cane, but they don't seem to be as anxious to get into it as I was. They do love those cookies, though, so maybe they will try it someday. We still have the mill to grind the cane and the boiler to cook the molasses. I found the recipe for the cookies early on and I am still baking them."

Molasses

Mountain home
Out by the fire.
'Lassey smell
　in the air
As we stirred
Slow smoke
　drifted upward
Soft voices from
　the dark
Entertained and
　intertwined
　our lives
So briefly.

Molasses Cookies

Helen Cockram – Meadows of Dan, VA

1½ cups shortening	2 eggs
1 cup sugar	½ cup molasses
1 cup brown sugar	

Beat above ingredients thoroughly. Mix following ingredients and beat in gradually:

4½ cups flour	1 tsp. cloves
4 tsps. soda	2 tsps. cinnamon
1 tsp. salt	1 tsp. ginger

Chill dough at least 1 hour. Roll dough into balls and then roll into granulated sugar. Put on ungreased cookie sheet and bake at 350° for 7 minutes. Do Not Over Bake. The time and temperature may have to be adjusted to your oven. When the cookies crack on top they are done. Remove from oven and leave in pan 3 to 4 minutes.

"My Dad, Frank Lynch, was a county constable for Patrick County. The first year he began the job, he was involved in busting up 17 copper stills in the Lovers Leap Mountain. Dad said one of the stills was a work of art. The same man built back three times - three perfect stills - Dad busted it up three times. After the third time, the moonshiner gave up and went to West Virginia to find work – so he told dad in later years. He also informed dad, 'Frank, you know the time you found my still that was under the big ledge, almost a cave? Well, I was laying right on top of that ledge watching. I could'a dropped a rock on your head if I'da been a mind to.'

One night my uncle, Raleigh Lynch, had been to a frolic where he had taken in a substantial amount of liquid refreshment. He had to walk back home by an old graveyard. As he approached the cemetery, he saw a man. He kept seeing the fellow and finally figured him out to be an old man who'd been dead for years. Frightened, he pulled out his pistol and shot several times. Raleigh then ran, jumped an 8-ft rail fence, and fell in the door gasping and panting. He was fairly sober by that time and worried he had shot a person and not a ghost. He wanted dad to go back and see. Dad waited until daylight and walked up to the cemetery. Along the edge of the graves was a hill with a large white rock overhang – missing several pieces that had been shot off."

Peanut Butter Frosts

Ruffin Lynch – Meadows of Dan, VA

1   cup all-purpose flour
1   cup quick-cooking oats
½   cup sugar
½   cup firmly packed brown sugar
½   tsp. soda
½   cup butter or margarine, softened
1/3 cup peanut butter
1   egg, beaten

Combine flour, oats, sugar, and soda in a large bowl. Add butter, peanut butter, and egg; stir until thoroughly blended. (Mixture will be crumbly.) Press in the bottom of a greased 9-inch square pan. Bake at 350° for 20 to 25 minutes or until the edges begin to pull away from sides of pan. (The center will be soft.) Cool completely. Top with Peanut Butter Frosting. Sprinkle with chopped peanuts, if desired.
Cut into eighteen 3- x 1½-inch bars. *(continued on next page)*

Fairystone State Park, named for the unique crosses found in the area, opened in 1936. The largest of the original six state parks in Virginia, it was built by the Civilian Conservation Corps on 4,537 acres of land donated by Junius B. Fishburn, once owner of the *Roanoke Times*. Swimming, camping, hiking, fishing, as well as nature and history programs are available all summer. Organized fairy stone hunts may be taken. Picnic shelters and cabins are located among shaded areas. www.dcr.state.va.us/parks

Peanut Butter Frosting:
¼ cup butter or margarine, softened
1½ cups powdered sugar, divided
¼ cup peanut butter
1 Tbsp. plus 2 tsps. milk
1 tsp. vanilla extract
  chopped peanuts, optional

Combine butter and 1 cup sugar in a small mixing bowl; beat until creamy. Add remaining ½ cup sugar, peanut butter, milk, and vanilla. Beat until fluffy. Add additional milk if needed. If you like peanut butter, you will like this!

Oatmeal Pie
Carol Turner – Woolwine, VA

2 eggs
2/3 cup melted oleo
2/3 cup white sugar
2/3 cup white-Karo syrup
2/3 cup, uncooked oatmeal
1/8 tsp. salt
1 tsp. vanilla

Beat eggs well. Add remaining ingredients and pour into unbaked pie shell. Bake 35-45 minutes at 350°.

Potato Candy
Margaret Noonkester

1 small potato (boiled and still hot)
1 box powdered sugar
  peanut butter

Mix powdered sugar with potato (using a fork) until it makes a dough. Then roll the dough out and spread the peanut butter on top. Roll it in a log and slice it in small pieces.

Hudson's Drug Store

A Hudson operated a drug store in Stuart, VA for the biggest part of the 20th century. George Hudson arrived in Stuart in the early 1920's and bought the Conner Drug Store. He operated under the name until 1941 when a new store was built and became Hudson's. Richard (Dick) Hudson started working there "when I was big enough to look over the counter."

Dick, a pharmacist, moved away after completing school but came home in 1954 to help his dad after the death of his brother. "We had a fountain and served food until sometime in the '60's when it became hard to find someone to run it."

Daughter, Cathy, remembers the cherry smashes as a favorite treat. "I also liked the ice cream at the fountain as a kid. And when he closed, we found out how expensive many things were that we took for granted he would bring home from the store."

"I used to know everybody in Stuart," says Hudson. "If somebody got sick at night, I went to open the store for them no matter what time it was. They usually didn't call unless it was important. I would be open part of the day on Sunday, too."

Any interesting stories about life as a pharmacist in a small town for almost fifty years? "Well, not really. But I did once find some old prescriptions for alcohol written back during prohibition. That was one way to get hold of some, I guess. Threw them away, but now wish I had kept them," he states.

Old Meadows of Dan Store. (L-R) Owner Lee Handy, Floyd Lawson, Pauline Handy Clifton, Guy Lawson, unknown, Harry Lawson. Photo compliments of Irene Handy Joyce.

Rice and Beans Spanish Dish
Kathleen Guynn

1	(15 oz.) can red kidney beans
2	(8 oz.) cans tomato sauce
1	medium onion, chopped
½	pod green sweet pepper, chopped
1	stalk celery, chopped
2	pks. Sazon (seasoning)
	garlic, salt & pepper to taste
1	bean can of water
1	cup long grain rice
1	Tbsp. oil
2	cups water

Mix 1st eight ingredients together. Cook until onions, celery, and peppers are done. Cook rice with oil in 2 cups water for 20 minutes. Take off stove and let set in covered kettle until all water is evaporated. Mix sauce and rice together and serve.

> If you love browsing and you're anywhere near Stuart, don't miss the *Just Plain Country Antique Mall*. Besides antiques, you may find local arts and crafts, collectibles, and surprises. With over 170 vendors, it's well worth a look!
> **276-694-5556**

Rum Cake
Patsy Baliles – Stuart, VA

1	cup pecans	½	cup cold water
1	box yellow cake mix	½	cup oil
1	pkg. vanilla pudding mix	½	cup rum (80 proof)
4	eggs		

Grease and flour tube pan or bundt pan. Sprinkle nuts over bottom of pan. Mix cake ingredients and pour over nuts. Bake 1 hour at 325°. Let cool, put cake on a plate or server and prick top of cake and spoon on glaze.

Glaze:

¼	lb. butter	1	cup sugar
¼	cup water	½	cup rum

Melt butter in saucepan. Stir in water and sugar. Boil 5 minutes, stirring constantly. Remove from heat and stir in rum.

Sammy and Sue Shelor in the corn maze.

Bluegrass, Banjos, a Wink, and a Mountain Farm

"I've been all over the world and there's nowhere I like more; it's a combination of the countryside and the people that keeps me here," states Sammy Shelor emphatically. "Meadows of Dan is definitely an old hometown type place. I like that."

Eighteen years spent on the road with the high-energy bluegrass Lonesome River Band has given him an appreciation for down time at home on the crest of the Blue Ridge. Though his family moved "below the mountain" to Stuart when he was eleven years old, summers were spent with a grandfather, Sandy Shelor, in the manner of rural kids. Putting up hay for local farmers, fishing, roaming the woods and fields, and visiting neighbors grounded and established in the young boy an affinity for older people. Grandpa Sandy knew where the best cooks lived, so they often dropped by those houses around midday when the biggest meal of the day was generally being served. Playing the banjo with musicians like Cap Ayers, Tump Spangler or his maternal grandfather, Cruise Howell, rounded out the summer.

"My two grandfathers are the biggest influence on my life - period," says Shelor. "Without them, I would not have learned musically what I needed to know."

At four years old, Sammy was enthralled by grandfather Cruise Howell's banjo picking. So much so that Howell built a little banjo out of a pressure cooker lid, whittling out the neck and constructing a tin head. It was put together with tractor bolts and coat hanger wire, but had real strings that could be tuned. Though given as a toy, the makeshift instrument was taken seriously.

"Grandpa Sandy told me if I could learn to play two songs on it, he'd buy me a real banjo," laughs Sam. "In fact, he went ahead and bought it. The day I managed that second song, I took off across the field to his house. I played the songs for him and drug that real banjo back home with me."

Shelor learned all he could about music, listening to numerous records and practicing. By ten years old, he was playing in an adult band. A friend, Gale Shockley, was the same age and played a guitar. They often performed together and got the opportunity to be on a couple of television shows called "Southern Exposure" and "The Old Rebel Show." Grandpa Shelor and he traveled and camped at fiddler's conventions within a two hundred mile radius - where Sammy listened, played with bands, and competed solo. "I've never had stage fright," he says, "probably due to being exposed to it so young. It seemed normal to me."

Before joining Lonesome River Band in 1990, several years were spent right out of high school with Heights of Grass and Virginia Squires, honing skills and working out a sound all his own. Legendary banjo player Sonny Osborne influenced and mentored the younger musician during these years, teaching, among other things, the importance of a quality instrument. By becoming a master of flawless timing, he was ready for the hard-driving, distinctive sound of Lonesome River Band and they were ready for his picking on their breakout CD, *Carrying the Tradition,* which propelled them to critical and commercial success. It's been said that two words could describe the LRB sound of the 90's: They Rock! Through many changes, that statement remains true.

Nominated for fourteen years in a row as Banjo Player of the Year by peers in the International Bluegrass Music Association, Sam has won four consecutive times. Honors have come from the Society for the Preservation of Bluegrass Music in America. (SPBGMA) He has been a guest player on any number of recordings, did a solo CD *Leading Roll,* and contributed great picking as well as vocals on a Crooked Road music series release, *Taking the Crooked Road Home,* which featured the versatile voice of Linda Lay. (Tom T. and Dixie Hall wrote the title cut from that CD.) Mid-October, 2007, saw Sammy joining other keepers of a historical musical legacy on the West Coast

Crooked Road Tour, also sponsored by the National Council for Traditional Arts. The tour was a rousing success.

After a decade with LRB, Shelor became the owner and leader of the band. Not anything that he had envisioned, just the way it happened. "Lonesome River Band is really a trademark, a business, and a job that could easily take a sixty hour workweek," he states. "There are always transportation issues; road bands have personnel changes and various details to attend to." Still, like most traditional and Bluegrass musicians, he makes time to help out at benefits and be a vital part of the local community.

Generations of Shelors have called the Blue Ridge Mountains home, so Sam's roots extend deep and wide into the rich soil. Though his wife, Sue, is a Connecticut Yankee transplanted to rural Virginia, she has adopted the area with a vengeance. No native could be a bigger advocate and seller of Patrick County and the artisans who live and work there. From the beginning, she was taken by the beauty and potential of the Blue Ridge Parkway and the region as a whole.

As a member of 'Round the Mountain, Sue works toward community and economic development for folks in Southwest Virginia. All items sold in her Mountain Meadow Crafts Market are made by artisans in the county, giving tourists something to take home that is an authentic memento of the area visited.

The two first met at a festival in Connecticut. She was a big fan of bluegrass music, but had only recently heard of Lonesome River Band. Upon seeing the first performance, she admits to having a thing ("the hots") for the banjo player, so stood in line to buy a CD and get an autograph. Sammy winked at her. "A couple of weeks later, in Pennsylvania, I saw him again," she says.

Sue Shelor in her shop at Mountain Meadows Crafts.

"You winked at me at the last festival," Sue told him.

"Naw, I don't do that sort of thing," he replied.

Their first date took place on Labor Day weekend. A long-distance relationship ensued, with Sammy remembering well all the 600-mile journeys from his driveway to hers for the next couple of years. Sue and her young son, Hunter, moved to Virginia and the wedding took place in September of 2000.

Coming from an artistic family, Sue had explored a number of mediums but hadn't found a niche until she decided to try gourd art. The first endeavor was a birdhouse, but she felt something more creative could be done. Because of being a self-described "earthy type person," who loves natural things, Sue and Hunter began exploring the woods and picking up items to decorate gourds. Pine needles, duck and other bird feathers, and even opossum teeth have been used, along with carving and wood burning. "I always try to make one of a kind items."

After Sammy inherited Grandfather Sandy's farm, an idea that perhaps selling vegetables would compliment the gourd art emerged. Gardening had been part of her life growing up as the youngest of five children, though never on a large scale. Undaunted, they had fields plowed and Sue decided to try heirloom tomatoes, different varieties of squash, two sweet corns, and seven types of beans. She tries to introduce more diversity of vegetables than might ordinarily be grown locally.

The first year was hard work, as gardens tend to be, with lots of rocks to be picked up. The selling took place under a tent by the side of the road. The following year, 2006, a friend and fellow banjo picker, John Arnold, suggested a corn maze as a possible agri-tourism use for part of the farm.

Because of being located on the Crooked Road and associated with the music industry, a decision was reached in favor of a maze featuring a musical theme each year. Sue appeared before the Crooked Road Executive Board to request the use of their logo for the first acoustics maze. With permission, and the help of John Arnold's graph, they managed an "amazing" recreation of the crooked road emblem, down to the little trademark ™. To begin the design, John and Sammy went into the knee-high corn with spray paint, a measuring wheel, and a square. They determined each square as closely as possible and sprayed the corn in that area. And on – and on - through the whole six acres, a little at a time. Following that, the two men spent thirty hours with weed eaters in hand, cutting two feet on each side of the sprayed corn. Afterwards, it took Sue about six hours per week with a lawn mower to keep it trimmed.

Hunter designed and built a Kid's Maze with bales of hay in the shape of a farm tractor. They were on their way!

The 2007 "Acoustics Corn Maze" was actually two: a large and a small one side by side. The smaller one was laid out to show *LRB 25,* in honor of their twenty-fifth anniversary. The larger one, cross planted to be thicker than normal, was more a musical trail depicting the trials, tribulations, and sometimes the dead ends of a musician's life. Questions planted throughout the journey added interest.

"We keep working out kinks as best we can," Sue says of the maze and the farm. "We're definitely learning the hard way."

So how many balls can two people keep up in the air at one time, doing most of the work themselves? Quite a few it seems, especially during the summer months through October, when record numbers of tourist travel the Blue Ridge Parkway, which runs beside their farm and craft shop. "About November it gets pretty quiet around here. The bad part of the farm is that the busiest time for Bluegrass and the gardening season run together," explains Sam.

Toward the end of autumn, Sue begins thinking of new gourd creations and hunting season right around the corner – she is an avid hunter. "We eat the meat I bring in," she states. "I have a great recipe for squirrel pot pie."

"And she makes the best deer tenderloin dish ever," adds Sammy.

As for Lonesome River Band…well, it's on the road again. "I've been doing this for thirty years. It's all I know. I like traveling, enjoy the music, the people we meet, and even problems are part of the deal" Sam laughs.

Simple Grilled Striped Bass

Sammy Shelor – Meadows of Dan, VA

2   striped bass fillets – skinned
    juice from 1 fresh lemon
1   Tbsp. olive oil
¼   tsp. parsley
¼   tsp. dill
1/8 tsp. tarragon
If using fresh herbs – increase the amounts.

Place the fillets on heavy-duty foil. Drizzle on the olive oil and lemon juice. Sprinkle the herbs over the fish. Wrap up foil leaving some room for air. Heat outside grill to medium; place foil inside and close lid. Do not turn fillets during grilling. Fish will be done when meat is white and flaky. Garnish with lemon wedges and fresh parsley sprigs.

Scalloped Potatoes
Phyllis Overby – Stuart, VA

Always offer to bait your date's fish hook, especially on the first date. Of course, if she's the better fisherman, the least you can do is buy or dig the bait.

7 medium potatoes
1 (12 oz.) can evaporated milk
1 (10 ¾ oz.) Campbell's Cheddar Cheese Soup
1/3 cup chopped onion
1/3 cup butter (melted)
1 tsp. salt
¼ tsp. McCormick ground black pepper

Preheat oven to 375°. Arrange sliced potatoes in greased 2-quart rectangular baking dish. In bowl, combine milk, soup, onion, butter, salt, and pepper; pour over potatoes. Bake, covered for 45 minutes. Uncover and bake 15 minutes more. Serves 6 or 8. Delicious!

"Sometimes you stumble upon a recipe that is easy to make and the ingredients combine for a delicious flavor. That was the case when I received the following recipe from my Aunt Nancy."

Spinach Casserole
Betsy Wilds - Stuart, VA

1 pkg. frozen chopped spinach
1 (8 oz.) container sour cream
1 can cream of potato soup
1 cup sharp cheese

Cook spinach by directions on package; drain well. Combine with soup and sour cream. Sprinkle cheese on top. Bake at 350° for ½ hour. So simple and yet so tasty!

Squirrel Pot Pie

Sue Shelor – Meadows of Dan, VA

2 squirrels – skinned and cleaned, cooked and diced
1 medium onion – chopped
¾ cup celery – diced
¾ cup fresh or frozen peas
¾ cup carrots – sliced
½ cup mushrooms – sliced
¼ cup lemon juice
   dried tarragon – to taste
   dash of salt and black pepper
3 Tbsps. butter
1 Tbsp. oil
1 bay leaf
5 peppercorns – whole
2 cans chicken broth
2 Tbsps. flour
1 pie dough – ready made

Place squirrels in a large pot. Add chicken broth and enough water to cover. Drop in the bay leaf and peppercorns. Let simmer till squirrel is tender, (about 45 minutes). Remove from pot to cool, saving water. In a heavy bottomed skillet, add 1 Tbsp. butter and 1 Tbsp. oil. Sauté the vegetables in this order: carrots, celery, onion, mushrooms and then peas. Add tarragon, salt, and pepper to your taste. Remove vegetables and set aside. In the same skillet add 2 Tbsp. butter and 2 Tbsp. flour. Melt and whisk till blended. Pour in the ¼ cup lemon juice and water from the squirrel pot (a little at a time while whisking!). Keep your gravy thick. Remove from heat.

    Pull meat off the bones of the squirrel and dice. Mix meat and vegetables into the gravy. Place the mixture in baking dish and cover with pie dough. Put 4 fork holes in top. Bake for 1 hour at 350° or until dough gets light to medium brown. Enjoy the taste of the outdoors!!

God gave you a gift of 86,400 seconds today. Have you used one to say thank you?

Sweet Broccoli Slaw

Recipe of Mary Pendegraph - submitted by: Jean Scott – Ararat, VA

2 (12 oz.) pkgs. broccoli slaw mix	½ cup craisins
1 cup mayonnaise	4 bacon slices, cooked and crumbled
1/3 cup sugar	
2 Tbsps. vinegar	½ cup chopped pecans
1 red onion, chopped	

Rinse broccoli-slaw with cold water and drain. Stir together mayonnaise, sugar and vinegar into a large bowl. Add slaw, onions and craisins. Toss gently to coat. Cover and chill for 8 hours. Sprinkle with bacon and nuts before serving.

Historic Star Theatre

"We have heard many stories about the theatre but the funniest has been from a gentleman who remembered when some boys came to a show one night with a jar full of lightening bugs which they let loose in the theatre before leaving.

The theatre was built in 1947 and has been restored back in the art deco era style décor. It features local, regional, state, and world-class talent in music and drama throughout the year. Visit our website at www.historicstartheatre.com for upcoming events."

-Carol Beasley

> Some folks here remember when their parents used a piece of fat meat tied around a bad cut to help it heal. Also, stock powder was used for cuts.
> — Carol Beasley

Sweet Potato Balls

Maude Booker's recipe - Carol Beasley – "The Depot Emporium" – Stuart

1 cup crumbled Corn Flakes	
4-5 sweet potatoes, mashed	1/3 cup packed brown sugar
1/3 cup butter	¼ tsp. nutmeg
dash salt	1 bag large marshmallows

Boil sweet potatoes and mash. Add butter, salt, brown sugar, and nutmeg. Make balls with potatoes around one marshmallow. Bake at 350° for 15 minutes or until warm.

Greenberry House / Leslie Shelor

Winters were long and cold in Maine in the 1980's when Leslie Shelor lived there. She had dogs that shed lots of hair. Having grown up with family members who were all artistic in some way, she possessed a natural affinity for creativity. Since she had seen people spin and "kinda knew the process," well, why not find a use for the hair that was so imminently available? That's the short story of how and why Leslie acquired a drop spindle and taught herself to spin.

Of course, there is no easy route to becoming really good at what you do. After moving back to Virginia, Shelor found a guild in Independence. "They were a very generous group of people. From them I learned all the things I was doing wrong, as well as many refinements."

Raising Angora rabbits is a passion and often their fur is incorporated into yarn spun with sheep and alpaca. "All of my fibers come from Virginia and North Carolina. I know by name most of the sheep whose wool I spin. Silk is the only product I use that is not local."

Hundreds of books made the trip back to Virginia with Shelor, because they had been collected for years and couldn't be left behind. A washer and dryer could, to make room for the collection. So, on the Internet or in a room separate from the hand spun and hand-dyed yarn at Greenberry House, you might find a treasure of a book you have been searching for! www.greenberryhouse.com

Sweet Potato Dumplings

Pat Hammons – Stuart, VA

- 2–3 raw sweet potatoes
- 1 can hungry jack biscuits
- 2 cups sugar
- 2 cups water
- 2 sticks margarine
- ¼ tsp. salt
- dash of cinnamon

Slice sweet potatoes ¼ inch thick, and then slice the circles in half. Divide biscuits in ½ sections. Flatten biscuits; wrap biscuit around sweet potatoes and place in pan. Bring margarine, water, sugar, and salt to a boil. Pour over biscuits. Sprinkle very little cinnamon on top. Bake 350° for 45 minutes. If browns too quickly, reduce heat to 325° after first 15 minutes.

Turkey Hash

"Tina, Herbert and Cathrine", Gospel Music – guitar, Autoharp, tub bass, mandolin, and vocals – CD's available

*"Herbert and I started to sing **gospel music** together in 1990, and we married our best friends (each other) in 1993. When Cathrine was born, I turned 40 and Herbert turned 50 the same year. Cathrine went with us everywhere to sing. She lay on a pallet on the floor in front of the church we were singing in. She got a little older and would sit in Herbert's guitar case. Now she is playing mandolin and singing with us. We are truly blessed.*

Even before we were married, Herbert would come over to practice music and sometimes I would cook supper. I introduced him to one of my family's traditional meals, turkey hash. We decided long ago that this was truly the <u>best</u> part of a turkey. It makes the house smell so good while it is cooking. I remember, before I married, a Christmas when my Great Uncle Abie and Great Aunt Alma had to leave the day after Christmas. The weather turned very cold and they had gotten a call from a neighbor that the house pipes had frozen. She told us later that when they got home, she said to her husband, "I wonder if they are having turkey hash tonight?" Then again the next morning, she asked again, "I wonder if they are having turkey hash this morning?" I have to laugh at this because, occasionally my parents would tell me on the phone that they were having chicken or turkey hash and I would say, "Stop, don't tell me!" Make this dish a traditional for your family."

Turkey Hash
Tina Conner – Stuart, VA

- 2 cups chopped turkey
- 1 cup chopped onion
- 4 cups turkey or chicken broth
- 1 tsp. salt
- ½ tsp. pepper
- 2 cups small, diced potatoes

Place turkey, onion, broth, salt, and pepper in kettle and boil until onions are tender (10 minutes). Place potatoes and simmer another 8-

10 minutes. Potatoes should be done, but still firm. **To thicken**: In quart jar with tight lid, shake thoroughly:

1½ cups cool water   1 cup plain flour

While ingredients are at a soft boil, gradually add flour/water mixture until thick like gravy. Test for enough salt and pepper. Pour hash over toast, biscuits, pancakes, or waffles. It is good for breakfast, lunch or dinner. You can also prepare hash with chicken. I have really never used a recipe as such, but this will be a start.

Whitt Farm Grape Salad
Cindy Hoback – Wolf Creek Farm

- 4 lbs. grapes, white and/or red seedless
- 1 pkg. fat free cream cheese
- 1 (8 oz.) fat free sour cream
- ½ cup Splenda
- 1 tsp. vanilla

Topping:
- ½ cup Splenda brown sugar
- ½ cup pecan or walnut pieces

Mix cream cheese, sour cream, Splenda, and vanilla until smooth. Pour over grapes and mix well. Combine brown sugar with nuts and sprinkle over grapes. Chill and serve! Does NOT taste as healthy as it is!

> *"Blessed be God, even the Father of our Lord Jesus Christ, the Father of mercies, and the God of all comfort; Who comforteth us in all our tribulations that we may be able to comfort them which are in any trouble, by the comfort wherewith we ourselves are comforted of God"* **II Corinthians 1:3-4**

Wanda Ayers-Slate, of Wanda's Estate and Custom Jewelry in Stuart, VA is the granddaughter of Civil War Veteran, Noah Martin, who served with Company D, 5th Virginia Infantry. He recalled how sad it was when the news came that Abe Lincoln had been shot. In 1901, at 64 years old, he married Naomi Moran who was 16. They had six children and a happy marriage for 22 years until his death. Slate's mother, Ethel, was their youngest child.

Henriedda Crafters / Lover's Leap Birdhouses

Historic Lover's Leap Tavern has been a place travelers have hastened toward since 1850. It sat by the trail that wound up the crest of the Blue Ridge Mountains from the Piedmont and Taylorsville (Stuart) toward Meadows of Dan for many years before there was anything built worth the name road.

Since 2000, the building has become a destination for bird lovers and others who love birdhouses, especially out of the ordinary birdhouses. Browsers often stop and are welcomed. Henry and Edna Mickles have combined their talents – he as a builder and painter, and she as an artist – to produce exceptional birdhouses.

The Mickles are an excellent source of information for attracting specific birds to your yard. All their birdhouses are built to accommodate Eastern Bluebirds as well as others. It seems that where you place the house has much to do with which birds will frequent your place. To make feathered visitors happy, bird food is available as well.

Henry Mickles offers a fantastic warranty. He will clean and paint small birdhouses free each year and larger ones for $10. If a birdhouse is damaged, he will repair it for a $10 fee as well. No wonder much of their business is repeat or sent by satisfied customers.

People from all 50 states and 26 countries have visited the shop and taken home a handcrafted souvenir – made right in the same building where it was purchased

Floyd County

Contents

Apple Marmalade..........................303	Nolen Applesauce Cake......................318
Best Apple Dump Cake..................303	Old Time Apple Butter.........................319
Butter Pecan Cake..................303	Open-Faced Omelet For Two............322
Cherry Fluff Salad..........................304	Penne With Artichokes,
Chocolate Cherry Candy.................304	Olives and Capers.........................323
Cornbread Salad............................304	Philly Cheese Ball...............................323
Creamy Chicken and Corn Soup....306	Pimento Cheese..................................325
Crock Pot Beef Stew 308	Rosemary Feta Cheese.......................325
Easy Oven Baked Potatoes............308	Salmon Croquettes..............................326
Gay Gay's Orzo Salad...................310	Salsa..326
Ground Beef & Noodle Casserole..310	Shooting Creek Potato Salad...............327
Hominy, Eggs, and Tomato Bake....311	Sour Cream Pound Cake....................332
Ice Cream Sandwich Cake.............311	Sauerkraut..332
Judy Lowrance's Cornbread...........311	Strawberry Soup.................................333
Leather Britches.............................331	Toffee..333
Lye Hominy....................................312	Tomato Muffin Treat..........................334
Mama's Soft Molasses Cookies.....314	Waldorf Salad
McCabe Coolidge's Sure Fire	With Peanut Dressing...................336
Bread Recipe............................315	Walnut Pate'.......................................336
Mountain Oysters...........................316	White Bean Chicken Chili
No Bake Fruit Cake.......................316	or Chili Soup...............................337

Painting by Edna Mickles of Henriedda Crafters, located at Lover's Leap on Rt. 58, Meadows of Dan, VA. She specializes in wonderful hand-painted birdhouses, built by her husband, Henry Mickles.

Apple Marmalade
Jane Williams – Floyd, VA – Gourd Artist

1   orange, peeled, remove seeds, sliced thin
6   medium apples, peel, coarsely chopped
2   cups water
3   Tbsps. lemon juice
5   cups sugar

Combine the orange, apples, water, and lemon juice together and cook for 10 minutes, or until apples are tender. Add sugar. Cook and stir until sugar is dissolved. Cool until 220° on candy thermometer. Skim off foam. Pour into canning jars; then seal. Process for 10 minutes in boiling water bath.

Best Apple Dump Cake
Pauline Bolt – Willis, VA

2   cans apple pie filling
½   cup sugar
1   tsp. cinnamon
1   box yellow cake mix
1   cup chopped pecans
    margarine

Put pie filling in greased 13x9-inch glass dish. Sprinkle with sugar and cinnamon. Spread dry cake mix evenly over apples. Mix a little cinnamon with pecans and sprinkle over top. Slice thin pats of butter all over the cake. Bake at 350° until golden brown.

Butter Pecan Cake
Merita Hylton

1   butter pecan cake mix
4   eggs
¾   cup oil
1   cup water
1   can coconut pecan frosting

Mix cake mix with eggs, oil, and water. Beat 2 minutes. Stir in frosting and pour into greased tube cake pan. Bake at 350° about 55 minutes. Sprinkle with powdered sugar.

Cherry Fluff Salad
Rhonda Spangler

1   lg. container Cool Whip
1   can sweetened condensed milk
1   can cherry pie filling
1   lg. can crushed pineapple
1   cup chopped pecans

Drain pineapple well. Stir all ingredients together in large bowl. Refrigerate.

Chocolate Cherry Candy
Jane Williams – Floyd, VA

1¼ lbs. confectionery sugar
¼   lb. butter (margarine)
3   Tbsps. cream
1   tsp. vanilla
52 candy cherries

Mix above ingredients together except for cherries until creamy. Form into a ball around the candy cherries. Melt the following in a double broiler. Dip cherry balls in melted chocolate. Cherries with stems make dipping easier.

8   ozs. semi-sweet chocolate
    (old recipe calls for 1/3 cake of paraffin wax) I use Crisco
3   tsps. confectionery sugar

Cornbread Salad
Cindy Salyer

2   boxes Jiffy cornbread mix
2   green peppers
4   cucumbers
6-8 roma tomatoes

2   sweet onions
2   stalks celery
1   cup grated cheese

topping:
1   cup mayonnaise
2   Tbsps. sugar
2   Tbsps. pickle relish
1   tsp. vinegar

Mix and bake Jiffy cornbread according to directions on package. When cool, crumble ½ the cornbread in bottom of large casserole dish. Cube vegetables, place over crumbles. Add topping mix, remaining crumbles, and cheese on top. Optional: Few slices of cooked and crumbled bacon over cheese.

The Haunted Kitchen Table

My grandfather, Willie Underwood, always believed in "haints." He stayed on guard and looked out for ghosts and out of the ordinary happenings. This did not mean that he was particularly fearful, just watchful when he traveled about after dark.

On the night of this event, Pa had been visiting a neighbor who had passed the bottle with him several times. The hour was pretty late when he got home and he went on up to bed, leaving the kitchen door open.

The old house was built into the lay of a hillside, with the kitchen on one level and steps leading up into the parlor, and on up to the bedroom. In the early morning hours, Granny heard a noise and began nudging him awake. Pa finally woke up enough to hear a strange scraping sound that couldn't be identified. He crawled groggily out of the feather tick, lit the lantern that had been left by the bed, grabbed his gun, and started toward the swishing, plunking, rustling sound.

He could look down into the parlor – nothing amiss there. Pausing a few seconds, he listened to determine the direction of the noise. Upon approaching the doorway leading down to the kitchen, a strange sight stopped Pa in his tracks. Something was moving about! As the lantern was held out to send a shaft of light into the darkness, the kitchen table seemed to float a foot or so across the floor, and then scrape slightly.

"Who's there?" demanded Pa.

No answer. The table moved again, headed toward the outside door. A sort of snort and soft steps could be heard. "Dag gum it, you better answer or I'll shoot!" shouted Pa.

The wooden table hovered a few inches off the floor but no one replied. Pa filled the tabletop full of bullet holes. With a whoosh and a plop, the legs settled to the floor.

Apprehensively, he approached the unruly piece of furniture and bent over with the lantern - to see a sad sight. Under the table lay his best brood sow. She had rooted out of the hog pen and wandered into the open door. Somehow she had gotten wedged underneath the table but couldn't get back out. The sow's back was lifting the table a couple of inches off the floor as she walked.

Now, warm weather ain't the time for dressing hogs but meat couldn't be wasted back then. Granny had to rise early and they got started on the job of cleaning, cooking, and canning Pa's ghost, hangover be danged. – *Roger Bolt*

In a slow cooker, vegetables don't overcook as they do on top of the stove, making it easy to put everything in at one time. The exception is milk, sour cream, or cream cheese, which should be added during the last hour.

Patricia Robin Woodruff is an artist who explores imagery that connects us to nature, beauty, peace, serenity, joy, and love. This is the second cookbook she's illustrated, the first being "The Complete Pressure Cooker Book" by Barb Baur. Woodruff is best known for her spiritual art, but her mother taught her that the spirit of hospitality is extended through feeding guests, so she is delighted to be able to create a warm and welcoming cover for "Grazing Along The Crooked Road." Woodruff divides her time between her homestead in Cameron County, PA and her studio in creative Floyd, VA.

Creamy Chicken and Corn Soup
Patricia Robin Woodruff – Floyd, VA

- 6 Tbsps. butter
- ½ cup onion, chopped
- 6 Tbsps. flour
- 2 cups water
- 2 bullion cubes (dissolve in water)
- 1 (16 oz.) can creamed corn
- 1½ cups half-and-half
- 3 Tbsps. grated carrot
- 1 Tbsp. chopped parsley
- 1/8 tsp. black pepper
- ½ tsp. ground nutmeg
- 1 cup shredded cooked chicken (or omit for a vegetarian version)

In a large pot, cook the onion in the butter over medium heat, until translucent (about 3 minutes). Stir in the flour and cook for 5 minutes longer, until it is thick and golden. Slowly add the bullion water, constantly stirring until it is smooth and thick. Stir in the remaining ingredients except for the chicken. Simmer for 5 minutes. Add the chicken just before serving.

Buffalo Mountain

Photo by Judy Hylton

Buffalo Mountain, the easily identifiable mountain that looks remarkably like the hump on a buffalo's back, is considered one of Virginia's greatest natural treasures. At 3,971 feet, it dominates the landscape of Floyd County. Native Americans must have found the height useful, as did the forestry service in the mid 1900's when a fire tower was manned to watch for fires. The tower was taken down in the 1990's when it had outlived it usefulness and became hazardous to climb because so many steps were missing. The skyline has never looked the same to natives who grew up seeing the silhouette of the tower against the sky every day.

Two fire towers were built about the same time, Haycock Mountain near Floyd, and Buffalo Mountain. Together, they could spot smoke over the 383 sq. miles of Floyd County and as far away as Bent Mountain and Fairy Stone State Park.

Buffalo Mountain has long been a place for recreation. Young people as well as families once walked for miles to climb the mountain for picnics. In the earlier years of the twentieth century, a tradition of going on top of the Buffalo on the first Sunday in May became popular. It was a celebration of sorts – winter was over and young men's fancies turned to romance. So did the fancy of young ladies. Pictures show the men in suits and ties and the girls in their Sunday dresses, proving again that a couple of generations back, people were made of strong stuff!

The mountain was once owned by Light Horse Harry Lee who received it as a land grant for his service in the Revolutionary War. His son, Carter, is said to have practiced law in a cabin just off what is now Buffalo Mountain Road. It is now owned and operated by the Virginia Department of Conservation and Recreation.

Crock Pot Beef Stew
Sadie Goad – Willis, VA

2	lbs. stew beef	2	tsps. salt
2	cups onion	¼	tsp. pepper
2	cups carrots	1	Tbsp. sugar
2	cups peas	5	Tbsps. cornstarch
4	cups potatoes	1	(46 oz.) can V-8 juice

Put all ingredients in crock-pot in order given. Cook for 10 – 12 hours. Do not stir while cooking. Turn on high until it starts to boil, then turn to low. Can cut this recipe in half.

> "THE LORD is my light and my salvation; whom shall I fear? The LORD is the strength of my life; of whom shall I be afraid?"
>
> *-Psalms 27:1*

Easy Oven Baked Potatoes
Sadie Goad – Willis, VA

- 6 medium potatoes
- 6 medium onions
- ½ cup margarine, melted
- 1 clove garlic crushed (I use 1 tsp. powdered garlic)
- ¼ tsp. salt
- ¼ tsp. celery seed
- ¼ tsp. pepper
- ¼ tsp. paprika

Cut potatoes in ½ inch slices, leaving skins on if desired. Alternate rows of sliced potatoes and sliced onions in a 13 x 9-inch baking dish. Cover dish with Reynolds wrap and bake at 400° for 40 minutes. Combine margarine, garlic, salt, and celery seed. Pour over potatoes and onions. Cook an additional 20 minutes uncovered.

"I moved to this beautiful county in the late 60's and can't even imagine living anywhere else. I love Floyd and it's wonderful people. Over the past 25 years, I have been involved in several businesses here in the county. In the early 80's I purchased the Blue Ridge Restaurant and ran it for almost 6 years. In fact, I sold it to Lee and Gail Hooks, who presently own the restaurant. During the time I owned the restaurant, my husband and I were also Christmas tree growers in the county. In this connection, we had retail Christmas tree lots, a choose and cut Christmas Tree Farm, and a Christmas Bed and Breakfast.

In 1990, my husband, David and I started traveling with VA Tech to help with International Development for the University. We traveled to Russia and Ukraine before the breakup of the Soviet Union. Since my husband and I are both amateur radio operators (ham radio) we started a 509 (c) (3) non-profit foundation called FAIRS – Foundation for Amateur International Radio Service – to help foster international goodwill via amateur radio. We knew amateur radio operators all around the world, therefore it was easy to communicate and keep in touch with the people we met for VA Tech. Our foundation is very active and we are still traveling to countries all around the world. At the present time, we are working in the eastern Caribbean Island of Dominica to help them set up emergency communication systems for their country. We also work in some other Caribbean Islands.

Every day is a good day and we really love what we're doing – especially living in Floyd county and being on the Crooked Road Music Trail. Come visit Floyd and experience a slower life!" -*Gaynell Larsen*

FAIRS was created as an idea during a train ride from Moscow to the Western Ukraine to distribute donated ham radio equipment. It seemed that a formal group was needed to do this type of volunteer work in an organized manner. They work to build global friendships, disaster preparedness, training, and medical assistance, among other services. N4USA www.fairs.org

Good Neighbor Recipe

1 Tongue that does not slander
1 Mind full of tolerance
2 Ears closed to gossip
2 Eyes overlooking other's faults
2 Hands extended to help others
1 Dash wit, smiles, and sunny disposition

Blend together the above ingredients. Form into one being. Serve generous portions to everyone you meet

Gay Gay's Orzo Salad
Gaynell Larsen – Floyd, VA

3 cups cooked Orzo (cook Orzo in salted water and drain well)
1 pkg. baby spinach
1 large bunch of fresh basil – chopped
1 red sweet pepper cut in small pieces
1/3 - ½ cup olive oil
   salt & pepper to taste
   dash tomato & basil seasoning
2 cups halved cherry tomatoes

Cook the Orzo and set aside. Break up spinach in microwave bowl. Add the basil and pepper. Pour the olive oil over the spinach, basil & peppers. Microwave until spinach is wilted, approximately 1½ minutes. Pour over cooked Orzo and season to taste!!! I use salt, pepper, and lots of Dash tomato & basil seasoning. You may want to add more olive oil if needed at this time. Serve hot. Add cherry tomatoes just before serving!

Ground Beef and Noodle Casserole
Pauline Bolt – Willis, VA

2 lbs. ground beef
1 medium onion, chopped fine
½ green pepper
3 cans tomato soup
1 can water
1 medium size bag of noodles
   salt & pepper

Brown the ground beef with the onion and green pepper. Cook the noodles. Combine all ingredients together and put in a 9x13-inch glass dish. Cover with Velveeta cheese and bake at 350° until cheese is melted.

Hominy, Eggs, and Tomato Bake

Hilda Collins – Meadows of Dan, VA

1 can hominy	4 fresh tomatoes
3 eggs	cheese, optional
3 slices bacon	

Fry bacon. Meantime, take pulp from tomatoes and chop, preserving the shells. Mash hominy slightly. Lightly scramble eggs with salt and pepper, then mix with hominy, tomato pulp, and crumble bacon. Place into tomato shells and bake at 350° for 20 minutes. Sprinkle with cheese if desired and melt.

Ice Cream Sandwich Cake

Judy Mannon

12 ice cream sandwiches	1 small chocolate instant pudding
1 8 oz. Cool Whip	8 Oreos, crumbled
½ cup fudge ice cream topping	

Warm fudge topping in bowl. Add 1 cup Cool Whip and dry pudding mix; blend well. Stir in Oreos and a little milk if needed. Layer 4 sandwiches, then 1/3 of pudding mixture. Continue with 4 more and pudding mixture until finished. Cover with Cool Whip. Freeze and serve. Yummy!

Judy Lowrance's Cornbread

Judy Lowrance - Floyd, VA

3 eggs, beaten	1 (8 ¼ oz.) can Del Monte cream style sweet corn
2/3 cup non-fat skim milk	
1 (6 oz.) pkg. Martha White Buttermilk Cornbread Mix	1 cup shredded cheese (Mexican Mix, optional)
few shakes red pepper flakes (a pinch)	1 medium onion, chopped
	1 tsp. - 2 Tbsps. sugar (optional)

Preheat oven to 425°. Grease well an 8 x 12-inch glass Pyrex dish. Beat eggs slightly and then add other ingredients. If you don't want to have a strong onion taste, cook in butter briefly before adding. Bake for about 24 minutes until it starts turning brown on top. This is great hot. It is even good at room temperature the next morning for breakfast! It is moist and not crumbly like many cornbread recipes.

Lye Hominy
Hilda Hancock Collins

Shell 8-10 ears of field corn into enameled pot; wash and drain. Dissolve 1 level teaspoon of Red Devil Lye in enough warm water to cover corn. Cook two hours at slow boil, stirring occasionally. When the cornhusks start to separate, the water will turn red. Drain, being careful to keep off hands. Rinse with warm water. Cover with water again and cook about 2 hours. Drain and rinse and repeat until corn is white and the water is clear. Hominy can be canned with 1 tsp salt to each pint jar. To prepare, drain and fry in butter with salt and pepper until brown.

A Birthday Sleepover

We went home, my two brothers, two sisters, and I, to spend the night with our Mother for her eightieth birthday. Our ages were: S.G. – 58, Virginia – 57, Lloyd – 54, Barbara – 51, and me, Brenda – 37 years old. It was the first time the five of us ever slept under her roof at the same time.

The reason for this was simple. My oldest brother had married and his wife delivered their first child three months before I was born. As I grew up, my nieces and nephews were more like siblings than my real brothers and sisters. As a youngster, it was hard for me to distinguish who was the in-law and who was my real sibling because I only saw them together. Since they all lived nearby, they came to visit but not to spend the night.

Years passed and I grew up and married. As an adult, my relationship with my older siblings developed into maturity. It didn't occur to us for many years, however, that we had never all lived together in one house as a family. My sister, Barbara, who was always known as Burr, had serious health issues and was in the hospital a long time. After a liver transplant and much recuperation, she was doing better as Mom's birthday approached. Perhaps almost losing her was our inspiration.

Traditionally, every child came by to see Mom or did something special on New Years day, the date of her birth. Since we are a mischievous bunch, we decided not to go by or tell her anything but planned a meeting time at her house. Each of us telephoned but talked about what we were doing, this and that, and nothing about her birthday. By afternoon, she was getting somewhat flustered and irritated with us.

She was downright aggravated with her children by the time we all showed up on her doorstep, arms filled with sleeping bags, snacks, pizza, birthday hoopla, and all sorts of stuff. She couldn't believe it.

We ate and played jokes and pretty much hurrahed most of the night. One brother got his air mattress blown up and laid on it long enough to drift off to sleep. We let the air out of it. The other brother decided to sleep in the recliner, so every time he dozed off, we jerked the lever on the side to set him in an upright position. We pranked and ate until about midnight when Mom said, "Now that's enough. Go to bed."

Not a lot of sleeping went on, and we left fairly early the next morning, our mother fully aware of what it was like having everyone under one roof at the same time. I'm not sure which made Mom happier, seeing us coming through the door or seeing us going out!

Mabry Mill

Ed and Lizzie Mabry would be aghast at the sheer numbers of visitors to their water powered gristmill each day, much less each year. One can only imagine their astonishment at it becoming the most photographed place situated near the Blue Ridge Parkway, where scenic beauty abounds. It was a business to them, a way of making a living and helping out their neighbors. Who knows what they'd have to say if they were told that the National Park Service tore down the original house they built with wonderful chestnut wood because it was too modern? It was replaced with a cabin from Galax in 1956. It seems likely that they'd approve the living history demonstrations and interpretive programs that teach about life in the Blue Ridge of yesteryear. After all, they were pretty progressive thinkers themselves.

> Life isn't about waiting for the storm to pass. It's about learning how to dance in the rain.
> –Unknown

"I grew up on these cookies. Mama made them often when we were kids. We grew our own cane and made our own molasses. Sugar was scarce. Molasses were plentiful. So they used molasses to make desserts instead of sugar. I remember one time on a Sunday, my brother Laythan and I were outside playing. Mama and my sister Gladys made cookies for dinner. They cut out men for us and baked them and laid them at our plates. When we came in for dinner, I grabbed mine and bit his head off before I saw what it was. I guess I never lived it down.

We also made stack cakes from the same recipe. Just roll out the dough to fit an 8 or 9-inch cake pan. Bake. Put apples butter between the layers, on top and sides of the cake. I think we sprinkled it with granulated sugar. We lived in an apple orchard, so apples were plentiful. We made a big kettle of apple butter every fall. We also made stack cakes from sugar cookies and apple butter."

Mama's Soft Molasses Cookies
Helen Hylton – Willis, VA

1	cup butter or margarine	1	cup brown sugar packed
1	cup molasses	3	eggs
½	tsp. soda	6	cups flour
	spices as desired		

Cream butter. Add sugar and molasses. Mix well. Add the eggs and mix thoroughly. Add soda and spices to mixture. Add flour one cup at a time. Roll into balls. Flatten and bake at 300°. Watch carefully and remove while the cookies look only half done. They will be chewy.

Floyd has been listed as one of the top 100 Small Art Communities in the U.S. Artist and artisans who work in numerous mediums have studios and make their homes in the community. Quality craftsmanship is pretty much guaranteed, as is variety and quantity. Expect lovely paintings in restaurants and visit galleries such as Old Church Gallery, Art Under the Sun, Junebug Center, Over the Moon Gallery and Cafe, and others. Go slow, you might miss a gallery, you know!

McCabe Coolidge's Sure Fire Bread Recipe for Beginners and Experts, adapted from the Tassajara Yeast Bread Book. "Back in the early 1970's, I started using the Tassajara Bread Recipe and just this afternoon I baked another two loaves, so I pass it on to you."

McCabe Coolidge's Sure Fire Bread Recipe

McCabe Coolidge – Floyd, VA – Wildfire Pottery

In a large pottery bowl, pour **three cups of lukewarm water** - put your forefinger in it, if your finger is quite warm but not hot, that's it.

Add **2 Tbsps. of dry yeast** - (I buy mine in a small plastic sack at the natural health store, otherwise use **2 commercial packets** like Red Star.

Add ¼ **cup of molasses** then **3 cups of whole-wheat flour** (King Arthur is my choice), a **couple of handfuls of buckwheat flour** and **2 handfuls of cornmeal**.

Stir, stir, stir, 100 whirls and let it rise for 30 to 45 minutes in a warm place.

Fold in **4 tsps. of salt** and **1/3 cup of olive oil** (or your favorite cooking oil). Add in **white flour** (King Arthur) until the dough comes easily off the sides of bowl.

Pour dough onto the floured board and start kneading, using more flour to keep the batch from sticking to the kitchen counter or board. Do this for 10 minutes or until dough is smooth and not too sticky. Place bowl in warm place and let rise, about 50 minutes, until doubled in size.

Punch down and let rise again for 15 minutes. In a hurry? Skip this step. Shape into 2 loaves and place in oiled bread pans or pottery vessels. Let rise until the center of loaf is above the side of the bread pan, 10-15 minutes.

While the dough is rising, turn the oven to 350°. Before placing the loaves in the oven, I mix **1 egg** with a little **milk** and stir it up. Use a brush and cover the surface with egg wash. Using a knife cut 2 slits on the surface of the loaf to let some air escape and then place in oven for 50 minutes or until the loaves are golden brown. Soon after taking the bread out, I shake it out of the pottery vessel and place it on the kitchen counter to cool down. Warn anyone in the house not to come by and pick a chunk out of it until it is cooled down. Say 15-20 minutes, at least. I love to cut a slice, slather some butter on it and every now and then I add honey.

Mountain Oysters
Anonymous

Bull Testicles – Prepare as soon after harvest as possible. Remove the thin membrane and soak in salt water overnight. This is believed to remove the male hormones and make tenderer. Rinse well. Slice oysters and dip in buttermilk and then into cornmeal. Have lard heating in cast iron skillet to cover oysters. When lard is melted and begins to "pop," drop in slices and fry until golden brown. Salt and pepper. Remove and drain on brown paper bag, sack, or paper towels. Enjoy!

County Sales

To find the world's largest selection of Bluegrass and Old-Time music, you must first find Talley's Alley in Floyd, VA. It's quite possible to pass it a couple of times, so be on the lookout. According to their website, they have over 4,500 CD's, cassettes, books, and videos to choose from.

According to Cindy Salyer, long-time employee, the business has been there for over thirty years, many of those spent in relative obscurity as a mail order business. Everything was done by hand for many years. Of course, real music fans found them and the company's fame spread. She also tells us that the owner, David Freeman, was inducted into the Bluegrass Hall of Fame and that he was born in New York City.

New York City! Yep, seems he fell for traditional music at an early age and scoured the city in search of old 78 recordings by fiddlers and pickers and singers most people had never heard of. His passion never wavered once he started anthologies and reissues on the County label in the 1960's. Today he owns Rebel records, a well-respected independent label. www.countysales.com

No Bake Fruit Cake
Peggy Wirt – Floyd, VA

1 lb. box graham crackers, crushed	1 lb. pecans
1 lb. raisins	2 lbs. candied mixed fruit mix
1 lb. English walnuts	¾ cup orange juice
	1 lb. marshmallows

Combine crushed graham crackers, nuts, raisins, and fruit. Melt marshmallows in orange juice (microwave for about 3 minutes stirring halfway through). Pour over the combined ingredients and mix well. Line miniature loaf pans or small pans with waxed paper, lightly rubbed with butter. Press mixture into pan, (really pack it)! Cover and put into the refrigerator for about an hour. Turn out and wrap with clear wrap. Keeps a long time or freezes well.

Temple Garrison

According to Temple Garrison, it would be hard to get lost in Floyd County. "Eventually, you come out on one of three roads, Rt. 8, Rt, 221, or the Parkway, so there's not much way to get lost."

Having traveled most of the back roads at an early age with her veterinarian father, Dr. Chris Harman, may have given her a little edge over newcomers, however. She remembers that she loved going out to farms when he made calls, especially a place called the Nolly Farm. Two brothers and a sister lived there and Miss Ruth Nolly would take young Temple into the house for a visit and ply her with goodies and milk. "Miss Ruth would feed me junk and then my Mom would be mad because I wasn't hungry for supper when I got home," she laughs.

"We had a two-way radio in the car, that's how Dad kept in touch. Mom would sometimes call to let him know that he needed to check by another farm for a sick cow or horse or other animal. He would tell me to pay attention, and then have me tell him which way to turn to get back home.

There were lots of fox hunters during that time, including Dad, who raised hunting dogs of all kinds: Walker hounds, black and tans, coon hounds, beagles, and you name it. Many of those old time hunters had a trick for breaking hunting dogs from chasing deer. They'd put a Billy goat in the pen with the young dogs. Goats smell similar to deer. When the dogs would get too close, the Billy goat would kick them, so soon the dogs learned they didn't want any part of anything that smelled like that goat."

"My grandfather, Jabez M. Harman, was a medical doctor in Floyd from the late 1890's until his death in 1944. He ordered a "kit" house that has been in our family over 100 years and my sister still lives in it. It's a brick Victorian, with a full basement and attic. Just a short distance from the house is a small brick building he used as a hospital.

While he was in medical school in Minnesota, he was issued a cadaver that was said to be a member of Jesse James's gang. My grandmother told us this secondhand from Granddad, so we can't say positively whether it's true or not. Anyway, that body helped him learn how to practice medicine. The skeleton has a crescent shaped indention fracture on the left side of the head. As the story goes, Jesse and his gang were robbing a bank and one of the tellers hid behind the door with a paperweight in his hand. As the robbers were leaving, the teller slammed the paperweight into the head of the last one out the door, killing him.

That's how our family came to have a skeleton with a past. Granddad kept it in his office and my father finally donated it to the Floyd County High School. That's where it is 'til today."

"Give for the joy of giving…
 If you only give to get….
 You are not giving….
 You are only trading."

Phadettia DeHart, Iva Hancock and Emma Belcher making applebutter early 1950s.

Nolen Applesauce Cake
Recipe of Sallie Nolen – Submitted by: Fern Nolen – Floyd, VA

Mix in two bowls, 1st bowl:
- 2½ cups flour
- 1 tsp. ground cinnamon
- 1-2 tsps. ground nutmeg
- 3 tsps. soda
- 1 tsp. salt
- 1 cup nuts

2nd bowl:
- 2 cups applesauce
- 2 cups sugar
- 4 eggs
- 1 cup oil
- 1 cup raisins

Combine and mix well the 1st bowl of ingredients. Combine and mix the 2nd bowl of ingredients. After mixing each individual bowl, pour bowl #1 into bowl #2. Stir real good with wooden spoon. Bake at 350° for 1 hour or until done.

Old Time Apple Butter
David and Annie Ruth Wood – Floyd, VA

12-15 bushels of apples
Suggested: (7-9 bushels of Golden Delicious - a sweet apple)
          (5-6 bushels of Winesap - a cooking apple)
          (You may substitute your favorite sweet or
          favorite cooking apple)
7   gallons of home-squeezed fresh apple juice/cider fermented 10-14 days
50 lbs. of granulated sugar
1   quart of red-hot cinnamon dots candy
1   oz. of pure cinnamon oil (no artificial stuff here, it won't work)
2   cups of apple cider vinegar

<u>Equipment</u>**:**
Several mechanical apple peelers, pans, and knives
1 – 50 gallon copper kettle with tripod stand
1 – large, sturdy stirrer with minimum 8-foot handle
1 – gallon dipper, heat resistant
2 – 3 gallon stockpots
1 – large washtub
30 gallons worth of pint and quart canning jars with lids and rings
Firewood–kindling to get started and a pile of locust logs 4–6" diameter, 4–5' long
A bunch of friends (a WHOLE bunch of friends)

      This is not an undertaking for the faint of heart. There are lots of details to learn as you do this year after year. If you know someone who has done this before, enlist him or her to help you get started. My parents and immediate family have been doing this for over 25 years for the "fun" of it and we are still learning.

      We get started making apple butter as a way to carry on the "old ways" of our ancestors who were just trying to survive. It has turned out to be a very enjoyable annual event. Although it's hard work, our family and friends will not give up due to the time that we get to spend with each other. The following instructions are the ways we have developed over the years and you will find that you will develop some of your own variations as you continue making apple butter year after year. I have taken some liberties in the processes assuming you have the means, knowledge, and equipment to perform some of the ancillary tasks. If you are taking this on, I'm sure you'll figure it out.

To begin with, 10-14 days before you make the apple butter squeeze approximately 3 to 4 bushels of a mixed variety of apples in a cider press to produce about 7 gallons of apple juice. Store in lightly capped gallon jars in a cool dark place (we use the can fruit cellar in our springhouse). This juice will start to ferment into a weak cider and will be used to start cooking the first apples put into the kettle. We used to use just plain water, but we found that the extra sugars and flavor the juice/cider adds is worth the effort. You can use plain water, but will have to increase the amount of granulated sugar that you add later in the process.

The night before making the apple butter get 5 or 6 buddies to come over and help peel apples. Don't tell them it probably takes them all together about 5 to 6 hours to get the job done. Peel, core, and slice the 12-15 bushels of apples into uniform size slices. To make this easier, try to get the kind of mechanical apple peeler that peels, cores, and spiral slices the apple. Be sure to trim any bits of peeling or core out of the cut apples. These don't cook up and will leave crunchy bits in the apple butter that are not very good. Store the apples in airtight bags to keep them fresh. Then get a good night's sleep.

GOOD MORNING! It's 5:30 am and you're out starting your cooking fire. Develop a good bed of coals in a pit 8 inch or so deep and 18 inch in diameter, this will take about 1½ hours. During this time drink your cup of coffee and watch the sun come up (or as we have done in years past, watch the snow come down!). Then wash the 50-gallon copper kettle. I'll suggest using a solution of salt and vinegar to start with to get the copper oxidation off the kettle then rinsing very, very well with plain water. Set the kettle in the tripod making sure that the kettle will sit level. Spray the rim and top 6 inches down into the kettle with spray Pam to help in the cleanup later that night. Start washing the apples with plain water, letting them drain thoroughly. Also during this time make sure you have somebody's Grandma come over and make sausage gravy and biscuits for everybody helping out; they'll need the energy.

Now it's 7:00 am and time to start the cookin'. Pour 3 gallons of the apple juice/cider you made 10-14 days ago; straining any impurities out as you fill the kettle. Place the copper kettle over the bed of coals in the pit and pour the remaining juice/cider in. Don't forget to strain out the impurities. Build up the fire by placing the ends of the logs into the coals and feed them in as necessary to keep the fire at an even temperature. You will need to maintain a fairly brisk boil in the kettle all day but do not boil too fast; there is a chance of burning and injury from splashing apples. When the juice/cider starts to boil start adding the washed, cut up apples. Get out that big stirrer and start stirring, constantly covering the bottom of the kettle so nothing sticks and burns. This is where the bunch of friends comes in. Keep adding apples slowly throughout the morning as they start to cook up in about 3 gallon additions at a time; bring the kettle back to a boil after each addition.

As a point of reference the last of the 12-15 bushels will go into the kettle sometime between 11:00 am and 12:00 noon. Keep stirring!

Cook the apples at a steady rate all day remembering to stir constantly (that's using that handy bunch of friends). Remember, if everybody decides to give up on you now, you'll have an awful lot of applesauce so treat them good with plenty of food and relief from stirring. I will suggest trying some of the other recipes in this cookbook – especially if there's a chili one.

Now it's 3:00 pm to 3:30 pm, MID-AFTERNOON and it's time to check the status of the cooking apples. Take a spoonful out of the kettle, being careful not to let any of the cooking apples splash up on you because it WILL burn! Put the apple sample on a plate and let the sample cool for a few minutes. Run the spoon through the apples making a little valley. Look at the edges to see how much liquid leaches out. Repeat this sampling every 15 minutes until there is very, very little to no liquid showing along the edges. Now let's start adding the sugar. Stir in the cinnamon dots candy and add the sugar 5 pounds at a time, stirring it in for a few minutes before adding the next 5 pounds. Cook for about another hour and check the liquid again with the above process. The reason we check the liquid level is so the apple butter will have a good thick consistency. Add the 1 oz. of pure cinnamon oil and stir for 15 minutes. Add the two cups of vinegar and if you're wondering, my grandmother says the vinegar is to help seal and preserve the apple butter in the cans. Stir another 10 minutes to mix thoroughly.

Now you're FINISHING UP. During the last hour or so, after stirring in the sugar, get your canning jars ready, warm up the jar and heat the lids. Line up the necessary canning supplies and some of your bunch of friends to fill and seal the jars. Pull the fire out from under the kettle and start dipping the now ready apple butter out of the kettle into the 3-gallon stockpots. Carry these over to the canning table; being careful not to burn yourself. You have to still keep stirring during this time until the kettle gets light enough to remove from the coal pit. Remember, when you start the canning process to send Grandma back to the kitchen to make fresh biscuits. Clean everything up and take a jar in and join Grandma.

This process should produce 25-30 gallons of good old time apple butter. Be sure everybody that helped out gets lots of thanks and a jar of apple butter. Good Luck!

Open-Faced Omelet For Two
Ed Cohn – Miracle Farm – Floyd, VA

Miracle Farm Bed and Breakfast Spa and Resort is an 1880s farmhouse. It is a sustainable living center and animal sanctuary in the Blue Ridge Mountains 7-8 miles outside Floyd, VA. The B&B offers daily complimentary breakfasts; Pilates workouts and massage services are available. You can go hiking, fishing, and bird watching. All of the guest accommodations at Miracle Farm include private bathrooms and kitchens, and offers views of the creek and surrounding fields. *www.miracle farmva.org*

3 large eggs
1 Tbsp. olive oil
1 onion cut in half top to bottom and sliced thin
 Handful of mushrooms sliced or coarsely chopped
2 Tbsps. pine nuts
1/8 cup tomatoes, chopped, sun dried <u>or</u>
½-¾ cup tomatoes coarsely chopped, fresh or canned
1 large clove garlic, crushed through press
 sliceable cheese to cover one layer on a 9-inch pan
 (I like very sharp cheddar but use your choice)
 goat or Parmesan cheese – enough to crumble on top
1 tsp. fennel seed
½-1 tsp. dried thyme (1 Tbsp. if fresh)
½-1 tsp. dried oregano (1 Tbsp. if fresh)
 paprika
1 Tbsp. fresh parsley minced

In an ovenproof, 9-inch pan (cast iron is good – stainless steel is better) over medium heat add 1 Tbsp. olive oil and onions. Sauté onions until translucent. Add fennel seed and pine nuts and sauté another few minutes. Add mushrooms and sauté until their released liquid is almost gone. Turn off heat and scrape mixture into a bowl. Add herbs, tomatoes, and garlic. Mix and set aside. Use the unwashed pan for the next step.

In a bowl, break eggs and mix until uniform. Turn oven to "broil". Bring pan back up to medium heat. Add 1 Tbsp. olive oil or butter and coat pan. Pour in egg mixture; turn heat to low. Sprinkle onion/mushroom mixture evenly over eggs before they set. Cover with slices of cheese. Add crumbled goat or Parmesan cheese evenly. Put pan under broiler until cheese starts to brown, then sprinkle with paprika, minced parsley, and fresh ground pepper. Cut in half; remove to warm plates.

Obviously you can experiment with other ingredients. Add to filling mixture, cooked spinach or chard, cooked, cubed potatoes, and other herbs. Yum!

Penne With Artichokes, Olives And Capers
Barbara Spillman – Floyd, VA

1 lb. penne	2 Tbsps. capers
¾ cup breadcrumbs	2 Tbsps. lemon juice
3 Tbsps. grated Parmesan cheese	½ tsp. dried oregano
1 cup grated or sliced mozzarella cheese	½ tsp. crushed red pepper flakes
¼ cup plus 2 Tbsps. olive oil	salt and pepper to taste
5 or more cloves of garlic, chopped	½ cup pasta cooking water
½ cup chopped flat leaf parsley	
1½ oz. jar marinated artichoke hearts, drained	
1¼ oz. tin artichoke hearts, drained	
3 or more scallions, chopped	
½ cup Greek olives, chopped	

Preheat the oven to 350°. Cook the penne and reserve ½ cup of the cooking water. In a small bowl, combine the breadcrumbs with the Parmesan cheese and 2 Tbsps. of the oil and reserve. In a large bowl, combine the other ingredients, except the mozzarella, toss with the pasta. Don't forget the ½ cup of pasta water. Put the pasta mixture into an oiled 9 x 13-inch baking dish. Top with the mozzarella, and then top that with the Parmesan breadcrumb mixture. Bake for 20 minutes or till heated through.

"Philly" Cheese Ball
Dianne Hamm – Willis, VA

1 (8 oz.) pkg. finely shredded sharp cheddar cheese
1 (8 oz.) pkg. Philadelphia Brand cream cheese
1 tsp. Worcestershire sauce
½ tsp. lemon juice

Combine shredded cheese and softened cream cheese. Mix until well blended. Add remaining ingredients and mix well. Form into a ball. Chill until firm. Serve with crackers of your choice. You may add any or all of the following ingredients if you desire: 2 tsps. chopped pimiento; 2 tsps. chopped green pepper; 2 tsps. chopped onion. You may also roll in nuts or parsley flakes.

Rising young bluegrass gospel group, "Statement," performs

Floyd Country Store

      They operate on Granny's rules: No smoking, No drinking alcohol, No bad language, and No conduct unbecoming to a lady or a gentleman. The place is packed every Friday night and spilling over into the streets. Travelers come from great distances to visit and see what all the fuss is about. Don't you know Granny is always right?

      The Friday Night Jamboree at the Floyd Country Store is all about fun, good music, good food, and shaking a leg if you're able. If you can't, it's still great entertainment to listen and watch. Good traditional and bluegrass music is a given, often as much outside the store as inside at this major venue of the Crooked Road.

      For most of the twentieth century, a hardware and general store occupied the building that now has been remodeled by the Crenshaws. It's been said that the Friday night jam began when two former owners would close the country store to practice with their bluegrass band. People would knock on the door so often, wanting to come in and listen, that the band just left the door open. Soon other musicians showed up, along with more listeners, some dancers dropped in and the whole thing mushroomed. For a few years, the store was only open one evening a week, for the music. Luckily that has changed. It's now a great place to come to browse, have a meal of home made soups, salads, and sandwiches with desserts worth saving room for. And music is not *just* on Friday nights, anymore! www.floydcountystore.com

"I'd like to share with you a simple Floyd Country Store recipe. It's a popular sandwich that melts in your mouth on our homemade buttermilk bread."

Pimento Cheese
Jill Mackin – Kitchen Manager of the Floyd Country Store – Floyd, VA

- 6 ozs. cream cheese at room temperature
- 2 cups grated sharp cheddar cheese
- 2 cups rated Monterey Jack cheese
- 1 cup mayonnaise
- ½ tsp. salt
- ¼ tsp. pepper
- ½ tsp. garlic powder
- ½ cup pimento, smashed
- 2 tsps. diced onion

Beat cream cheese until fluffy. Add the rest of the ingredients. Beat until well blended.

Rosemary Feta Cheese
Barbara Spillman – Floyd, VA

- 1 pint jar and lid, both very clean
- ½ lb. feta cheese
  - several sprigs of rosemary, washed and dried
  - extra virgin olive oil
  - rosemary and olive oil triscuits

Remove the green rosemary leaves from the woody branches. Sprinkle some of these leaves into the bottom of the jar. Add the feta cheese to the jar in the biggest chunk possible. Then fit in any smaller pieces that may remain. Fill the jar with extra virgin olive oil. Screw on the lid and store in the refrigerator till you are ready to serve it. If your fridge is so cold that the oil becomes opaque remove the jar a few minutes before you want to serve it so that the oil can warm a little. Decant a big chunk of the cheese along with oil and rosemary onto a small, rimmed plate. Serve with rosemary and olive oil triscuits or the cracker of your choice. Try adding a garlic clove or a small hot red pepper in addition to the rosemary.

A good 40 miles of the scenic Blue Ridge Parkway wander through Floyd County. Rocky Knob Campground and Picnic Area, situated at the crest of the mountains, is a wonderful place to spend the day, hiking and picnicking. For a longer stay, the campground has tent and RV sites, no hookups or showers, but has bathrooms, water, and comfort stations.
www.nps.gov

Nico is a musician of the Crooked Road, who makes the creative town of Floyd, VA, her home. In 2006 she was the reader's choice in the Floyd Press and was voted, "Best of Floyd County Virginia!" in the Music/Entertainment category. Her amazing voice has often been compared to legendary Joni Mitchell. Nico can be found playing Celtic and folk music around Floyd and the surrounding areas, accompanying herself on guitar or playing the bowed psaltery. www.sonicbids.com/NicoWoodruff

Salmon Croquettes
Nico Woodruff – Floyd, VA

2	Tbsps. butter	1	cup water
2	Tbsps. flour	1	bullion cube

Dissolve the bullion in the water. Melt butter. Stir in flour and cook until thick and golden. SLOWLY stir in liquid bullion. When the sauce is smooth and hot, remove from heat and add:

1   egg yolk (do not use a whole egg)
1   (14 oz.) can of skinless boneless salmon
    or substitute 2 small cans of tuna in water – drained
1   cup bread crumbs (add more if the mixture is still sticky)
1   Tbsp. Worcestershire sauce or Tamari soy sauce
    Italian breadcrumbs (for coating)

Roll into ball (about the size of a golf ball), coat with Italian breadcrumbs and deep fry.

Ambrosia Bed and Breakfast is a historic pre-civil war log farmhouse. It was used as an inn in the early 1800's. They offer summer camps for children and retreats for adults. Located 4 miles from Floyd. www.ambrosiafarm.net

Salsa
Caroline Thomas – Ambrosia Farm Bed & Breakfast & Pottery – Floyd, VA

4	tomatoes, ripe, chopped	1	cucumber, chopped
1	onion, minced	1	bell pepper, chopped
2	cloves garlic, minced	½	cup fresh cilantro, chopped
1	jalapeno pepper, minced		salt and cracked pepper to taste
	juice of 2 limes		

Mix all together and serve with your favorite chip.

"Potato salad was made this way by Sallie Nolen, a resident on Shooting Creek farm from 1939 until her death in 1963. Her husband, Cab Nolen, was the owner of Nolen Mill, now known as Pine Creek Mill. Her daughter-in-law, Lucille, has added her own touch to the recipe by using Honey Mustard and paprika that may not have been available in the old days. She recently made several gallons for her granddaughter's wedding reception. It sure seems to be a big favorite with everyone that eats it." - *Judy Nolen Hylton*

Shooting Creek Potato Salad
Lucille T. Nolen – Floyd, VA

- 8 cups creamed potatoes
- 1½ cups mayonnaise
- 2 Tbsps. honey mustard
- 3-4 boiled eggs, chopped
  (2 additional boiled eggs for top if desired)
- 2 cups chopped sweet pickles
- 1 cup chopped onions
  paprika

Peel approximately 5 lbs. potatoes, slice and cook until tender, drain. Cream with an electric mixer until fluffy as you would for mashed potatoes. Adding salt and sugar to taste (approximately level Tbsp. of sugar) and only margarine, no milk. Add mayonnaise, mustard, chopped eggs, pickles, and onions. Put in bowl. If desired, after putting potato salad in bowl, chop or slice the additional 2 boiled eggs and lay around on top of salad, sprinkle with paprika.

Angels in the Attic has been operating for the good of various local service agencies since 2000. All funds above operating costs are distributed. Volunteers staff the thrift store, located up the street from the Floyd Country Store, where one can find ordinary and sometimes extraordinary items. They're open on Friday nights during the summer. It's worth a look! www.angels intheattic.org

Rock Castle Gorge National Recreation Trail can be accessed at milepost 167 on the Blue Ridge Parkway. It extends on an almost 11 mile loop trail with another access point in Woolwine. Expect a bit of a rugged climb back uphill. For a milder trail, enter the old roadbed near the driveway to Rocky Knob Cabins just off the parkway. Also ends at the access at Woolwine.

Two Brothers
As told by Judy Nolen Hylton

They were born into a family of five siblings, four boys and one girl, in the early years of the twentieth century. They learned to farm with horses and mules and to help out at the gristmill their father ran. Whether there was any special connection between Edd and Louis Nolen in their early years is not known, but circumstances and possibly their personalities created a bond beyond that of most brothers. They literally became each other's "right and left-hand man."

Though Louis never married, Edd met Lucille Thomas on an outing to the Pinnacles Dam near Meadows of Dan with other young folks in 1939. "Bet I can walk faster than you," he told her as they came back uphill from the dam. From that day, they became a dating couple and married on December 27, 1941. The young couple set up housekeeping, but in just six months he was called up by Uncle Sam to go to war.

It seems unlikely that Edd Nolen knew at the time what an outstanding match he had made. Though Lucille was a mild and kindhearted young lady, she was made of strong stuff. At sixteen, she went to work at the J. Freezer & Son Shirt Factory in Floyd for $3.00 a week, later going to 15 cents an hour. With this, she helped her parents add on to their house, bought furniture, and a 1937 Ford for $350.00. Two payments were still owed on the car when Lucille married Edd and she insisted on paying them herself.

Edd went to war and Lucille went to live with her parents, still working at the shirt factory while awaiting the birth of the couple's first child who would be named Joyce. He did not see his daughter until she was over two years old. After being wounded in his left hand, arm, and hip in North Africa, several months were spent in a hospital. He was discharged in January 1945 with a Purple Heart, Two Bronze Stars, and several medals.

The Nolens moved into a small house that, like most others of the time period, had no running water, an outdoor johnny house, and a springhouse to keep food cold. Edd farmed and worked at a sawmill. Lucille canned vegetables from the garden, cooked on a wood stove, milked cows, churned, and made lye soap to use in washing clothes on a washboard. She raised chickens and sold milk, finding time somehow to work at the factory and sew clothes for her increasing family. Two boys, Curtis and Kenneth, were born during the forties and in 1954, another daughter, Judy, came along.

During these years, Edd and his brother, Louis, worked at sawmills and farmed a large tract of land they purchased together. Because Louis didn't drive, it was more convenient for him to stay at the Nolen house. He became part of the family and Judy Nolen Hylton says, "We never knew anything except Uncle Louis living with us. He was a big part of our lives and there was something missing if he wasn't there. Later, the grandchildren felt like he was another grandpa – always willing to take them for a ride on the tractor or to see the cows, or just to play games with them."

A new brick house, complete with running water and a bathroom was completed and moved into in October 1959. On the morning of February 11, 1960, the brothers climbed into a green '52 Ford truck and went to work at Huff's sawmill where Edd usually logged and Louis cut timber. This particular day, they loaded and hauled slab wood that they had cut the day before to Tom Huff's house. A friend, Rural Shortt, stopped by and helped them cut more slab wood.

It had rained hard the night before. As Louis picked slabs off the pile and handed them to Edd to feed into the cut-off saw, the large slab pile behind them fell, covering the tractor and knocking first Louis, and then Edd into the saw. It was over in a matter of seconds with Louis yelling, "I've lost a hand!" and Edd answering, "I have, too."

Shortt immediately grabbed anything in sight to stop or soak up the blood. He got them into his car and drove them to the clinic in Floyd, blowing his horn as he sped through the red light.

Upon arrival at the clinic, (now the Community Action Building) Dr. Patton gave Rural a shot because he appeared close to being in a state of shock. Edd and Louis were given a shot as well and the clinic staff rushed to bandage their arms and phone an ambulance to transport them to Lewis Gale Hospital in Roanoke. Neither one lost consciousness and sat up all the way to the hospital.

Five year old Judy Nolen was home with her mother when Rural and his father, Dave Shortt, came to bring the brother's wallets, the truck, and the bad news. When her husband's green truck pulled into the driveway, Lucille looked out the window and said, "Oh, no, what has happened?" Judy was left with a neighbor and Lucille headed for Roanoke. The State Police went to the accident site and retrieved Louis's arm in hope of saving it for reattachment. Another student told Curtis about the accident, but Kenneth and Joyce didn't hear about it until they were on the school bus coming home.

Both men were in surgery when Lucille arrived. Dr. Fisher reported to her about Edd, "If I can keep the one blood vessel alive in the thumb, I can save his left arm." The only thing holding Edd's left arm was one blood vessel, the skin, and his coveralls.

Louis's right arm could not be reattached, so it was donated to someone else for use of the bones. Dr. Fisher explained to Lucille, "Louis has lost his right arm just below the elbow and we are smoothing up the rough edges of his arm and sewing it up." He remained in the hospital for five days and later returned for a skin graft.

Edd's arm was saved but numerous surgeries were involved. It was damaged so much as to never be of much use and was always held in an angled position. A two-week stay was required, followed later by more surgery, bone, nerve, tendon and skin grafts. One of the skin grafts involved opening the skin of Edd's left side and stomach section, putting his arm inside the skin, pulling the skin over the arm and attaching the arm inside the skin. It stayed this way for six weeks and then he went back to the hospital to have it removed. Once he went to McGuire Veteran's Hospital in Richmond, where they gave him no encouragement, instead advising amputation. This he chose not to do.

The day after the accident, it started snowing. This was the beginning of the famous big snow of the 1960's that's still talked about today. The mountains were battered with snowstorm after snowstorm of foot-deep snows. The wind caused drifts that covered roofs of houses in some places and roads that could hardly be found. School was closed for a month and most places had no electricity. For water, the Nolen family melted snow and somehow tended the cattle and farm with the help of family and neighbors.

The two remarkable brothers came home to begin adapting. They didn't sit down or think of disability income; they went back to work, teaching themselves through trial and error. It was an amazing thing, even to their families, how much work the brothers could do and how they did it. Edd's right hand and Louis's left hand made a pair and that's how they used them. There is a picture showing Edd baling hay in June, just four months after the accident. In fact, they learned to farm, plant garden, harvest corn, work on farm equipment, mow and bale hay, and do whatever needed doing.

While working on the farm equipment, tractors, etc. one would hold the screw, bolt, or whatever, and the other would use the wrench or screwdriver to complete the repair. They built and repaired fences – one held the nail and the other hammered. Both would mow hay, and then Louis would rake while Edd would bale. Edd drove and Louis packed hay. Edd would go buy gas for the tractors, Louis would plow the gardens, and Edd would mow the yard. Louis would tie a string around his arm stub with the other end of the string tied to the power saw and cut firewood while Edd held the wood or loaded. They would feed the cattle, give them shots, and help deliver calves in the middle of the night. They worked out their routine and there was not a job that the two could not do together.

Edd always drove the truck and Louis rode along, both wearing the same style hat. Edd wore dark colored work clothes and Louis preferred bibbed overalls. In cooler weather, Edd liked to wear coveralls but Louis wore a jacket. What do you do with a pair of gloves when you only need one? Well, they turned them inside out and made it work for the same hand. It stands to reason that they could have shared a pair of gloves, but Edd liked brown jersey gloves while Louis favored the yellow, fuzzy, gloves. Acquaintances always spoke of them as Edd and Louis, as if that were one name. No one ever stopped by to see just one of them. "Is Edd and Louis here?" they'd ask.

On winter days, they'd play checkers, dominoes, or cards with the children. Playing cards with one hand could be tricky but they figured it out. Edd held them in his injured hand and Louis made a contraption that held his just fine.

One year after the accident, Louis went back to work at the sawmill and Edd returned two years later, working as a team again. The brothers always helped neighbors and family as well, mowing hay, cutting corn, pushing snow off driveways, or taking someone to the doctor. When the children grew up, they helped build houses, worked gardens, and even fed the cat or dog while someone was on vacation.

Lucille was not idle during these years. She cooked, sewed clothes for the family, washed for four children and three adults, canned, and worked at the shirt factory. She retired in 1979 in order to help her mother and father. Somehow she found time to crochet beautiful doilies and learn to quilt, making one for each child and grandchild.

Life took a turn for the worse when Edd was diagnosed with cancer. While he was sick, Pastor Richard Thomas came to visit and talk about salvation. "Would you like to be forgiven for all your sins and accept Christ into your heart?" he asked Edd.

"Yes," answered Edd. From across the room Louis said, "Me, too." And so the two who had worked together side by side made their religious conversion for Christ at the same time, which seemed fitting, somehow.

Edd Nolen passed from this life in January 1998, ending the walk he and Lucille had continued from that first step they'd begun on an outing in 1939.

Leather Britches
Hilda Hancock Collins – Ballard area

Pick tender green beans and remove strings. Do not wash. There are two good old-fashioned ways to prepare. (1) String with large needle and cotton thread and hang to dry. Worked well over wood cook stoves! When dry they will be slightly darker in color and shriveled but can be bent without breaking. (2) Place in a single layer on old window screen and cover with another. This will take about 4-5 days out in the sun. Best to take them in at night away from dew and critters. Since the britches are prone to weevils, heat them in a 250° oven. Cool and store in tight jars.

Wash the britches and soak overnight. Drain, add clear water, and simmer until tender with fatback or ham hock, salt, and pepper. Takes up to 4 hours. Eat with strong onion and cornbread. YUM, YUM!

"This was one of Mama's (Effie Burnette) favorite cakes. She made one almost every week for her and Daddy (Red). She would have some kind of fruit to go with it."

Sour Cream Pound Cake
Hilda Underwood – Willis, VA

3	sticks butter	3	cups plain flour, sifted
6	eggs	½	tsp. baking powder
1	cup sour cream		pinch of salt
3	cups sugar	1	tsp. vanilla flavoring

Cream butter and add sugar slowly. Add eggs one at a time, beating well. Add dry ingredients slowly. Add sour cream and flavoring. Bake at 325° for 1 hour and 15 minutes.

Sauerkraut
Sadie Goad – Willis, VA

40 lbs. cabbage & 1 lb. salt **OR**
5 lbs. cabbage & 3 Tbsps. salt

Quarter and chop cabbage depending on the amount you use, 40 lbs. or 5 lbs. and add salt accordingly. Mix with hands in large pan, pack gently into crock with potato masher. Repeat until crock is nearly full. Cover with a cloth, plate weighed down with jar of water on top of plate. During the curing process kraut requires daily attention. Remove scum as it forms and wash and scald the cloth often to keep it free from scum and mold. Fermentation takes 10-14 days, as soon as kraut is thoroughly cured; pack in Kerr jars adding enough of the Kraut juice or a weak brine of 2 Tbsps. of salt to a quart of water to fill jars. Process in boiling water bath; 25 minutes for quarts, and 20 minutes for pints.

Though the Country Store is best known, there's lots of music in them thar hills of Floyd County. Chateau Morrisette, Sun Music Hall, Oddfellas, and Café del Sol are all places for music of great variety.

"Here's a recipe I concocted for something I call "Strawberry Soup". I serve it in fancy dessert dishes (like you would use for ice cream)."

Strawberry Soup
Kristin Gillenwater – Meadowood Bed & Breakfast – Meadows of Dan, VA

1   cup sugar
1   cup half-and-half
1   bag of frozen strawberries
½   cup sour cream

Put sugar, half-and-half, and sour cream into blender. Add strawberries a few at a time to avoid burning up your blender motor. Blend until smooth.

Toffee
Judy Lowrance – Floyd, VA

1   cup brown sugar
2   sticks butter
1   pkg. semi-sweet chocolate chips
1   cup nuts (I used chopped walnuts)
35 saltines (mystery ingredient!)

Preheat oven to 350°. Line cookie sheet pan with tin foil. Cover foil with Saltines. Cook butter and sugar in microwave for 4 minutes or until bubbly. Pour over crackers and bake for 20 minutes. Take out and pour chocolate chips over hot cracker mixture. Smooth with spatula. Cover with nuts (push them in). Let cool. Put in fridge for one hour. Break into small pieces.

I believe in the sun, even if it does not shine.
I believe in love, even if I do not feel it.
I believe in God, even if I do not see Him.

Meadowood B&B is located in Floyd County, VA on 20 acres, with hiking trails and a spring-fed pond. They are located right off the Blue Ridge Parkway just 15 minutes from the town of Floyd. They offer a home-cooked four-course breakfast, free high-speed wireless internet, on-site massages, and a variety of specials and packages. www.blueridgebedandbreakfast.net

Schoolhouse Fabrics

In 1971, Clester Duncan started selling boxes of scrap fabric from the Donkenny factory in one room of the old Floyd Elementary School, which closed in 1962. She gradually expanded, renting the first floor and later, the second floor. In a few years, sewing items and material were filling up the 15,000 square foot building. By 1986, she purchased the schoolhouse that now housed specialized rooms - a paradise for crafters, quilters, and sewers.

Jerry J. Duncan, her son, recalls a statement made to him by a friend. "Who would have ever thought someone in a small community like Floyd, VA could buy an old schoolhouse and fill it up with fabric and become successful?"

He adds, "Rationally, I guess it shouldn't have worked. The whole county doesn't have the population of most cities. But by some miracle and God's help, it did."

Many changes have taken place through the years, according to Duncan who has worked there since the beginning. Textile seconds used to be bought and sold by the pound in the building behind the schoolhouse, but few textile mills remain in the U.S. Nothing much is considered seconds now. To Duncan and other family members who run the large family business, service is important and changes are taken in stride. All in all, "Textiles have been a good life."

Home Remedy for Constipation
Lois Mabery's concoction submitted by Hilda Collins

1 cup bran
1 cup apple juice
1 cup prune juice

Mix well and take 2 Tbsps. daily.

Tomato Muffin Treat
Bill Spillman, Jr. – Floyd, VA

2 English muffins	virgin olive oil
1 large ripe fresh tomato	1 lemon or lime
	salt and pepper

Split the 2 English muffins with fingers or with a fork, then toast. Rinse the tomato, core out the stem portion, and slice off the top and bottom. Cut the remainder of the tomato into 4 equally thick circular slabs. Place the 4 toasted English muffin halves on a plate and drizzle with virgin olive oil. Place a slab of tomato on each of the English muffin halves. Salt and pepper to taste. Squeeze fresh lemon or lime juice over each tomato slab. Serves 2.

"This is basically a summer dish during the period when delicious fresh tomatoes are abundant."

Tuggles Gap

A brief overview of the history of Tuggles Gap: In 1768, Benjamin Tuggle IV surveyed and platted about 1,000 acres in the Blue Ridge Mountains of Patrick and Floyd counties in Virginia. This gap is located about eight miles from Floyd, the county seat of Floyd County and about twenty miles from Stuart, the county seat of Patrick County.

Benjamin Tuggle never married, so he divided the land between his two nephews, who settled on the land about the close of the Revolutionary War. The children of Reuben and Joshua Tuggle lived on the land for many years.

Tuggles Gap Restaurant & Motel has been in continuous business for almost seventy years. It was built in 1938 near the location of the Blue Ridge Parkway and Rt. 8 interchange. At first, it was to be a gas station, with soda pop, candy, and a few groceries. The need for food and lodging was recognized as the Parkway was completed through the county, thus an addition onto the original structure became the restaurant and the first eight motel units were built.

Currently, the business is owned and operated by Neil and Cheri Baker, who have been here for over fifteen years. They are only the third family to own and operate the motel and restaurant. Two of the most popular and well-known dishes served here are the pan-fried chicken and Tuggles Gap pie.   *– Cheri Baker*

Tuggles Gap Pan-fried Chicken

Use fresh chicken breast and leg-thigh quarters. Bread them with lots of pepper, flour, and salt. Cook in a black skillet about one hour – turning constantly in about ½ inch of olive oil.

Every evening I turn "worries" over to God. He's going to be up all night anyway.

"Virginia is the number six apple producing state and is seventh in peanuts. This delicious salad can be on the sweet side if the apple variety is also sweet. If not using semi-tart apples, you might want to add a tsp. or two of lemon juice"

Waldorf Salad With Peanut Dressing
Judy Lowrance - Floyd, VA

2 cups diced semi-tart apples, not peeled (I used more because there's quite a lot of sauce).
1/3 cup raisins
1/3- ½ cup diced celery
½ cup chopped salted peanuts
¼ cup creamy peanut butter
¼ cup honey
¼ cup mayonnaise
1-2 tsps. lemon juice (optional) if using sweeter apples

In a bowl, toss together apples, raisins, celery, and peanuts; set aside. In a small bowl, blend peanut butter, honey, and mayonnaise. Toss with apple mixture and serve on a bed of lettuce.

Walnut Pate'
Patricia Woodruff – Art Under The Sun Gallery – Floyd, VA

2 cloves garlic
1½ cups walnuts
¼ cup olive oil
   cayenne pepper (to taste)
1 Tbsp. dried basil (better yet 3 Tbsps. fresh basil)
½ tsp. black pepper
½ pkg. (4 oz.) low fat cream cheese
½ stick butter
½ tsp. balsamic vinegar

Blend in food processor the garlic, walnuts, and olive oil. Add the remaining ingredients and blend in food processor. Serve with crackers.

Dutchies View Bed and Breakfast is a quaint country farmhouse perched atop a knoll with a panoramic view of the Blue Ridge Mountains. Actually located in Patrick County, both Floyd and Stuart are easily accessible. The original farmhouse was built in the mid 1800's as a two- room farmhouse. The house had no electricity or plumbing until 1952, when it was moved from its original location to where it sits today. In 1952, an addition was built to accommodate a family of seven, then plumbing and electricity was added. In 1995, a Dutch couple purchased the poorly maintained home, refurbished it and added six guest rooms. In 1997, Dutchies View was born and opened for business.

In the fall of 2004, Patrick and Crystal Powell were on a quest to find a B&B with panoramic views. When they stumbled across Dutchies View, they instantly fell in love with its gorgeous setting. They have added a larger dining room, a larger living room, and more deck space for their guests.

Each of the six rooms has its own private bath. In the evening, guests sit around the porch soaking up the view and enjoy coffee and fresh homemade desserts, and lively conversation. In the morning, guests are roused from sleep by the delectable aroma of Dutchies View's own private blend of coffee. Guests start the day with a large country breakfast complete with homemade breads and jams, fresh fruit, bacon, eggs, Patrick's famous lemon ginger pancakes! www.dutchiesview.com

White Bean Chicken Chili or Chili Soup

Patrick and Crystal Powell – Dutchies View B&B

1   lb. skinless/boneless chicken breasts and ½ cup water
1   can each: Navy beans, northern beans, white kidney beans, chili beans, and   Pinto beans (do not drain)
1   (4 oz.) can green chilies chopped
½   cup chopped Vidalia onion
1   Tbsp. minced garlic
1   Tbsp. favorite hot sauce
1   tsp. each: cumin, oregano, chili powder, and natures seasoning
2   Tbsps. extra virgin olive oil
    If making soup and not chili, add 1 ½ cups chicken broth

Cook chicken in skillet with water covered until completely cooked. (Will easily fall apart when cooked). Let cool, then shred chicken with fingers into varied sizes. In a large stockpot, combine all ingredients and cook on medium heat for 2 to 3 hours stirring occasionally. Serve with a dollop of sour cream and sprinkle with oregano. Leftovers can be served in a large tortilla with all the fixings for a great tasting burrito.

<u>Life By the Side of the Road</u>

Uncle Irvie's Barn by the side of the road.

Rushing by, you may glance my way and think me quite dull. Here I sit with my doors hanging cock-eyed on rusted hinges, my boards warped and sagging, pieces of tin missing from my roof. But wait; there are marvelous stories I could tell of life in these parts during the past century. Being built here close to the road has given me a chance to see adventure that I would never have known had Marion Burnette, my original owner, put me in a far meadow.

In my early years, people traveled mostly by shank mare or on horseback. Any number was overtaken by darkness and sought shelter in my loft. Travelers were thankful for the warmth and also for the food my owner provided; it gave them strength to make the rest of their journey. This occurred often during the great depression, but was commonplace throughout the years. In those days, men walked twenty miles past me to catch a train seeking work

Visitors or not, I was never lonesome. Along with the twelve children of Marion Burnette, there were cousins who played hide and seek in the hay and visited the kittens that roamed about my stalls. Later the grandchildren came along, toddling after grandpa. Oh, the laughter that has rung within these walls! Some complaining has been heard, too, when the hay had to be gotten in and milking had to be done early on a cold morning. Not as much as you might think, because farm kids knew that work had to be done so they invented games and played jokes to lighten the load. I can hear them now, talking to the farm horses as they bridled them up for a day's work in the fields.

A few miles down the road, there was two country stores where local folks went to buy necessities, learn the news, and spin a yarn or two. On rainy or snowy days it was not out of the ordinary for Marion or his son Irva, (Irvie) who later owned the property, to come through my doors at milking time and find a bag or two of groceries sitting near the wall. I have offered protection for livestock feed and for corn on the way to the mill to be ground as well. When the owner got time, he would return and find his items waiting in the same spot.

"I'm much obliged to you," he'd say to my owner, who would reply back to him, "Glad to help you out. Anytime."

High-octane spirits from a fruit jar occasionally overpowered young men out sowing their wild oats, rendering them incapable or unwilling to complete the trip to their homes. They wound up needing a sleeping-it-off place and I was that place more than one time.

I can just hear Irvie saying to a couple of groaning young men, "How y'all doing this morning, boys?" as he went about his chores, chewing tobacco and spitting. He probably recalled, as I do, that he and his brothers spent some nights under my roof in their younger days.

Throughout the years, I have served my purpose as a barn for horses and cows. Travelers' horses have been fed and numerous cows and calves have called me home. But the world is different and life has changed as people zoom about in gas-powered vehicles. They don't notice me any more. Maybe it's because the road is no longer dirt, with ruts and mud and big rocks to slow the vehicles down. No one is out working around my yard, doing this or that, to entice passers-by to stop and chew the fat. A way of life has gone, most likely forever, and I was a part of the old way. But - I have been loved and I have been useful to strangers, neighbors, and friends as well as to my owner. No one can take away the memories I have of the precious years I've spent sitting by the side of the road!

May God give you:
For every storm ~ a rainbow
For every tear ~ a smile
For every care ~ a promise
And a blessing in each trial.
For every problem life sends,
A faithful friend to share.
For every sigh ~ a sweet song
And an answer for each prayer.
    -Irish Blessing

Wanda Hylton Dalton

"My claim to fame happened just this summer (2008)," says Wanda Dalton, as we talked to her at the Floyd Country Store. "Rhonda Vincent played at the high school and invited me up on stage to sing *Slippers With Wings* with her. It was such a privilege to get to sing with her and be backed up by her band. I was terrified when I got up on stage but she helped me by singing. It was a nice moment for me."

Why would Rhonda Vincent randomly pick a nice lady who lives in Floyd, VA to come up on stage and sing with her? Perhaps it wasn't too random. Dalton wrote the song. Vincent and many others have sung and recorded it through the years. Of course, having Randall Hylton, well-known singer and songwriter, for a brother to help polish it up and make it shine didn't hurt anything.

The words to the song came because she was bored. "I sewed in a sewing factory for many years," she states. I was so bored I started thinking of songs. The title came first and the song afterward. Randall helped me get the words in proper order, so it was really co-written. The Lewis Family first recorded the song. Randall recorded it, too, and it was one of his most requested songs wherever he performed. People have told us that it brought comfort and hope to them. I am really glad if it does."

Music was a big part of the Hylton family. Their father played a guitar and mouth-harp and their mother sang. They did appearances on WBOB in Galax, VA and on WPAQ in Mt. Airy, NC. Wanda's sister sang and brother, Randall, began playing guitar while he was very young. "He was always trying to learn more," she laughs.

"We grew up on the side of the road in Willis," she says. "I remember during the early 1940's, that a car would come by from Hillsville with a big bullhorn. We could hear them coming from a good ways up the road. They were announcing what was going on at the Hillsville, Floyd, or Stuart Theaters. The same person owned all three. Sometimes there were live shows and we'd go if at all possible. Ten or fifteen cents would get you in."

"I will never forget going to see Charlie and Bill Monroe at Hillsville. I was about three or four years old and Daddy was holding me in his arms as he talked to Bill. I just reached out and hugged Bill Monroe around the neck. I have no idea why. He laughed with a distinctive giggle that I still can hear, though I was so young. Our car broke down on the way home and someone brought us the rest of the way. Daddy had to go back and get it the next day."

Though retired after thirty years with County Sales, or possibly *because* of being there, Wanda has written a new song. *Country Folks* will be on the latest CD by bluegrass greats "Lost and Found," slated for release in the autumn. She expects to keep enjoying singing in church, as she has through the years. "My preference is singing harmony," she states.

And if ever I am certain of one certain thing,
Susie is wearing golden slippers with wings.
<u>-Wanda Hylton Dalton / Randall Hylton</u>

Franklin County

Contents

Banana Pudding..............................345	Grandma Hatcher's Homemade Games.364
Barbequed Groundhog....................345	Ham Bites.......................................365
B-B-Q Corn Chip Salad.................345	Ham Salad Spread..........................366
Bertha's Pound Cake......................346	Hot Crunchy Chicken Casserole...........366
Blackberry Cobbler........................346	Irene's Country Fried Chicken.............366
Blackberry Pie...............................346	Lady Baltimore Cake.........................368
Blackberry Wine Cake....................349	Mama's Sugar Cookies........................370
Buffalo Chicken Dip........................350	Mary D's Poppy Seed Dressing............369
Chicken and Cheese Tostadas.........351	Oat Cakes...370
Chicken and Dumplings..................352	Ol' Timey Fit As A Fiddle Beans..........374
Corn and Pea Salad........................351	Pavlova..374
Cottage Cheese Ice Cream..............354	Pineapple Cheese Ball........................375
Cream of Potato and Tomato Soup..355	Rolo Pecan Pretzel Turtles....................375
Creamy Rice Pudding......................354	Skillet Beans.....................................379
Deviled Eggs...................................358	Slumgullion......................................379
Eggplant Parmesan.........................359	Southern Coconut Cake......................382
Filling for Coconut Cake.................359	Southern Pecan Pie............................383
Franklin County Sweet Mash Corn Liquor 1940's............................360	Spoon Bread....................................385
French Bakes..................................363	Teriyaki Sauce for Deer Meat..............385
Fritters From Greens......................363	Tomato Rarebit................................385
Grandma Daniel's Rolls..................363	Wilted Lettuce..................................386
	Zucchini Pineapple Bread...................387

Photo taken at Rt. 40 Dairy Queen in Rocky Mount, VA. Scenes are changed on the pig periodically by the manager and "painter of the pig," Leanne Dickerson. Locals, as well as travelers, take notice. Some love it and some don't, but all check out *The Pig* as they drive by or stop in!

About Franklin County

As early as 10,000 B.C. – before the time of Christ - Native Americans lived in the area that would become Franklin County, Virginia.

Historians tell us that the climate was much cooler here then, and that those early Indians hunted huge mastodon, moose, and caribou that roamed here. Their recipes no doubt began with taking off the hide and involved an open fire.

The Native Americans were called "Indians" because the first white people to arrive in the new world thought they had found the Indies and they called the people they found "Indians." The explorers later realized they were wrong but the name stuck.

We know that Indians lived here because the first white people to settle in the area in the 1740's found evidence, some of which you can see today. There are Indian caves in the Penhook area and stonefish traps at Waid Recreation Area and on the Pigg River near the Blackwater Bridge on U.S. 220. Farmers and people building houses today still uncover spear points, arrowheads, and other items.

Native Americans living here often made war with members of other Indian tribes that came through on a route called Warrior's Path. This path was one of the main trails used by Indian warriors from the Creek nations in Georgia and Alabama on their way to attack enemies in Pennsylvania and New York. Northern Indians came the same way as they went south to seek revenge.

The Warrior's Path became part of the Great Wagon Road from Philadelphia to the Yadkin Valley in North Carolina near today's Augusta, GA. Around here, the route was called the Carolina Road. You can see a highway sign marking part of the old Carolina Road in the grassy median of U.S. 220 north of Boones Mill. This road was busy in those days. A lot of settlers used the road. German Baptists from Pennsylvania settled in northwest Franklin County and Scots-Irish settled the southwest part.

Robert Hill, deemed the first permanent white settler in the Rocky Mount area, was among the 1740's travelers. He had two young sons killed by Indians – one as he stood in the doorway of a blockhouse/fort built by Hill as protection from the savages. Another Hill son was killed by an Indian standing on Bald Knob (behind today's county high school) and buried about where he fell to start what is today known as Tanyard Cemetery. The fort built by Robert Hill is in ruins but is being preserved through a project by Franklin County Historical Society.

Franklin County's history is older than our modern calendar – and older than the United States. Two of our citizens were at the debate in Richmond in 1788 voting no to ratification of the proposed Constitution. Thomas Arthur and John Early said no, based on advice from Patrick Henry.

"You will sip sorrow," Henry told the delegation during the 20-day debate. "I look on that paper (the proposed Constitution) as the most fatal plan that could possibly be conceived to enslave a free people."

Much of the county history is on display or in written form in the History Museum and Research Library operated by Franklin County Historical Society, 460 S. Main St., Rocky Mount. No admission charge, donations welcome.

The Historical Society presents character tours, group tours, and conducts monthly meetings, all with history themes. History is fun. Let the Historical Society show you. www.franklincountyvirginiahistoricalsociety.org   - *Linda Stanley*

Dairy Queen Band

Way before the Crooked Road idea took shape, the Dairy Queen in Rocky Mount was a place to hear traditional and Bluegrass music on Thursday mornings. The popular band that played was even named the Dairy Queen Band. Members are Dewey Prillaman on fiddle, Junior Montgomery on banjo, Allen McBride on mandolin, Fulton Dillon on guitar, and James Guilliams on bass and sometimes guitar. After the formation of Virginia's Heritage Music Trail, the Dairy Queen was designated an affiliated partner of the Crooked Road, and it's namesake band has received widespread attention.

The Dairy Queen band plays from September to May, taking the summer months off so many travelers miss them. However, a plan is underway for music on the second and fourth Thursday nights with other bands participating.

"My son, Zach Brown plays mandolin in the Blackwater Bluegrass Band in Franklin County."

Banana Pudding
Twyla Brown – Wirtz, VA

1 (12 oz.) carton Cool Whip, thawed
1 (8 oz.) carton sour cream
1 large box instant vanilla pudding

In large bowl mix together the Cool Whip and sour cream. In another bowl mix pudding according to package directions. Pour pudding into sour cream mixture and mix well. Put this mixture between layers of vanilla wafers and sliced bananas. Keep refrigerated until ready to serve.

"Glen plays music with Cedar Ridge Bluegrass Band in Franklin County."

B-B-Q Corn Chip Salad
Glen and Peggy Turman – Penhook, VA

6 cups lettuce
1½ cups crushed barbeque corn chips
¼ cup diced onion
½-1 cup crumbled bacon
¾ cup grated cheese

Dressing:
¼ cup sugar
¼ cup oil
1½ Tbsps. vinegar
1 Tbsp. water
¼ tsp. salt
black and red pepper to taste
¼ tsp. onion powder
1 Tbsp. mayonnaise
2 tsp. mustard

Combine the lettuce, corn chips, onion, bacon, and cheese. Blend well the sugar, oil, vinegar, water, salt, black and red pepper, onion powder, mayonnaise, and mustard. Add dressing to salad just before serving.

Barbequed Groundhog
-Susan Justice- Ferrum

Catch a young groundhog and fatten him about two weeks on milk and bread before slaughtering. Clean inside and out, cut up or boil whole in water with some garlic cloves. When tender, place in pan and cover with your favorite barbeque sauce. Bake in slow oven for about 30 minutes. Raccoon can be prepared the same way.

Bertha's Pound Cake
Marilyn A. Clements

3	cups plain flour	6	eggs
3	cups sugar	1	tsp. baking powder
2	sticks I Can't Believe It's Not Butter, softened	2	tsps. lemon flavoring
		2	tsps. vanilla flavoring
1	(8 oz.) sour cream	½	cup Wesson oil

Cream sugar and eggs (1 at a time). Add flour and baking powder alternately with sour cream. Add flavoring and oil. Pour into greased and floured bundt pan and bake at 325° for 1 hour and 15 minutes or until toothpick comes out clean.

Blackberry Cobbler
Brenda D. Raine – Penhook, VA

4	cups fresh blackberries	1	stick butter, melted
1¼	cups sugar	1	egg
1	cup flour		

Put the berries in a 9-inch buttered baking dish and sprinkle with ¼ cup sugar. Mix together the flour, butter, egg, and remaining sugar. Press over the berries. Bake at 375° for 45-60 minutes or until golden brown. Serve warm with vanilla ice cream. For variety mix in raspberries or blueberries.

Blackberry Pie
Jean Brown - Snow Creek, VA

1½	cups self-rising flour	2	Tbsp. butter	1	stick of butter
1	tsp. soda		buttermilk	1½	Tbsps. lemon juice
1	Tbsp. Crisco		sugar to taste		blackberries

Mix the flour, soda, Crisco, and butter. Stir in buttermilk to form a soft pastry. Roll out ½ of dough and line bottom of baking dish. Fill with blackberries (fresh or frozen). Add sugar to sweeten to your taste. Cut 1 stick of butter into pieces and add to berries. Add water mixed with lemon juice to where you can see the water level with berries. Roll out rest of pastry for the top and bake in 350° oven until brown to suit your taste. Serve hot with vanilla ice cream. Delicious!

Summer Fruit

It seems like we were always picking, eating, preserving and savoring fruit in my growing up years. Late spring sent me down the lanes and roads clutching a handful of sugar to dip wild, sweet strawberries in as I meandered along. The cherry trees were ripe with their crimson sweet-sour fruit in early June. Before school was out for the year, the children on the school bus would reach out the bus windows and grab cherries as they rode by the cherry trees that lined the white fence by the road. Luckily, there were always plenty for utterly delicious pies Mama or Grandmamma would bake for us.

July 4th would usually mark the start of blackberry season. Oh, what a hot, sticky, "buggy" task! We would go early in the morning when it was fairly cool, clad in long pants, long-sleeved shirts and sturdy shoes or boots to keep the briars from scratching us or the chiggers and ticks away. By the time we got back, we were so hot! The black, juicy, fragrant fruit found its way to our mouths and buckets, though. There also was always the underlying fear of snakes and any wildlife we might step on or flush out of hiding. Of course, when we got back, we had to have a thorough tick check. Even this day, my most favorite dessert is blackberry pie or cobbler.

(A family joke for many years was my finding a big fat June bug in a pie Mama had made. Somehow it escaped during the berry washing.)

My aunt who lived up the hill raised "blackcaps" – black raspberries. She cultivated and coddled the vines, which produced wonderful fruit. She always shared them, but somehow the blackberries we sweated and strained over were best.

When August came, it was time to make a trip to the best peach orchard around. (This was one fruit we didn't grow.) Not just any peaches would do. They must be perfect. One time we rode up on a mountain to the back of beyond, but we came home loaded down with the most perfect peaches around. I can still feel the fuzz as I bit down on one of these perfect fruits and the warm juice running down my chin. O, heavenly smell! O, scrumptious taste!! We would spend the next few days peeling, cutting up, and canning (later freezing) the peaches. They would also be made into a variety of wonderful desserts: peach shortcake, peach ice cream, peaches on pound cake, peaches over vanilla ice cream, peach pie, or just a bowl of plain peaches sweetened with brown sugar.

September meant a trip to another kind of orchard – apple. We always went to Alexander's Orchard, as we thought there was no better one. I often thought what a nice place to live, but I'm sure there was a lot of hard work to do. The packing house always had a fascinating smell – so winey and rich and fall-like. Those apples were so sweet, crisp and fine smelling. A big bowl of polished apples on the table made a lovely centerpiece, but it didn't last long!   - *Brenda D. Raine*

Brown Family Square Dancers

      Franklin County, VA was home base for a family that loved old-time music and square dancing so much they were inspired to form a dance group that entertained local folks and throughout surrounding areas.

      The Brown family consisted of fourteen children, including five sets of twins. None were identical though a strong family resemblance existed among them all.

      One boy-girl set of twins was named after Little Jimmy Dickens and Patsy Cline, though Jimmy Brown didn't turn out to be little. A Smith-Douglas Fertilizer sack was the inspiration for naming my husband, Ruben Douglas.

      The parents of the Brown children, W.C. and Sally Kate, were good dancers and would have dances in their home in the mid-forties. One set of twins would have to hold the oil lamps on the mantle because the old wooden floor would vibrate when several people were dancing. (Some of you seniors might remember what that was like!)

      The Brown children all married spouses who were good dancers. That is how it came about that we could have 18-24 people dancing at one time. On occasion, some would have to work and our number would be smaller, like 4-6 couples.

      The Brown Family Dancers traveled to fiddler's conventions all around and appeared at the Dogwood Festival in Vinton for several years. For seventeen years, the program at the Roanoke Fiddler's convention included the dancing Browns.

They danced at a convention at the Homestead Resort in Bath County, at the Hotel Roanoke, and for a special benefit for the Martinsville Hospital. Ten or twelve couples were on the stage at the Martinsville High School at one time for that. There was a Japanese businessman at Hotel Roanoke who was particularly interested in and seemed to really enjoy the music and the dance steps.

In the 1970's a phone call came asking the Browns to dance at the Roanoke Convention Center. George Jones and Tammy Wynette were scheduled to appear, but they were breaking up their marriage and their tour. "Can you get everybody to come put on a show for us?" they asked. "We need you to be part of our program tomorrow night."

"Well, we scurried around and got eight couples together. We danced and George put on a great performance, but Tammy was the no-show that time." -*Jean Brown*

The Franklin County conspiracy case of 1935 was a trial of 23 defendants that lasted 10 weeks, making it the second longest trial on record in Virginia history at that time. The longest was the treason trial of Aaron Burr that took place in Richmond in 1807.

Blackberry Wine Cake
Sharon K. Tudor – Rocky Mount, VA

- 1 box of white cake mix
- 4 eggs (room temperature)
- 1 cup oil
- 1 cup of blackberry wine (I use Manischewitz wine)
- 1 (3 oz.) box blackberry or raspberry Jell-O
- 1 (3 oz.) box of instant vanilla Jell-O pudding mix
- ½ cup of chopped pecans or walnuts

Preheat oven to 325°. Beat eggs until fluffy; then add oil, both boxes of jell-o; mix well. Gradually add wine and cake mix, mixing well. Fold in nuts. I use a tube pan for baking. Bake 45–55 minutes (or until cake test reveals cake is done).

Glaze:
- ¼ cup blackberry wine
- 3 cups of confectioners sugar

Mix the wine and sugar together. Place in a saucepan, stirring and bring to a boil. Boil for about 1½ to 2 minutes. Remove from heat and allow to rest until the glaze begins to thicken. After the cake is cool, drizzle the thickened glaze over the cake. This cake becomes very moist if made the day before serving. DELICIOUS!!!

Bootleg Express Draft Farm

If only everyone could just once stand in the first frost of the year, shivering in the paddock with chill and anticipation only to see the warm breath from their nostrils and then the blur of mane and feathers in a full gallop coming to meet you. Purely God's Magic…
www.bootlegexpressdraftfarm.com

"Located in the eastern part of Franklin County on a few acres of green pasture, you will find a small horse farm nestled amongst the natives. Several names came to mind when we started this venture several years ago, but wanting to show our pride in the history of this county, we call it "Bootleg Express Farm."

When we moved to Franklin County, we knew we wanted to raise our family here. Originally from Southwest Virginia, we had lived in the Northern VA suburbs and wanted to find a place to call home. After having our two daughters, we knew that with this country changing so fast, we had to find something that kept their interest and that we could focus on as a family. There was one love that we could agree on, our horses. Not just any horses, but horses that had passion and that created passion among anyone that became familiar with them. Here on our farm, you will find Shires and Clydesdales. With their size and majesty, they definitely demand attention, but our future lies in a horse from a different culture and a different land - The Gypsy Cob. The Gypsy people love nothing more than they love their horses, with their long feathered feet, colored coats, and gentle nature, these horses have made their way into the heart of America and we are striving to make sure they stay there.

We don't get much rest and we sure aren't going to make a fortune, but our girls are happy and we are living a life we can be proud of. God blesses us everyday with the beauty that surrounds us." -Travis & Tabatha Adkins

Buffalo Chicken Dip
Tabatha Adkins – Union Hall, VA

2	(10 oz.) cans chunk chicken, drained	2	cups shredded cheddar cheese
2	(8 oz.) pkgs. cream cheese, softened	1	(8 oz.) box chicken-flavored crackers
1	cup Ranch dressing		
¾	cup hot sauce		

Heat chicken and hot sauce in a skillet over medium heat until heated through. Stir in cream cheese and ranch dressing. Cook, stirring until well blended and warm. Mix in half of the shredded cheese and transfer the mixture to a slow cooker. Sprinkle the remaining cheese over the top, cover, and cook on low setting until hot and bubbly. Serve with crackers or tortillas.

Chicken and Cheese Tostadas
Teresa McCollum – The Vintage Spa – Rocky Mount, VA

6   Taco Bell home originals flour tortillas
1   (¼ oz.) pkg. Taco Bell home originals taco seasoning mix, divided
1   lb. boneless skinless chicken breasts, cut into ½-inch pieces
½   cup water
2   cups chopped tomatoes, divided
2   cups Kraft shredded cheddar cheese, divided
6   Tbsps. sour cream
¼   cup chopped cilantro

Preheat oven to 400°. Place tortillas in single layer on large baking sheet. Spray tortillas with cooking spray; sprinkle with 1 tsp. of the seasoning mix. Bake 7 to 8 minutes or until crisp and golden brown. Meanwhile, mix chicken, remaining seasoning mix, and the water in large skillet. Bring to boil on medium-high heat. Reduce heat to medium-low; simmer 5 minutes or until chicken is cooked through, stirring occasionally. Add 1½ cups of the tomatoes. Cook until heated through, stirring occasionally. Remove from heat; stir in 1½ cups of the cheese. Spoon chicken mixture evenly over tortillas. Top with the remaining ½ cup cheese, remaining ½ cup tomatoes, the sour cream, and cilantro.

In 2004, Franklin County Fun was launched as a website dedicated to recording positive events taking place around the county. From 500 hits per month, it has grown to nearly 2 million hits yearly. It is now an eagerly awaited quarterly magazine, too.

Corn and Pea Salad
Janie Murphy – Snow Creek, VA

1   (15 oz.) can corn, drained
1   (15 oz.) can peas, drained
1   small onion
1   small sweet pepper
1   tsp. celery seed
1   cup shredded cheese
1   cup tomato, chopped
¼   cup mayonnaise
¼   tsp. mustard seed
    ranch dressing to taste

Mix all ingredients together, putting ½ cheese in salad, ½ of cheese on top. Refrigerate over night, add ranch dressing at serving time.

"When we were children, Mama (Betsy) raised chickens, so when chicken was needed she would gather the chicken, chop its head off, and when it quit hopping around, she would have scalding hot water ready and douse that chicken in the water. The feathers were then plucked off, the chicken "cleaned", cut up, and left to soak in salt water for an hour or so. We did not appreciate helping with this chore."

Home remedy:

Cut beets in blocks. Fill ½ gallon jar, add 1 lb. rock candy. Fill jar with bootleg whiskey. Take 1 Tbsp. before meal for ulcerated stomach.

Chicken and Dumplings

Recipe of Betsy Guilliams – submitted by Jackie Siler – Callaway, VA

1   whole chicken or chicken breasts
1½ cups flour
    chicken broth
    shortening
    milk

Cook chicken, remove any bones, and skim the broth, getting some of the fat off. Reserve the chicken to serve with dumplings, or you can leave the chicken in the dumplings. Use as much flour as needed to make amount of dumplings needed (1½ cups flour usually a good amount). Use either self-rising or plain (if plain, add baking powder). Use shortening or broth from cooked chicken to make up biscuit like mixture. If a rich broth for dumplings is desired, make up with evaporated milk. If the broth in the pot is not thick enough, add butter or margarine. Make up dumplings, then roll out and cut in squares. You will "stretch" dumplings when they are added to broth. After preparing dumplings, have the broth hot, then add milk to the broth. After it comes to a soft boil, add dumplings to the pot (remembering to stretch them) and bring back to boil. Let boil for short while and then lower heat until they are the right texture. Do not overcook.

If'n you hear somebody has been gossiping about you, jest reply, "They must not know me too well, or they'd know the rest of my faults. If'n they did, they wouldn't have mentioned jest these few."

Aaron Long/ Procon Foundations

For anyone who thinks the youth of America have become lazy and with little resolution - meet Aaron Long. At 23 years old, he is owner of Procon, a company specializing in concrete work, which employs around seventy people. Of course, there appears to be a wisdom that usually comes from years of experience flowing from him, leading one to picture a 45 year old brain in his young body.

Long has acquired several years experience, having started the business at 16. His youth prevented many from taking him seriously, so his girlfriend's grandfather did the estimating and dealing with contractors, while Aaron showed up with the other workers to do the job. He gives Mandy, now his wife, credit for handling the office work and being his support throughout the establishing of the business.

Nothing was easy. He now works a 12-hour day, down from the early years when he was "trying to do it all." Learning to delegate was hard, but has been one of the steps Long had to take in the process of growing. Education and a willingness to learn from others in the field, as well as to try new technology, has been an asset. Oh, yeah… he had to learn from the ground up, as he knew almost nothing when he started the business simply because a contractor told him there was a need.

The core purpose of Procon, as stated on their website, gives a great idea of the type of person who started and owns it:

> Be Good Stewards
> To Give:
> To Our Customers - Unequaled Value
> To Our Colleagues – Unlimited Opportunities
> To Our Families – Provision
> To Our Fellowman – Integrity
> To Our Community – Support
> To Our God - Honor

This I recall to my mind, therefore have I hope. It is of the Lord's mercies that we are not consumed, because his compassions fail not. They are new every morning: great is thy faithfulness.
-Lamentations 3:21-23

Franklin County is the seventh largest county in Virginia at 692 square miles of land. The highest point is Cahas Mountain at 3,553 ft. near Boones Mill.

"This recipe is over 100 years old. My mother-in-law, Ethel Naff, age 103, gave me this recipe. It was a favorite of her mother, Mary Ellen Ikenberry Jamison. She called the cottage cheese "smearcase" in the old days. She would put it in the ice house before serving."

Cottage Cheese Ice Cream
Angelia Naff – Boones Mill, VA

2	(3 oz.) pkgs. cream cheese	1	tsp. vanilla
2/3	cup cottage cheese	1	pt. whipping cream
1	cup sugar	3	stiffly beaten egg whites
3	beaten egg yolks		graham cracker crumbs

Cream the cream cheese and cottage cheese well. Add sugar and the egg yolks. Mix thoroughly. Add the vanilla, whipping cream that is already whipped, and fold in the egg whites. Line a 9 x 9-inch pan with graham cracker crumbs. Pour mixture in pan and top with graham cracker crumbs. Freeze, cut in squares, and serve. Serves 6.

Creamy Rice Pudding
Dot Webb – Callaway, VA

½	cup uncooked regular rice	3	eggs, beaten
1	cup boiling water	2/3	cup sugar
1	quart milk	1	tsp. vanilla
½	stick butter	½	cup raisins (optional)
1	tsp. salt		nutmeg

Combine rice and boiling water in a large saucepan (about 3 quarts). Cover and cook slowly for 7 minutes. Add milk, butter, and salt. Quickly add eggs, sugar, vanilla, and raisins if desired. Pour in baking dish and bake in slow oven for 1 hour and 15 minutes. Spoon into serving dishes and sprinkle top with nutmeg.

James Webb of Callaway began woodworking after retiring from the local telephone company. Before entering the military, he had worked for a short time with a sawmill; that was his only experience with wood. Now he is handcrafting fiddles, dulcimer, and mandolins that seasoned musicians are delighted to play.

"My history with Phoebe Needles Center for Lifelong Learning began in April, 2002, with a private retreat. Working on a Doctoral course on C. S. Lewis, I needed time, space, and beautiful scenery in which to think my own thoughts and take time away from extended-family-member concerns. It was perfect: a time "outside of time" and "a place apart." I was healed there, in so many ways.

When we moved from Amherst County to Franklin County in 2004, I was glad to be closer to this "beautiful place apart" and looked forward to spending more time at Phoebe Needles. My wish came true when I was allowed to temporarily fill in as food-preparer for occasional special events.

As a member of the planning team for the Center for Lifelong Learning, I decided to donate my time, food, and other materials toward providing elegantly served comfort food for the luncheons that followed the monthly seminars for retired adults. This has garnered much pleasure for me and satisfied the attendees to the extent that recipes for some of my dishes are often requested as our guests depart these events.

Here, then, is a recipe that I fall back on when, suddenly, more attendees arrive for a Seminar than were originally anticipated."

Cream of Potato and Tomato Soup

Karen Smith-Moretz – Phoebe Needles Center for Lifelong Learning – Ferrum, VA

6 (26 oz.) cans Campbell's cream of tomato soup
10 (10 ¾ oz.) cans Campbell's cream of potato soup
2 quarts half-and-half
filtered spring water
½ cup Sherry, optional

Empty soup cans into a large (6 quart size) crock-pot bowl. Turn heat on high. Fill one of the smaller soup cans with the spring water. Use this to scoop out the remaining bits of soup from each can. Pour it into the pan with the soups. Stir in the half-and-half (and Sherry, if used) and heat to 140-160°, stirring once each hour. Or, heat in a large, heavy, pan and keep warm in crock-pot until serving time. Serve in soup bowls with thick dollops of Crème Fraiche* and chopped green onions.

*Crème Fraiche is made the day before the soup, by stirring 1-pint whipping cream into 1-pint sour cream in a large bowl. After thoroughly, but gently, blending the ingredients, divide mixture into four (1-cup size) bowls and cover with Saran Wrap. Place bowls on a baking sheet and place in an oven with the oven light on. Leave – undisturbed – for 8-12 hours (8 hours in summer and 12 hours in winter). Place tray in refrigerator until thoroughly chilled (another 4-8 hours). Stir gently before serving.
Note: Serves two dozen persons.

My Mountain Home

My daddy was from Boone, NC and my mother was from a little town called Rural Hall, NC near Winston-Salem. My dad was a Lutheran pastor and by the time the children came along we moved to a little town in the sand hills near Columbia, SC. When I was 15 we moved to Florida and I stayed there until I finished college and other schooling.

I always had a sense of affinity for the hill country. Growing up in sand, something about clay seemed more appropriate. I spent the summers with my mother's parents. Once in a while, my dad and I would make the trip all the way to Boone. The roads were not what they are now. I thought the journey was so neat. A little outside Boone, we would take the road toward West Jefferson, a gravel road, and get off that road onto what we would call a Jeep trail today. I was the oldest by 6 years, so the younger ones would stay behind in Boone. To me, it was so great to get to drive right through this creek to go to my Granddaddy's house. I never knew my grandmother; she had 13 children and died before I was born. I always looked forward to being even further up in the mountains. When they get through with mapping the human gene system, they are going to find a Hillbilly gene and I've got one from my daddy and my mama. We could sit on my grandparent's front porch in Winston-Salem and way off at a distance, we could see Pilot Mountain.

I always had a sense the right place to live was in the mountains and that is what eventually brought Karen and me here. Her roots are in Kansas. She was a Navy brat, born in Kansas City, Missouri. After teaching 3 decades at George Mason University, we retired first to Amherst, VA, which we like but we wanted to get further south in VA, a little more in the mountains. We moved to Franklin County in August of 2004. We have never looked back; we love it here. I wouldn't trade living here for anything. Not only the scenery, but also the people here have hooked us both.   – *as told by John Moretz*

WYTI – 1570 on your AM dial

WYTI radio station went on the air April 1, 1957 and is still vibrantly serving their community, making a strong case that they must be doing something right. They were voted the Small Business of the Year (2007) for Franklin County as well. What the station does is part of what's good about small-town and rural America, which is to carry on a tradition of specialized programming for their area.

Bill Jefferson, who started to work the day the station went on the air and bought the business in 1970, has been adamant about maintaining true country music, according to his daughter and General Manager, Susan Mullins. "Every fourth song we play is bluegrass and a hymn is part of the lineup every hour," she states, although when she was younger, she questioned why they couldn't vary things more.

"I have come to appreciate our history and the heritage of mountain music," she continues. "I love it. I am so proud of my father for holding to tradition."

Mullins says she grew up in the radio station and has worked there thirty years. Her father and mother (the git 'er done lady) still work there as well. Three DJ's: Cliff Beach, Carl Castillo, and Bruce Jarvis, keep things happening from 6:00 AM to 9:00 PM daily. Chris Altice and Charles Durham make the weekends hum. Office manager, Don Mattingly and Sales Mgr. Jesse Ramsey round out the crew. "We have a family environment where each person is important," states Mullins. "It takes us all doing whatever needs to be done. Of course, we have some fun, too."

Paul Harvey, Focus on the Family, and other ABC network programs can be heard daily, as can Swap Shop, which features items for sale. Weekly programs such as med-talk and law-talk, featuring Carolyn Furrow, esq. are popular. "Our View" featuring guests, prizes, and folklore, etc, can be heard on Mondays with Peggy Conklin. Once a year is the special Christmas Shoppers Guide that gears everyone up for the holidays with tips, recipes, and games. Saturday mornings, Chris Altice hosts the Virginia Bluegrass Theatre, with interviews and music, often live, with local bands, that harkens back to the good ol' days of radio when all the well-known bands traveled to different radio stations to perform.

"And what is involved in being Vice-President and General Manager?" we ask Susan Mullins.

"Well, one day I was scrubbing the bathroom and someone came into the office and inquired what my job was here. I told them janitor. But today, the wind has blown our trashcans away and scattered trash everywhere. So I will be putting on boots and walking through the woods to pick it up and look for the trashcans, so I guess I'm the jack-of-all-trades," she laughs.

Because he is not crazy about the computerized equipment of today, Bill Jefferson, who worked at WPAQ in Mt. Airy many years ago and has been a lifetime musician and singer, isn't on the air as he was in former years. However, his band, "Bill Jefferson and the Country Playboys," do a television show that is broadcast each Sunday on Ion Media Network channels in Virginia, West Virginia, and North Carolina. Recording is done in the wonderfully restored train station in Rocky Mount with a very professional crew.

Jesse Ramsey plays fiddle for Bill Jefferson's band. He was in seventh grade at Henry School when he first was with a string group and through the years "has probably been involved with fifty bands. I played bass as much as anything but can play other instruments." He owned a Ben Franklin store in Rocky Mount and mostly used music as a hobby because, "making a living with music is not always reliable."

The vocalist for the band, April Altice, has quite a respectable background in music. Traveling and singing behind David Frizzell for five years, on the Grand Ol' Opry – the first time at twelve years old – and with many other recognizable names, she carved a career in the music business. While she hasn't exactly chucked Nashville, love got her to Franklin County and she enjoys bluegrass along with most every type of music. Having Merle Kilgore as a Godfather couldn't be a bad thing either, for someone with a voice and a desire to sing. She and husband, Chris, ("he is a musician and a half," she declares") are in about three bands each, but greatly enjoy the Bill Jefferson Band.

Deviled Eggs

Barbara Hunley – Rocky Mount, VA

6   eggs
1   heaping Tbsp. mayonnaise
1/3 cup Heinz sweet relish
     paprika

Hard boil 6 eggs. Peel eggs and cut in half lengthwise. Place whites on plate and mix yellows with mayonnaise and sweet relish. Spoon mixture into egg halves and sprinkle lightly with either chili powder or paprika, preferably with the paprika. Chill and serve.

Booker T. Washington National Monument

Booker T. Washington was born into slavery in 1856 on a small tobacco plantation owned by James and Elizabeth Burroughs. Thousands of people come each year to the National Park located on Rt. 122 in Franklin County, to learn about his life and see the type of farm that would have been typical of the time. The farm animals are there, an heirloom garden is maintained, and there are two walking trails, but the first stop should be the visitor's center. Here one can learn about a life of amazing accomplishments from a man who died at the relatively young age of 59. In a time of turmoil, few black schools, and poor transportation, he became a great spokesperson, author, statesman, and the founder of Tuskegee Institute. www.nps.gov/bowa

Eggplant Parmesan
Deborah Russell – Dairy Queen – Rocky Mount, VA

2   nice size eggplants
1   pkg. mozzarella cheese, shredded
1   jar tomato sauce, big size
    bread crumbs (spread out on wax paper)
2   eggs, beaten

Hughes Drive-In circa 1969
- photo courtesy of Arrington Enterprises

Skin the eggplant, dip in egg, and then bread crumbs. Put enough oil in frying pan to fry the eggplant. Just brown each side of eggplant. Drain on paper towels (after you take out of frying pan). Put a layer of tomato sauce on bottom of oblong glass baking dish. Then put 1 layer of the fried eggplant on top of tomato sauce already in baking dish and continue same pattern until you have used up all the eggplants. Bake at 350° for ½ hour. Put aluminum foil over baking dish. Enjoy!

Franklin County is the 2nd largest dairy farming county in Virginia.

"I was raised at Laurel Fork, VA. My mom, Nellie Bolt, always made a coconut cake for Christmas using this filling between the layers. I always looked forward to having the cake each year. I still make it every Christmas."

Filling for Coconut Cake
Glenn Bolt – Smith Mt. Lake

1½ cups brown sugar
4   Tbsps. butter
½   cup water
1¼ cups black walnuts
1¼ cups raisins
2   Tbsps. cream

Heat sugar, butter, and water in pan and cook until small amount of mixture forms a soft ball in cold water, 235°F. Remove from heat, add nuts and raisins. Add cream until right consistency to spread. Spread evenly between layers.

Franklin County Sweet Mash Corn Liquor 1940s
Franklin County Historical Society – Rocky Mount, VA

To make sweet mash corn liquor: boil water and transfer to the mash boxes. Add about 3 bushels of ground corn to each mash box and stir with a 'mash fork'. This swells and thickens the mixture to keep the water from running out the cracks.

Sprinkle dry barley or corn malt – ground shelled corn to hold the heat. Cook just under 1 hour to allow mixture to thicken. Stir to break up 'cap' on top. Continue stirring to keep mixture evenly heated, adding 40 lbs. barley malt. Bootleggers say the temperature should stay to a point where they can swipe a finger through the top of the mixture 3 times without being burned.

Add 40 lbs. rye. Allow mixture to set an hour and a half 'to sweeten' and cool to about 90 degrees. In warm water, dissolve a half-pound 'east' (yeast) to pour into each mash box. Any hotter than 90 degrees, the mash will sour before the yeast works. It takes 3 days for the mash to 'work off' and produce beer.

Then remove beer and put in the still. Heat, boil and stir constantly with a 'broom' (soft stir stick) to prevent sticking and a scorched taste. Stop stirring when mixture reaches a rolling boil. Place copper cap on still and chain tightly in place. Connect copper cap spout to the pipe in the thumper barrel. To retain steam, paste a strip of cloth around the cap and pipes. The pressure from the beer being heated in the still blows the steam into the thumper barrel. Heat evenly lest the beer flavor spoil and the beer be thrown into the cap and thumper barrel, ruining the liquor.

As the still is fired, peck on the cap to hear the clear sound that means only steam is coming through. If the 'dead sound' of beer escaping into the cap is heard, immediately throw water on the fire to cool it down. Pull peg on thumper barrel to drain out the hot beer. This means the 'backings' in the thumper barrel must be replaced. The backings are the last few gallons of a previous batch of whiskey, saved to put in the thump barrel to increase the proof of the next run. This is liquor but is not strong enough to hold a bead. Check for alcohol content by throwing a cupful into a fire. As long as it burns, it can be used for backings.

Once hot steam is built up in the thumper barrel, the backings in the bottom begin to bubble and make a thumping sound – something federal tax agents listened for with trained ears. When the thumping noise stops, the liquor has started out the copper worm. Steam travels from the thump barrel through the pipe to the slackstand where the copper worm condenses it into the finished whiskey product. A bucket in a tub under the hole at the bottom of the slackstand catches the first and strongest proof whiskey. Catch a bit in a zinc can top, strike a match to it, and look for the blue flame. As the liquor runs, the strength weakens.

Once the run is completed, pour all the whiskey into the proofing barrel to mix and even the proof. It usually averages ninety proof. Check the proof by pouring liquor into a jar and 'reading the bead'. This product is best when the bead separates in the middle. This first run is the choice liquor for family and friends.

Photo of "moonshine" exhibit at Blue Ridge Institute

Save the mash for the second run. Sugar is added to produce sugar liquor. Grain made the first batch ferment. The sugar makes the grain work again. Each 100 lbs. of sugar makes about 12 gallons of whiskey. Each mash box takes about 200 lbs. of sugar for the second run. Refill mash boxes with water, wait 3 days, and run the sugar liquor. This can be done 3 times before the mash becomes hog slop- something hogs of yesteryear loved.

Shively Store Mini-Museum

According to Lane Rakes, his family has been in the Shooting Creek area nearly 250 years. "Way back, the government would give you all the land you could clear. My Scots-Irish ancestors cleared land and started growing corn. They grew flax and buckwheat, too. But the corn was for making whiskey."

His grandparents, several greats back, owned a plantation in the area. "Their original deed was written on sheepskin. The other side still had the hair on it. My grandmother said they kept it rolled up, hanging from the ceiling, to keep mice from getting into it. It disappeared through the years."

Making moonshine was a family tradition. "There was nowhere to work, really, in the early 1900's, so people made liquor (likker) to feed their families. My granddad and my dad both made it. My job, when I was young, maybe 6 or 7, was to watch the mule's ears. They'd raise them straight up if anybody or anything came around. I'd get tired and lay down on some sugar sacks beside our ol' hound dog and sleep all night while Dad worked. People still tell me occasionally that my dad made the best whiskey in these parts."

Being raised around an operation may cause it to rub off on you, as in Rakes's case. His father stood the young lad up in the seat as a ruse while making deliveries of illegal goods. As an adult, Rakes laid a hard hat in the back window of his vehicle and joined the work traffic to make deliveries, always staying under the speed limit. He was more adventurous while working for the highway department. "I'd deliver six cases on the way to work and haul cornmeal home to start another run. The guys I worked with told me, 'you're hauling corn both ways. You're just working for a cover-up."

"And why were you working, since you must have been doing pretty well with your side business?" we ask. "Cover-up," he states with a grin.

Lane and his wife, Susan, have been working to establish a mini-museum in the old Sheriff Shively Country Store in the Crossroads community at the intersection of Rt. 40 and Rt. 605. After a number of repairs and help from the Historical Society and others, they are on their way. Musical events are taking place, displays have come together, and people stop by to "sit a spell" the way things used to be when the store was a hub of activity in the 1920's and 30's.

The store serviced the somewhat isolated community, supplying whatever farmers, housewives, and local distilleries needed. Not a law officer - Sheriff was a first name – the owner was well liked in the neighborhood. Locals are glad to see the old store being utilized again.

Survival by living off the land has become a dying art in the last few years, but the Rakes's could do well. Sue is dedicated to the use of herbs and is an outstanding cook of wild game. Lane knows the mountains and what's edible. "Especially in the spring, nobody should starve in these hills. There's plenty to eat," he states. He used to can squirrel heads for gravy in the winter, but thinks that's probably not a good idea anymore. Fish is great canned, he found, as is other game and vegetables.

The museum is open Friday and Saturday, 10:30 – 4:30. Drop In!

Blue Ridge Institute and Museum

According to their website, the Blue Ridge Institute was established by Ferrum College in the early 1970's to document, interpret, and present the folk heritage of the Blue Ridge Mountains. Having succeeded extremely well under the leadership of Roddy Moore, by 1986, the Institute was designated the State Center for Blue Ridge Folklore. Through the years, quality programs, exhibits, and Heritage Archives have made the institute a major consulting resource.

On the last Saturday in October, the Blue Ridge Folk Life Festival takes place on the Ferrum College campus, providing a visit to mountain life of yesteryear. It's also family-friendly. *www.blueridgeinstitute.org*

French Bakes
Mary Badman – Snow Creek, VA

3-5 large unpeeled potatoes, scrubbed and patted dry
1 Tbsp. extra virgin olive oil or canola oil
½ tsp. salt or to taste
garlic powder to taste

Preheat oven to 400°. Cut potatoes into sticks about the size of French fries. Put them into a bowl with oil, salt, and garlic powder. Toss them well. Spread them in a single layer on a lightly oiled baking sheet. Bake for about 35 minutes or until lightly browned and tender. Serve your oven baked French fries immediately.

"There is quite a history to this recipe. Grandma Daniel taught her daughter, my Aunt Bertha, to make her rolls and bread dough. Every Saturday that we visited Aunt Bertha, the door was opened to the tantalizing smell of homemade rolls and bread. She did not have a recipe, so one Saturday we went armed with measuring cups and spoons and measured her hand scooped ingredients. She would always triple the amount so she would have enough for the week. The recipe that follows is the result. It takes practice to get it right, because hands come in all sizes. To tell the truth, I have never measured that handful of Crisco, so you are on your own. Just keep the recipe going!"

Grandma Daniel's Rolls
Donna M. Guthrie – Snow Creek, VA

3 cups plain flour
¾ tsp. salt
1 Tbsp. sugar
1 handful Crisco
½ cup water
2 pkgs. dry yeast
5-7 eggs, depending on size

Dissolve yeast in warm water. Beat eggs well. Add sugar and salt to beaten eggs. Then add the yeast mixture. Work Crisco into flour. Make nest in flour and add wet ingredients. Knead well. Add water, if necessary (best if soft). Let rise until double. Work into rolls or loaves. Let rise until double. Bake at 400° for 15-17 minutes for rolls; 20-25 minutes for loaves.

Fritters from Greens
-Susan Justice

1 quart greens
1 egg
1 chopped onion
cornmeal
flour

Mix up like a batter and fry in bacon grease or oil. Can be fried in one large hoecake or smaller, like potato cakes. Fresh greens of any sort may be used - cook until tender first.

Homemade salve
-Nancy Vorhees

3 bars camphor
3 ½ oz. white Vaseline
2 Tbsps. kerosene
2 Tbsps. turpentine

Shave camphor and add all ingredients together. Set on stove and let set till camphor dissolves.

"My Grandma used to make this easy game for me (and my cousins). It would entertain us for hours (well, it seemed like hours for us). Grandma would play with me too, and she would use the game to help me learn how to count. Sometimes she would let me decorate the game with construction paper, glue, and crayons so it looked more like a game instead of an egg carton. Grandma and Grandpap also taught me how to count by sitting on the porch and watching the cars go by. They lived on Route 40 so cars drove by very regularly. Grandpap would pick a car color, Grandma would pick one and I would pick one. Then we would each count our color of car. The one who had the most after an hour won the game. I am sure it was Grandma's way of keeping me busy, teaching me to count, and giving her a little rest on the porch with a cold glass of lemonade or sweet iced tea, but I loved it all the same. I hope someone will try these games with their children or grandchildren.

My grandfather was James Walter "Peg" Hatcher. He was well known in the community for playing the fiddle at local community dances and family gatherings. As a little girl I remember flat-footing and swinging around with whoever would dance with me while Grandpap and other members of our musically gifted family played late into the evening. Those were simpler times, memorable times, times to be cherished."

Grandma Hatcher's Homemade Games
Stacey Jones – Henry, VA

1 egg carton
  ballpoint pen
  colored buttons
  paper to keep score

Take a clean egg carton; write numbers inside egg cup bottoms. You may want to use low, easy to count numbers for smaller children. Lay egg carton on the floor and stand back several foot lengths. Give each person 3 to 5 (a set) of one color buttons (one person gets red, one blue, etc.). Each person takes a turn tossing their buttons and counting up their points.

Grandmother Mamie Barker Holland

"My grandmother, Mamie Barker Holland, from Henry County near Turkey Cock Mountain, had a problem with two neighborhood cats digging up her newly planted boxwoods. Her cousin, Eugene, came to visit one day and she mentioned her dilemma. He suggested that she blow up a couple of balloons, wrap them in bacon, place them in a shallow furrow under the boxwoods and cover the balloons with pine straw. He said the cats would smell the bacon and pop the balloons, scaring them off forever from her bushes. Grandma thought that it was a brilliant plan. She just happened to have both balloons and bacon. They set to work and soon their trick was set. They retired back to the parlor to continue their visit but kept an open ear toward the raised window near the boxwood bed. Soon enough a loud bang was heard and Grandma and Eugene headed out the door at a trot. And there they were, six strange cats, each enjoying an unexpected afternoon treat. Grandma delighted in telling that story. She loved a good joke, even if it was on her."

-Lynn Holland Loveland

With an eclectic mix of primitive creations, handmade crafts, beautiful antiques, and a year-round Christmas shop, Rustic County Charm offers a friendly, country atmosphere to its customers. Located five miles south of Rocky Mount, VA, this is a convenient stop for those in need of a unique gift or a quick snack and cool drink. Pat Guilliams and Regina Cosgrove, owners, began their crafting careers with their design label Humble Heart Designs available at Rustic Country Charm. Traveling throughout Virginia, North Carolina, and West Virginia, the pair launched many popular creations including their exclusive "Bright Idea" and "Team Sprit" collections of light bulb ornaments. (540)-482-0807. rusticcountrycharm@yahoo.com

Ham Bites
Pat Guilliams

- 8 Grand biscuits
- 1 cup honey ham, chopped
- cheddar cheese, shredded
- ¾ cup mayonnaise
- 2 tsps. Dijon mustard

Quarter biscuits and place in mini muffin pan. Mix all ingredients and fill biscuit "wells" with mix. Bake at 450° for 9 minutes. Enjoy!

Ham Salad Spread
Elsie Harrison

3	cups cooked boiled ham (grated fine)	2	tsps. finely chopped onion
1	boiled egg, chopped	2	tsps. finely chopped sweet pickles
2	Tbsps. finely chopped celery	¾	cup mayonnaise
		1	Tbsp. mustard

Mix well. Can be used on crackers, on sandwich, or to fill dough shells.

Hot Crunchy Chicken Casserole
Nina F. Ross – Rocky Mount, VA

2	cups chopped cooked chicken	2	Tbsps. chopped onion
1	cup chopped celery	1	can cream of chicken soup, undiluted
½	cup slivered almonds	1	(2 oz.) can mushroom stems and pieces, drained
½	cup crushed Ritz crackers		
½	cup mayonnaise	½	cup crushed potato chips

Preheat oven to 375°. Combine all ingredients, except potato chips. Spoon into a greased 1½ quart casserole dish. Bake for 15 minutes. Sprinkle potato chips on top. Bake an additional 15 minutes.

Irene's Country Fried Chicken
Irene Davis – Rocky Mount, VA

1	whole fryer chicken, cup up
1	Tbsp. salt
2	cups flour, plain or self-rising
1	cup, flaked instant mashed potatoes
½	cup oil
	salt and pepper to taste

Put chicken in container with lid. Add cold water to cover chicken. Pour salt in water. Cover and refrigerate overnight. Remove chicken from water and rinse with cold water. Mix flour and instant mashed potatoes. Roll chicken in flour mixture. Add oil to electric skillet. Fry on 350°. Put rolled chicken in skillet, and cover. Keep chicken turned. Cook about an hour or until done. I never could get my chicken to brown, so I came up with this.

There are several great music jams in the county – check the newspaper, The Franklin News Post, or www.crookedroad.org

Left, Mr. Chapman Bryant, Walter Bryant, C.L "Dud" Prillaman, D.W. "Doc" Davis, D. Harvey Shumate and Jeff East.

Henry, VA

In the early 1900's my grandparents, Harvey and Lynn Prillaman Shumate, began their life together in the village of Henry. It was a wonderful place to rear a family. There were approximately twenty families in the village and many children to play with.

There were five girls born to the Shumate family in the first house on the right, next to the present Henry Post Office going "up the creek" toward Ferrum - Emma, Estelle, Ruby, Lula, and Hazel, my mother. Two children died between two and three years old, Thomas and Bettie Sue.

My grandpa was a mail carrier from 1904-1931 and started his route on horseback. He progressed to a two-wheel cart, a buggy, and finally a car. Mama told about the time Grandma got worried about Grandpa not getting back from the mail route. She kept sending Mama and Aunt Lula to the Post Office to see if Grandpa's horse was there and they kept coming back saying "no." As it turned out, he had traded horses that day.

The railroad was an important aspect of their childhood. Each year, a passenger train excursion called the Booster Train brought merchants from Rocky Mount. It usually featured a brass band. The merchants handed out advertising trinkets for about fifteen or twenty minutes. The people would put hands on one another's

What better place for a business called Antiques and Collectibles of the Crooked Road than downtown Rocky Mount, the Eastern Gateway to the Crooked Road Heritage Music Trail? With a large number of vendors, there's lots to look at and a sit-down deli, making the visit a treat for the eyes and stomach!

shoulders and shuffle around dancing. They called it a "snake dance." This was the Norfolk and Western Train, called the Punkin Vine, which ran from Roanoke, VA to Winston-Salem, NC.

Grandpa played a banjo and the piano. His brother-in-law, Doc, could fiddle up a storm. They would go to different houses to play for dances and the family would go along. Musicians who traveled in the area or played in Henry would stop by, including Charlie Poole.

Next door to Grandpa and Grandma's house was Grandpa's sister, Mary Lou Shumate Davis and her husband, Doc Davis, who had three children, Jesse, Hassell, and Mary. They also reared their nephews, Carroll and Tom Davis. This family, along with many other aunts, uncles, and cousins, was very close knit. Family meant so much to them and still does to those of us who are their descendents. To this day I treasure so many wonderful family gatherings and remember so many that have now passed away. *-Pat Jones*

"*Guess I was a young Paula Deen because before we had a refrigerator, my mom, Iva Hancock, would have to put the butter where I couldn't take a bite out of it. I have her butter printer and butter dish that held the many pounds of butter that we churned. This was one of her favorite cakes, using that butter. Nothing was better than frosting it with our homemade apple butter.*"

Lady Baltimore Cake
Glynda Hancock Bolt- Smith Mt. Lake

1	cup butter at room temperature
2	cups sugar
4	eggs
3	cups sifted self-rising flour
1	cup milk
1	tsp. vanilla

Preheat oven to 350°. Grease and flour three 9-inch cake pans. Cream butter until fluffy. Add sugar and continue to beat about 4-5 minutes. Add eggs 1 at a time. Beat well after each. Add flour and milk alternately. Add vanilla and continue to mix well. Divide into cake pans. For level cakes, hold pan with cake batter 3-4 inches above table and drop (gets rid of bubbles too). Bake 25-30 minutes. Cool 5 minutes in pan. Frost with homemade apple butter between layers and on top.

"Benjamin M. Goode and Fannie Ross Goode settled in the Henry Community in the 1880's and moved to the Village of Henry at the turn of the century. Ben was the son of David Goode, a confederate war veteran who lived near Providence. Ben ran a store and post office at Henry until his death in 1922. His wife, Fannie, was left to raise two teenage daughters. The other children, Mabel, Virgil, Clifford, and Maury were working or attending college at the death of their father.

Maury Goode ran the family store at Henry until he became a rural mail courier in the 1950's. Mabel and Katherine Goode taught at many schools in Virginia including the one at Henry. Virgil Goode was an attorney and served in the Virginia House of Delegates and was Commonwealth Attorney in Rocky Mount. Virgil and his family moved to Oak Level in 1947. Clifford Goode taught in Martinsville and Henry County before moving to Richmond. Beatrice Goode taught school in West Virginia, married and settled in Summerville, West Virginia." -Betsy Goode Madden and Virgil H. Goode, Jr.

Russell Cannady began music jam sessions in 1959 and continues them today at Cannady's Wholesale on Rt. 220, a few miles past Rocky Mount. There's usually two bands and his plays last, "so we won't run anybody off," he laughs.

Mary D's Poppy Seed Dressing

Betsy Goode Madden, Lucy and Virgil H. Goode, Jr. – Rocky Mount, VA

½ cup sugar
1 tsp. dry mustard
1 tsp. salt
1 tsp. pepper
¼ tsp. paprika
1 Tbsp. grated onion
1 cup salad oil
1/3 cup vinegar
1 Tbsp. poppy seed

Combine sugar, seasoning, and onion in bowl; add oil slowly, beating at medium speed; add vinegar and poppy seed, beat well. This dressing is excellent over all salad greens and tomatoes. Also, combine romaine lettuce and spinach, add oranges and/or grapefruit and sliced almonds; toss with dressing.

"Life is too short for bad coffee."
-Motto of Claiborne House B&B

"This recipe is handed down from my great grandma, Martha Helms Shumate."

Mama's Sugar Cookie
Pat Jones – Henry, VA

1	cup sugar
½	cup shortening
1	egg
¼	cup milk
2	cups flour
½	tsp. salt
3	tsps. baking soda
1	tsp. vanilla

Cream shortening, add the sugar gradually, and cream well. Sift the salt and baking powder with the flour. Add the milk gradually with the sugar mixture. Then add the well-beaten egg, vanilla, and the flour gradually to make a soft dough. Roll small amount at a time. Bake at 350° for 7–8 minutes.

Place apple in bag of potatoes to prevent the potatoes from sprouting.

Oat Cakes
Anne Snead – Boones Mill, VA

½	lb. fine oatmeal
½	lb. plain white flour
1	tsp. salt
1	tsp. sugar
½	oz. fresh yeast (2 pkgs. of yeast)
¾	pt. warm milk and water

Sieve the oatmeal and flour into a warm basin. Add the salt and stir. Dissolve the yeast with a little of the warm liquid and add the sugar. Set aside in a warm place for it to rise. Mix the dry ingredients with the yeast and the rest of the liquid to make a nice batter. Cover with clean cloth and let the batter stand in a warm place for about one hour. Then bake on a well greased bake stone. This quantity will make 12 oat cakes.

Anne Snead

"God has worked in my life so much," says Ann Snead in her charming British accent. "As long as I have breath, I will witness to his goodness. He has been with me through everything. I know He strengthens us as we are to strengthen each other."

Anne met Dave Snead when he came to England with the United States military. They married and traveled to many different places for the next twenty years, becoming the parents of four children, two boys and two girls. Dave often filled in as a lay pastor or speaker when a church needed someone.

In Germany, where she first accompanied Dave after their marriage, Anne came in contact with iced tea. "I really didn't like leaving England," she says, "but there were other wives on the military base who visited me. One day, some of us were together at one of the houses and the lady of the house asked if we'd like some tea. When she brought it, there was ice in it. I had never seen this before, having drunk only hot tea. I asked her what must I do with the ice?"

At a time when Anne was needed with her family in Staffordshire, God worked a miracle for them. Dave had been stationed at Fort Bragg four years when a colleague was ordered to an airbase near London. The fellow didn't want the assignment and asked Dave whether he would want the position. A position in England? They couldn't wait to go, especially Anne. It was such a pleasure to have her family in England, discovering the way of life and eating the foods she had known as a child. It was a sad time as well, because her sister died after a short illness and Anne's mother fell into a depression. The joy that helped them all was Anne's discovery that she was expecting her fourth child. Her mother began knitting and crocheting baby things and the Sneads moved to Texas with a trunk full of new handmade baby things, just in time for their son's birth.

When Dave finally answered a strong calling to go into fulltime ministry, they were in Arizona. Anne was not happy. She didn't feel qualified to be a pastor's wife. "I was so shy. I couldn't pray in public or speak in front of people. My mother always said I couldn't say *Boo!* to a goose." It was a confusing time.

After she tried to locate him all kind of jobs that he wouldn't take, the District Superintendent assigned them to a charge that included Baptist and Methodist congregations in Moneta. At the close of a meeting early on, someone asked her to pray. "I jabbed Dave with my elbow, he jabbed me back. I jabbed again and he prayed. On the way home, he said, 'I believe they asked *Mrs. Snead* to lead in prayer.' I went home and started asking God for help in saying a public prayer."

On a lonely night while Dave was gone to help a church member, Anne was miserable and questioning why her husband was not home with his family when they needed him, too. God spoke to her so plainly and so strongly, "Anne, I want you to be a helpmate for Dave."

"I felt that command from the top of my head to the tip of my toes. My life changed right then. It changed the way I looked at everything," she says. "From that time, I tried to do all I could to be what God wanted me to be."

She succeeded most admirably. Any member of the Methodist churches pastored by the Sneads during the 23 years of Dave's ministry, will likely tell you that they were blessed with two for the price of one. Her life was, and continues to be, a witness to the glory of God. "I used to be afraid to speak, now they can't shut me up," she laughs.

Anne believes God wants his own to have fun. She is quick to smile. While in Bedford County, Dave received notice that he would be going to Highland Methodist Church in Callaway. Congregation members kidded Anne and told her to "watch out for those bootleggers over in Franklin County."

"I didn't know what they were talking about – moonshine and bootleggers," she laughs in her lilting English voice.

"When we got to the parsonage, something was wrong and there was no water," she says. "The Board of Trustee members came over carrying jugs of water into the basement. I decided to have a bit of fun with them, so I went out and said to them, 'You can't be bringing those jugs of moonshine into the parsonage.' I thought they were going to drop the water, they were so stunned. I went on. I heard all about you moonshiners over in Bedford County. They told me you all make it and they drink it!"

It was a while before they believed she was joking. One of the men was especially hard to convince and kept repeating, "Mrs. Snead thinks we're sneaking moonshine into the parsonage."

Today Anne goes on without Dave by her side. Her memories of life as a minister's wife are good. "I know that Dave was truly called and did what he was supposed to do. It is rewarding work," she states. "God blessed us in so many ways. I wish more people would realize how joyful the Christian life is."

Romance Along the Crooked Road

Matt Kirwan and Jessica Shepard spent a good deal of time settling on a date for their wedding. Both knew they wanted to marry each other. They agreed on a simple wedding. They agreed August was a desirable month. But the Galax Old Time Fiddler's Convention takes up one week of August. "We definitely couldn't let it interfere with Galax because I want to compete and Jessica will be dancing,"

Jessica and Matt

states Matt. "Besides, if we did get married during that week, none of our friends would come."

The two met at a Fiddler's Convention in Sparta, NC – a stone's throw off the Crooked Road. She was dancing with Ben Harman, her partner in the dance group, Patrick Henry Travelers. (She considers Ben and his wife, Joan, her adopted grandparents.) Matt plays fiddle with the Loose Gap Loafers, who were supplying the music. It was not the first time they had seen each other. "A bunch of the older ladies had been trying to push us together," he laughs. "Iva Stilwell, our 84 year old bass player, was one who kept trying."

"They pushed him more than me," contributes Jessica. "I already wanted to meet him. In fact, after our first date, I told my mother I was going to marry him."

Floyd Country Store's Friday Night Jam was the scene of Matt and Jessica's first date. The Dry Hill Draggers were playing, a band they like dancing to. Chris Prillaman, fiddler for the band, remains their favorite fiddle player. Nothing could be more natural than Kirwan proposing there, a couple of years and many musical events down the road.

"Of course, I've been telling him he should propose at Floyd almost since we met," says Jessica, only half-joking. "But he took me totally by surprise when he did. I wasn't sure he was serious for a few minutes."

"I didn't have to get on my knees since we were outside sitting on the ground," explains Matt. "That was good for me. But I haven't had to try to impress her, anyway. Everything has been easier and totally different with Jessica. The two of us enjoy music and festivals together so it's been fun. Besides, she was crazy about me from the start!"

Jessica has been dancing "since I could walk," she says. Matt hated fiddle playing when his dad pressed him to take lessons as a youngster. "It took a lot of practice, once I started back to playing after I quit in high school. The skill seemed to come slow but I love it now. There's no better way to make friends than through music."

So in August, on a weekend free of major musical events, the University of Virginia junior will wed her prince, a geologist with the U.S. Geological Survey. They plan to live in a cabin in the mountains while she continues her education. "That may turn out to sound more romantic than it will actually be," Jessica chuckles.

What lesson can be learned here? Why, listen to your elders, of course. They knew the laughing, dancing, music making pair was right for each other from the start!

Ol' Timey Fit As A Fiddle Beans
Tony & Shellie Leete – The Claiborne House Bed & Breakfast – Rocky Mount, VA

5 cups fresh grown green beans or 4 (8oz.) cans green beans	¼ cup Parmesan cheese (grated or shredded)
4 slices of bacon	2 garlic cloves, chopped and minced
	black pepper to season

Heat a large fry pan or skillet on medium heat. Cook bacon until crispy. Take out bacon and set aside to cool, once cooled, crumble the bacon. Empty pan of bacon fat leaving a nice generous coating on inside of pan. Add garlic to heated pan and sauté garlic until it begins to brown slightly. Add topped and tailed green beans to heated pan and stir into garlic. Heat thoroughly for 5-8 minutes until green beans start to lose bright color. Toss in Parmesan cheese and sprinkle with black pepper. Add crumbled bacon into mixture last. Toss together and serve hot. Make 8 side dish servings or "two big ol' heapin' bowlfuls if ya can't resist these thangs!" www.ClaiborneHouse.net

"I have been living here in Franklin County for 9 months and love the region; this is my recipe for Pavlova, which is considered New Zealand's most favorite dessert. It has berries and grated chocolate on top."

Pavlova
Tania Rohlfs – Glade Hill, VA

6 eggs	1½ tsps. white vinegar	1½ Tbsps. cornstarch
2 cups sugar	1½ tsps. vanilla essence	

Preheat oven to 350°. Using an electric mixer, beat egg whites until stiff and add the sugar gradually. Continue mixing for 10 minutes until mixture is thick and glossy. Mix vinegar, vanilla, and cornstarch together. Add to meringue. Beat on high speed for 5 minutes. Line an oven tray with baking paper. Draw an 8-inch circle on the baking paper. Spread the pavlova mixture to within 1 inch of the edge of the circle, keeping the shape as round and even as possible. Smooth top surface over. Place pavlova in oven then turn temperature down to 210°. Bake pavlova for 1 hour and 15 minutes. Turn oven off. Open oven door slightly and leave pavlova in oven until cold. Carefully lift pavlova onto a serving plate. Decorate with whipped cream and fresh fruit. The secret to a great pavlova is in the beating.

Pineapple Cheese Ball
Cindy Hodges – Wirtz, VA

2   (8 oz.) pkgs. of cream cheese
1   pkg. of hidden valley ranch mix
1   (8 oz.) can of crushed pineapple, drained
2   cups of sharp cheddar cheese
1   cup of chopped pecans
1   cup of chopped walnuts

Mix together first 4 ingredients until well blended. Then form it into a ball. Then coat with nut mixture.

"We serve these at our Christmas Open House each year and they are always a big hit! It's a simple snack that is fast to make and very delicious."

Rolo Pecan Pretzel Turtles
Reginia Cosgrove – Rustic Country Charm – Rocky Mount, VA

mini pretzels   **Rolo candy**   **pecans**

Preheat oven to 200°. Lay mini pretzels out on a baking sheet. Place a Rolo candy on each pretzel and then a pecan on top of the candy. Place in oven, but turn the oven off at this time. That's right, turn the oven off. You only need enough heat to melt the candy. Leave in oven about 5 to 10 minutes. Test by pushing a pecan down into the Rolo. Take out of oven and push the pecans down into the candy and let cool.

Live simply.
Love generously.
Care deeply.
Speak kindly.
Leave the rest to God.

PINEAPPLE

The "Pineapple", imported from the Caribbean Islands was a rare delicacy on the tables of the early colonists. Because of the pineapple's aroma and interesting flavor this expensive fruit became the symbol of the spirit of hospitality and was used extensively in eighteenth century decorative art. This tradition has been continued until today. We see this attractive fruit carved, cast and painted in many traditional and modern motifs.

Allen Mills / Lost and Found

Bluegrass music seeped into the soul of Allen Mills from an old arch top Philco radio as he lay on the floor after lunch beside his father. Noonday Jamboree with Charlie Monroe was broadcast from station WBIG out of North Carolina at twelve o'clock every day in the mid-forties. "At eleven o'clock, we quit plowing corn, pulling tobacco, priming tobacco, or whatever our job was that morning. We took the team to the branch for water, gave them six ears of corn, put them in the stable and came in the house to eat. Then we went in the front room and lay on the floor to rest and listen to Charlie Monroe. That was our ritual every day."

He bought his first musical instrument - a mandolin - in 1953 from a pawnshop. He picked with neighbors, Wayne Scearce, and some Gibson boys who lived down the road. "I always liked being around where people were making music. Nobody else in my family played an instrument, although they enjoyed listening."

In the late 1960's and early 70's, Mills and Gene Parker played together at the old T-Bird Club in Danville. Later in the summer, after they had quit, Gene called up and said, "Let's get together and pick some grass." So they did. Soon they included Marvin McDaniel, "just playing everything we knew, for the fun of it."

"One day Gene said there was a boy up in Rocky Mount who played the mandolin and was gonna make a real good player, name of Dempsey Young. So he brought him down to pick with us and Gene put him through his paces. I reckon we played "Red Apple Rag" about thirty minutes. Gene would play it a little different each time. Dempsey would say, 'Let me try it again.' He was determined to get it just right."

To say Dempsey got it right would be an understatement. He had won top honors at the Galax Old Fiddlers Convention in his teens and continued to develop his own unique style with Lost and Found. With his baritone voice and sleek playing, Dempsey helped define the music that became known as the band's signature sound.

About the time the four men were practicing and picking for pleasure, Martinsville started a local cablevision TV show. Cable was in its infancy and reached a limited number of people though it was a big deal for a small town. Allen, who had done some radio, "busted" into the studio one day and talked to Rick Shultz. "How about some bluegrass on your television station?" he asked him.

"All right, when do you want to do it?" Rick replied.

After stuttering a minute, Mills settled on a couple of weeks away and they set the date. When he told the other guys who'd been playing together, it turned out that McDaniel wanted nothing to do with being on television. They checked with a guy named Roger Handy who came on board. They began rehearsing about five nights a week in order to get six songs ready to do on the show

A band needs a name and no one could come up with anything that seemed to fit. Finally, Mills began thinking that they had "found" each other and come up with a pretty good sound, so maybe they'd been "lost" before. He figured, "why not Lost and Found?" Since the other members couldn't contribute a better handle, it was decided to use the name until something else could be decided upon. A better one never turned up.

Lost and Found Band

The live TV show turned into an eighteen-month gig. "We got to be well-known in Martinsville. Of course, nobody in the next county had ever heard of us!"

Some good breaks came their way. Buddy Pendleton asked the band to go to Union Grove, the biggest festival and competition on the east coast at the time. Ben Bolling, of VA State Parks, invited Lost and Found to play in several parks on the weekends, gaining them wider recognition. They cut an album and Gary Henderson, of WAMU, American University Radio, played it on air to good reviews. He called to ask if they'd like to come to Washington.

"We were a bunch of ol' country boys and getting a chance to go play in Washington, DC, sounded pretty good. It was a way to get the world acquainted with our music. Then Gary said he was gonna pay us! Wow, I thought, what kinda deal is this?" laughs Mills. "Of course we wanted to go."

In Washington, the band met Joe Wilson who was Director of the National Council for the Traditional Arts for many years. "I didn't know who he was, what the NCTA was or what it did. In the words of Vince Gill, I was dumb as a fence post," states Allen. "But Joe had us booked into a hall downtown and we managed to find it so we could perform."

"I don't know how many people came out to hear us. It didn't matter at the time. We were playing for fun, having a real good time, and we didn't care whether anybody was there or not. Besides, we weren't thinking of ourselves as anything but a bunch of 'ol country boys without a lot going for them, just goofing off and picking together."

All the band members had other jobs, including Mills who owned a paint and body shop in partnership with another fellow. "I finally had to make a decision to get out of it because the band was traveling so much. It wasn't fair to a partner when I might not be there to do my share of the work. In the end, he bought me out and I made a vow on December 31, 1977, that I would make a living from music or starve to death. That was almost thirty-one years ago. The other day at the doctor's office I was down to 226 pounds. Sounds like I'm drawing up all the time, huh?"

Early on the band learned to be entertainers. According to Mills, a band can perform well but if they don't entertain the audience, they don't go back the next week. A good fan base is important too, because fans spread the word and travel to support a band they like. "We've been lucky," says Allen. "Whether it was from pity or for whatever reason, people accepted us. Bluegrass fans are warmer and more caring than most. They are outstanding people. Some of them feed us and treat us like family. Of course, if we got booed off the stage, we just didn't go back there anymore," he chuckles.

A road band goes through many changes; it is the nature of that type of work. The first to go on to something else was Roger Handy. After years of traveling, Gene Parker grew weary of life on the road. That left Mills and Young of the original members to carry on the Lost and Found sound, along with the talented musicians who filled the empty slots. The loss of Dempsey, who passed from this life in December of 2006, was one Mills has had a hard time bearing. It still brings tears. "Thirty-three years of playing together can't be erased. He was family and friend – a great musician."

After losing their mandolin player and vocalist, the band considered how or whether to go on. All agreed that they wanted to keep performing. Scott Napier, a mandolin player who often jammed with Dempsey, agreed to come on board with their group. "We're so thankful to have him," states Mills. "He's not only a great player, but a great person, too, as all my band members are. When we add Ronald Smith on banjo and vocals and Scottie Sparks on guitar and vocals, well, we've got a good thing going."

On the new album due out this fall, Young had already recorded eight of the songs; the other six are by Napier. Pete Goble, considered an authority by Mills, gave it a listen and stated that he could not detect the difference. "That's saying a lot," says Mills. "It is amazing to hear him playing what Dempsey created."

Because Allen is a fan of theirs, *Trail of Sorrow*, from Don Reno and Red Smiley is included, as has been one of their recordings on each Lost and Found album. This wasn't planned, it sort of happened as a tribute to these early innovators of bluegrass. *Don't Let Your Sweet Love Die,* a Roy Hall song from the 1940's, is included as well. As it sounds, fans can expect some old stuff and some great new material. What is the name of the album? "I wish I knew, I'd tell you," is the reply.

Deb Mills, Allen's wife, is one of his greatest assets, as he readily admits. "I've got the best partner and supporter anybody could have," he emphasizes. "She comes from a musical family and plays a couple of instruments herself, so she understands the passion for music. We've been together 29 years and we try to make the most of each and every day."

And how long will he keep touring? "As long as the good Lord gives me air to breathe. At this point, if I quit, I'd be turning my back on the people who put me where I am. I can't do that."

Skillet Beans
Deb & Allen Mills – Ferrum, VA

| 1 | lb. hamburger | 1 | green pepper |
| 1 | medium onion | 2 | cans pork and beans or baked beans |

Brown hamburger with chopped onion and green pepper and drain well. Add beans and simmer for 20-30 minutes. This works well in a crock pot as well.

"Like many people of my generation, my family did not have a lot of money. My father did not have a steady job and my mother was a schoolteacher. We did not have a car, telephone, TV, or indoor bathroom. The only time I really felt poor was when friends would come and need to use the bathroom.

A garden was a necessity; we lived on the Pamlico River, so fish and crabs were available for the catching.

I don't have the recipe for one of my favorite meals, but can remember that rock stew. It contained rockfish, potatoes, onions, and WATER! We ate quite a bit of creamed chipped beef and creamed tuna, and they tasted fine to me. Meatless recipes were some of my favorites, also, and I passed them on to my children."

Slumgullion
Joan Seifred - Moneta, VA

| | green lima beans | 1 | tsp. salt. | | okra, sliced |
| 1 | tsp. sugar | | tomatoes, pared and quartered | 1-2 | Tbsps. bacon fat corn |

Cook lima beans with sugar and salt. Add the tomatoes and okra to the limas when about done. Cook okra and limas about 10 minutes. Add tomatoes and their juice. Add bacon fat and simmer. Add cut-off corn and cook 10-15 minutes. Add water as needed. Add salt, but don't add until last, it toughens beans. My adaptation is to cook frozen limas to nearly done; add a can of tomatoes, corn niblets and sliced okra; simmer until okra is cooked; season as desired. Makes a nice hot lunch for a cold winter day.

Scene at Ferrum Folklife Festival

Franklin County

    Franklin County is full to the brim with history, mystery, music, scenery, and fantastic Smith Mountain Lake as a bonus. But the authors of this book found another treasure: porches. Porch sitting should not be allowed to become a lost art; it's way too pleasurable a pastime – and little training is required to be good at it.

    On a spring morning, with birds calling loudly in the background, we sat on the porch belonging to 95-year-old Nancy Voorhees ("If I live til June, I'll be 96") and learned about tatting. The breeze was pleasant, bushes were blooming, and we gazed at a pastoral farm scene as we talked. She told us about learning to tat with a ten-penny nail as a young girl. "I spent the night with Stella Austin, and her grandmother was sitting in the corner busily doing something. I watched her until she asked if I wanted to learn, then she showed me how to hold the thread. My fingers seemed to know what to do."

    Voorhees has demonstrated tatting at the Blue Ridge Folk Life Festival the past few years. She also has given lessons at Michael's in Roanoke, and keeps busy, even with a recently broken arm. She shows us some lovely work. Later, we discover nice paintings she has done and wooden chairs bottomed by her hands.

    We learned about Valley Grocery Store in Bassett, which was owned by her father. Her mother ran a boarding house upstairs. "There was Ramsey's Factory, the railroad, and then our store," she explains. As we leave, she tells us, "Come back some time and I'll teach you how to tat."

Nancy Vorhees demonstrates her tatting.

The boards of Sheriff Shiveley's old store porch have surely seen and heard some tales through the years and they're still a good place. Some have been replaced, making it a safer place to sit a spell while chewing the fat, as we did during the official opening of the Eastern Gate to the Crooked Road. We met Mr. J.D. "Grandpa" Jones, who grew up on Shively Road, behind the store during the 30's and 40's with six brothers and one sister. He has two sons, two grandsons, and two great-grandchildren.

"The preachers up here got paid with moonshine money," he said. "There wasn't any way to make a living and nobody had cars to drive out to work. We farmed to live through the winter and feed the animals. I used to have to churn butter with a dasher churn. It took over 300 licks to make the cream turn to butter."

While not admitting to making any personally, he could tell us how to test good moonshine. Folks up here took pride in making good liquor back then, he tells us, not like the dangerous stuff sometimes made today. Fill a jar half full of the liquid, then cap it and shake. It should bead to about half bubbles and half "shine." Lane Rakes nodded his head affirmatively as he walked by.

Allen Mills and his wife, Deb, live just over the line in Patrick County, but his band, *Lost and Found,* is so associated with Franklin we put 'em there. Besides, a good spitter should be able to take aim and land a hit into Franklin from their driveway. We didn't try and in fact did not spit a single time while enjoying one of the greatest porches anywhere around. Good porch sitting manners seemed to be the best policy since we're better sitters than spitters, but enough of that. All I can say is, Deb and Allen have a fine porch to come home to and our visit was a little slice of happy.

This is a moist, tender, and beautiful cake. A special hint – measure all ingredients before you start cake and make the zesty lemon filling first so it will have time to cool."

Southern Coconut Cake

In memory of Nancy Lee Divers by her mother, Nancy Vorhees- Rocky Mount, VA

Notes about coconut

To remove shell from coconut: Open the eyes with an ice pick or sharp point of a knife. Drain out milk. Put coconut in slow oven (325° F.) until it cracks (about 30 minutes). Remove from oven and allow shell to cool. Meat should separate easily.

4 cups sifted cake flour	1 cup shortening
5 tsps. baking powder	2 cups sugar
1½ tsps. salt	2 cups milk
6 egg whites	1 tsp. vanilla extract
½ cup sugar	1 tsp. almond extract

Sift together flour, baking powder, and salt. Beat egg whites until foamy and gradually add ½ cup sugar, continue beating until meringue will hold up in stiff peaks; set aside. Cream shortening and sugar and continue to cream until light and fluffy. Add flour mixture alternately with milk, a small amount at a time, beating well after each addition. Add vanilla and almond extract. Add beaten egg whites and fold into batter thoroughly. Line bottom of three 9-inch cake pans with wax paper and lightly grease and flour pans. Pour in batter. Bake at 375° for 20-25 minutes. Let cool. Spread Zesty Lemon Filling between layers. Ice with Coconut Marshmallow Frosting.

Zesty Lemon Filling:

¾ cup sugar	1 cup water
¼ cup cornstarch	1/3 cup lemon juice
¼ tsp. salt	1 Tbsp. butter
1 egg yolk, slightly beaten	2 tsps. grated lemon rind

Combine sugar, cornstarch, and salt in top of double boiler, set aside. Stir egg yolk, water, and lemon juice. Add to sugar mixture; blending well. Cook over boiling water, stirring constantly about 5 minutes or until thick. Remove from heat; add butter and grated rind.

(Continued on next page.)

Coconut Marshmallow Frosting:

2 egg whites, unbeaten
1½ cups sugar
    dash salt
1/3 cup water
2 tsps. light corn syrup
1 tsp. vanilla extract
16 marshmallows
1½ cups shredded coconut

Combine egg whites, sugar, salt, water, and corn syrup in top of double boiler. Beat about 1 minute until thoroughly mixed. Then place over boiling water and beat constantly with hand beater electric mixer for several minutes or until frosting will hold its shape. Remove from heat; add vanilla extract. Add marshmallows, cut into pieces. Beat until blended. Frost cake and sprinkle with coconut.

For over 25 years Sterling Belcher and his family have promoted traditional, gospel, and bluegrass music at their Triple Creek Park. The Virginia Folk Music Association honored him on the occasion of his 25th year.

Southern Pecan Pie

Katie Anderson – Rocky Mount, VA

1	cup chopped pecans	½	tsp. salt
½	cup sugar	3	Tbsps. shortening
1	tsp. vanilla	1	cup Blue Label Karo Syrup
3	eggs		

Beat eggs; add sugar, syrup, melted shortening, salt, vanilla, and nuts. Mix well, pour into partly baked crust and bake in moderate oven 325° about 45 minutes. The nuts float to top and form a crisp delicious crust.

Slow oven	250 to 325 degrees
Moderate oven	350 to 375 degrees
Hot oven	400 to 450 degrees
Very hot oven	450 to 500 degrees

"Growing up I had wonderful parents, but I also had Aunt Callie and Uncle Bill who were just like a second set of parents to me and my siblings. They made each one of us feel very special and loved. We spent many hours and days enjoying their company. When we were with them we did not do anything special, it just seemed like it was.

In the summer, we often helped move irrigation pipe in the tobacco field and when the time came, some of us were usually right there helping wire that tobacco. After a long hot day in the tobacco field we may have enjoyed sitting on the porch with a glass of sweet tea or a coke float talking and watching the cars go up and down the road or listening to the creek that flowed right beside the house. How I loved hearing the sounds of the creatures at night and possibly catching lightening bugs and putting them in a jar. Sometimes when Uncle Bill was staying at the barn at night keeping the fire going to cure the tobacco, Mother and Daddy would take us to visit him and keep him company. We loved that because we got to roast marshmallows and there was usually a watermelon in the creek just waiting for us.

If we were spending the night we got to sleep later than we did at home. We would play in the creek, check out the coon dogs, play cards, board games, watch TV, and make doll clothes out of scrap material. If it was washday, we helped wash clothes on a ringer washing machine that took most all day. We thought that was fun, but now we know it was hard work. When Aunt Callie churned her butter, she would give me some and let me make individual pats from a small wooden mold. I thought I was really something doing that. Many times we would go visiting. That was exciting for me because I would get to play with the children in that neighborhood.

I loved Aunt Callie's flowers. She always had geraniums, irises, petunias, and beautiful rose bushes. I liked picking the roses and bringing them to the house. One day I decided to pick a cluster of roses and put them behind my ear. Aunt Callie called me in for dinner. I came into the house with those roses behind my ear and sat down at the table. I was just waiting for them and their guests to tell me how pretty I looked, but they didn't say anything for a little while. I found out when I got older, they didn't say anything right away because they were trying not to laugh out loud. The roses were so heavy that my head was leaning to one side.

One of the best things about being at their house was the wonderful home cooked food. Aunt Callie had homemade biscuits, cornbread, and sweet tea with her meals. The table was always full of fresh vegetables right out of the garden. She would can and freeze a lot of the vegetables so you knew whenever you stopped by you were going to have a great meal.

Holidays were always spent together. The day would not have been the same without our aunt and uncle. When I started dating the man I married, I took him to visit with Aunt Callie and Uncle Bill to make sure he met with their approval. They were so much a part of our lives. The cherished times we spent together and the wonderful memories of those two special people are still with me daily. I will never forget the feelings I had for them and the life lessons they instilled in me."

Spoon Bread
Recipe of Callie Haynes Fortune, submitted by Libby Bondurant

2	cups sweet milk	1	cup meal	½	tsp. baking powder
1	cup buttermilk	1/3	cup melted butter	¼	tsp. soda
2	eggs	½	tsp. salt	1	Tbsp. sugar

Combine all ingredients together and beat well. Bake in greased dish at 400° for 15-20 minutes.

Teriyaki Sauce for Deer Meat
Mindy Mahan

½ cup soy sauce
¼ cup salad oil
4 cloves garlic, minced
1-2 tsps. ginger
3 Tbsps. brown sugar

Mix above ingredients together and add meat. Slice meat thin to marinade. Marinate meat 4-24 hours. A plastic bag works great. Less messy and more evenly distributes marinade. This marinade is great with chicken and pork also.

Tomato Rarebit
Joan Seifred – Moneta, VA

1 can tomato soup
1 egg, beaten
1 chopped onion, optional
8 ozs. cheddar cheese, chunks
Worcestershire sauce

Pour undiluted soup from can into skillet; add egg, stirring constantly. Add chopped onion, if desired. Cut 8 ounces of cheddar cheese in chunks, and add to soup mixture. Stir over medium heat until cheese melts. Finish with a few dashes of Worcestershire sauce; serve over toast.

*May you have the hindsight to know where you've been
The foresight to know where you're going
And the insight to know when you're going too far.*

"I have been collecting recipe books for over 40 years. I have a little over 300 in my collection. I have read all of them at least once and some, many times. In years past I would enjoy preparing a new recipe each week from one of my cookbooks. I also have many old recipes that have been passed down from family and friends, and some that I clipped from newspapers and magazines.

I enjoy cooking from scratch. I believe this is one way to keep some of the preservatives out of our family's diets. When my children were growing up we raised a big garden and in the early years I canned outside over an open fire pit. We raised and butchered two hogs and a beef cow every November.

My oldest daughter often recalls the times when she carried wood and helped me keep a fire going under an old cast iron kettle when I made lye soap. My youngest daughter also recalls that when she heard me ringing the ol' big dinner bell on the post in the front yard, that she knew she was to come running home. The cast iron kettle and the dinner bell belong to them now.

These days I'm cooking for two, however, I still cook my home made vegetable soup and spaghetti sauce in a large stockpot and can this in a pressure canner. I spend two days cooking and have fourteen meals. What a time saver!

Life is easier, but I am older. This recipe was passed down from Maw-maw (grandmother born in 1895). She used fat back instead of bacon and didn't use the dry mustard. My mother knew this was our family's favorite dish; she would always serve this with cornbread and pinto beans."

Wilted Lettuce

Noeta Blevins – Ferrum, VA

5 cups leaf lettuce torn into bite-size pieces	
3-4 green spring onions	1 Tbsp. water
5 slices bacon crumbled	¼ tsp. salt
2 Tbsps. sugar	pepper to taste
3 Tbsps. vinegar	¼ tsp. dry mustard, optional

Put lettuce and onions in salad bowl. Fry bacon crisp and cool on a paper towel. Cool bacon grease slightly before adding sugar, vinegar, water, salt, and mustard; bring to boiling point and pour over lettuce and onions. Toss to mix. Sprinkle bacon on top and serve immediately.

Zucchini Pineapple Bread
Susan Williams

- 3 eggs
- 2 cups sugar
- 1 tsp. vanilla
- 1 cup vegetable oil
- 2 grated unpeeled zucchinis
- 1 (15 oz.) can well drained crushed pineapple
- 1 cup chopped pecans
- 3½ cups flour
- 1½ tsps. salt
- 1½ tsps. baking soda
- ¾ tsp. baking powder

Mix together using a mixer the eggs, sugar, vanilla, and vegetable oil. Add the remaining ingredients and mix well. Bake at 325° for 50 minutes in a greased bread loaf pan. Makes 5 small loaves, or 3 regular loaves.

Phoebe Needles Center

The mission statement of Phoebe Needles is: To serve the people of Southwest Virginia by offering a variety of educational, spiritual, and renewal programs designed to nurture people in their spiritual formation. To this end, hundreds of children use the facilities through an annual summer camp program. The Lifelong Learning Program held monthly for adults offers diverse topics and learning experiences for about 60 people each meeting. Retreats are offered for large groups and there's a new high ropes course with the aim of building teamwork.

A century of history is behind the accredited camp and conference center and the rock church nearby, Saint Peter's-in-the-Mountains, owned by the Episcopal Diocese of Southwestern Virginia. Mr. Esom Sloan and Reverend Alexander Barr built a two-room mission school in about 1901 to educate the children of the fairly isolated community located in the shadow of the Blue Ridge Mountains. It was called St. Peter's Mission School. Reverend W.T. Roberts had the vision for a church beside the school, to be called Emmanuel Church. It was consecrated in 1904.

In 1917, Mr. Arthur C. Needles, president of the Norfolk and Western Railroad, donated land and money to build a school in honor of his daughter, Phoebe, who died at age 7 of meningitis. The old church had been destroyed by a snowstorm in 1914. The church and school have been a vital part of the community ever since, with expansions and renovations to upgrade and better serve as the years have gone by.

Phoebe Needles School Days

I lived in Calloway and started going to Phoebe Needles School when I was about five or six years old, tagging along with my older siblings. Because I did not go on a regular basis, I was around seven before I finished the first grade. My teacher was Miss Etta Davis, who was also the principal. We always had two teachers and sometimes a teacher would come from our sister school in Endicott.

In the second grade, I had a teacher from Boston, Mass., Miss Alberta Booth. She was a single, young girl. She and the other teachers were truly missionaries. At that time, you might say this area was backward. In my family there were eight children. We came to Phoebe Needles because it was free. Our textbooks were free and we had a hot lunch each day, either a stew or a soup of some kind. It was convenient and we walked to school.

We lived at the foot of Five Mile Mountain and had a lot of cousins who lived in the community. We didn't always walk the road, but would go through the woods and pick up the cousins and by the time we got to school, it might be a dozen of us. It probably was a little over a mile to school. We went in all kinds of weather because we grew up on a farm and had to get out and do our chores so we might as well go to school.

Most of my brothers and sisters finished the seventh grade at Phoebe Needles and then went to public school at Calloway and finished high school there. My family moved away in 1940 to operate a dairy farm in another community, so I left here in the fifth grade and began going to Fairmont School. I graduated from Calloway High School.

At Phoebe Needles, our teachers were Ms. Etta Davis, Alberta Booth, and Louise

Wood, who was a music major. On Wednesday of each week, there was a radio program called the Wednesday Morning Club. It was a program of classical music. She would take us down to the living quarters to hear this program. I really liked it because they served us cookies.

Each morning around 10:00 a.m. after we had one or two of our regular classes, we would go upstairs for devotions. That is also where we would practice for a religious play to perform for our parents. There was a stage area with a dressing room on either side and a fairly large auditorium. We also had a rhythm band. My sister has a picture of me leading the band. You can see me from behind and I had on my bib overalls and they were twisted in the back. I guess I was in a hurry that morning.

We had a lot of fun there. We had a playground just outside the school. The facility was modern compared to what the community had. There was a spring located over the hill and it had a pump that pumped water uphill to a reservoir, a tank on stilts that furnished the school with running water. We had two restrooms, one for boys and one for girls; they didn't always work but we had them. We also had water fountains. There was a hand dug well where we sometimes pumped drinking water.

I attended school at Phoebe Needles from around 1936 to 1939-40. I feel fortunate to have attended this school because I think we were exposed to some things that the public schools didn't have, like the classical music.

I had a cousin, Carter Agee, who had a beautiful tenor voice and Miss Louise Wood trained him to use his voice. He started out singing in church and then he took up bluegrass music. When he sang a solo, you could tell he had some voice training.

There were dances held at the school for the community. When I attended Phoebe Needles, World War II was about to begin. I would hear the teachers talking about the situation in Europe and I knew something bad was going on. There were not a lot of social events occurring during the war. However, after the war, the square dances revived and were held there again. I missed out on both of those periods.

When the school closed, Miss Alberta Booth became a teacher at an Indian reservation in Colorado. She married and came back to visit a couple of times. When she passed away, there was a memorial service for her at St. Peter's Episcopal Church and I told the story of how I had a crush on this young, single woman in the fifth grade.

We have a reunion for all the students that attended Phoebe Needles, on the first Saturday in October of each year. About twenty years ago, Grace Sowder Pendleton attended and she was the oldest one at the reunion. She said she attended Phoebe Needles the very first day it opened in 1907.

The man that donated the land for the first building at Phoebe Needles was my great uncle, Easom Slone. He is buried under the tree outside the school. The legend has it, he requested to be buried there so he could hear the children sing.

-as told by Rudolph Jones

The Shooting Creek area, which encompasses parts of Floyd and Franklin counties, was famous (or infamous) for moonshine stills. Lane Rakes, who knows a thing or two about the business, and his friend Susan Justice, wrote the following song in memory of the moonshinning times.

Memories of Shooting Creek
Written by: Susan E. Justice and Edker Lane Rakes.
Recorded by Sandy Via and Steve Shively at Outlet Studios

Coming down Shooting Creek around the Crooked Road
If you listen, you might hear the mountain people's bluegrass in the air
Echoing off the mountaintops and along the creek bottoms where the corn crops growed
Coming down Shooting Creek, around the Crooked Road.

Where some late night you might hear their mountain cur's bark,
Treeing a coon in the dark… It will never leave their hearts
The mountain music's in their souls and whiskey making in their blood,
All along the hollows low.
Coming down Shooting Creek along the Crooked Road.

If you stare into the night air you might see
the Ghost of the liquor makers at their stills,
As the moon shines high in the night sky, way back in them there hills.
Coming down Shooting Creek around the Crooked Road.

In the still of the night air, if you listen you might hear the shooting of their guns
Where mountain justice long ago did run.
They was protecting their stills, it was the only income they had to feed their loved ones.
Coming down the Crooked Road, where Shooting Creek does flow.

The old time religion where songs were sung so low,
Their mountain beliefs that are trying to survive.
The 21st century has arrived and is taking all their southern pride.
Coming down Shooting Creek, along the Crooked Road.

There are only memories of a long time ago,
No more heritage in their hearts are sown.
Where no more corn is grown, no more moonshine sold.
The memories of Shooting Creek in stories now are told…

- Used by permission of the authors

Friends

Contents

Apple Brown Betty In A Pumpkin.....393
Applesauce Pie...................................393
Aunt Edna's Peanut Surprise.............395
Awesome Fish Filets...........................395
Baked Buffalo Stew............................396
Baked Fruit..398
Banana Split Cake..............................398
Blueberry Coffeecake........................399
Brown Sugar Pie.................................399
Cabbage and Corn Beef Casserole....400
Cake' N – Cheese Cake.....................400
Chocolate Cherry Cake......................401
Chocolate Gravy.................................403
Clam Sauce Spaghetti.......................403
Corn-Jalapeno Dip.............................403
Cream Cheese Tarts..........................404
Creamy Potato Soup..........................405
Crystal Pickles....................................405
Debbie's Peanut Butter Delights........406
Grandma Bea Carper's
    Angel Biscuits..............................406
Granny's Popsicles............................405
Granny's Slaw....................................408
Homemade Bisquits..........................408
Hungarian Style Cabbage Rolls........409
Jelly Roll...410
Low Calorie Salad.............................410
Mame's Chicken' N Dumplings.......411
Million Dollar Rice Salad.................410
Mother Rucker's Cornbread...........413
No Bake Chocolate Peanut Butter
    Oatmeal Cookies......................414
Orange Crush Pound Cake.............414
Peanut Butter Pie.............................415
Pease Pudding..................................416
Phyllis's Pecan Pie...........................416
Poundies...417
Pumpkin Fluff...................................418
Ranch Style Baked Beans...............418
Sea Foam Candy..............................420
Simple Fruit Cobbler........................419
Singing Hinnie..................................421
Snow in the Vineyard.......................422
Sweet and Sour Chicken 422
To-Po Chops....................................423
Vegetable Salad...............................424
Whipping Cream Pound Cake........424
Whole Wheat Bran Bread...............424

A representative collage of some of the fine folks
who visit, live or work in Southwest Virginia.

Apple Brown Betty In A Pumpkin

Sherri Hyder - Historical Re-enactor of the 18th Century - Hampton, TN

4	cups large breadcrumbs
¼	tsp. ground cinnamon
	pinch of salt
¾	cup brown sugar
4	cups chopped cooking apples sliced thin
1	cup raisins
	butter
	pumpkin

Cut hole in top of pumpkin large enough to stick hand in. Clean out seeds and strings. Save seeds to roast later. Layer breadcrumbs, apples, raisins, nuts, brown sugar, butter, and cinnamon, alternating until pumpkin is filled. Top with butter. Put top on pumpkin. Put pumpkin in front of fire, not as close as to burn the pumpkin, but close enough so the contents will cook. Turn every 15 to 20 minutes until apples are tender inside. It will take 3 to 4 hours for this to cook. May cook at 250° to 300° in oven by placing pumpkin in large ovenproof dish and covering with aluminum foil. Cook for several hours.

Nat and Sherri Hyder have been demonstrating 18th century fireplace and outdoor cooking for the past 25 years. They do workshops and soap making as well. 423-725-2298

"My husband Odell Shelton is a member of the Shelton Brothers Gospel Bluegrass group."

Applesauce Pie

Freeda Shelton – Ridgeway, VA

3	eggs		1	stick margarine, melted
2	cups sugar		1	Tbsp. vanilla
20	ozs. applesauce		1	tsp. pumpkin pie spice
2	Tbsps. flour		1	deep-dish piecrust
¼	cup milk (canned is fine)			

Mix sugar and flour together. Then add other ingredients. Bake at 350° for 1½ hours or until center is set.

Childhood Memories

"As a child I always enjoyed summer. No school, we could ride our bikes, play with the neighbors and have fun. Of course, we had to do a few jobs around the house and in the garden. I still have not figured out why the garden needs so many weeds.

We were fortunate that we got to go visit our relatives during the summer months more often than in the winter. My mother was raised in Tazewell County and we had fun going to visit her family. Granddaddy raised a patch of strawberries on my uncle's dairy farm so I got to help pick berries to sell. Being Pruett's we had to rise real early at 5:00 a.m. to get to the patch. Of course, I got to eat my fair share of strawberries. We would finish picking in time to have breakfast with my uncle and aunt after they had finished the morning milking.

My dad was raised in Scott County just outside of Dungannon. We really enjoyed our trips to visit my two uncles and aunts there. We would time a visit in late summer so we could get some pawpaws. They taste great and we did not have them in Tazewell County. Some of Dad's extended family had ended up in Texas, Arizona, North Dakota, and Rhode Island. We made family trips to visit them sometimes camping along the way. On one trip across Texas the gas stations were having a gas war. We could pay 14¢ to 18¢ for a gallon. We need to turn back the clock and enjoy those prices again.

I really do enjoy looking at cookbooks. While I was looking through one of the books I inherited from my mother, I found a recipe that brought back a lot of good memories. When Dad's Aunt Edna Stair from Arizona came we would make peanut cookies from one of her favorite recipes. In order for the peanut cookies to be their best, we had to go to the Woolworth's 5¢ and 10¢ store to get roasted peanuts with the red skins. Cookbooks can also contain other very important information. My mother had written down dates like birthdays and anniversaries, their social security numbers, and notes from friends. I found an article written in my mother's handwriting about a daily routine of her Grandmother:

How Did Grandma Manage?

Mama's mama on a winter day, milked the cows and fed them hay, slopped the hogs, saddled the mule and got the children off to school, did a washing, mopped the floors, washed the windows and did some chores while cooking a dish of home dried fruit. Then she pressed her husband's Sunday suit, swept the parlor and made the bed. Baked a dozen loaves of bread, split some wood and lugged it in— had enough to fill the bin. She cleaned the lamps and put in oil, stewed some *apples she thought might spoil, churned the butter, baked a cake, then exclaimed "for mercy's sake, the calves are out of the pen" went out and chased them in again. Gathered the eggs and locked the stable, returned to the house and set the table, cooked a supper that was delicious, and afterwards washed the supper dishes. She fed the cat, sprinkled the clothes, and mended on a basket full of clothes. She opened the pump organ and began to play, "When we get to the end of a perfect day."*

I am not sure if this was really a true accounting of my great grandmother but it could possibly be a normal day for a lady in the country before we became modern housewives. - Carolyn Haynes

Aunt Edna's Peanut Surprise

Carolyn Haynes – Martinsville, VA

- 1 cup shortening
- 2 cups brown sugar
- 2 eggs
- 2 cups flour
- 1 tsp. baking powder
- 1 tsp. soda
- 1 tsp. salt
- 2 cups oatmeal
- 1 cup Wheaties
- 1 cup coarsely chopped peanuts

Cream shortening and brown sugar. Add eggs, mix well and add dry ingredients. Drop by tablespoon and bake at 350° for 12-15 minutes.

Awesome Fish Filets

Ken Henderson - Pounding Mill, VA

- 4 filets of rainbow trout
- 2 eggs
- 1/4 tsp. black pepper
- 1 small bag pork rinds
- 4 Tsps. Canola oil

Wash filets and dip into mixture of beaten eggs and pepper. In a food processor blend pork rinds into mixture and pour into plastic bag. Shake filets in pork rind mixture and fry in skillet in Canola oil. Yummy!

"Brush Creek Buffalo Farm started in October, 1993, by Jim and Jan Politis. We started raising buffalo (bison) and in February, 1994, we started selling the meat. Buffalo is lean, healthy red meat, lower in fat and cholesterol. The buffalo are raised naturally, without hormones, steroids, or antibiotics.

The farm has been in Jan's family since the early 1900's and in 1999, we put the farm in conservation easement to make sure it would remain a farm. We love raising the buffalo and having visitors come and share the beauty of these wonderful animals.

This stew recipe was served in our restaurant, Brush Creek Buffalo Store in Riner, VA. We sold the restaurant in July, 2007, to spend more time at the farm. Everyone loved this stew and we hope you will too."

Baked Buffalo Stew
Jan Politis – Brush Creek Buffalo Farm – Riner, VA

- 2 lbs. Buffalo stew meat
- 2 cloves garlic, fine chopped
- 2 cups finely chopped onion
- 2 bay leaves
- 1½ tsp. salt
- ¼ tsp. pepper
- ½ cup unsifted flour or ½ cup cornstarch
- ¾ cup red cooking wine and 2 cups of water or
- ½ cup red wine vinegar and 2½ cups of water
- 1 can (6 oz.) tomato paste
- cooked noodles or rice

Place buffalo stew meat, onion, garlic, and bay leaves in shallow pan; sprinkle with salt and pepper. Bake uncovered in a hot oven at 450° for 10 minutes, reduce heat to slow, 300°, and continue baking for 30 minutes longer until juices are released from the meat. Make sauce of flour or cornstarch, red cooking wine, water and tomato paste. Cook until smooth. Pour over meat, cover and bake in slow oven, 300° for 1 to 1½ hours or until meat is very tender, but not dry. Serves 6.

**Make it easy, mix all ingredients together and pour into crock pot. Cover on low 8-10 hours or high 5-6 hours. (Low is best.) May substitute carrots and potatoes for noodles or rice, just put carrots and potatoes in bottom of crock pot, and then add meat mixture. *(From National Buffalo Association cookbook)*

"Have you ever wondered why it is when one thinks of a kid as being a "show-off" you always think of boys? Well, I'm not so sure that is always the case, though I never thought of myself as a "show-off." I felt that proud would be more appropriate.

By the time I reached the age of eleven, I had graduated from a bicycle to the car. My brother, Mike, had tried to teach me to drive a tractor. I wasn't too good at that. The clutch and brake were too hard to push down. The side of the barn worked great to stop the tractor. Teaching me to drive a car was somewhat more successful. He taught me to drive a '53 Chevy, straight gear on the column. I could barely see over the steering wheel and had to sit on the edge of the seat to change gears and press the gas pedal. I was in that car driving around and around the house every chance that I got. Boy was I proud! Though not too much when I had left the car in neutral and it was slowly rolling past the dining room window at suppertime and Daddy had to run and catch it before it rolled into the fence and down the hill. Nor was I too proud, when my sister, Libby, and I were joy riding in the hay field when the car came to a complete stop for what I thought was no reason. The reason was – I had run over a hay bale that I could not see. Daddy to the rescue again.

Speaking of being proud – I once wanted to show some of my cousins how good I was at driving since I had been doing so for a while. The family had gathered at our grandmother's house. (Her house was on a long dirt road, which would have given me the opportunity to be proud for a right good ways). My grandmother, aunts, uncles, and younger sister, Martha, were all on the front porch. This gave them a perfect view of the road. I told my sister, Libby, and a couple of cousins, Connie and Darnae, that I would take them for a ride. This time, I was driving the family '57 Ford. We all climbed in the car. I was sitting up straight and on the edge of the seat so that I could see over the wheel and press the gas. To my dismay, that ride didn't last long – I gave the car a little too much gas and sort of ran up on the bank on one side of the road. (Just a little). With all the hollering from the aunts, it made me nervous. Therefore, I couldn't drive as well as I had told everyone that I could. For a proud twelve year old, that was a little too embarrassing. Daddy to the rescue again. This time, he did not think it was too funny. Needless to say, joy riding was not too high on my list for a while. That is until school started. Picture this – PTA meeting, my best friend and a '57 Ford in the school parking lot – the temptation was too great. I was really proud that night!"

Baked Fruit

Jane Poore – Louisa, VA

1½ cups sugar
2 Tbsps. cornstarch
4 cups sliced peaches, drained
4 cups sliced pears, drained
2 cups pineapple chunks, drained
1 tsp. cinnamon
½ tsp. nutmeg
¼ tsp. curry powder

Combine sugar and cornstarch, set aside. Sprinkle spices over fruit, then combine with sugar/cornstarch mixture. Bake in 2½-quart casserole for 1 hour at 350.

A good cook adds a pinch of love.

Banana Split Cake

Margaret Vest – Salem, VA

1½ cups Honey Maid graham cracker crumbs
1 cup sugar, divided
1/3 cup butter, melted
2 (8 oz.) pkgs. Philadelphia cream cheese, softened
1 (20 oz.) can crushed pineapple, drained
6 medium bananas, divided
2 cups cold milk
2 (4 serving size) boxes Jell-O vanilla flavor instant pudding & pie filling
2 cups thawed Cool Whip whipped topping, divided
1 cup Planters chopped pecans

Mix crumbs, ½ cup of the sugar and the butter; press firmly onto bottom of 13x9-inch pan. Freeze 10 minutes. Beat cream cheese and remaining ¾ cup sugar with electric mixer on medium speed until well blended. Spread carefully over crust; top with pineapple. Slice 4 of the bananas; arrange over pineapple. Pour milk into medium bowl. Add dry pudding mixes. Beat with wire whisk 2 minutes or until well blended. Gently stir in 1 cup of the whipped topping; spread over banana layer in pan. Top with remaining 1 cup whipped topping; sprinkle with pecans. Refrigerate 5 hours. Slice remaining 2 bananas just before serving; arrange over dessert. Store any leftover dessert in refrigerator.

Blueberry Coffeecake
Joyce Mills – Wolf Creek Band – Mount Airy, NC

½ cup vegetable shortening
2 eggs
1 cup sugar
1 tsp. vanilla extract
2½ cups all purpose flour
2/3 cup milk
1 Tbsp. baking powder
2 cups fresh or frozen blueberries

Picture taken at Phoebe Needles. Then Director of The Crooked Road, Bill Smith, joined local musicians. Music jams abound throughout the ten counties of The Crooked Road.

Preheat oven to 350°. Lightly grease and flour two 8 or 9-inch round pans. Prepare cake, beat shortening and sugar together until fluffy. Add eggs and vanilla, beat well. Combine flour, baking powder, shortening, milk, and sugar. Mix until smooth. Spoon batter into baking pans, sprinkle 1 cup berries over batter in each pan. **Topping** is below:

2/3 cup sugar   ½ cup margarine
2/3 cup flour   ¼ tsp. almond extract

Combine sugar and flour with a pastry blender. Cut in butter, add almond. Sprinkle over berries. Bake for 35 minutes. Cut into wedges.

Brown Sugar Pie
Harold Osborne – Kingsport, TN

1 frozen piecrust   1 Tbsp. flour
1 cup brown sugar   1 Tbsp. milk
1 egg   1 tsp. vanilla
1 Tbsp. butter

Mix ingredients in bowl until thoroughly blended. Pour into crust. Bake at 350° at least 35 to 40 minutes or until brown.

Johnny plays Banjo and Bass with the Bill Jefferson Band He has played with Don Reno and Carl Perkins.

Cabbage and Corn Beef Casserole
Johnny & Lessie Smith – Hurt, VA

1   can corn beef
1   small head cabbage, chopped
1   can mushroom soup

1   can water from the soup can
2   medium size potatoes, sliced
1   medium onion, chopped

Layer in casserole dish ½ of each of the following ingredients, potatoes, onions, cabbage, and corn beef. Repeat layers. Mix the mushroom soup and water together and pour over casserole. Cook for 20 to 30 minutes until brown at 350°

"My Mama was crawling through a wire fence so we could go blackberry picking when a big brown fence lizard jumped on her back. She yelled for my sister or me to get it off her and ran toward us. We in turn ran away from her because we were afraid of the lizard. She said when I get this thing off me and catch you I will beat the living daylights out of both of you, but she didn't."

Cake-N-Cheese Cake
Inez Chandler – Waynesville, NC

1   cup flour
2/3   cup sugar
1   tsp. baking powder
½   tsp. salt
1   tsp. vanilla
1   egg
½   cup butter

Cheese filling:
1   (8oz.) cream cheese
2/3   cup sugar
1   cup sour cream
1   tsp. vanilla
3   eggs

Topping:
1   tsp. vanilla   ¼   cup sugar   1   cup sour cream

Combine all cake ingredients. Beat on medium speed until blended. Spread in a 9-inch square floured and greased pan. Pour cheese filling over this and bake 35 to 45 minutes at 325° until firm when touched lightly in center. Let cool and spread with topping. Chill at least 4 hours before serving.

"I grew up with music. Although I lived in Kentucky, I wasn't exposed to "traditional" music until later on in my college days.

I'm a music teacher and presently live in Knoxville, TN. Every year I teach a unit on Appalachian music. I demonstrate my dulcimer, psaltery, and pennywhistle. I teach primary age students, so we learn about the culture through singing games, photographs, and anything else I can get my hands on. I try to instill a love for all kinds of music, especially the music of our area.

Our culture is changing way too quickly. Children only know what is popular right now, and I mean **right now!** They may know all about the latest rap artist, but they have no clue who Daniel Boone was. I realize we have to live in the present, but honoring our past is also important.

Last summer my husband and I rented a car and drove all around Ireland, staying in B&B's along the way. It was wonderful to witness how so much of our traditional music and culture has been influenced by our Celtic ancestors.

One of the teaching methods I use in class is the Kodaly Method. This method stresses that a child should use his mother tongue – the folk music of his native language. What a rich heritage we have in our own backyard. I just hope our future generations understand what we need to preserve.

Chocolate Cherry Cake
Jane Dill – Knoxville, TN

1   (18¼ ozs.) pkg. chocolate fudge cake mix
2   eggs
1   tsp. almond extract
1   (21 ozs.) can cherry pie filling
1   cup sugar
1/3 cup milk
1/3 cup butter
1   cup semisweet chocolate chips

In a bowl, combine the cake mix, eggs, and extract. Add pie filling; mix well. Spread into a greased 15x10x1-inch baking pan. Bake at 350° for 20-30 minutes or until a toothpick inserted near the center comes out clean. Meanwhile, in a saucepan, combine sugar, milk, and butter. Cook and stir until sugar is dissolved and butter is melted. Remove from the heat; stir in chocolate chips until melted. Pour over warm cake; spread evenly. Cool completely before cutting. Store in the refrigerator.

(L to R) Vera Dew, Dorothy Turner, Lois Black, Libby Bondurant, Mary Badman, Janie Murphy, Frances Jamison, and Nell Draper

The Pleasant Quilters never had a formal beginning, unless you count when they started a bank account in 1991. Nevertheless, the group certainly withstood the test of time. Some older ladies in the neighborhood, including Janie Gardener, Kate Jamison, Imogene Bondurant, Gertrude Jamison, and Gracie Brown got together for many years to quilt. Most of them attended Pleasant Grove United Methodist Church. Gradually, others from the church and neighborhood began joining the group to learn or to help out. By the mid-1980's, a day each week was set aside to get together, generally at Jewel Jamison's or Dick and Frances Jamison's. Each Tuesday about ten or twelve ladies (anybody who's interested!) show up at either Dorothy Turner or Frances Jamison's house, according to the size of the quilt being done. Dorothy's basement is perfect for larger sized quilt frames.

Fun is a big part of the day but a tremendous amount of work gets done as well. Many individuals as well as the church, have benefited from the proceeds of their work. For instance, $3,000 dollars was given when the church parking lot needed paving. "Anyone can bring up something they think we need to do and we talk about it and make a decision. There's no friction and we do a great deal of good," states Frances Jamison. "We give ourselves a little treat and go out to eat once in a while, too. The bonus is all the nice people we've met who bring quilt tops to be quilted. God blesses us."

"My kids and grandkids love this. They still call and come home occasionally for this."

Chocolate Gravy

Edith M. Hess – Russell County, VA

2½	cups sugar	4½ or 5	cups milk
4	Tbsps. flour	4	Tbsps. chocolate

Put sugar, chocolate, and flour in pan, make up with ½ cup milk. Then add rest of milk. Put on stove; bring to a boil while stirring, on medium heat. Cook until a little thick but not real thick. Make some homemade biscuits and eat with butter on them

Clam Sauce Spaghetti

Kathy Fleming – Blountville, TN

2   cans clams & juice (Snows minced 6½ oz. can)
¾   cup extra virgin olive oil
½   cup chopped fresh parsley (no stems)
3-4 cloves garlic, sliced
½-1 lb. cooked spaghetti

Brown garlic in hot olive oil, strain to remove garlic. Return hot garlic oil to skillet; add clam juice, salt, and pepper to taste. Simmer 15 minutes. Add parsley and clams. Simmer 10 minutes. Pour over spaghetti.
Enjoy.

Corn-Jalapeno Dip

Christine A. Bradley – Cobb County, GA

2   (8 oz.) pkgs. cream cheese, softened
1   pkg. frozen cream-style corn, thawed
1-2 jalapeno peppers, chopped, with seeds

Combine all ingredients; pour into a greased casserole dish. Bake at 350° until bubbling hot and lightly browned. Serve with tortilla chips.

Don't go for looks; they can deceive. Don't go for wealth; even that fades away. Go for someone who makes you smile, Because it takes only a smile to Make a dark day seem bright. Find the one that makes your heart smile.

"I was married on October 25, 1969. This was the day after my husband turned 18. I turned 18 on December 9, 1969. I knew how to cook two things, fudge and cornbread, and my husband didn't like either. One of my first cooked meals was fried pork chops, gravy, and mashed potatoes. I don't remember biscuits, so I am guessing they were canned! When my husband came to the table, he asked why I had two bowls of mashed potatoes. The gravy was white and thick! The pork chops were so dry and tough, the dog chewed on them for days. I remember our parents shaking their heads because we were spending about $20.00 a week for groceries. That was a lot to spend in those days. I ruined a lot of food learning how to cook, but we survived and laughed about those first meals for many years. In April of 1971, my husband enlisted in the Navy. After basic training, we were stationed in Pensacola, FL for six months. Thanksgiving was our first holiday away from home and family and I was terribly homesick. We joined three other couples for a wonderful Thanksgiving dinner and the following recipe is the dessert that one of the wives prepared. After 36 years, it still remains a favorite in my family and is always a hit with everyone. For me, it not only tastes good, it brings back a happy memory."

Cream Cheese Tarts

Julia Quesenberry – Austinville, VA

Crust
1   (3 oz.) pkg. cream cheese
1   cup flour
1   stick margarine

Having the cream cheese and margarine at room temp. makes this easier to mix. Do <u>not</u> melt the margarine. You have to use your hands, it is very thick. It also works better to mix the crust mixture several hours or the day before and refrigerate.

Filling
1   (8 oz.) pkg. cream cheese
½   cup sugar
½   tsp. vanilla
1   egg

Using a mixer, beat room temperature cream cheese until smooth. Roll the crust mixture into 24 balls (about 1 inch). Press into small tart pans. Fill almost to the top with the filling mixture. Bake at 325° for about 20 minutes or until just golden brown. Cool. Top with cherry or blueberry pie filling. My family loves it topped with strawberry freezer jam. I just put the toppings in bowls and let people choose their favorite. I also suggest making more than one batch. They go quickly and are very pretty!

Creamy Potato Soup

Dorothy Turner – Martinsville, VA

1	(30 oz.) pkg. frozen shredded hash brown potatoes
6	cups water
1/3	cup chopped onion
2	(10-3/4 ozs. each) cans condensed cream of celery soup, undiluted
4	ozs. process cheese (Velveeta), cubed
1	(8 oz.) cup sour cream
½	tsp. salt
¼	tsp. pepper

In a large saucepan, combine the potatoes, water, and onion. Bring to a boil. Reduce heat; stir in soup and cheese. Cook and stir until cheese is melted. Stir in the sour cream, salt, and pepper. Cook and stir until heated through (do not boil). Makes about 3 quarts.

Crystal Pickles

Violet Viars

Wash and place **25 small cucumbers** in brine strong enough to float an egg. Add about **2 cups of pickling salt.** Let stand 2 weeks. Take out and wash, slice and put in fresh water. Add **alum** the size of a walnut (**about 2 Tbsps.**). Let stand overnight. Drain and wash again. Now you are ready for the syrup. Boil and pour over pickles each day for 3 mornings. On the 4th day, repeat, heat, and seal.

1	quart white vinegar	2	sticks of cinnamon
2	quarts sugar	1	tsp. whole cloves

The Lord bless thee, and keep thee:
The Lord make his face shine upon thee,
*   and be gracious unto thee:*
The Lord lift up his countenance upon thee,
*   and give thee peace.* -Numbers 6: 24-26

Granny's Popsicles

Carolyn Haynes – Martinsville, VA

1	small box Jell-O
1	pkg. kool-aid
¾	cup sugar
2	cups hot water
2	cups cold water

Mix well and pour into molds. You can use any kind of jell-o and use same flavor of kool-aid as jell-o. Freeze until hard and enjoy.

Debbie Bennett won "Songwriter of the Year" from the Country Music Gospel Association in 2007. She has five # 1 songs in this country and has sung at the *Pageant of Peace* at the White House. Bennett was born and raised in Stuart, VA. She is an uplifting, spirit filled, and energetic singer with a devotion to serving God in the music field and most importantly in her everyday walk of life. An inspiring singer/ songwriter who writes songs about life's experiences that touch hearts in the United States and abroad. www.sonicbids.com/ DebbieBennett

Debbie's Peanut Butter Delights

Debbie Bennett – Danbury, NC

- 2 cups sugar
- 1 stick margarine
- 2 Tbsps. Hershey's cocoa
- ½ cup milk
- 1 cup peanut butter (loosely packed)
- 3 cups quick cooking oats
- 1 tsp. vanilla

Mix first 4 ingredients in saucepan, boil for 1 minute. Remove from stove and stir in remaining ingredients; mix well. Drop by teaspoon onto wax paper or aluminum foil.

Grandma Bea Carper's Angel Biscuits

Donna Carper – Craig County, VA - www.locustmountainboys.com

- 5 cups flour
- ¾ cup shortening
- ¼ cup sugar
- 1 pkg. dry yeast (dissolve in ¼ cup warm water with Tbsp. of the sugar)
- 2 cups buttermilk
- 1 tsp. baking soda (leveled)
- 3 tsps. baking powder (leveled)
- 1 tsp. salt

Cut shortening into flour (until resembles corn meal) and add remaining dry ingredients. Add buttermilk and yeast and then mix well until you have a stiff dough. Let stand in refrigerator for an hour. (Better to let stand overnight if possible). Roll dough and cut biscuits. Place on greased cookie sheet. Bake at 400° for 10 minutes. Enjoy!

Granny Mitchell

Granny was born Armaine Mae Merriman on December 8, 1903. She married Papa Mitchell from the Stuart area and they settled in Bassett. From the time I was born in 1947 until she died in 1998, she and Papa were a big part of my family's life. My mother, father, two brothers, and sister and I lived next to them while growing up. Granny looked after us in the summer and any other time my parents were working, and was like a mother to us. She was a very hard worker, washing clothes, cleaning house, and cooking for our family until long after I was married and had children of my own.

I didn't see the mischievous side of Granny until after we were grown with families of our own. I guess this was so because she was busy all the time with chores and watching over her grandchildren. My brother Larry moved his wife and children to North Carolina when he got a new job. Somehow, when he came in on the weekends, the "feud" began. He would walk up the hill a short distance to Granny's house to see her and would leave some acorns or rocks, maybe a stick, in her refrigerator or under her pillow. She would retaliate by putting rocks in between the sheets of the bed he was sleeping in at mom's house. This went on for many years. One time Granny put a banana peel in his loafers after he had returned to his home in North Carolina. The next weekend that Larry came in, he had maggots in those shoes when he got ready to put them on for church on Sunday. Another time, Granny put acorns in his bed. He and his wife came in very late on Friday night, got in bed, and discovered that the bed was full of worms. Shelia, his wife, good-naturedly shook out the sheets over the porch rail, remade the bed, and went on to sleep.

One time, I was mowing the yard for my mom. I felt something whizzing past my head, looked around, and there stood Granny, throwing apples from a nearby apple tree at my head. I was so glad she didn't have a good aim! She had the biggest blue eyes, dancing with mischief when she pulled those pranks.

When Granny died in 1998, she left a million memories! I can still see her with her wringer washer, carrying out washing tubs of water to soak her flowers, all 5 foot 2 inches and maybe a 100 pounds. I remember her cooking a full meal for us at lunch over a wood stove. We dined on potatoes, beans, biscuits, and apple pies…delicious!!! Just before her viewing, our family gathered at the funeral home. Larry slipped a handful of rocks in her coffin and said, "Gottcha last Granny!" There were a few puzzled faces as visitors passed by and saw those rocks lying there. I'm sure Granny is in heaven, just waiting for Larry to get there, with something up her sleeve.   *- Linda Martin, granddaughter*

Granny's Slaw
Linda Martin - Martinsville, VA

1 medium head of cabbage	1 or 2 onions	1 or 2 green peppers
		1 cup sugar

Shred cabbage fine. Slice peppers and onions thin. Put a layer of cabbage, layer of peppers, and layer of onions. Sprinkle with sugar and continue until all is in bowl. Boil following ingredients. Pour over cabbage mixture while hot. Cover and place in refrigerator at least 4 hours or overnight, if possible.

¾ cup vinegar	2 Tbsp. sugar	½ cup oil
1 tsp. dry mustard	1 Tbsp. Salt	1 tsp. celery seed

"The very first time I tried to make biscuits, I was taking care of a niece and nephew in Carroll County while their mother was having some surgery. At the time I was a mother of a 2 year old and expecting our 2nd child due in May. This was December. I had never made a biscuit in my life – so I asked the kids what they wanted for breakfast, thinking of Corn Flakes, Cheerios, or even Bacon & Eggs; but oh, no... not these kids. They wanted Biscuits and Gravy. Needless to say they were absolutely terrible. Their Father would not allow these poor little kids to complain – but dear ole Auntie came to the rescue. My first bite was sickening and I strongly stated my feelings, quickly scooped up the biscuits, and tossed them out to the pigs. We had a good laugh and then ate some oatmeal. What a 10- day experience. One I will never forget. And I thank the Good Lord for this time with a wonderful family. I learned a lot and yes, eventually how to make some edible biscuits."

Homemade Biscuits
Mary Ann White – Marengo, Ohio

A couple hands full of flour	**Water to hold together**
Add a couple teaspoons full of baking powder	**Salt to taste**
Enough Lard to make flour crumbly	

In large bowl, combine ingredients. Form batter into ball, roll out to about ½ inch thickness on a floured board, take glass and cut out biscuits, place on baking sheet. Bake at 350° till brown (not burned), serve. In the event you cannot eat these biscuits, throw them out to the pigs, open up a sack of frozen Pillsbury Biscuits, bake and enjoy.

"My stepfather, Pete Sabo, was a big man with a heart to match. He won me over when he came for his first date with my mother carrying a box of candy and a rabbit with a sack of candy eggs attached. She thought one was for her, but he gave both to me! His parents were from Hungary and he told me about riding to Southwest Virginia on a flat bed railroad car. It was crowded with other Hungarians coming to find work and they were told, 'If you fall off, we won't stop to pick you up.' They were very industrious, thrifty people and could bake the best bread ever. We lived in Moorefield and his parents ran Sabo's grocery in St. Paul. He worked for the railroad."

Hungarian Style Cabbage Rolls
In memory of Alex "Pete" Sabo - by Mary Lou Vance – Erwin, TN

1 large leaf cabbage head	1 large onion, chopped
2 jars kraut, juice included	1 large egg, beaten
2 lbs. ground meat (such as ground sirloin)	salt & pepper to taste
3 garlic cloves minced (or garlic powder to equal 3 cloves or to taste)	1 large can tomato juice
1 small can tomato sauce or tomatoes	1 pork chop, meat taken off bone and ground
½ cup long-grain rice (minute rice can be used)	

Prepare large pot of water to boil. Remove leaves from cabbage head, very gently making sure leaves remain whole without tearing. Put in boiling water, very gently making sure leaves are submerged in water with a wooden spoon. Replace lid on pot for 2-3 minutes. Drain in colander. Rinse in cold water until easy to handle. With a sharp paring knife, cut thick vein out of cabbage leaf.

In a large bowl, put ground meat, garlic, tomato sauce, rice, onion, salt, pepper, egg, and pork. Mix as you would a meatloaf. Very gently so as not to break leaf, take one cabbage leaf and depending on size of leaf, put 2 Tbsps. of meat mixture in center of leaf and very gently fold leaf around meat mixture.

In large Dutch oven pour one jar of kraut. Place cabbage roll on top of kraut, seam side down. Repeat. Stack rolls on top of each other until all meat mixture is used. Pour jar of kraut on top. Very gently pour tomato juice down side of pot. Rinse bottle out with a little water. If all of second jar is not used, pour water in pot. Start on medium/low heat. Put lid on. After about 30 minutes, very gently shake pot. DO NOT STIR. Shaking keeps them from sticking. Tomato juice or water may have to be added as cooking goes on. Temperature may have to be reduced to low.

Jelly Roll
Maggie White – Austinville, VA

4	eggs, separated	1	tsp. vanilla
¾	cup sugar	¾	cup sifted flour

Beat egg yolks until light, add sugar and vanilla; mix well. Add sifted flour. Lastly, fold in well-beaten egg whites. Line a 15x10-inch (cookie sheet) with wax paper. Bake in moderate oven 6–8 minutes. Batter will be real thin while cake is hot; trim off hard edges and spread with jelly, roll up. Sprinkle with powdered sugar.

Low Calorie Salad
Betty L. Dillon – Henry, VA

1 can pineapple and juice
1 carton light'n lively cottage cheese
1 (3 oz.) pkg. strawberry jell-o
1 (9 oz.) container of Cool Whip

Heat pineapple and juice until jell-o dissolves, then cool. Add cottage cheese and Cool Whip. Put in refrigerator and chill.

Million Dollar Rice Salad
Iris McGrady – Martinsville, VA

1	(8 oz.) cream cheese	2	cups rice, cooked and cooled
1	Tbsp. sugar	1	small jar maraschino cherries, chopped
1	Tbsp. mayonnaise		
1	large pkg. miniature marshmallows	1	cup whipped cream
		¾	cup chopped pecans, optional
1	large can crushed pineapple, drained		

Blend cream cheese, sugar, and mayonnaise together until smooth. Add marshmallows, pineapple, rice, and cherries; fold together. Fold in whipped cream and pecans; turn into 9x13-inch pan and chill. Cut into squares to serve.

NOTES:

"A little while ago my daughter called and asked me for our Mame's Chicken'n Dumplings recipe. She wanted to prepare it for her two little ones. She told me that it was a big favorite of hers when we used to go visit with Mame. I told her that when I came for my next visit I'd bring the recipe and we could prepare the meal together. My daughter and grandchildren live in Tucson, AZ, and it was a couple of months before I had a chance for a visit.

When I arrived at her place I told her that I would need to go shopping for all of the ingredients. I wanted to make certain that it turned out just like Mame's. So off we went to the supermarket where I purchased everything needed for the dish. The next day when it came time to prepare dinner, my daughter, grandson (he loves to help in the kitchen) and I got out the items I had purchased. When I started cooking the dish, my daughter's eyes kept getting bigger and bigger. She couldn't conceal her surprise when the dish was finished. We starting laughing and laughed so hard that we couldn't see for the tears of joy. You see Mame, my grandmother, raised my brother, two sisters, and me after our mother passed away. Times were tough back then and we had to scrape by. Although we never went hungry we did eat some 'interesting' dishes. I never imagined that some day this recipe would be something that would be handed down and become a family favorite. Even my picky grandchildren love this new dish.

In case you are interested in trying the recipe for Mame's Chicken'n Dumplings, here are the ingredients and directions:"

Mame's Chicken'n Dumplings
Peggy Morgan – Gardena, CA

1 can cream of chicken soup
1 can of refrigerator biscuits

Heat the can of soup (following the directions on the can) in a saucepan until it starts to steam. Drop in the biscuits. It's best if you pull the biscuits apart so they will be lighter and fluffier. Heat and stir until done. Season to taste and enjoy.

Healing Skin Wounds
Cornelia W. Elgin – Ridgeway, VA

This Folk remedy was used back in the 1800's and it still works today! If you have scraped the skin off anywhere on your body, just go get you a little <u>raw</u> honey and apply to wound. Your wound will heal quickly.

Mother Rucker's Cornbread
James "Sparky" Rucker – Maryville, TN

"Being an African American folk performer from east Tennessee and coming from a family well versed in the Church of God Sanctified, I am well acquainted with cornbread. At every district meeting, the church always provided a meal. "You'll get the earthly food downstairs and then you'll come back up here and get the spiritual food!" Of course, that earthly food would consist of Sister James' turnip greens, and Sister Minnefee's (Lillie Mae) candied yams, and my Mother's (Louretta Thomas Rucker) lip-smacking cornbread. Not that yellow cornbread that you get in the Midwest… or that yellow and sugar sweet cornbread that you get up north…but I'm talkin' 'bout that good old white cornbread that you get here in east Tennessee. Cornbread that "sticks to your rib!" Cornbread that you can scour out the iron skillet with…the same skillet that you cooked it in!!!

I don't know why folks think that you need sugar in cornbread. Corn itself is sweet…so why do you need to add sugar??? If I wanted cake…then that's what I'd cook!

As a musician I travel a lot around the country. I sometimes have to eat in restaurants and …occasionally there is "cornbread" on the menu…especially in these "food bar" places…and I take a chance and order it from the menu. It comes to the table and my mouth waters as I let it soak up the "pot likker" from the turnip greens…or let it float in my bowl of pinto beans…or maybe slather it in good creamy butter! Well, anyway I put it in my mouth and arrgh!!! It's too sweet!

Well, one day, up in Northern Virginia I was sitting around the kitchen table of a friend's place and we were all discussing the just consumed meal and the topic of "cornbread" arose. I, of course, offered my opinion on the adverse use of sugar in cornbread when a woman who was also there at dinner related this story…

It seems that her daughter was in her history class and the teacher asked what was the main cause of the Civil War. The teacher was, of course, expecting the answer to be "slavery." In her eagerness to answer the question, the little girl raised her hand and wiggled anxiously and yelled out, "I know! I know!"

The very pleased teacher rejoined, "What is the answer, young lady?"

The little girl, with a satisfied grin on her face, blurted out the answer, "it's because the Yankees put sugar in the cornbread!"

Well there you have it from the mouth of babes…**no sugar in the cornbread or suffer the consequences!**

Here's the way I learned to make cornbread…directly from Mother Rucker's recipe: First you'll need a greased iron skillet (I use a 10-inch skillet). Of course, if you remember to NOT wash the skillet with soap and water, but to just scrub it out with plain water immediately after using it (while it's still hot), the skillet will retain some of the oil and will not rust. If you just forgot…or if the skillet is new…slowly melt some Crisco or any other vegetable based shortening (I'm a vegetarian) in the skillet over a low flame while you mix the ingredients for the cornbread. This oil should make about a tablespoon of cooking oil once it is melted, and incidentally making your skillet good and greasy. Remember that old song "Keep Your Skillet Good and Greasy?" Well now you know why!

You'll also need some buttermilk! Now if you can't get good buttermilk…or if you've had the urge for some good cornbread…and it's in the middle of the night…and your craving for cornbread is so insistent that you can't wait till next day for the store to open…well you can make buttermilk by adding 4 tsps. of vinegar to 1 cup of milk and letting it sit for a spell until it clabbers (ask some older person what "clabber" means). **www.sparkyandrhonda.com** **http://www.myspace.com/sparkyrhondarucker**

- 1½ cups of white cornmeal (OK so you can't find white cornmeal…go ahead and use yellow)
- 1 tsp. baking powder
- ½ tsp. salt
- 1 egg
- 1 cup buttermilk (is it clabbered yet?)
- 1 Tbsp. cooking oil (that same melted shortening which you will pour from the warm skillet)
- ½ tsp. baking soda

Pre-heat oven to 400°. Combine the white cornmeal, baking powder, and salt. Add the egg, buttermilk, and cooking oil. Now add the baking soda. Pour mixture into that well greased still-warm skillet. Bake in pre-warmed oven for about 25 minutes until the bread is brown and separated from the sides of the skillet (and after the smell of the cornbread is so good it is making your mouth water). Let it cool slightly until you can take the cornbread from the pan without it tearing up. Place it on a plate…slice a wedge…butter it…or sop up some good turnip greens pot liquor…have it with some pinto beans…or with a cup of milk…well…use your imagination. By the way…did you notice that the recipe did not call for wheat flour? Of course not! It's CORNBREAD! You can now enjoy Mother Louretta Rucker's cornbread. And when you cook cornbread…you don't need precise directions either…just let it be an adventure!

The Moose Family, a friend of the Crooked Road, resides in Surry County in Lowgap, N.C. Following in the footsteps of David Moose, the group sings old-time gospel music and demonstrates Shape Note singing. The group is a longtime performer at the Blue Ridge Folklife Festival held annually at Ferrum College. Shape Note demonstrations are given yearly at various sites along the Blue Ridge Parkway including Brinegar Days. Other performances include The Rex Theatre, Galax, VA, WPAQ Merry-Go-Round, Mt. Airy, NC, and a special performance at *Whitetop Folk Festival Remembered* at the Barter Theater.

"I have seen grown men weep, docile women wrestle, and hound dogs bay when my wife, Janice, places these cookies on the table. Incredibly quick and tasty. One thing Janice left out of the recipe is the stance to take while stirring. She always stirs with her right hand, her left arm forming an isosceles triangle with a fist placed defiantly on her left hip. I am firmly convinced this is required to make these wonderful cookies!" -Tony Scales, author of **Natural Tunnel: Natures' Marvel in Stone**

No Bake Chocolate Peanut Butter Oatmeal Cookies

Janice Scales – Submitted by Tony Scales – Wise, VA

3	cups sugar	¾	cup milk
1	Tbsp. cocoa	3	heaping Tbsps. peanut butter
1	heaping Tbsp. margarine	2½	cups oatmeal (minute)

<u>Note</u>: use regular tablespoon, not measuring spoon**.** Stir sugar and cocoa together in a Teflon skillet. Add margarine and milk, stirring constantly on medium heat. Bring to boil and cook for one minute. Remove from heat and stir in peanut butter. Add oatmeal and stir. Drop by tablespoon on wax paper. Cool completely and store in airtight container.

Orange Crush Pound Cake

The Moose Family Singers –Lowgap, NC

2¾	cups sugar	5	eggs
1	cup Crisco	½	tsp. salt
½	stick butter	3	cups cake flour
1	cup orange crush (can sub. Sunkist)	1	tsp. vanilla
		1	tsp. orange flavoring

Cream together butter, Crisco, and sugar. Add eggs one at a time. Cream until light and fluffy. Sift dry ingredients. Add alternately with orange drink. Then add flavorings. Pour in a lightly greased and floured tube pan. Bake 325° for 1 hour and 10 minutes. Cream the following ingredients together to make a topping and spread on top of cake.

1	cup powdered sugar	½	tsp. vanilla
1	(3 oz.) cream cheese	½	tsp. orange flavoring

Scalded Milk
Linda Fain – Martinsville, VA

Many older recipes called for you to scald milk, that is, to bring it nearly to a boil (185°F, 85°C, or more), preferably in a thick-bottomed pan, and stirring actively, to keep a protein skin from forming on the surface and keep the proteins and sugar from sticking to the bottom. Scalding served two purposes, to kill potentially harmful bacteria in the milk, and to destroy enzymes that keep the milk from thickening in recipes. Pasteurization, however, accomplishes both of those goals, and since almost all store-bought milk in Western countries is pasteurized these days, scalding is essentially an unnecessary step. Another reason some recipes continue to call for scalded milk is that they simply want you to heat the milk first, as it will speed the cooking process, help melt butter, dissolve sugar more easily, etc. To help keep a scalding project from turning into a scorching one, try some of these tips:
    Rinse your pan with cold water before adding and heating the milk, keep the heat to medium, and stir attentively.
Heat the milk in a double boiler and stir occasionally.

Skillet Good and Greasy Lyrics

*Fatback and beans
And them good old collard greens
Keep your skillet good and greasy
All the time, time, time.*

Peanut Butter Pie
Barbara Bryant – Sullivan County, TN

½ cup peanut butter
1 cup powdered sugar
½ cup sugar
3 Tbsps. cornstarch
½ tsp. salt
3 cups milk, scalded
3 egg yolks beaten (save egg whites for meringue)
1 Tbsp. butter
1½ tsps. vanilla

Blend peanut butter and powdered sugar until mealy. Sprinkle 2/3 of this mixture over bottom of baked pie shell. Combine egg yolks, salt, cornstarch, and sugar. Then stir into scalded milk. Cook over low heat, stirring constantly until thick. Add vanilla and butter. Cool slightly. Pour into baked pie shell. Top with meringue. Bake at 375° for 8 to 10 minutes. Combine the following and beat until stiff for meringue.

3 egg whites   ¼ tsp. cream of tartar   6 Tbsps. sugar

'Pease pudding hot, Pease pudding cold, Pease pudding in the pot, nine days old'
(North Country rhyme)

"Pease pudding has been served for generations in County Durham. The nursery rhyme describes the dish as finding favour whether served hot, cold, or in a pot nine days old; so it is a versatile meal with variation given in old recipe books. It is certainly one of the oldest dishes in the English culinary repertoire well beyond the North East and Durham. It was originally made from dried peas with their skins still on, rather than with split peas or old fresh peas."

Pease Pudding
Yvonne and Peter Banks – Northumberland, England

1	large potato	1	egg, beaten
8	oz. yellow split peas	1	tsp. sugar
4	oz. bacon or ham scraps without rind		black pepper
			salt
1	skinned onion		chopped parsley

Wash and drain the peas. Tie them loosely, along with the potato in a cloth or a piece of muslin. Put in a pan and cover with fresh cold water. Add the ham or bacon scraps and the onion. Bring to the boil, skim and boil gently for 2 hours or until tender. Drain the peas and the potato and pick out the onions as much as possible. Whizz the mixture with the butter, egg, sugar, and a little pepper and salt. When this is smooth, add parsley (optional). Turn this into a mold or a warm serving dish and serve it with boiled ham, roast pork or sausages. Any left over can be fried the next day. (I like it cold on bread and butter with a little brown sauce).

Phyllis's Pecan Pie
Phyllis Flippin – Mt.Airy, NC

2	Tbsps. flour	2	tsps. vanilla flavoring
3	eggs, beaten	1	cup chopped pecans
1	stick butter	1	box brown sugar
¾	cup milk	2	pie shells
			pecan halves

Mix ingredients together and pour in unbaked pie shells. Place pecan halves in desired pattern on top. Bake at 350° for 45 minutes.

After playing piano eight years, Jimmy Mullen picked up the guitar and began picking – mostly bluegrass. Well, maybe it wasn't that simple, but that's his short version. He writes songs as well, many for church.

"I don't think I have a big talent," he says. " It just seems like a natural thing."

After visiting his sister who lives in Chilhowie several times, Mullen got acquainted with Lisa Reedy and members of the Whitetop Mountain Band. While in America, he enjoys the jam sessions at Mt. Rogers School and other musical events.

One thing he really loves doing on Christmas morning is to go play and sing for older folks. "I go home feeling a lot better," is his explanation. - *As told by Jimmy Mullen*

"Poundies, also known as, Champ, Cally, and Pandy, is one of the most famous ways of serving Ireland's best loved vegetable, the potato. Poundies is Ireland's way of serving mashed potatoes."

Poundies

Jimmy Mullen – N. Ireland – Fair River Valley String Band

2 lbs. potatoes, unpeeled
¼ pint milk
4-5 spring onions, finely chopped
2-4 ozs. butter
salt & pepper

Heat a pan of salted water and boil the potatoes in their skins until tender. Drain and dry over a low heat covered with a piece of absorbent kitchen paper. Peel and mash well. While the potatoes are cooking put the milk and chopped spring onions into a saucepan, bring to the boil and simmer for a few minutes. Gradually beat into the mashed potatoes to form a soft, but not sloppy mixture. Beat in half the butter and season with salt and pepper. Divide between 4 warm plates or bowls. Make a well in the center of each serving. Cut the remaining butter into 4 pieces and put one piece in each of the hollows. Serve immediately.

Traditionally, poundies would have been served as a main meal, with a glass of milk, or buttermilk. Nowadays, however, it is used to accompany meats such as boiled ham, and grilled sausages. Preparation time is 5 minutes. Cooking time 20-25 minutes.

Smith Mountain Grass started as a seven-member band in 1999, composed mostly of musicians from communities along the shore of Smith Mountain Lake. Four members now perform at various venues, have won 1st place honors at fiddler's conventions, and have several CD's, including a gospel one. They always try to provide a show consisting of many types of music. 540-721-2417

"My husband, Jack and son, Spencer are members of the Smith Mountain Grass Band."

Pumpkin Fluff
Becky Blankenship – Bedford, VA

1   (16 oz.) can pumpkin
1   small box vanilla instant pudding
2   Tbsps. pumpkin pie spice mix
1   small container Cool Whip

Mix together pudding and pumpkin spice. Add can of pumpkin. Mix well. Fold in Cool Whip. Chill and serve with graham cracker sticks or ginger snaps.

Ranch Style Baked Beans
Loretta Edwards – Vansant, VA

1   lb ground beef
1   envelope dry onion soup mix
½   cup water
1   cup ketchup
2   Tbsps. prepared mustard
2   tsps. vinegar
2-3 cans pork & beans - not drained
1   can red kidney beans, well drained.

Cook ground beef over medium heat until lightly browned. Stir with fork to break up meat. Drain off fat. Add the remaining ingredients and mix well. Turn into a casserole dish & bake at 400°degrees for 30 minutes or I put mine in a crook pot for about 2 hours.

Recipe For A Wonderful Day
Margaret Vest – Salem, VA

1 cup friendly words
2 heaping cups understanding
2 cups milk of human kindness
4 heaping teaspoons time and patience
   pinch of warm personality
   a dash of dry humor
   and the spice of life

Instructions for mixing ingredients: Add heaping cups of understanding to milk of human kindness….Sift together three times before using….Make a smooth sauce….not too thick….Use generous amounts of time and patience and cook with gas on front burner….Keep temperature low….Do not boil….Add dash of dry humor….A pinch of warm personality….Season to taste with spice of life….Serve with individual molds….Works best when made by a good mixer. That's a recipe we all might try.

"This is a recipe from my mother."

Simple Fruit Cobbler
Karen Chandler – Waynesville, NC

1 stick butter, melted
1 cup sugar
1 cup milk
1 cup self-rising flour
2 cups or 1 can cooked fruit

Mix first four ingredients together, pour in 8x8-inch dish and then pour fruit on top and do not mix. Bake at 350° until golden brown. You can use strawberries, peaches, apples, blackberries, and etc.

To comfort sore fingers; soak them in a mixture of magnesium salts and warm water or in alum water.

"This recipe was given to me when my children were young, my oldest now 59 and my youngest 50. It came from a dear friend from Pennsylvania."

Recipe for Croup
Maggie White – Austinville, VA

1 Tbsp. butter-melted
2 Tbsps. honey or brown sugar
½ tsp. lemon juice

Warm and drink. Repeat in 30 minutes if necessary.

"I'd like to share with everyone a recipe from my childhood, that I remember my mother, Gillie Haynes, preparing for me and our family. It was included in my favorite food groups as a child and still is, CANDY. For me, this is the best and most important food group and there are only two categories, good and real good. I'm convinced that my survival comes from eating a little bit of chocolate everyday. Growing up, I thought I was the luckiest kid around because I had two country stores within walking distance of my house, which sold lots of candy. That was when the candy was cheap and the candy bars and soft drinks were big. As a child, my favorite candy shopping experience was at a "dime store" in town that had a candy department with some fancier sweets. This was the kind where the candies were unwrapped and displayed behind a glass case and an employee would scoop up and weigh the amount you wanted and put the candy in a nice little white paper bag for you. So in keeping with the theme, the recipe that I am submitting is called Sea Foam Candy. Not only is it tasty, it was a little mysterious for me as a child. I remember my mother saying that if the weather was bad, it wouldn't work. Now I know there is some scientific reason for its failure. All I knew back then was that I was not going to enjoy Sea Foam candy on a rainy, cloudy or some other bad weather day. So, on a beautiful, sunny day, try this sweet treat and enjoy."

Sea Foam Candy

Martha Sue Bryant – Ashland, KY

3	cups brown sugar	2	egg whites, beaten
¼	tsp. salt	1	tsp. vanilla
¾	cup water		

Dissolve brown sugar and salt in water. Cook without stirring, to hard ball stage. Pour gradually over egg whites that have been beaten stiff. Beat constantly. Add vanilla and continue beating until cool. Drop by teaspoon on wax paper.

"This is a recipe from the region. It's a rural area with an isolated population in the North and around Newcastle. It was an industrial area, shipbuilding and coal distribution. Hence, coals to Newcastle.

Hinnie is a term of endearment, still much used in Northumberland. The Singin' Hinnie from Northumberland contains dried fruits. The Singin' Hinnie is so called because it sizzles as it cooks. You will discover, if you make it, why there was a special implement called Singin' Hinnie hands to turn it over. This operation is quite difficult, best carried out with a fish slice (spatula) in eight hand. The Singin' Hinnie is served hot, straight from the griddle, slit crossways and buttered and cut into wedges. It is a wonderful, easy, hot snack, good to welcome people home with on cold winter evenings."

Singing Hinnie

Yvonne and Peter Banks – Northumberland, England

- **12 ozs. plain flour**
- **1 tsp. salt**
- **½ tsp. bicarbonate of soda**
- **1 tsp. cream of tartar**
- **3 ozs. lard or butter**
- **4 ozs. currants**
- **7½ fl. ozs. milk**

Put the flour, salt, bicarbonate of soda, and cream of tartar into a bowl and rub in the lard or butter. Toss in the currants, make a well in the centre and mix in the milk. Mix everything to a dough. Knead the dough lightly and roll it into a round, about 10 inches across and ¾ inch thick. Heat a lightly greased griddle on a low heat. Put on the dough and cook it until it is golden brown on each side and cooked through, about 15 minutes altogether. If you are using an electric with a concentrated circle of heat, you may find that you will need to turn the electric off completely for a time and let the hinnie cook on heat stored in the ring and the griddle. Serve the hinnie hot, split, and buttered.

Some folks cause happiness wherever they go; others whenever they go!

"Snow In The Vineyard"
Jean Rood – Martinsville, VA

1   (8 oz.) softened cream cheese
½   cup granulated sugar
1   (8 oz.) sour cream
3-4   lbs. seedless grapes

Combine the first 3 ingredients in the above order. Add the grapes; I like to mix red, purple, green, and white grapes. Cover and chill for several hours or overnight. I take it to a lot of family meals and church dinners. Make it a day ahead. It's wonderful!

Sweet and Sour Chicken
Linda E. Maxwell – Axton, VA

¼ cup butter or margarine	1 Tbsp. soy sauce
½ cup chopped onion	½ tsp. garlic salt
½ cup chopped green pepper	½ tsp. salt
½ cup chopped carrots	¼ tsp. pepper
¾ cup catsup	dash ground red pepper
1 cup pineapple juice	dash ground ginger
2 Tbsps. vinegar	1 cup pineapple chunks drained
¼ cup firmly packed brown sugar	1 (3 lb.) chicken, cut up

Preheat oven to 400°. In medium skillet melt butter, add onions, peppers, and carrots. Cook 5 minutes stirring constantly. Stir in catsup, pineapple juice, vinegar, brown sugar, soy sauce, garlic salt, salt, pepper, and ginger. Cook until it boils. Add pineapple chunks. Arrange chicken pieces, skin side down in 13x9-inch baking dish. Pour sauce over all. Bake covered 45 minutes, uncover and bake 30 minutes longer or until done.

The Nunn Brothers Festival

Olin and Alzry Nunn were blessed with 10 children. They passed their love for music on to them. The youngest of these children were twins, Arnold and Alden. When they were 8 years old, their father decided to start each boy out on an instrument. Alden began by playing the piano but soon switched to the fiddle. Arnold began with the fiddle and later switched to the piano and guitar.

After they were grown, with the pressures of work, they found that their love of music became their favorite pastime to alleviate the stress of their business.

Out of that passion came their 1st festival in the year of 1999. Alden and Arnold wanted to have a place to continue the old-time traditions of bluegrass and a family oriented environment. Now in it's 10th year, the crowd has grown from 500 to 2000.
The Nunn Brothers Festival runs each year during the last weekend in July (Thursday through Sunday) with local bands filling the afternoon and night air with the sound of years gone by…Bluegrass at its Best!
www.nunnbrothers.com

Just as the repetition of a pattern makes an attractive quilt, a life well lived inspires others to repeat the proven pattern.

To-po Chops
Marjorie Richards – "Old Dominion Cloggers" – Stuart, VA

6 pork chops, ¾ - in thick	¾ tsp. crushed basil
½ tsp. salt	1/8 tsp. pepper
¼ tsp. pepper	4 medium potatoes, pared and cut into 1/8-in slices
1 can tomatoes (1 lb)	
¼ cup water	1 medium onion, sliced
1 tsp. salt	

Trim excess fat from chops; lightly grease heavy skillet with fat from one chop. Brown chops slowly on both sides; season each side with ¼ tsp. salt and 1/8 tsp. pepper. Remove chops; drain fat from skillet. Add tomatoes to skillet; break up with fork. Mix in water, 1 tsp. salt, basil and 1/8 tsp. pepper. Layer potatoes in tomato mixture. Arrange onion over potatoes. Top with chops. Cover tightly; simmer 45 min. or until potatoes are tender and chops done. 6 servings

Vegetable Salad
Elsie Gray – Lebanon, VA

1 head cauliflower (cut small)	2 Tbsps. white vinegar
1 head broccoli (cut small)	1 cup white mozzarella cheese (shredded)
1 package bacon (cooked and crumbled)	1 cup cheddar cheese (shredded)
1 small red onion, chopped	2 cups Mayo
¼ cup sugar	salt and pepper to taste.

Combine cauliflower, broccoli, onions, and cheese in a bowl. Fry bacon and break into bits. Combine the sugar, vinegar, mayo, salt, and pepper to make a dressing. Pour this over the vegetables and cheese. Toss and sprinkle bacon on top and serve. This is good for church dinners. It feeds a lot of people.

"My husband, John, is the steel guitar player on the Bill Jefferson TV show."

Whipping Cream Pound Cake
Debbie Cullers – Mount Gilead, NC

3 cups cake flour	7 eggs (room temperature)
3 cups sugar	1 cup whipping cream
½ lb. butter (room temperature)	2 tsps. vanilla

Cream together butter and sugar until fluffy; add eggs one at a time. Beat after each egg. Mix in ½ of flour and ½ of whipping cream; beat well, then add remaining flour and whipping cream. Mix vanilla in batter, (beat for 5 to 8 minutes) then pour batter into prepared tube pan. Set cake in cold oven, then turn oven to 350°. Bake for 75 minutes. Cool in pan for 5 minutes.

Whole Wheat Bran Bread
Iris McGrady – Martinsville, VA

1½ cups bran or wheat germ	1 tsp. salt	¼ cup brown sugar, optional
2½ cups whole wheat flour	1½ tsps. soda	½ cup molasses
		1¾ cups buttermilk

Mix dry ingredients together. Mix soda in buttermilk and stir liquid into dry ingredients. Bake 1 hour at 325° in greased bread pan.

The Cro[ok]
Virginia's Heri[tage]

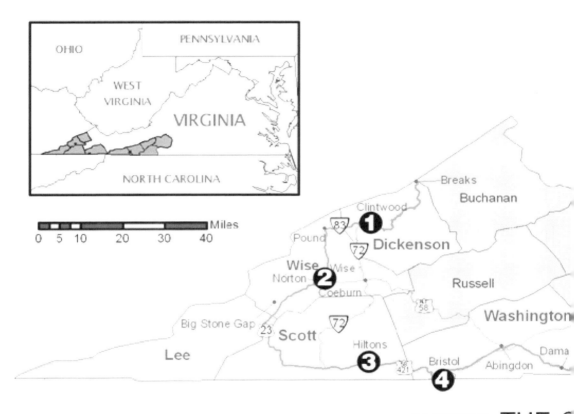

1. RALPH STANLEY MUSEUM, CLINTWOOD
2. COUNTRY CABIN, NORTON
3. CARTER FAMILY FOLD, HILTONS
4. BIRTHPLACE OF COUNTRY MUSIC ALLIANCE, BRISTOL